D0947020

WITHDRAWN

PIETY
AND POVERTY

Europe Past and Present Series

PIETY AND POVERTY

*Working-Class Religion
in Berlin, London
and New York
1870–1914*

HUGH MCLEOD

Holmes & Meier
New York/London

Published in the United States of America 1996 by
Holmes & Meier Publishers, Inc.
160 Broadway
New York, NY 10038

Book design by Robert Sugar

This book has been printed on acid-free paper.

Library of Congress Cataloging-in-Publication Data
McLeod, Hugh.
   Piety and Poverty : working-class religion in Berlin, London and
New York, 1870–1914 / Hugh McLeod.
      p.   cm. — (Europe past and present series)
   Includes bibliographical references and index.
   ISBN 0-8419-1356-0 (alk. paper)
   1. Working class—Germany—Berlin—Religious life.   2. Working
class—England—London—Religious life.   3. Working class—New York
(N.Y.)—Religious life.   4. Secularization (Theology).   5. Berlin
(Germany)—Religion—19th century.   6. London (England)—
Religion—19th century.   7. New York (N.Y.)—Religion—19th
century.   8. Berlin (Germany)—Religion—20th century.   9. London
(England)—Religion—20th century.   10. New York (N.Y.)—
Religion—20th century.   I. Title.   II. Series.
BR477.M34   1996
270.81′08′624—dc20   94-36428
                                                                        CIP

Manufactured in the United States of America

CONTENTS

v

MAPS

TABLES

ACKNOWLEDGEMENTS

I first started collecting material for this book slightly over fifteen years ago. Since then I have been diverted into writing various other books and papers, but this project was always partly in my mind. During this time I have often thought that the one necessary quality in a social historian is persistence. Of the many and varied places my research has taken me to, perhaps the most unfamiliar was Ocean Terminal in Bayonne, New Jersey, a military base with some spare capacity which was used to house a federal archive: getting access to the archive involved first of all negotiating an armed guard, then travelling by military bus to the building where the records were kept, and finally enduring soft music while in the record room. More familiar has been the constant struggle to persuade those who have historical documents in their care to allow me to consult them. Watchful receptionists determined to protect their employers from time-wasters have often proved more formidable obstacles than the armed guards at Ocean Terminal. A less expected obstacle was provided by a group of anarchists who occupied a Berlin church shortly before I was intending to use its archive—said to be one of the best in the city. I never did find out if this was true. When, after several letters or phone calls, access to an archive is finally achieved, there is, of course, no guarantee that the records will prove to be of any relevance. So I have plenty of memories of the frustrations of historical research. But I also have vivid memories of the pure delight of being alone in an old building, with all around me cupboards stuffed full of the letters, minute-books, registers, and crumbling pamphlets that have been temporarily entrusted to my care.

I would like to begin, therefore, by expressing my great gratitude to the people—mainly priests, pastors and church secretaries—who trusted me with the records in their keeping, and often gave up time to help me in other ways. Next I would like to thank the librarians and archivists, who provided essential help at many points in this project. This study would also have been impossible without various research grants, and I would like to acknowledge my debt to the former Social Science Research Council, the British Academy, and the University of Birmingham. I would like to thank Harry Buglass for drawing the maps. Another debt is to those who provided me with beds to sleep in, lent me tapes and unpublished papers, helped me get access to sources, or discussed aspects of the book with me: I would like specially to thank Flavia Alaya, Alan Bartlett, Michael Bäumer, Ursula Baumann, Gerlinde Böpple, Callum Brown, the late Harry Browne, Jeff Cox, Jay Dolan, Owen Dudley Edwards, Clive Field, Jean Fischer, Manfred Fischer, Stephen Fischer, Sheridan Gilley, Larry Glickman, David Hempton, Lucian Hölscher, Paul Joyce, Karen Kearns, Christa Ressmeyer Klein,

Rob Lewis, Peter Marsh, Stuart Mews, Philip Murnion, Jim Obelkevich, Stephen Pattison, Gillian Rose, Ellen Ross, Raphael Samuel, Meredith Tax, David Taylor, Pamela Taylor, Dorothy Thompson, the late Edward Thompson, Paul Thompson, Thea Thompson, and Sean Willentz. I would also like to thank all members of my family, and particularly Paul, Damien, Louise, Dominic, Mark, Luke, and most of all Jackie, for their patience and their encouragement.

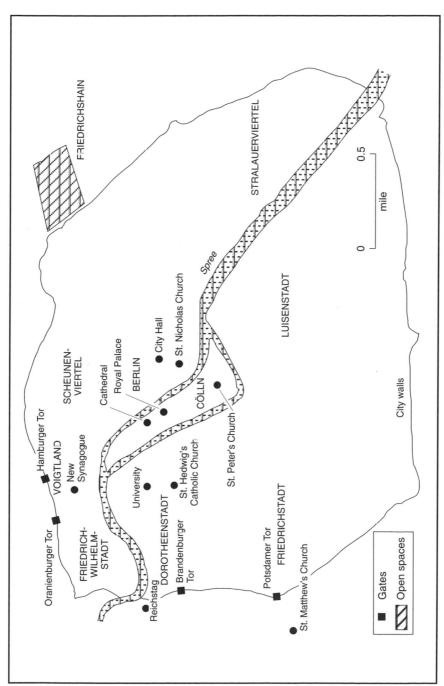

Map 1. Central Berlin. Showing city walls (demolished 1870s) and major public buildings and places of worship.

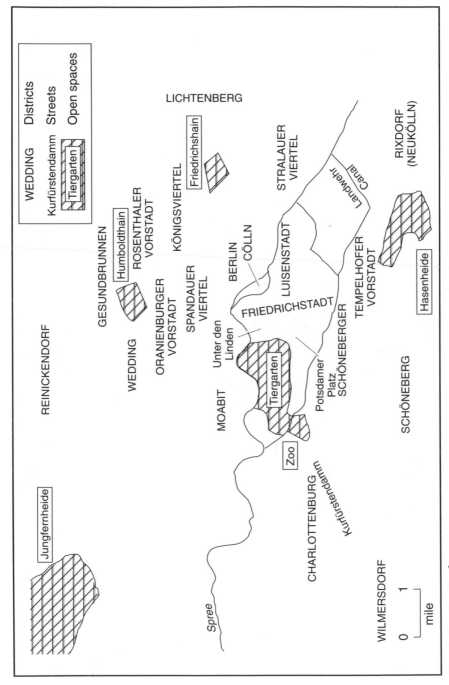

Map 2. **Greater Berlin.**

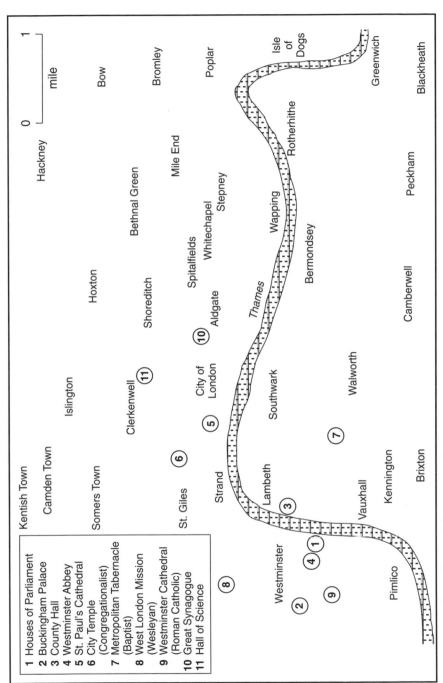

Map 3. **Central London and the East End.**

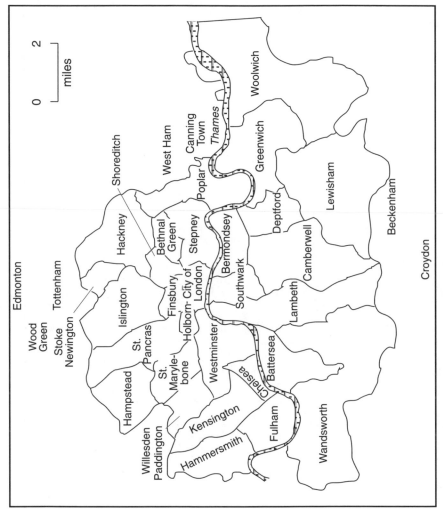

Map 4. The County of London and other districts mentioned in the text.

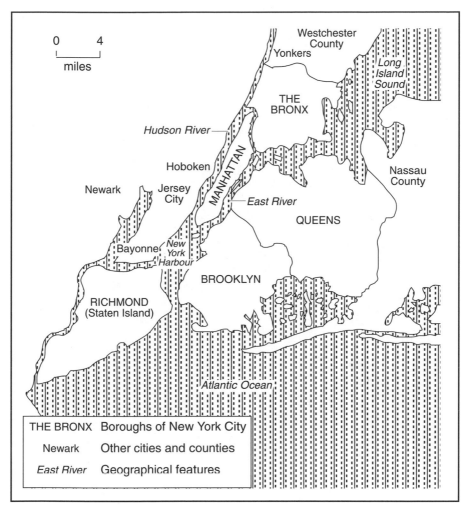

0   4
miles

Westchester
County
Yonkers

Long
Island
Sound

THE
BRONX

Hudson River

Hoboken

MANHATTAN

Nassau
County

Newark   Jersey
City

East River

QUEENS

Bayonne *New
York
Harbour*

BROOKLYN

RICHMOND
(Staten Island)

Atlantic Ocean

THE BRONX	Boroughs of New York City
Newark	Other cities and counties
East River	Geographical features

Map 5. **The New York Metropolitan Area.**

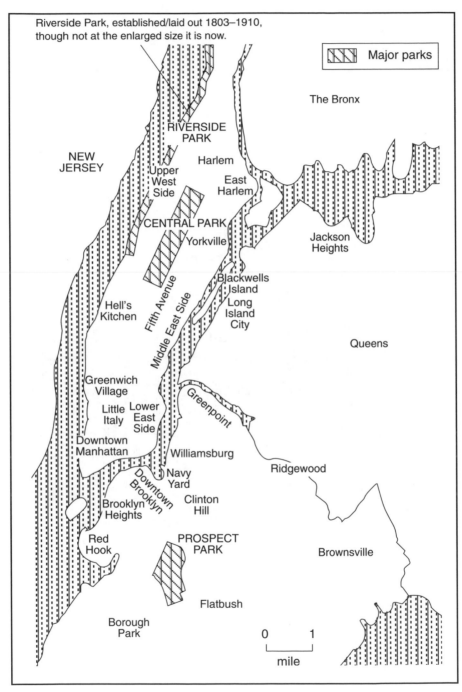

Riverside Park, established/laid out 1803–1910,
though not at the enlarged size it is now.

Major parks

The Bronx

RIVERSIDE
PARK

NEW
JERSEY

Harlem

Upper
West
Side

East
Harlem

CENTRAL PARK

Yorkville

Jackson
Heights

Blackwells
Island

Long
Island
City

Hell's
Kitchen

Queens

Greenwich
Village

Greenpoint

Little
Italy

Lower
East
Side

Downtown
Manhattan

Williamsburg

Ridgewood

Navy
Yard

Downtown
Brooklyn

Clinton
Hill

Brooklyn
Heights

PROSPECT
PARK

Brownsville

Red
Hook

Flatbush

Borough
Park

0   1
mile

Map 6. **New York City.**

INTRODUCTION

THE LATER NINETEENTH and early twentieth centuries were regarded in many Western countries as a time of religious crisis. The crisis was generally believed to be most acute in the cities and especially among the working class. This book focuses on working-class religion in three of the world's greatest cities in this period of crisis.

My first objective is to get behind the generalizations and the rhetoric that prevail in most accounts in order to provide a more precise and nuanced description of the part played by religion and irreligion in the daily life of working-class people. I shall show how, for instance, belief and unbelief related to their experience of poverty and social exclusion, to the ways in which they celebrated or survived the turning points and crises of life, to the relationships between women and men, and to political organizations. By focusing on the part played by religion, and sometimes by secularism, in the everyday life of working-class communities, I hope to demonstrate the importance of a dimension that is far too often ignored, dismissed or mentioned only in passing.[1] The salience of sectarian differences in such major industrial regions as Lancashire and the Ruhrgebiet is so obvious that most historians are forced to take the issue seriously.[2] However, the task of defining the nature and meaning of working-class religion in more religiously homogeneous cities and regions has proved more difficult, and many historians have solved it by resorting to clichés, such as the concept of 'apathy', or by reducing working-class religiosity to the search for material assistance.[3] Historians of religion in Britain have for some years been keenly interested in the question of the relationship between the churches and the working class, though as yet no consensus has been reached. Because of the nature of the most widely used sources, these scholars have often been more successful at seeing the question through the eyes of the clergy than through those of working-class people.[4] In Germany, on the other hand, very little research has been done on working-class religion in regions other than the Ruhrgebiet.[5] In the United States the theme has been studied mainly in terms of immigration history.[6] This study will break new ground in two ways. First, by exploiting a wide range of hitherto underused sources, most notably various oral history surveys, it will attempt to go further than any previous history of urban working-class religion towards seeing the subject through the eyes of the people themselves. Second, it is the first study of working-class religion that has attempted to solve the problems of interpretation by using a comparative framework. I shall return later to discuss the rationale for this approach.

My second objective is to define the nature, extent and causes of the secularization of the working class during this period, and to explain why these varied so considerably as between different parts of Western Europe and North America. The question of the extent and causes of the secularization of Western societies has been hotly debated by sociologists, especially over the last thirty years; and most historians of modern religion have had at least half an eye on the debate. The classical approach to the question, which goes back to Max Weber, and which is championed by such historians as Alan Gilbert, and such sociologists as Bryan Wilson and Steve Bruce, sees secularization as an inexorable, pervasive and universal process, intimately related to other aspects of modernization, such as mechanization and bureaucratization.[7] As Weber put it: 'The fate of our times is characterized by rationalization and intellectualization and, above all, by the "disenchantment of the world".'[8] A number of historians have, however, criticized what they regard as the determinism and the weak empirical foundations of the classical theory of secularization.[9] Jeff Cox, for instance, has stressed the varied religious histories of modern Western nations, and has argued that the introduction of a free market in religion has presented churches with a challenge to which some have responded effectively, while others have been defeated. In particular, he suggests that the decline of the churches in England in the later nineteenth and early twentieth centuries was due not to any universal and inevitable secularization, but to specific weaknesses and failures to adapt: in the United States the churches adapted more successfully and survived, although the social and intellectual changes that they confronted in that period were similar.[10]

One of the most important matters at issue in the debate is that of the relationship between secularization and urbanization, which therefore requires some discussion here.

I

The nineteenth century saw a growth of cities on a scale far beyond anything seen before in the world's history. Most spectacularly, London grew from around one million to a stupendous six million. But by 1900, New York, Paris and Berlin were also close to the three million mark, and thus far larger than any city of a previous era. The century also saw the proliferation of second-rank cities: by 1900 there were about thirty Western cities with more than half a million inhabitants—which would have qualified them for metropolitan status in the eighteenth century. Furthermore, the growth in the number of smaller cities meant that even in countries which lacked a major metropolis, there was often a considerable increase in the proportion of the population living in urban areas. The change was most dramatic in England and Wales where, between 1801 and 1891, the proportion of the population living in towns of more than ten thousand inhabitants increased from 21 per cent to 62 per cent. But Scotland, Germany, France, Belgium, the United States and many other European and American nations also saw substantial increases.

From the start, there have been two opposing views as to what this social revolution meant for the religious traditions of the Western world. By the 1830s and 1840s, there were many voices proclaiming that the cities were strongholds of irreligion. Most famous, perhaps, was Engels' study of the English working class in 1844, in which he claimed that religion had effectively died out.[11] While most such comments concerned the working class, some observers saw the city as a whole as a religious desert. One of Engels' contemporaries, a London clergyman, claimed in a sermon of 1844 that 'the life of cities is essentially a worldly life,' whereas 'the country with its pure serenity—oh, how unlike the hot thick breath of the towns—of itself inspires some feelings of religion.'[12] Meanwhile, a Berlin clergyman was comparing his city to Sodom and Gomorrah, and suggesting that it would be a suitable site for a mission to the heathen.[13]

But at the same time there were also those who saw the cities as the most dynamic centres of religious activism. To a Scottish Evangelical in the 1830s Glasgow was 'Gospel City', leading the nation in its religiously inspired reform movements and its evangelistic enterprises.[14] And Robert Vaughan, the English Congregational minister who published *The Age of Great Cities* in 1843, was equally optimistic about the influence that these cities could exercise over the nation.[15] Of course, most of these commentators were deeply involved in the religious controversies of their time, and their commitments strongly coloured their judgements. For instance, the enthusiasm of Nonconformists for urbanization was influenced by the fact that they saw the cities as a powerful counterweight to the religious traditionalism of the countryside: their sectarian partisanship may have blinded them to the less welcome aspects of city life.

The same differences of interpretation are to be found among modern historians and sociologists writing the religious history of the nineteenth century. The most familiar view is that of Alan Gilbert, who sees urbanization as essentially synonymous with secularization—in spite of a temporary religious revival in the early stages of the English Industrial Revolution. Gilbert, like most other writers who have seen urbanization and secularization as intimately related, argues that both are to be seen as aspects of a process of 'modernization', which revolutionized Western societies in the nineteenth century. Exponents of modernization theory generally argue that religion was in severe decline in the cities of nineteenth and early twentieth-century Europe and North America, and that its strength lay in backward rural communities, where the modernizing forces had not yet penetrated.[16] However, there is a rival school, represented by such historians as Callum Brown, which holds that nineteenth-century urbanization frequently stimulated religious growth.[17]

The former view is customarily argued in three ways. The least controversial form of the argument is that which focuses on the demographic upheavals associated with the growth of industries and of cities in the nineteenth century. It is generally accepted that the major population shifts of this period confronted established churches with enormous logistical problems, which most of them failed adequately to solve; that some workers, after moving to cities or industrial regions, remained highly mobile, and found it difficult to form close links with any particular clergyman or congregation; and that some more settled workers gave up in the town religious practices which had derived their meaning from the rural context in which they had first been learnt. It should be noted, however, that these arguments refer to the forms taken by urbanization in the specific context of nineteenth-century Europe and North America, and are not necessarily relevant to other times and places.

The two other kinds of argument, however, are more ambitious and posit a more general relationship between urbanization and secularization. The second argument suggests that cities with populations running into hundreds of thousands, or even millions, such as those that appeared in large numbers during the nineteenth century, are by their nature pluralistic: they lend themselves to the formation of numerous discrete subcultures, since the supervision of such matters as morals, beliefs and religious practices by employers, magistrates or the church was no longer practicable. In the circumstances of nineteenth-century Europe, this meant that religion declined, or at least appeared to be declining in the cities, as the urban population enjoyed a degree of freedom that was not available elsewhere. This argument is sometimes extended to suggest that the pluralism of urban life leads to the development of a relativistic outlook, which breeds religious scepticism. The third, and most ambitious argument posits a general relationship between urbanization and industrialization on the one hand, and secularization on the other, on the grounds that the former bring about a mental revolution, as a result of which a rationalistic and mechanistic outlook comes to prevail, and all forms of supernaturalism lose their credibility. Of course, not all proponents of the view that nineteenth-century urbanization and secularization were related would accept all three arguments. Many historians, for instance, would accept the first argument, or the first and second, while rejecting the third.[18]

The counterargument, that urbanization stimulates religious growth, has been presented in its most ambitious form by the American sociologists Roger Finke and Rodney Stark. They contend that urbanization tends to be associated with increasing religious pluralism, and that the greater the degree of pluralism, the higher the proportion of the population that is likely to be religiously active. This is partly because competition keeps religious denominations on their toes, and partly because the multiplication of denominations permits each religious group to cater for the needs of a particular section of the market: the greater the variety of 'brands' available, the more likely it is that every 'customer' will find something which she or he likes the look of. Finke and Stark draw explicit parallels between America's religious free market and its free enterprise economic system, and they see state churches as the religious equivalents of state-owned monopoly industries. They are clearly influenced by the a priori assumption that a free market is best suited to supply the customer's needs; they also seem to assume that the demand for religion is more or less constant, and that the main question therefore is how this demand can be most effectively met.[19]

Callum Brown makes less ambitious claims. He is not arguing that there is a universal relationship between urbanization and the nature of religious change. But he suggests that so far as nineteenth-century Britain was concerned, secularization was not caused by urbanization, and that in the case of Scotland urban growth did more to stimulate revival than to hasten decline. The 1851 religious census showed that Scottish church attendance was higher in towns than in rural areas, and Brown's study of church statistics leads him to argue that religious influences in Scottish society reached an all-time peak in the late Victorian period. While the nineteenth-century religious boom affected all parts of Scotland, it was the towns which generated most of the instruments of revival—the new, highly active Dissenting churches, the missions, Sunday schools, and a wide variety of reforming crusades with objects that ranged from sabbatarianism, to temperance, to the provision of parks, to stricter control of house-building and sanitation.[20]

There is also a third view, hinted at in the work of some historians yet not fully spelled out, namely that the significance of urbanization in the long-term history of European religion has been exaggerated, and that the most important changes happened before industrialization or the great surge of urban growth in the nineteenth century. Thus Lucian Hölscher's work on long-term trends in religious practice in Germany suggests that in many parts of north German towns the collapse in communion rates took place in the eighteenth century. The significance of social changes in the nineteenth century was that secular tendencies, already predominant in many towns, spread out to the more pious countryside.[21]

II

While the overall religious consequences of nineteenth-century urbanization were, and continue to be, widely debated, there was and is much more consensus with regard to the religious trends among one very large section of the urban population, namely the working class. In the years around 1900 there was much evidence to suggest that the working class of European cities went to church less frequently than members of other classes. Their level of church-going was sometimes very low indeed, and many observers spoke of a general working-class alienation from the churches.[22] American observers seldom made such sweeping claims. But here too there was a considerable body of literature published in the years around 1900 on 'The Workingman's Alienation from the Church' (the title of an article by a Chicago Baptist minister, published in 1898–9).[23]

In more recent years, the question of the relationship between the church and the working class during this period has generated an extensive historical literature, much of which has focused on the causes of this alienation. The picture presented in this literature has often been exaggerated and oversimplified. In particular, too little account has been taken of gender differences. It has also been too readily assumed that non-churchgoers were irreligious. I shall return to these issues in later chapters. But alienation there was, even if it was a far more complex process than is sometimes suggested.

Three main lines of interpretation have been advanced to explain this alienation. The first concentrates on the failure of the churches to meet working-class religious needs; the second focuses on proletarian living conditions and culture; the third relates declining involvement in the churches to growing class-consciousness and political organization.

The first interpretation can be summed up in Pope Pius XI's famous claim that 'The greatest scandal of the Church in the nineteenth century was that it lost the working class.'[24] The implied assumption, of course, is that there was nothing inevitable about working-class alienation, and that if the church had understood the situation better, and responded more adequately to working-class needs, the story might have ended differently. Indeed, this argument was used explicitly by the American historian Henry J. Browne, who praised Cardinal Gibbons and other American bishops for preserving links between the church and the labour movement, and thus helping to avert the clear-cut division between church and workers that took place in many parts of Europe.[25] Historians who have argued that the churches 'lost' the working class have done so in a number of ways. Most commonly they have focused on the failure adequately to address the 'Social Question'.[26] Other analyses have focused on the inadequacy of the resources devoted to working-class parishes[27] or on the prevalence of humiliating social distinctions within the churches.[28] All of these arguments, it should be noted, focus on the failures of specific churches. They are not sufficient to explain a generalized decline of organized religion, since, at least in theory, it was possible for the worker alienated from one church to turn to another—indeed, in some countries, many did so, though the factors constraining such changes of allegiance were much stronger in some places than others. For instance, switches between Catholicism and Protestantism were rare; whereas switches from one form of Protestantism to another were quite common. The constraints were probably weakest in the United States, with its pluralistic and fluid religious atmosphere, where hereditary allegiances had been weakened, and members of one church would fairly readily switch to another. They were much stronger in Germany, where even wholly nonpractising Evangelicals often retained a good deal of their prejudice against 'sectarians'.

The argument that focuses on working-class living conditions and culture can take a specific form and a more general form. The specific form focuses on the situation of large sections of the working class, and especially of recent immigrants to the city, at the time of rapid urban growth in the nineteenth century. A characteristic example occurs in Charpin's study of Marseilles. In the first half of the nineteenth century levels of religious practice remained high among the artisan and labouring population of the city, in spite of some decline among the bourgeoisie. But in the third quarter of the century, when the population was growing very fast, there was a severe decline, especially in the poorer suburbs, inhabited by recent immigrants. According to Charpin, these newcomers were preoccupied with the struggle for survival: they worked very long hours, often including Sundays, and they were continually moving house, so that they were unlikely to form strong ties with a particular priest or parish; in any case, the fact that many of them spoke only Italian or the patois of some part of rural southern France made it likely that they would keep themselves to themselves, and avoid institutions, such as the city's churches, which were dominated by natives of Marseilles.[29]

A more generalized version of the argument which links working-class detachment from the church to working-class living conditions and culture was presented in my study of religion in late Victorian London. Here I focused on the implications of life at the bottom of a hierarchical society, in which working-class people had little experience of power or responsibility and frequently suffered humiliation at the hands of those in authority: the powerful sense of community solidarity led to a suspicion of anyone who was conspicuously different or seemed to be putting on airs; the recognition that life is hard, and rogues abound, tended to produce scepticism, fatalism and an exaggerated distrust of idealists and the apparently virtuous; the experience of subordination, of being victim rather than agent, tended to produce cynicism about the possibility of significant change, or the value of action, except ad hoc and on a very limited scale.[30]

The line of interpretation that associates working-class detachment from the church with growing class-consciousness is in a sense incontestable. Clearly the two processes were often associated in nineteenth-century Europe. What is less clear is the relationship between them. Gustafsson's research on Sweden in the 1880s suggests that Social Democracy grew in those working-class communities that were already substantially detached from the Lutheran church. He explains this detachment largely in terms of the declining status and living standards of certain sections of the working class, and a consequent sharpening of their sense of separate identity and avoidance of situations which involved mixing with 'superiors'.[31]

On the other hand, Eric Hobsbawm suggests that it was politicization that led to detachment from the church, and that a substantial degree of secularization was an inevitable concomitant of nineteenth-century working-class radicalism.[32] Hobsbawm's explanation for this is that all forms of religion were in the context of nineteenth-century Europe essentially backward-looking and archaic—they could still provide powerful support for those who wanted to return to the past, but they could not offer a coherent way forward. Admittedly, there were Christian Socialists, but they were of 'marginal' significance. Radical and socialist propagandists accordingly were obliged to attack religion, which they saw as an obstacle to the total reformation of humanity that they desired, and their plebeian audiences— though not interested in secularism as an end in itself—bought the anti-religious message, because they bought the political message that went with it.

In my view, each of the theories of working-class alienation cited above has at least some validity, but they suffer from excessive rigidity. Most are framed to fit the facts as they obtained in one particular place and time, but they do not help us to grasp the great variations in the extent and nature of the phenomenon. We need an explanatory framework that will make it possible to understand both why the phenomenon of working-class alienation from organized religion was so widespread in the cities and industrial regions of later nineteenth- and early twentieth-century Europe and America, and why the actual extent and the precise nature of this alienation varied so widely.

III

The historical literature on religion and the working class, on religion and urbanization, and on secularization has been dominated by two kinds of study. On the one hand, there have been very generalized works, which are strong on the history of ideas, on personalities, and on ecclesiastical politics, but include little detailed study of specific localities.[33] On the other hand, there have been very detailed local studies, which are often particularly successful in handling the relationship between local religious conditions and the local economy.[34] At a descriptive level, these latter studies are often superb; but they are not so helpful in explaining the general phenomenon of, for instance, working-class alienation from the church, since factors that appear to be decisive in one place may prove to be of little relevance in another. Valuable as both kinds of study often are, there is a need for a third kind of study, which is both local and comparative. By being locally based, such a study would remain close to the day-to-day realities of life in urban working-class communities, and would retain a sense of the specific histories that make every city unique, and not just an example of universal tendencies. At the same time, by being comparative, it should make it possible to identify both the general factors which contributed to, for instance, the secularizing trend in most Western countries at this time, and the specific factors which meant that the trends were much more marked in some countries and cities than others.

The choice for this study of a German, a British and an American city was determined by a combination of two kinds of consideration. On the one hand, as the world's three most economically advanced nations, all of them having predominantly Protestant religious traditions, they had a good deal in common. Moreover, there were many-sided influences of each country on the others: German and British emigrants went to America; Irish emigrants went to both Britain and America; and there was an enormous traffic in ideas, including religious ideas, between the three countries. On the other hand, there was one major area of difference between the three countries, which is particularly interesting from the point of view of the present study: the nineteenth-century trend toward working-class alienation from the churches, and, indeed, toward secularization more generally, had gone further in northern Germany than in most other countries; on the other hand, among the more economically advanced nations of Europe and the Americas, the United States was the one most noted for the flourishing state of its churches, and for relatively high levels of working-class participation; Britain lay somewhere in the middle. So a three-way comparison between a German, a British and an American city seems a particularly interesting way of approaching these issues.

The decision to focus on the three metropolitan centres of those countries was made for the pragmatic reason that a medium-depth study of this kind depends heavily on the availability of printed sources, such as social surveys and memoirs, and metropolitan centres tend to generate unusually large quantities of literature of this kind. Of course, no category of city is 'typical'. For instance, metropolitan centres have a crucial role in intellectual and cultural life, where they tend to be the most important sites for experimentation and for advanced thinking within each field. They also tend to differ from other large cities in having unusually high concentrations of the very wealthy, and of the established elites in such fields as literature, the arts, entertainment, journalism and religion; they are also able to find a place for large subcultures of those who are for one reason or another on the margins of society, ranging from bohemians, to professional criminals, to members of exotic ethnic communities, whose numbers are too small to permit a distinctive presence in smaller cities.

On the other hand, I see no reason to think that working-class life in the metropolitan centres was very much different from that in other large cities with comparable economic structures or ethnic make-up. So far as levels of religious participation were concerned, London and Berlin seem to have ranked low by national standards, but to have been fairly much in line with other large cities. For instance, in the late nineteenth and early twentieth centuries, Berlin's Protestant communicant rate was generally higher than that of Hamburg or Bremen, but lower than that of Dresden or Nuremberg.[35] Church attendance in London was lower than in Liverpool or Bristol, but higher than in Birmingham, and about the same as in Sheffield.[36] Church membership in New York was below that in Boston, but slightly above Chicago and Philadelphia—though comparisons among the crude figures mean little, since denominations calculated their statistics in different ways, and American cities varied considerably in denominational composition.[37] While few, if any, of the metropolitan centres of Europe and America in the years around 1900 were noted for exceptional levels of piety, there is no reason to think that they were exceptionally secularized by the standards of their time and place.

IV

At the end of the nineteenth century, London, New York and Berlin ranked respectively first, second and fourth in size among the world's cities. All three were growing very rapidly, though the sources of immigration to the cities differed considerably: at one extreme was New York, where immigrants from overseas and the children of immigrants made up the great majority of the population; at the other extreme was Berlin, where, although there were small Polish Catholic and East European Jewish communities, the great majority of the population were German speakers from Brandenburg or the eastern provinces; London's population was somewhat more heterogeneous than Berlin's, but much less so than that of New York. As metropolitan centres of their respective nations, the three cities had their districts of wealth and fashion, their communities of writers and artists, and their dormitory suburbs for white-collar workers, and they were the major sites of such characteristically metropolitan industries as clothing manufacture and printing and publishing.

There were, however, three major differences in economic structure among the cities: first, London and Berlin were capital cities, whereas New York was not even the capital of New York state; secondly, the ports of London and New York were of central importance in the economy of those cities, whereas the river Spree had a much more limited role in the economy of Berlin; third, heavy engineering had a major role in the Berlin economy, whereas London and New York were primarily cities of small workshops.

In religious terms, the three cities had important points in common, and also major differences. All three cities had a mainly Protestant elite; a Catholic community that was predominantly working class; and a Jewish community that included both a long-established and predominantly middle-class element, and poorer recent immigrants. New York differed from the other two cities in that Protestants, though powerful and wealthy, were a minority of the population, and the proportion both of Catholics and Jews was considerably higher than in Berlin or London. London resembled Berlin in that both had an established church, and the distribution of the three main religious communities was roughly similar; London resembled New York in the variety of different religious denominations that flourished in the city. In all three cities, secularization was an important issue at the end of the nineteenth century. In particular, the apparent irreligion or religious apathy of large sections of the working class was a matter of concern to the churches, and there were suggestions that a more general decline of the churches, or even of religion in general, was underway.[38]

In my study of the three cities I have narrowed down what is potentially an impossibly large field by concentrating my use of primary sources on certain districts or ethnic groups, and otherwise relying on secondary sources. For instance, I relied very largely on secondary sources for information about the Jewish communities in the three cities, and there were also other ways in which I limited my use of primary sources. In the case of Berlin, I concentrated on primary sources relating to the northern side of the city, and to Protestantism. In New York, I focused on the Irish and Germans, and on two sections of Manhattan, the Middle West Side and the Upper East Side. In London, I gave priority to primary sources which were not available, or which, for other reasons, I did not use in the late 1960s and early 1970s when I was preparing a thesis, and subsequently a book, on religion in late Victorian and Edwardian London;[39] in particular, I have made systematic use of interviews conducted by oral historians in various parts of the city during the 1970s and 1980s.

One potential problem in a comparative study of this kind is that the information obtained from the three cities is not always strictly comparable. The aspects of religious life in Berlin that are well documented are not always the same as the ones that are well documented in New York or in London. For instance, I was able to obtain excellent material on the social composition of members of various churches in New York; some such material is available for London, but it is less helpful; and in the case of Berlin, there is plenty of information about lay office-holders, but very little about the rank and file of churchgoers. On the other hand, the city of Berlin published annual statistics of the numbers of baptisms,

confirmations, weddings and funerals conducted, and of communions adminis-
tered in the churches of the various denominations, so we are much better informed on these subjects for Berlin than for the other two cities.

Historians of religion in London are able to benefit from the availability of a
much wider range of oral history material. This latter source makes it much more
possible to comment on the beliefs and attitudes of those who were neither committed church members nor convinced secularists than is the case with the other
two cities. In Berlin, hostility to the churches is unusually well documented, as
those resigning from the church were obliged to go through a formal procedure,
and we have information about who left the church and why. So the picture that I
have drawn of working-class religion in each of the three cities sometimes draws
on different kinds of evidence, and certainly the quality of evidence is uneven,
often being better for one city than for the other two. Nonetheless, I would argue
that the evidence, though differently constituted, is sufficient to permit a reasonably full picture of working-class religion and irreligion in the three cities, and to
permit explanations as to why they differed.

V

In part I, I adopt a mainly descriptive approach, looking in turn at the religious
situation in each of the three cities. Working-class religion and working-class secularism are placed in the context of the distinctive religious history of each city and
the wider patterns of religious affiliation and practice. In the section on New York,
the major emphasis is on the importance of ethnic divisions within the city's working class, whereas in the chapters on Berlin and London there is more stress on the
points that the various sections of the working class had in common.

Parts II and III use a comparative approach. In part II, I return to the themes
of religion and urbanization and of working-class religious alienation. I propose
new ways of approaching these questions, and attempt to explain the differences
among the situations in the three cities. I argue that the relationship between
urbanization and religion has been understood in too mechanical a way, with insufficient regard for the specific social forces which came to the fore in different
cities. In particular, differences between the religious role of the bourgeois elites
of Berlin, London and New York help to explain the differences between the
religious histories of the three cities in the nineteenth century. I then attempt to
explain why the proportion of working-class people who were militant secularists
was much greater in Berlin than in London or New York, and why the proportion
of working-class people who were active church-members was considerably higher
in New York than in London or Berlin.

In part III, I move away from the rather generalized approach adopted in part
II, in order to look more closely at some of the factors affecting the religious
outlook of individual working-class people. I focus on the relationship between
working-class religion and the experience of poverty, challenging the popular view

that religion helped the poor to accept their poverty: this underestimates both the extent to which the experience of poverty alienated the poor from God, and the frequency with which religion helped the poor to find ways of fighting against their poverty. I then look at the differences between male and female religiosity, and consider how far the contrast often drawn between pious women and irreligious men is valid. There is, in fact, some truth in this picture, but it is very oversimplified, and, in particular, obscures important differences among the situations in the three cities. Finally, I consider how far secularization had progressed in the working-class communities of this period, arguing that the pattern is very uneven and that even in Berlin the extent of secularization has generally been exaggerated.

PART ONE

THREE
CITIES

CHAPTER 1

Berlin

BERLIN GREW UP IN the shadow of the Royal Palace. The *Schloss* stood right in the middle of the city on the Spree Island, opposite the cathedral, and within sight of City Hall. And the dominant position which it enjoyed in the city's topography accurately reflected the dominant influence over the city's life which the Hohenzollern dynasty exercised until the nineteenth century, and which continued in somewhat attenuated form even when Berlin had become a commercial, industrial and cultural metropolis in its own right.

In 1680 Berlin had a population of only 10,000. It then began to grow very rapidly, reaching 72,000 in 1730, 172,000 in 1800, 450,000 (inclusive of suburbs) in 1848, 900,000 (with suburbs) in 1871, and slightly under 4 million in 1920, when the suburbs were linked with the old city to make Greater Berlin. The Great Elector started the Hohenzollerns on the path that led to the triumphs of 1815 and 1871 and ultimately to the catastrophe of 1918. The city's rapid growth began in his reign (1640–88), and he left the city three important legacies that continued for many years afterwards to give Berlin something of its distinctive personality: ethnic and religious diversity, toleration and a strong military presence. The late seventeenth century brought to Berlin 'the Colony' (of French Huguenots), smaller settlements of Bohemians and of south German Catholics, and (of even greater long-term significance) the Jews, who remained until the 1940s a vital element in the city's life. The military were a very visible feature throughout the eighteenth century, and in 1803, soldiers and their dependents still made up 14 per cent of the population. With the growth of the 'residence' into the 'metropolis' during the nineteenth century, the proportion of soldiers fell substantially, but barracks and parade grounds continued to occupy large areas, and army officers continued to form an important element in the city's elite. Under Frederick the Great (1740–86), Berlin's tradition of religious toleration acquired a new twist, as the city became an important centre of the German Enlightenment, and one with a reputation for heterodoxy. Prussia's monarchs also took a keen interest in the planning of their capital city: the layout of the streets, the leading monuments and the names of the districts on Berlin's more fashionable western side all owed their existence to members of the ruling family. Another royal foundation was the university, which started in 1810 and soon became the most important in Germany.

But the biggest boost to Berlin's growth was given by the Congress of Vienna (1815). In keeping with their policy of establishing strong monarchies, the victorious powers gave Prussia control over large areas of northern Germany, including the Rhineland and Westphalia. With the beginnings of German industrialization in the 1830s and 1840s, Berlin soon emerged as the most important centre of commerce and communications and of the engineering and clothing industries. After the establishment of Berlin as capital of the new German Empire in 1871, even more spectacular growth ensued. By then, Berlin was comfortably ahead of Vienna, and its position as the German metropolis was already assured.

In 1846 the radical journalist Friedrich Sass wrote that

> Berlin is a city that, under more favourable conditions than Potsdam, was raised up by the ruling dynasty. Only in recent, or very recent times, has it tried to develop as a European city with its own perspectives, and to exchange the court dress of the reigning house for civilian dress. . . . As a royal city Berlin has become more accustomed than other cities to the play-acting and the external glitter that is always tied up with monarchy. This enthusiasm for monarchical pomp has contributed a lot to the people's tendency to support the existing order of things as being the most natural, the simplest, the most indispensable and the most necessary.[1]

Popular enthusiasm for the Hohenzollerns had reached a peak during and immediately after the war against the French in 1813–15. As the city grew in size and importance as an economic and intellectual centre, the role of the court diminished somewhat. After the defeat of the 1848 revolution, a substantial section of the population was alienated from the ruling house. For ten years Friedrich Wilhelm IV directed the triumphant forces of reaction. Newspapers were closed down, political associations dissolved, radicals imprisoned, schools and universities purged. But the basis had been laid for a long-lasting democratic and radical tradition, well rooted both in the middle and the working class. With the beginnings in 1858 of the 'New Era,' the democratic forces began to come back into the open. 'Forty-eighters' returning from exile found jobs with the city's revived Liberal press; in 1862 the first of a succession of Liberal mayors was elected, and the Left Liberals dominated city government for the rest of the imperial period. However, in Reichstag elections, where a 'one man, one vote' system operated, the Social Democrats were soon able to mount an effective challenge. In 1877, they won two of the city's six seats, and by 1912 the Socialist dominance of Berlin's proletarian districts was so complete that they won no less than 75 per cent of the total votes cast in the capital.

Bismarck was said to dislike Berlin so much that he considered moving the imperial capital to Kassel, and Wilhelm II preferred to spend most of his time in Potsdam.[2] Yet the Hohenzollern dynasty continued to exercise considerable influence over the city's life, and 'monarchical pomp' remained a highly visible aspect of the city. It was perhaps this contrast that gave Imperial Berlin much of its distinctive flavour. For an important section of the population, loyalty to the King and Emperor was a professional requirement and, often, no doubt, quite sincerely felt. This section included the military, a variety of other state officials, and the Protestant clergy. Royalist sentiment was also strong among the aristocracy and among many of the lower middle class.[3] On the other hand, the Left Liberals, with their strongholds in the educated middle class, were distinctly lukewarm toward the ruling dynasty and toward the cult of royalty, and the Social Democrats were openly scornful. Critics of the established order tended to express their scorn in a tone of biting sarcasm, which became characteristic of a large part of the Berlin press. All the things that one half of the population regarded as sacred were continually subjected to *Hohn* and *Spott* (sneering and jeering—two favourite Berlin terms) by the other half.[4] And this applied as much to the Protestant church as to other national institutions. Meanwhile, the champions of tradition hit back with abuse and name-calling, in which anti-Semitism often played a part—Liberalism, for instance, was often presented as a Jewish conspiracy, and 'the Jewish press' was a favourite scapegoat.[5] This style of controversy was repeated within the church: liberal Protestants sneered at their conservative co-religionists as uncultured obscurantists, and conservatives referred to the liberals as 'Jewish Protestants' and tried to call in question their patriotism, and even their honesty.[6] So the tone of religious, as well as political, debate in nineteenth- and early twentieth-century Berlin was bitter.

I

The Prussian kings of the nineteenth century took very seriously their duties as 'supreme bishops' of the Prussian church,[7] and Berlin church life was among those aspects of the city in which they interested themselves very closely. The most visible reflection of this relationship was the fact that members of the royal family were frequently present at the consecration of new churches in the capital city. At the Grace Church, for instance, in 1895, all the bells of the city's churches began to ring as the royal couple arrived at the main door of the church, where they were met by a group of church leaders, the parish council and the architect. The architect gave the key to the king, who gave it to the superintendent, who gave it to the pastor, who opened the door, after which the king and queen entered first, and the others followed in hierarchical order, with the parishioners going in last.[8] The Grace Church had been built 'under the protection of Her Majesty', and many other Berlin churches had special associations with the royal family. This included most notably the city's two most conspicuous ecclesiastical monuments—the cathedral, where many members of the House of Hohenzollern were buried, and the Kaiser Wilhelm Memorial Church. In the heart of the working-class and Socialist district of Wedding, the Thanksgiving Church, opened in 1882, was so called because it was built in thanksgiving for the emperor's escape from an assassination attempt—the same attempt that was used by Bismarck as a pretext for banning the Social Democrats.[9]

The symbolism of these buildings was obvious enough. But the Hohenzollerns also influenced the church in deeper ways. Back in the seventeenth century, the Calvinism of the ruling family had been a source of conflict with the Lutheran majority of the local population. In 1817, Friedrich Wilhelm III forcibly brought the two together in the Prussian Union, and the resulting disputes—in particular, the opposition from strict Lutherans— overshadowed Prussian church life for several decades. By the second half of the nineteenth century, confessional differences were no longer a major issue in Berlin, but Prussian kings took a close interest in the intense conflict between the liberal and orthodox factions of the city's clergy. Many city churches were under royal patronage—that is, the king held the right of presentation (appointment) of the pastor. Successive kings (and queens) were generous to these churches with gifts of money. They also made sure that new appointments went to men who shared their own views. Friedrich Wilhelm IV, in particular, and to a lesser extent, Wilhelm I, preferred theological orthodoxy, while Wilhelm II supported the *Mittelpartei*, which steered a middle course between the more strident advocates of orthodoxy and liberalism, both of whom were numerous in Berlin. All these kings also attempted to influence the political pronouncements of the clergy. Criticism of the king by Berlin clergy was out of the question, and as long as the monarchy lasted it would have been equally out of the question for a Berlin clergyman to declare his support for the Social Democrats. The Brandenburg Consistory, the principal organ of church administration for the province in which Berlin lay, and the *Evangelischer Oberkirchenrat*, which was the supreme administrative organ of the Prussian church, both consisted of royal nominees. While they usually had a balanced membership, with members of varying confessional backgrounds and theological tendencies, the choice of president reflected the views of the king (or sometimes of the government) as to the overall direction that the church should be taking.[10]

The relationship of the church with the monarchy was a factor of central importance in the history of Protestantism in nineteenth-century Berlin. Two other factors of general relevance were the city's famous shortage of churches, and the legacy of the 1848 revolution. Of course, the failure to build enough churches or assign enough clergy to meet the needs of rapidly growing urban parishes was nothing unique to Berlin. In greater or lesser degree the same situation existed in most of the larger cities of nineteenth-century Europe, and in most cases there was a considerable time-lag between the onset of rapid growth and the framing of a church response. But the shortage of churches in Berlin was of longer standing than most and by the later nineteenth century it was among the most acute. In 1881 a speaker at the city synod noted that Berlin was regarded by foreigners as 'the most irreligious city in the world'.[11]

Up until the accession of Frederick the Great in 1740, the Prussian capital had been well provided with Protestant churches. The original medieval parishes were supplemented by the building of fourteen new churches in the later seventeenth and early eighteenth centuries. However, there was then a complete standstill until the building in 1835 of the four famous churches designed by the city's leading architect, Karl Friedrich Schinkel, in the impoverished northern suburbs. By then the largest parishes in the city contained over 50,000 people. With the onset of very rapid population growth in the 1850s, the trickle of new church buildings and pastorates was quite inadequate to provide for the religious needs of more than a quite small proportion of the population. The problems were most acute in the working-class suburbs on the north, south and east. In 1890, when the deterioration in religious provision reached its lowest point, Holy Cross, with 128,000 people, held the record for parish size. Over the city as a whole, there were 9,593 Protestants for each Protestant clergyman, and 26.5 Protestants for each seat in a Protestant church.[12] The generally low attendances at Sunday services meant that there was seldom a danger that anyone would be hurt while pushing their way to a seat—though churches could be crowded on major festivals, as on Good Friday and Easter Sunday in 1879, when people were being turned away from some churches half an hour before the service began. However, the still fairly considerable demand for the assistance of a clergyman at the four major turning-points in life meant that pastors had their time fully taken up in performing ceremonies and instructing confirmees, and other aspects of their work were likely to be neglected. In 1900, by which time there had been a slight amelioration, each of the 56 clergymen on the north side of the city took an average of eight baptisms, six funerals and two weddings for each week in the year, in addition to instructing 170 confirmation candidates. Before the division of parishes and the establishment of new pastorates in the 1890s there had been more extreme cases in which the number of baptisms rose to thirty a week, the funerals to sixteen and the weddings to eight. One solution was the mass baptism or mass wedding, which could be a source of resentment among poorer parishioners, who pointed out that the rich were able to pay for personal attention.[13]

In March 1848 religion still provided a common language through which the martyrs of the revolution could be mourned. After the barricade fighting of 18–19 March the barricade fighters sang the funeral hymn *Jesus, meine Zuversicht* outside the palace and demanded Christian burial for the fallen. This took place on 22 March when large numbers of people attended early morning services before the funeral in the afternoon. In keeping with Berlin's pluralist traditions, the ceremony began with sermons in the New Church delivered by a Protestant pastor, a Catholic priest and a Jewish rabbi. Most of the city's Protestant clergy subsequently took part in the procession to the Friedrichshain, where a graveside oration was delivered by Adolf Sydow, a leader of the church's liberal wing. One prominent Berlin preacher, Pastor Karl Büchsel of the fashionable St Matthew's Church, was, however, hostile to the revolution from the start, and in the course of the year the Pietist wing of the church became increasingly closely identified with the cause of counter-revolution. The Pietists, who combined an emotional religious style with a strongly conservative approach to doctrine, enjoyed great influence at the time because of their close links with the royal family and the court. The royal coup d'état of November 1848 received the outspoken support of a large section of Berlin clergy.[14] From this time on, we can see a more pronounced split between the city's powerful tradition of political radicalism and the Protestant church. On the one hand, a large section of the church unequivocally identified Christianity with political conservatism. On the other hand, democratic and radical movements in the city tended to acquire a secular tone. This applied most emphatically to the Socialists, who began to be a force in Berlin in the 1860s. But Berlin liberalism also tended to have an anticlerical edge, which quite frequently broadened into a more generalized secularism. There was always a mediating element within the Berlin church which challenged the stark opposition between a secular radicalism and a conservative church. But the scepticism or indifference of most radicals was as discouraging for them as the hostility of large sections of the clergy and devout laity.

Until 1906 the overwhelming majority of Berliners belonged to one of the three great religious communities, namely the Protestants, the Roman Catholics and the Jews. After 1906 the proportion of church members in the population fell somewhat as a result of the movement of mass resignation from the churches (*Kirchenaustrittsbewegung*), mainly supported by members and followers of the Social Democratic Party. But in 1914 about 95 per cent of the population were still affiliated to one of the three major communities. During the period when Berlin was capital of the German Empire, the proportion of Protestants slowly fell, the Roman Catholic share of the population increased, and the proportion of Jews remained more or less constant. But the Protestants remained by far the largest community. In 1871 they comprised 89 per cent of the population, as against 6 per cent Catholics and 4 per cent Jewish. By 1905, the proportion of Protestants was down to 83 per cent, with 11 per cent Catholic and 5 per cent Jewish.[15]

The Protestants, as well as being by far the most numerous group, were also the most socially varied; by contrast, household incomes were far above the city average in the Jewish community, which included a disproportionately large number of middle-class members, whereas the Catholic community was strongly working-class, and had the lowest average income levels. Within the Jewish community, there was a fundamental division between the German-speaking and mainly prosperous majority and the poorer Yiddish-speaking *Ostjuden* from Germany's eastern provinces. From about 1895, the former were moving westward in large numbers into the middle-class suburbs of Charlottenburg, Schöneberg and Wilmersdorf; the latter remained concentrated in the Scheunenviertel, a slum district on the northeast side of the city centre, which was Berlin's nearest equivalent to the working-class Jewish districts of London and New York. The former were predominantly liberal in religion; the latter were much more traditionalist. Jews were a vital element in Berlin's middle class and intelligentsia—and, indeed, those of Jewish descent who had converted to Christianity were also a distinctive and important group. But they made up only a very small part of the city's working class.[16]

II

In terms of nominal affiliation, then, the great majority of Berliners were members of the Prussian *Landeskirche*. In terms of actual religious practice, however, they varied considerably, and here we need to say something about the geography of Berlin in the later nineteenth century. By the 1870s it was evident that there were at least three geographically concentrated patterns of religious observance in the capital. The simplest contrast was between central and peripheral parishes. In 1876, 81 per cent of legitimate children born to Protestant mothers were baptized in the central parishes, but only 57 per cent in the peripheral parishes; the proportions of religious burials were 82 per cent and 44 per cent, and of church weddings 37 per cent and 21 per cent.[17]

Among the central parishes, however, there were differences between those in the old city and those in the west. The highest congregations were found to the west, in the elite Dorotheenstadt, around Unter den Linden, and further out in the Tiergarten, with its aristocrats, army officers and higher civil servants. Here religious and political conservatism were often interlinked, loyalty to the Crown was an important factor, and the dominant religious tone was Pietist. Under Friedrich Wilhelm III (1797–1840) a strongly religious tone was reintroduced into the Prussian court, and this trend went further under the Pietist Friedrich Wilhelm IV (1840–61). Officers and officials were expected to attend church, and a reputation for piety was an advantage. Aristocrats became presidents of Bible Societies, foreign missions, and numerous other Protestant organizations, and their wives were frequently very active in charity. In this respect, queens and princesses often gave the lead: in particular, Friedrich Wilhelm IV's wife, Queen Elisabeth, was a keen supporter of hospitals and orphanages, and her carriage with its four white horses became a familiar sight in the various remote corners of the city where such institutions were to be found. The last empress, Auguste Viktoria, set a very similar example.[18] A survey of church attendance in 1869 showed that the largest congregations in the city were to be found in the cathedral, with its team of court preachers, and at St Matthew's in the Tiergarten, where the pastor, Karl Büchsel, was an outspoken champion of religious and political conservatism. In the 1870s, Sunday morning services at St Matthew's were said to rank among Berlin's major social events, and one of the few occasions when members of the different branches of the city's elite would meet in the same place.[19]

By comparison, the old cities of Berlin and Cölln were more bourgeois, and thus more politically and theologically liberal in tone. St Peter's and St Nicholas were partly, and St Mary's wholly under the patronage of the city council, as were the neighbouring New and Jerusalem churches in Friedrichstadt, and as a result all were noted for their Liberal clergy. The educationalist Eduard Spranger, who received confirmation instruction in the New Church in the 1890s, recalled that 'no exaggerated supernaturalism was demanded of us', but that 'our religious faculty was stimulated in a way that did not bring us into immediate conflict with the enlightened atmosphere of the capital city around us'. Later he took an enthusiastic part in 'parish evenings', where the clergy and educated laypeople listened to lectures on theological topics, and where Friedrich Schleiermacher, the patron saint of Berlin's liberal Protestants, was still regarded as the supreme authority. Here the population had deep local roots, and often long-standing family ties with particular churches or clergymen. Baptisms, church weddings, religious burial tended to be seen as a matter of course. But demonstrative piety was not the fashion, and church attendance and communicant statistics tended to be lower than in the west of the city.[20]

At the opposite end of the spectrum socially and religiously from the pious and wealthy west were the impoverished working-class districts to the north. In the 1830s and 1840s, the area around the Hamburg Gate (the Voigtland) was known as the poorest in the city, and the nearby Oranienburg Gate was developing as the main focus of heavy industry. In the 1840s and 1850s the factories were beginning to move out to Moabit and Wedding, which were among the major centres of heavy industry under the Empire. During the later part of the nineteenth century, new industrial districts also developed on the east and southeast sides of the city. In contrast to the giant factories of the north, Luisenstadt, on the southeast side, developed as the principal centre of the city's clothing industry—its courts filled with small workshops, and its tenements packed with women working at home on their sewing machines.[21]

In 1875 as part of the programme of secularizing measures imposed by Bismarck in his so-called *Kulturkampf* against the Roman Catholic Church, civil registration of births, marriages and deaths was introduced in Prussia. This was followed by a sharp drop in the proportion of couples going through a church marriage ceremony or baptizing their children. In the eyes of many church commentators this revealed a state of semiheathenism among the population of Berlin. All were agreed that church attendance was low and contact with the clergy infrequent in poorer districts of the city.[22] A survey in 1869 suggested that in working-class areas of the city, morning congregations averaged 1 per cent of the Protestant population. In 1877 a Protestant pastor, E. Hülle, produced a statistical study of Berlin church life, in which he divided parishes into four groups, according to the social status of their inhabitants. The average ratio of annual communions to Protestant population was 16.5 per cent in the richest group, 12.4 per cent in the second group, 6.6 per cent in the third group and 4.9 per cent in the poorest group. By 1890, there had been a general increase, but the rank order remained the same: the ratios were now 23.1 per cent, 15.8 per cent, 13.8 per cent and 9.5 per cent (see also figures in table 1). Hülle concentrated mainly on living conditions in the poorer areas of Berlin as an explanation for the low levels of religious practice. He referred to 'the frightening degree of indifference with regard to anything that is not directly concerned with the business of making a living'.[23] Other commentators stressed such factors as the influence of socialism, the prevalence of irreligious ideas, the distance between clergy and people and the high rates of mobility within the city.

To begin with the last of these points: it was widely believed among Berlin clergy that the mobility of the population made it particularly difficult to maintain

TABLE 1

**Protestant Communicants in Berlin Districts, 1900, as a Percentage
of Protestant Population**

	SOCIAL RANKING	COMMUNICANTS (%)
Central districts[a]	1	16.5
Friedrichsvorstadt and Tempelhofervorstadt West	1	18.9
Moabit East, Tiergarten and Friedrich Wilhelm Stadt	1	18.1
Friedrichs- and Schönebergervorstadt	4	16.2
Tempelhofervorstadt East	5	10.2
Moabit West	6	11.8
Rosenthaler Vorstadt South	7	6.3
Stralauer Viertel West	8	9.2
Königsviertel	9	12.8
Inner Luisenstadt	9	9.3
Spandauer Viertel	9	11.0
Outer Luisenstadt West	12	4.4
Oranienburger Vorstadt	13	21.8
Stralauer Viertel East	13	13.0
Outer Luisenstadt East	15	12.7
Rosenthaler Vorstadt North	16	6.7
Wedding	17	3.4

SOURCE: *SJSB*, 27 (1900–2) provides communicant statistics for each parish and figures for infant mortality and for housing in each district—the social ranking has been calculated on the basis of the latter two indicators.
[a]Central districts comprise Berlin, Cölln, Friedrichswerder, Friedrichstadt, Dorotheenstadt.

contact with their parishioners. For instance, Pastor Baumann of the Thanksgiving Church said in a lecture of 1885 that half the population of Berlin changed their address during the year. He saw his parish in terms of a series of 'rings'. On the periphery were 'thousands of soldiers, young men, women workers,...servants [who] enter our giant city, without there being, under present conditions, the slightest chance that the church will have any influence on them.' Official statistics confirmed that changes of address were very frequent, but it is less clear how far people moved. Frequent moves within a small area of the city would clearly be less destructive of ties with such bodies as the church than would moves from one side of the city to another. In fact, Günther Dehn, who became an assistant pastor at the Reformation Church in Moabit in 1911, stated that although the workers moved frequently, they preferred to stay in the same part of the city. This kind of pattern is illustrated by an interview with a woman born in Lichtenberg in 1912: because her father was often out of work, they were always on the move, from one back court to another; but since the flats were all in the same area, she continued all the time to attend the same school and the same branch of the Good Templars, and to use the same library.[24] Before the significance of the high rates of mobility can be properly evaluated, therefore, more precise information is needed as to the patterns that it took.

The pastor was a member of the educated bourgeoisie, and as such, a person who might be respected, but with whom an intimate relationship was scarcely possible. Information is available on the social backgrounds of the majority of Berlin clergymen, and as an example I have taken the twenty-two clergymen who officiated in the strongly proletarian north Berlin district of Wedding in 1905. Of these at least twenty had attended university. In twenty cases the occupation of the pastor's father was known. The lowest in social status of the fathers were two master craftsmen and a farmer. The others comprised three teachers, a headmaster, five pastors, a musical director, an engineer, three state officials, two merchants and a factory owner.[25] There seems to have been some feeling among working-class Protestants that the clergy identified with their own kind. An oral history survey of the 1950s, which interviewed workers born in the 1870s and 1880s about their early experiences, reported several complaints of this kind. For instance, a woman from Reinickendorf, who had worked as a domestic servant, recalled that in the confirmation class the pastor had placed the children from the mainly middle-class *Vorschule* in the front rows and addressed them by their first names, while the children from the more plebeian *Gemeindeschule* were addressed by their surnames. She eventually left the church, feeling that 'pastors never helped people, and preached from the sole motive of earning a living'. A woman from Schöneberg remembered that the principal pastor would not have any *Gemeindeschule* children at all in his classes, but left them to his assistants, and a pastor who had been in a Charlottenburg parish in the early twentieth century claimed that his colleagues had given 'preferential treatment to children from the middle class, with whom they felt most at home'.[26]

The sense that the clergy were too far distant from the ordinary parish member was one of the considerations that lay behind the foundation in 1877 of the City Mission, which became one of the most important, and the most controversial, instruments in the church's efforts to win back the loyalty of working-class Berliners.[27] The Mission used evangelists drawn from the working class, and set up simple meeting rooms in poor areas. As Adolf Stoecker, the Mission's director, put it, the people regarded the missionary as 'someone like themselves', who 'knows where the shoe pinches'.[28] Pastor Kraft of the Zion Church, speaking to the local synod, justified the work of the city missionaries in these terms:

> Certainly there are many parishioners who do not want pastoral care from a city missionary, but there are many who prefer a city missionary to a clergyman, because they feel more social affinity with the missionary. Especially in democratically tinged families a city missionary can achieve more than a pastor, if they are in poverty, as the sight of the pastor's better coat can awaken feelings of antipathy and class hatred.[29]

City missionaries might be resented as intruders; but on the other hand there were many people who appreciated their willingness regularly to visit poor families, and who expressed pleasant surprise at the fact that the church was interested in them. Admittedly, the question of whether a visit should come from the missionary or from the pastor was a somewhat delicate one: some people would have felt that their social standing was in question if a missionary called; and many people who had little else to do with the church felt flattered by a visit from the pastor.[30]

If the clergy were regarded as somewhat distant, the same could be true of regular churchgoers, and even religiously minded working-class people might not feel at home in their parish church. At the Twelve Apostles Church in the 1870s, the parish council decided to hold separate services for middle-class and working-class parishioners, because it was found that the poorer churchgoers felt ill at ease in the presence of well-dressed people, and gave up going.[31] For similar reasons, the city missionaries found that some of their working-class converts would attend a Bible class in a meeting room, but would not go to the main service in the parish church. In 1900, a city missionary complained that when he looked around the parish church during a service very few artisans or workers were to be seen.[32]

Unfortunately, I have not been able to find any more precise information on the social composition of congregations. However, lists of officeholders, with their occupations, are frequently available, and sometimes there are lists of leading members of the rival church parties. The two main parties, the Liberals and the Positives (Conservatives), were both highly organized and elections to parish councils or the city synod generally took the form of a battle between them. It is clear from these lists that the lay elite of working-class parishes during this period was heavily middle class (see table 2). In St Paul's, Gesundbrunnen, one of the poorest parishes in Berlin, none of the elders elected in 1874 was a manual worker, and only three out of thirty-six parish representatives. Subsequent elections, continuing right up to the 1930s, led to the choice of only the occasional worker, to sit beside the factory owners, landlords, shopkeepers, master artisans and teachers who made up most of the parish corporations. In another north Berlin parish, Zion, where about 80 per cent of the population belonged to the working class in the mid–1860s, the 1874 elections produced no working-class elders and only one worker among the thirty parish representatives. During the same period, Nazareth Church in Wedding (also ranked by Hülle among the poorest parishes in the city) was said to be dominated by members of long-established Wedding families, who regarded with considerable suspicion the mass of poor factory workers who had flooded into the area.[33] By 1897, when a characteristically bitter church election generated a large amount of polemical literature in that parish, there were some factory workers and craftsmen among the leaders of the rival parties, but they were very much in a minority. Out of twenty-seven leading supporters of the theologically conservative Positive Party, seven were manual workers; a leaflet put out by the Liberal Party named many leading supporters without their occupations, but out of twenty-two whose occupation was given, only five were manual workers; none of the seven committee members belonging to the Peace Party was a manual worker (see table 3). The highest number of working-class parish representatives I have seen is in Reconciliation parish where eight out of twenty-eight were manual workers in 1919.[34] This relatively high proportion was no doubt re-

TABLE 2

Occupations of Elders and Parish Representatives in St Paul's Parish, Gesundbrunnen, 1873 and 1906

	1873	1906
Rentiers, property owners	12	7
Merchants, factory owners	12	8
Officials	3	3
Professions	1	1
Teachers	4	8
Pharmacist	1	—
White-collar workers	3	—
Shopkeepers	2	—
Master artisans	5	8
Skilled workers	3	5
Unskilled workers	—	1
Not stated	2	2
Total	48	43

SOURCE: *Geschichte der St Pauls-Gemeinde zu Berlin-Nord* (Berlin 1935).

TABLE 3

Occupations of Leaders of Church Parties in Nazareth Parish, Wedding, 1897

Positives	
Rentiers, property owners	2
Merchants, factory owners	1
State officals	6
Teachers	2
White-collar workers	2
Police	1
Master artisans	7
Skilled workers	3
Unskilled workers	3
Total	27
Liberals	
Merchants	1
Professions	1
Innkeepers	6
Master artisans	9
Skilled workers	5
Total	22
Peace Party	
Merchants	2
Teachers	3
White-collar worker	1
Master artisan	1
Total	7

SOURCE: election leaflets in file on Hermann Neubauer, pastor of Nazareth parish 1891–1932, in Brandenburgisches Konsistorium: Personalia (EZA).

lated to the proximity of one of the housing projects of the church-sponsored Patriotic Building Society, which was also a major base for the Protestant Workers' Associations and Christian Trade Unions.[35]

Out of sixteen branches of the Protestant Workers' Association in Berlin in 1905, fourteen were based on localities. But the cemetery workers and coffin carriers were sufficiently numerous to have their own branches. According to one parish history, these posts were mainly filled by rural immigrants from the eastern provinces, and in appointing such officials, pastors would presumably give preference to those who were known to be loyal church members. Apart from church employees, the section of the work force that seems most often to have had close ties with the Protestant church were state employees—presumably because they identified themselves with the Protestant church's fervent patriotism and loyalty to state and emperor. A high proportion of the residents in the Patriotic Building Society's housing project were employed by the post office or the railways, and the thirty-eight elders and parish representatives in Reconciliation parish in 1919 included no less than ten employees of the post office and five members of the police. The patriotism of state employees even seems to have extended to voting for the more conservative candidates in parish elections—the liberal faction in Capernaum parish complained that the local concentration of employees of the police, the post office and the tramways put them at a disadvantage.[36]

During the period of very rapid urban growth in the later nineteenth century, the majority of adult Berliners had moved in from other parts of Germany, and so far as the working class was concerned this meant very largely Brandenburg and the eastern provinces. It was frequently observed by the clergy that many immigrants came to Berlin with habits both of churchgoing and of close contact with the clergy, but soon lost touch with the church on arrival in the city. The statistics of religious practice in the various Prussian provinces indicate that this was very probably correct. In the years 1891–5, when the annual number of communions per 100 members of the *Landeskirche* was 16 in Berlin, it was 24 in Mecklenburg-Strelitz, 34 in Mecklenburg-Schwerin, 41 in Brandenburg, 44 in East Prussia, 45 in West Prussia, 49 in Silesia and 65 in Posen.[37] The reports of the City Mission suggest that many immigrants regretted having lost touch with the church since coming to Berlin. Such people were often quite responsive to the efforts of the city missionaries, and featured prominently in their reports. Thus it was, for instance, with a Wedding carpenter and his wife, whom the missionary persuaded to join his Bible class, though they were reluctant to attend the main church service because they had no suitable clothes. The wife told him: 'Earlier, before we came to Berlin, we went to church every Sunday. We sang hymns at home, and we continued to do that in the early days here, but then the neighbours made fun of us, so we gave it up. Then we went to church less often, and for a long time we have not gone at all.'[38] Stoecker described how recent immigrants to the city who had little contact with the church would nonetheless welcome the missionary's suggestion that they gather round to read the Bible together; neighbours would join in; and the basis would be laid for a new bible class in a meeting room.[39]

There was thus a considerable section of the population who had largely lost touch with the church but retained certain religious beliefs and customs, or at least an interest in religious questions. In times of sickness, especially, there were many otherwise indifferent people who welcomed a visit from a missionary who would pray with them or read the Bible. Sometimes they hoped that the missionary's prayers would aid recovery; sometimes their concern was with the fate of their souls in the event of death; sometimes, they simply gained strength from the feeling that they were not alone, and from the missionary's assurance that God cared for them.[40] If Berlin meant for some a welcome freedom, for others it meant disorder and disruption, and the resumption of some form of religious practice was a way of reentering a world in which there were clearly defined landmarks and boundaries.

But while there were some who looked back with a certain nostalgia to the religiosity of their rural youth, and remained essentially loyal to the beliefs they had learnt in the village, there were others, probably more numerous, who saw the rural church as part of an oppressive authority structure from which they were grateful to have escaped. The latter point is suggested by a collection of six interviews with former workers in an East Berlin light-bulb factory, conducted around 1980. The interviewees had all been born in the early years of this century. The only one who had kept up her ties with the church was the single native Berliner. Resentment of the church as a symbol of authority was particularly explicit in the case of a man who had been effectively forced to go to church in his Silesian village, where the Catholic priest owned half the land. Later, he reveled in the freedom of life in Berlin.[41] One of the young men who filled in Günther Dehn's questionnaire about their religious ideas made a similar point. He had been brought up in a village where the school teacher was church organist, and punished those children who had not been in church on Sunday. At one point the children had been required to learn a biblical passage by heart, and this boy had not done so, as his parents were too poor to own a Bible. When the teacher heard this he got the class to chant the saying: 'Wo keine Bibel ist im Haus, da sieht's gar öd' und traurig aus' ('Where there is no Bible in the house, everything looks desolate and sad'). The young man commented: 'As a result of this and hundreds of other cases, thousands of German workers have been alienated from their God.'[42]

The mission journal for 1880 included a section on 'unbelief and ridicule', and it was widely agreed that rejection of Christian beliefs was widespread in working-class districts of Berlin. It was not always clear what specific form this criticism took. However, the journal quite often gave accounts of conversations between missionaries and unbelievers. The main lines of criticism mentioned were claims that religion was unscientific, questioning of passages in the Bible and claims that if there were a God he would not allow so much suffering. Criticism of the Bible frequently included claims that it was 'a book of fairy-tales', though sometimes it took the form of identifying specific inconsistencies. Another missionary reported a series of conversations he had with a man who was for long a sceptic, though he was later converted. In one of their early conversations, the man made a number of characteristic assertions: 'God cannot be living, for otherwise he could not stand by and watch such need. No, no, there's nothing in it. Nature is God. You won't get anywhere with me. I am a freethinker and a Social Democrat. If you can *prove* there's a God I shall believe in it. Otherwise not.'[43] Social Democracy and religious unbelief were bound together in the minds of many Berliners. This was certainly true of conservative Protestants, like those who supported the City Mission, who tended to assume that socialism and Christianity were incompatible, and who blamed Social Democratic propaganda for much of the prevalent unbelief.[44] The Socialists themselves were more divided on the question of the relationship between Christianity and socialism. Frequently they simply asserted that religion was out of date or unscientific; on the other hand, they sometimes claimed that socialism was true Christianity. For instance, one missionary quoted a worker who told him: 'Although I have left the church, I am still a Christian. However, I want to have my heaven here.'[45] Indeed criticism of the Bible tended to focus on miracles or on the biblical account of the Creation; references to the teaching of Jesus, while rare, were always favourable.[46] In 1878, the Socialist orator Johann Most initiated the first of the movements of mass resignation from the churches that were a periodic feature of Berlin life for several decades. While Most condemned religion as unscientific, the main point of his criticism was political: the church is a pillar of the state, and to attack it is thus to undermine the state. Although some four thousand people attended the opening meeting of his campaign, the number of resignations was at this stage small.[47] While support for the Social Democrats was growing, and many workers were partly alienated from the church, relatively few were ready to make a definite break. Again, the reports of the City Mission throw some light on the complexities of popular attitudes to religion and the churches.

The importance attached to baptism and other religious rites will be discussed in chapter 8. Two other aspects of popular religiosity will be mentioned here: the appeal of religious music and the importance of the Bible. The City Mission exploited the evocative quality of music, in the hope that it would reawaken suppressed religious feelings: one of their best known institutions was a team of boys, known as the *Kurrende*, who sang hymns in streets and courtyards. Those who liked the singing would throw coins down into the courtyard. According to the Mission, 'the singing of the children often does wonders', as it 'finds the way to the heart of those who no longer hear the word of God, and also disdain the printed word'.[48]

According to the pastor of Zion Church in 1865, most households in his parish had a Bible, but in few was it read.[49] However, two kinds of evidence indicate, from opposing directions, the continuing centrality of the Bible in Berlin's religious culture. One is the relative popularity of Bible study groups, which seem to have been attended by many working-class people who, for one reason or another, would not go to the main church services. One missionary who had started a particularly flourishing group described 'the joy with which the last remaining coins are spent on buying the Book of Books', and another quoted various testimonials from satisfied customers along the lines of 'These hours are quite different from church. You are taken so deeply into the Bible and learn to understand it.' A woman with an irreligious husband always felt unhappy at home, but 'God's Word' gave her peace. And a lengthy account by another missionary of a former atheist who had been converted and eventually got a job with a firm that sold Bibles includes a description of the man in the period immediately before his conversion, sitting up late at night poring over the Bible.[50] A more backhanded tribute to the continuing fascination exercised on German Protestants by the Bible was the enthusiasm with which some sceptics searched for inconsistencies and absurdities in the sacred text with which to confound the preachers of the gospel. Here is one example, where a group of men tried to prove to a city missionary that there were obvious inconsistencies in the Bible: ' "Cain went into a strange land, and there he took a wife." That's what the Bible says. Well that shows that besides the first human couple and their children, there must have been other people.' Confident of victory, they brought me the Bible, and very shamefacedly, they then saw that they had got it wrong. (This mistaken idea about Cain's wife is very widespread in Berlin.)'[51]

Those who lost faith in the clergy but continued to believe in the Bible were promising material for the free churches or 'sects' (as they were commonly known) which were active in working-class areas of Berlin. Of these, by far the largest were the Apostolic churches, which claimed 1,191 members in 1881, rising to around 10,000 in 1910, when they were also represented in many of the suburbs. However, there were many smaller groups. A study by Eberhard Büchner[52] included, besides the New Apostolic church, the Christian Zion church (followers of Alexander Dowie), the Dissenting Christians, the Salvation Army, the Christian Theosophists, and a group named Oschm-Rahmah-Johjihjoh, whose members lived communally, and whose ideas were derived partly from Swedenborg and partly from Buddhism. The latter two groups were very small, and their teachings had little in common with those of mainstream Christianity (though in the case of the Christian Theosophists there was some degree of overlap). The first four groups, in spite of some idiosyncracies of teaching or practice, had unmistakably evangelical Protestant roots and in this they had affinities with the other more conventional 'sectarian' bodies, such as the Methodists and Baptists. The first two preached an imminent Second Coming, the first and third practised prophecy, and common to the first three groups was the part played by miraculous healing in their meetings. As a representative of the Zion Church told Büchner, 'Above all, we see Christ not only as saviour, but also as healer.' At the Dissenting Christians, Büchner met a 'poor little needlewoman . . . who has already laid hands on who knows how many people, and, in her own words, experienced bright wonders . . . . All sorts of illnesses are healed in this way, even severe abdominal pains, which can otherwise be cured only through dangerous operations. The precondition is that God "wills" the cure.'[53]

All commentators agreed that these movements offered a tight-knit supportive community, an informal atmosphere and a strict moral code, all of which appealed to dissatisfied working-class and lower middle-class members of the *Landeskirche*. Indeed they established themselves in the heart of the city's working-class communities. The most notorious of the city's giant tenements,

Ackerstrasse 132/3 in Wedding, with a population of over 1,500 in the 1880s, was said to have its own Methodist church, and the working-class districts to the north and east of the city were the main centres of sectarian activity.[54] Büchner described as follows the environment of the typical Apostolic parish: 'They mostly meet in back corners. You have to cross dirty courts and climb up steep steps, before you get to the doors of their assembly rooms. Filled with curiosity, you open the door and find yourself in a cheerless whitewashed room in which it would appear that factory workers once carried out their difficult duties.'[55] This was in dramatic contrast to the grandiose buildings of the official Protestant church, towering above the neighbouring tenements, and sometimes standing in partial isolation from them on a little island of greenery. But for many working-class people the very familiarity and inconspicuousness of the surroundings in which the sectarians met may have been part of the attraction. According to Büchner, the members of the Apostolic congregation were 'all drawn from the common people...You can see that they have to struggle for their existence. Their faces are mostly worn with care.'[56]

III

In the 1870s the Protestant church in Berlin appeared to have hit rock bottom. The 1880s, however, saw an upturn in religious practice, especially in working-class areas, where the figures had been lowest. One factor that must have helped there was the change in church finances that came into operation in 1882: the charging of fees for baptisms, weddings and funerals was abolished, and the 'church tax' was introduced, which was fixed at a certain percentage of income tax. This had the advantage for the church that it ensured a more predictable income, and one that could be more easily redistributed to the areas of greatest need; it had the advantage for poorer church members that more of the burden of supporting the church was shifted onto the shoulders of those with large incomes.[57] The proportion of parents baptizing their children rose again to a high level in the 1880s, and there was a more modest rise in the proportion of church weddings and religious funerals. Numbers of communicants and churchgoers also rose.[58] A popular explanation for this at the time was that the depression of the later 1870s and early 1880s caused dedicated hedonists to turn back to God: 'The time of need taught people to pray again.'[59] Another interpretation stressed the role of the City Mission in reviving religious practice in working-class areas.[60] It may also be relevant that the Anti-Socialist Law of 1878 held back the growth of the great new force in Berlin life, and the one that presented the churches with their biggest challenge at that time. The Social Democracy of the later nineteenth century was, as innumerable commentators pointed out, a complete interpretation of life, indeed, a new religion, and for twelve years the churches were partly protected from the competition it offered.

In the early 1890s, the Protestant church at last embarked on its long-discussed church-building programme.[61] The church tax provided a large part of the necessary funds. The victory of the conservative Positive Party in the 1889 church elections removed one important barrier to progress: the previous Liberal majority on the city synod had made the allocation of new funds for church building dependent on the provision that pastors of new parishes were to be elected, rather than nominated by a patron, whereas the president of the Consistory held strictly to the principle that existing patronage rights must be respected. The accession of Wilhelm II in 1888 may also have helped, as he and his wife were both enthusiastic supporters of the cause of giving Berlin more churches, and they were willing both to devote royal money to the cause and to throw their own prestige behind fund-raising efforts. The 1890s saw so many new church-building projects that soon anticlericals were complaining as loudly of the excessive number of churches in the city as church-people had once complained of the shortage. As a sardonic city guide published in 1905 wrote: old churches were 'beautiful, though not numerous', while new churches were 'merely numerous'.[62] The evolution of the northwestern industrial district of Moabit was typical. In 1835 it got a 'Schinkel church', and by 1895, the population had risen to 120,000, but there was still only the one church. Then, however, four were built in the next eighteen years, while the population grew to 200,000. Even then, with one church for 40,000 people (of whom close to 90 per cent were Protestants), the provision was scarcely extravagant.[63]

These new churches were for the most part large and imposing buildings. Typically they seated around twelve hundred people. Liberals were inclined to suggest that there was something Catholic about big churches, and that new churches should be 'simpler, cheaper and more in keeping with Evangelical ideas'.[64] With the aid of the church tax, they were able to employ several pastors and a considerable corps of assistants, usually including one or more nurses. The pastors would carve up the parish, so that each had special responsibility for one section, and the intimidating size of the total parish area could be reduced to somewhat more manageable proportions. The means by which the Protestant parish tried to reestablish its presence in the life of working-class districts were social work (*Diakonie*) and clubs (*Vereine*). More theologically conservative parishes also supported the evangelistic efforts of the City Mission.[65] The later nineteenth and early twentieth centuries saw the development in Germany of powerful ideologically based subcultures, Protestant, Catholic and Social Democratic, each with a very wide range of organizations, designed to protect their members from the contamination of over-close contact with those who did not share their world-view.[66] The Protestant subculture never developed in Berlin anything like the strength it had in its strongholds on the Rhine and Ruhr and in Saxony. But Berlin, too, in this period saw the formation of such organizations as men's clubs, workers' clubs, clubs for young women and young men, and sports groups.

In the field of social work the efforts of Protestant parishes were very extensive and many-sided. All had a poor fund and a nurse or nurses. But this period saw many more ambitious schemes. One of the most ambitious, and one well in keeping with the trend toward the establishment of discrete subcultures, was the

Patriotic Building Society, associated with the Reconciliation Church in Wedding.[67] This society was formed in 1902, and in 1903 it started building its own small estate of superior working-class flats, in a style halfway between the traditional Berlin tenement block and medieval Nuremberg. Some of their members 'had suffered at the hands of colleagues and neighbours because of their [the members'] patriotic, Christian outlook'—hence the establishment of a ghetto where everyone thought alike, an idea developed more extensively in the 1920s by the Social Democrats and Communists, who developed whole 'settlements' on the outskirts of the city.[68] Other initiatives of this period were directed at the non-churchgoing population, or at people in general, regardless of religious affiliation. As an example of the former, the Schrippenkirche, also associated with the Reconciliation parish, provided meals of coffee and bread rolls (*Schrippen*) combined with religious services for homeless men.[69] As an example of the latter, the Nazareth parish, also in Wedding, established a whole series of charitable institutions in the 1880s and 1890s, including a team of parish nurses, a children's hospital, a home for abandoned children and an institution providing work for unemployed men.[70]

Protestants took great pride in these initiatives, and saw them as a refutation of the accusations that the church did not care about the poor.[71] And the pastor of Nazareth parish, who was sick of arguing with people who had resigned from the church, decided that the only effective answer was 'love in word and deed': 'The pastor with his faithful pastoral care of the parishioners, the parish sisters with loving service at the sick bed, achieve more than meetings and resolutions.'[72] No doubt there was much truth in both these arguments. Yet in some ways, the high priority given by the church to welfare work added to its problems in relation to the working class.

In the first place, *Diakonie* was expensive, and could only be funded with the help of wealthy patrons—so, the church's already close links with aristocrats and, to a lesser extent, industrialists, were further strengthened. For instance, when in 1865 an energetic new pastor, who was planning numerous social projects, was appointed to St Sophia's, he was able to achieve these because of the support of the banker Adolf Lösche, and his wife Sophie; the Lazarus hospital in Wedding depended crucially on the support of Louis Schwartzkopff, the head of one of the city's largest engineering firms; and the Berlin YMCA, soon after its foundation in 1883, was able to build an impressive headquarters on the Wilmelmstrasse only as a result of a five-hundred-thousand-mark gift from Count Waldersee.[73]

Secondly, the recipients of help sometimes objected to what they regarded as the patronizing tone and the heavy-handed religious message that went with it. The Workers' Colony in Wedding, which provided work and accommodation for the unemployed, was a particular subject of complaint, as religion was bound up with the strict discipline, in a way that was entirely counterproductive so far as the aim of achieving a religious conversion was concerned—for instance, religious texts covered the walls, and only religious reading matter was allowed.[74]

Some Protestants also tried to mobilize the masses for the cause of fatherland and emperor. The key figure here was Adolf Stoecker (1835–1909), who came to

Berlin as court and cathedral preacher in 1874.[75] His life-long objective was to make the Protestant church a *Volkskirche* (church of the people) and the leading agent of social reform. This was to be achieved partly by evangelism, designed to reawaken the dormant religious faith of the masses, above all through the City Mission; partly by revitalizing the church's network of charitable institutions; partly by politics—which meant confronting the 'godless' forces of Liberalism and Social Democracy. The most famous and controversial episode in Stoecker's career was the attempt in 1878 to found a Christian Social Workers Party, which would undercut the appeal of Social Democracy by combining social reform with patriotism and loyalty to the Kaiser. For a brief period in early 1878 Stoecker's new party was the sensation of the moment: large crowds turned out to hear him address rallies in beer-halls in working-class districts of the city. These usually ended in fights between Social Democrats and members of the Evangelical men's and youth clubs, and with rival singings of 'The Workers' Marseillaise' and 'Ein' feste Burg ist unser Gott'. Before long, however, the Berlin police, which had initially given Stoecker protection, concluded that the new party was not an effective means of fighting Social Democracy: beyond a small hard core of churchgoing workers, the main appeal, in their view, was to some of the very poor, who joined the new party in the hope of financial gain.[76] The 1878 election was a fiasco for Stoecker: his party received only 1,422 votes in Berlin, as against 60,000 for the Social Democrats. With that, his attempt to create a new political movement of the Berlin working class came to an end. From 1879, there was an increased emphasis in his speeches on anti-Semitism, and he began to direct his appeal to the lower middle class. This was the beginning of a more successful political career. In 1880 and 1881 he was elected as a Conservative, first to the Prussian Landtag and then to the Reichstag, from west German constituencies in predominantly rural areas, where he was able to build on a stronger base of popular Protestantism than existed in Berlin.

Even after the failure of Stoecker's political efforts in Berlin, he remained an important and highly controversial figure in the city's religious life. His keenest supporters were found among those connected with the City Mission, who included a large proportion of the clergy and the churchgoers in working-class areas of the city. For them, Stoecker was like a breath of fresh air. Fiercely outspoken, and never afraid to antagonize those in authority, he was proud of his own humble origins and his ability to communicate with ordinary people. An enthusiastic adoptive Berliner, he reveled in the vigour of big-city life. Whatever new Protestant initiatives were attempted in the 1880s and 1890s, Stoecker usually had a leading role. Thus he was prominently involved in the ultimately successful campaign to build new churches in the capital, and also in the largely unsuccessful movement to form Protestant workers' associations. He was one of the founders of the Evangelical-Social Congress, which flourished in the early and mid-1890s, before the church authorities tried to suppress it.[77]

Stoecker faced opposition on many fronts. He was regarded with suspicion by many church leaders, Conservative politicians and members of the royal family, who saw him as a noisy and irresponsible demagogue, and in 1890 he was finally dismissed from his position as court preacher. The large liberal element in the Berlin church disliked his conservative theology, which they saw as a major cause of estrangement from the church. And so far as the majority of working-class Berliners were concerned, his emphatic loyalty to state and emperor had little appeal. In later nineteenth-century Prussia, the possibility of any politically significant clerical radicalism was severely limited by the fact that the clergy were bound by the church authorities to a loyalty to state and king from which large sections of the working class had already moved away. In some parts of west central Germany, Stoecker's form of 'Tory radicalism' was still a viable possibility; but when Stoecker appeared on the stage in Berlin, it was already dominated by the highly secular Social Democrats and the almost equally secular Progressives.

Nonetheless, Stoecker was the major influence on the Berlin working-class parish as it developed in the later nineteenth and early twentieth centuries. Analysis of voting patterns in church elections in the early twentieth century shows that whereas the Liberals were on top in the mainly bourgeois parishes of central Berlin and Charlottenburg, the Positives had their strongholds in the plebeian north and east.[78] The face of Protestantism in working-class areas of Berlin was to a considerable degree shaped by Stoecker—highly organized, active in social welfare, theologically conservative, monarchist and patriotic, implacably opposed to Social Democracy and with tendencies toward anti-Semitism.[79] Stoecker's attempts to reinvigorate the Berlin church had a polarizing effect. He helped to bring about something of a revival in the 1880s and 1890s, by reactivating the dormant church loyalties of some working-class people, and by further strengthening the church's position among groups like the lower middle class, where it was already relatively strong. But this was achieved at the cost of further alienating large sections of the working class and the liberal bourgeoisie, who could not stomach Stoecker's political and theological conservatism.[80]

IV

Meanwhile the Roman Catholic and, more especially, the Social Democratic subcultures were developing rapidly. So far as Catholicism is concerned, a turning point seems to have come with the appointment of Joseph Jahnel, an energetic publicist and church builder, as Provost of St Hedwig's in 1888. Berlin Catholics had their own smaller-scale version of the Berlin church shortage. With the aid of the national Catholic press Jahnel set about raising money from Catholics in southern and western Germany to aid the mostly poor Catholic minority in the national capital.[81]

Catholic accounts of the church situation in early twentieth-century Berlin mainly emphasized the difficulties which the church faced. Apart from the poverty suffered both by Catholics as a community and by most Catholics as individuals, the chief problem was that of maintaining Catholic identity in an environment dominated by Protestantism and Social Democracy. Catholic priests sometimes made rueful comparisons with the situation in those parts of southern Germany where Catholics were in an overwhelming majority, and the church could use the weight of public opinion to ensure that the clergy were obeyed and treated with deference. In Berlin, they complained, only the children greeted the priest in the street, and if the clergy asked people to give more to the church, some would respond by threatening to leave the church or convert to Protestantism.[82] But a more relevant comparison would be with those parts of western and north-western Germany where Catholic minorities succeeded in creating a powerful Catholic subculture. The vital factor here seems to have been that the Catholic minority should be either large enough to support a large network of institutions (as in some predominantly Protestant areas of the Ruhrgebiet), or concentrated in Catholic enclaves (as it was, for instance, in the mainly Protestant state of Oldenburg, which had exceptionally high levels of religious practice and of voting for the Centre Party by the Catholic minority).[83]

In Berlin, the 10 per cent of the population who were Catholics were spread fairly evenly across the city. In 1905 figures were published of the numbers belonging to each denomination within each of the city's Protestant parishes. In contrast to the Jews, who ranged from over 20 per cent of the population in some parishes to less than 1 per cent in others, the Catholic proportion varied little from the average, and there was only one parish where it exceeded 15 per cent. An analysis of the 1910 census, which looked at smaller units of population, showed that there were some heavier concentrations in the immediate vicinity of certain Catholic churches or of factories with large numbers of Silesian or Polish workers—though even in these areas the proportion of Catholics only reached about 25 per cent.[84] One consequence of the high degree of dispersal of the Catholic population was a high rate of intermarriage between Catholics and Protestants. In the years 1901–5, 60 per cent of Catholics marrying in Berlin were choosing a Protestant partner, and the majority of the resulting children were being brought up as Protestants.[85] One priest complained that Catholic Berliners had 'unconsciously absorbed the Protestant spirit', which he saw reflected in a relatively casual attitude toward the sacraments.[86]

Overall, levels of Catholic practice were low by comparison with most other parts of Germany, though in most respects higher than for the Protestant population. For instance, estimates of the proportion of Catholics receiving Easter communion varied between about 30 per cent and 50 per cent, but both figures compared well with the 15 per cent of Protestants who took communion during the year. Estimates of the proportion of Catholics attending mass each week tend to be vague; but once again it would appear that the level was low by comparison with Catholics in western Germany but high by comparison with Protestants in Berlin. Wilhelm Frank of St Pius, a large working-class parish in the east of the city, thought the proportion was 'less than a third' in the early twentieth century. Robert Schlenke, who took charge of St Boniface in south Berlin in 1900, suggested that the proportion was around a quarter—though he claimed that more would come if they had a larger church and more priests.[87]

An added problem was the tension between German-speaking and Polish-speaking Catholics. The same battles that went on in New York and Chicago were being fought on a smaller scale in Berlin, and the Catholic authorities in Berlin were less amenable to the demands of foreign-language speakers than their American counterparts. In 1900, though there were some Berlin priests who were able to preach and hear confessions in Polish, none was himself a Pole, and demands for separate Polish parishes on the American model were always rejected. Wilhelm Frank seems to have regarded the Poles of his east Berlin parish with a mixture of admiration and irritation. On the positive side he praised their basic loyalty to the parish and the strong sense of religious duty which led them to queue up for long periods at the confessional. On the other hand, he clearly regarded them as an awkward lot, who were always complaining, and would completely take over if given half a chance. The Poles partly satisfied themselves by forming networks of Polish organizations within the parish, but tensions continued, and there were periodic boycotts of services in particular parishes.[88]

In the early twentieth century, the Catholic Church, like the Protestants, maintained a wide range of facilities such as hospitals, orphanages and hostels, and like their Protestant counterparts, the Catholic clergy were founding a vast range of *Vereine* as a means of binding the Catholic people together. In spite of the difficulties already mentioned they were on the whole more successful. They did not labour under the disadvantage of being regarded as an arm of the state, and they were less sharply separated by education and social status from their people. Rather than enjoying the support of wealthy benefactors, the Catholic clergy built their churches only through a constant struggle, in which they involved their parishioners. This work was a constant strain, and sometimes a cause of popular resentment, but it did mean that Catholics had a greater sense of identification with their churches, and were less likely to see them as something imposed from outside.[89] Indeed, the development of a Catholic subculture seemed to be making such strides that alarmed Protestants were claiming that there was a Catholic 'threat'.[90] In fact, the growth in the proportion of Catholics in the population was entirely due to immigration of Poles (about a quarter of all Berlin Catholics in 1900) and of German-speaking Catholics from such areas as Silesia.[91] The Catholic clergy were far too busy taking care of the spiritual needs of their own people to engage in much proselytism.

The real danger to Protestantism at that time came from the growth of Social Democracy, which in the years from 1890 to the First World War developed an enormous network of organizations, claiming the active or passive loyalty of huge numbers of working-class Berliners. In 1906–14 a number of prominent Social Democrats were involved in a renewed campaign of mass resignations from the churches (*Kirchenaustrittsbewegung*), which now attracted quite impressive numbers. For instance, around eight thousand Berlin Protestants resigned from the church each year in 1908 and 1909, and after a drop in 1910 and 1911, the number rose to over ten thousand in 1912 and again in 1913. An analysis produced by the church authorities of those leaving the church during 1913 showed that the dissidents were predominantly working-class men, with the highest proportion being in their twenties. In that year 0.62 per cent of the members of the *Landeskirche* living in the area of the Berlin City Synod left the church, the proportion ranging from 0.06 per cent in the aristocratic Dorotheenstadt parish to 1.51 per cent in Capernaum parish in Wedding. Of the adults leaving, 62 per cent were men, and 63 per cent were not liable to the church tax, because of the low level of their income.[92]

As it happens, Capernaum parish, which had the highest rate of resignations in Berlin, also has good records, including forms completed by parishioners who resigned in 1908, with comments by a city missionary who visited them; it also has annual reports for the years 1911–13 by a parish helper who had taken on the job of visiting those who were leaving the church. In 1913, after a year in which he had visited 323 people who had indicated their intention of leaving the church, the parish helper took a gloomy view of the religious situation. 'One has the feeling,' he wrote, 'of working among a people who know nothing of Christianity, and it has been suggested that a "Society for Missions to the Heathen" is needed in the national capital.' He admitted that the term 'heathen' was a little crude, and that many of those who were leaving the church would take offence if the term were used. Nonetheless, he felt that it was not too wide of the mark, and he complained of 'being treated like a criminal...just because he belonged to the church'.[93]

An analysis of 54 forms completed by those resigning in 1908 shows that 33 related to married couples who were resigning together, 18 to men acting on their own, and 3 to women acting on their own. In most cases only the husband's occupation is given. The great majority were skilled manual workers. Of the 51 men, 48 were manual workers. Of these 13 were simply described as 'worker' or 'factory worker', but most claimed a skill of some kind, metal- and woodworkers predominating. Out of 87 individuals 35 had been born in Berlin or its suburbs. In the 54 cases, there were 2 in which the couples concerned were leaving to join the Apostolic Church.

Of the remaining 52, there were 16 where husband, wife or both stated that the church tax was not the main reason for the resignation, and that they objected to the church on other grounds as well; in 14 they simply stated that could not or would not pay the church tax; in 6 they said they were leaving because of inability to pay the tax, but wished to stress either that they had nothing against the church or that they still retained their religious belief; in 1 I could not decipher the comments; and in 15 the missionary failed to make contact with the people, or else no comment is recorded. If the comments made by the missionary are combined with the more general observations made by the parish helper, it appears that the reasons given for leaving the church were very varied. The reason most commonly given—inability to pay the church tax—did not explain very much, since, as the parish helper pointed out, the same people were often willing to contribute money to the Social Democratic Party. It was a matter of priorities, and for most of these people the church was a low priority.

Though the conclusion—namely, to leave the church—was the same, people reached this conclusion by a variety of routes. Four routes were characteristic. First, and probably most worrying from the church's point of view, was a simple

lack of interest in the church or religion. One such objector struck a characteristically twentieth-century note: the twenty-five-year-old Hamburg-born wife of a
cabinet-maker said that 'she found no pleasure in going to church. She wanted to
live and enjoy herself.' More typical was the comment of a forty-two-year-old saddler
that he did not want to pay taxes for something he never used. Second were those
who expressed objections to church doctrine, such as a twenty-five-year-old tech-
nician who said that his god was the scientist and antireligious writer Ernst Haeckel.
Admittedly, the doctrinal objections cited tend to be rather unspecific, and it is
difficult to know how considered they were, though the parish helper mentions
claims that 'The Bible is all lies' (which usually meant that they did not believe in
miracles), and references to Frederick the Great's formula, 'Everyone can be saved
in their own way'. Then there were those who stressed political objections—not
many of the comments recorded by the city missionary were explicitly political,
though the parish helper referred to claims that 'the church is only there for the
capitalists' and that 'Social Democracy is the best Christianity'.

Finally, there were those who claimed that the church was insufficiently Christian. These tend to be the most interesting criticisms, as they were usually more
specific. The main points tended to be either criticism of individual clergymen or
other church officials, or else complaints that rich and poor were treated un-
equally: for instance a forty-year-old country-born moulder complained of distinctions between different classes of funeral, 'which does not accord with the
Bible'. The parish helper referred to criticisms of seat rents in the church and
claims that 'Jesus was for the poor; the state church is only for the rich'. Disputes
over funerals were mentioned in two cases. A man complained of 'unfriendly'
remarks by the pastor; and several people referred to the treasurer of the
neighbouring Nazareth parish, who had embezzled church funds—this, presumably, being taken as an illustration of the claim quoted by the parish helper that
'the religious people are the worst of all'.[94]

The fact that a certain proportion of those leaving the church still claimed to
be Christians, and insisted that their objections were exclusively to the church
and/or clergy, was also indicated by a *cause célèbre* of 1912. In 1909 Emil Wenske,
a carpenter living in the Stralauer Vorstadt, had left the church together with his
wife, but in 1912 they wanted their six-month-old daughter baptized. Pastor Pfeiffer
of the Pentecost Church refused, whereupon Wenske complained to the
Consistory, which supported Pfeiffer, stating that baptism was only possible where
the Christian upbringing of the child was guaranteed—something that was excluded in this case, as the parents had left the church. To this Wenske replied:
'Although I do not formally belong to the church any more, I remain a follower of
Jesus's teaching of love for all people, and especially for children, of whom he said
"Suffer the little children to come unto me and forbid them not"!!' A subsequent
letter from the child's grandparents stated that the Wenskes had left the church
because of 'the intolerant conduct of some clergy'. Wenske himself claimed that a
more 'accommodating' attitude by the clergy and more 'pastoral care' could win
back many of those who were estranged, but that the line taken here by the pastor
and Consistory would only 'help to increase the present hatred of the top leader-

ship of the Protestant *Landeskirche* and lead to more resignations'. The saga ended with a liberal pastor in a neighbouring parish agreeing to baptize the child, having been satisfied by Wenske's assurances that the child would receive a Christian upbringing.[95]

One should not exaggerate the numbers of those who were converts to the socialist *Weltanschauung*. But the religious significance of Social Democracy lay in the fact that for the first time Christianity faced the competition of a total world-view with mass appeal. For the committed comrade, the Social Democratic Party and the socialist philosophy offered a complete way of life, providing an analysis of the present world and what was wrong with it, hope for the future, friendship, a complete range of social activities, and even life-cycle rituals and a calendar of annual celebrations.[96] Socialism as a quasi-religious movement reached its highest stage of development and attracted its biggest mass base in the Weimar Republic. In the German Democratic Republic it achieved the status of a state religion, and in the process began to lose most of its popular appeal. But already before 1914 the numbers of active Socialists in working-class areas of Berlin far exceeded the number of active churchgoers, though the majority of the population had a foot in both camps, and avoided a total commitment to either.

CHAPTER 2

London

VICTORIAN LONDON WAS a city on a scale such as the world had never seen before. In 1801, with just under a million people, London was close behind Edo, then the world's largest city.[1] By 1851, with slightly over two million people, it was comfortably ahead of its rivals; and in 1901 there were over six million Londoners— nearly twice as many as in New York, which ran second. By now a quarter of London's population lived beyond the county boundaries in places like West Ham, Tottenham or Willesden, which had their own independent local government, but were in all other respects no more than suburbs of the great city. The characteristic habitat of the Londoner was a terrace of two- or three-storey houses, with a family living on each floor, and a yard or small garden at the back. The prevalence of low-rise living meant that in proportion to its huge population, London spread even further than did cities of tenement dwellers, such as Berlin or New York. And as it grew, London had inevitably engulfed towns, like Woolwich, Greenwich and Croydon, as well as numerous villages and hamlets.

I

Victorian London had three focal points, each representing a different aspect of the city's economy and a different section of its population: the City of London, the City of Westminster and the river Thames. The City of London, the historic nucleus from which all else had grown, had a population of only twenty-six thousand at the end of the nineteenth century. But its banks, offices, law courts and newspapers provided employment for several hundred thousand people. Every weekday they poured in by railway, underground or tram from the northern and southern suburbs. Then there was the City of Westminster, which had grown up in the Middle Ages as the seat of royal government, a mile to the west. If the City of London was the base of British financial power, Westminster was the political centre of the Empire, the site of the Court, of Parliament, and of the town houses of the aristocracy—as well as being the main place for theatres and expensive shops. And the Thames was the site of the world's largest port, with its docks, its numerous riverside industries, and several hundred thousand working-class people who lived in Stepney, Poplar, Bermondsey and the other riverside boroughs of east and south London.

The religious traditions of these three parts of London were different. Westminster's traditions were unequivocally Anglican—appropriately so, since Westminster Abbey was the national church, the place where monarchs were crowned, and a mausoleum for Britain's most famous statesmen, writers and military commanders. The sovereign, the overwhelming majority of those who moved in 'Society,' and most members of Parliament all belonged to the Church of England. According to a guide to London 'Society' published in 1885, 'most of the smart people' went to church, with the Chapel Royal and St Margaret's, Westminster, being favoured by the 'political set', and 'many other shrines' being 'set apart for Society's elect'.[2] By this time Roman Catholicism was beginning to be accepted as a socially permissible, though highly idiosyncratic, alternative to Anglicanism, in a way that Nonconformity was not.

The City of London was famous for St Paul's Cathedral and for its many other Wren churches. But, like other centres of commerce, it also had important traditions of religious Dissent, going back to the seventeenth century. One legacy of this tradition was the City Temple with London's most famous Congregational pulpit, from which Joseph Parker, R. J. Campbell and Maude Royden each preached to huge congregations at various points in the later nineteenth and early twentieth centuries.[3] But, as successful merchants moved out of the City, they took their chapels with them. The heirs to City Dissent were the flourishing Congregational chapels of the northern suburbs.[4] Not that any of the suburbs was one-sidedly Nonconformist: Islington and, of course, Clapham were famous for their traditions of upper middle-class evangelical Anglicanism, and Hackney, in the early nineteenth century, had been a high church stronghold. Churchgoing reached a peak in the wealthier suburbs where, as a rule, both Anglicanism and various branches of Nonconformity were strong.

In most of the riverside districts, the Church of England got left badly behind by expanding population in the later eighteenth and early nineteenth centuries. When, in the 1840s, the Anglicans set in train a big church-building programme, they had a lot of catching-up to do.[5] At this time most of the more prosperous places of worship belonged to the Nonconformists, and certain parts of the East End were tightly packed with Congregational and Baptist chapels. On the other hand, there was some reason to think that the Dissenters were being no more successful than the Church of England in reaching the impoverished masses of the population. The national religious census of 1851 showed that the poorer districts of London had levels of church attendance that ranked among the lowest in England. The leaders of the churches were well aware of these weaknesses, and in the second half of the nineteenth century, working-class areas of London were the scene of numerous experiments designed to bridge the gap between church and people. These ranged from the Salvation Army, to the Anglican 'slum ritualists', to the Wesleyan Central Missions, to the Settlements.[6] Equally important, though less obtrusive, was the increasing concentration of religious plant and personnel on working-class London during the second half of the nineteenth century, as parishes were subdivided, new churches and church halls built, and increasing numbers of curates and voluntary workers were recruited to work in the area which was thought to present English Christianity with its biggest challenge.[7]

Two other kinds of district, though less conspicuous, also require a mention. First, there were the areas of small workshop production, extending across inner north London, and including the old silk-weaving district of Spitalfields, the shoemaking area of Bethnal Green, Shoreditch with its furniture industry, Clerkenwell, with its numerous artisan trades, notably watchmaking and the piano-making areas of Camden Town and Kings Cross. In religious terms this was the homeland of Secularism.[8] Charles Bradlaugh, the dominant personality of the secularist movement in the later nineteenth century, was himself a native of Shoreditch, and his Hall of Science stood on Old Street in Finsbury. The Nonconformists were also reasonably strong in this area. It was the territory of the self-taught working-class intellectual, and fertile ground for both religious and anti-religious enthusiasts.[9]

In the late nineteenth century many new suburban districts were springing up, with medium-sized houses intended for city clerks and other socially intermediate groups. Here was a largely new social stratum, recruited partly from socially mobile sons of the working class, partly from the rural lower middle class, partly from the families of shopkeepers. As a class without sharply defined traditions, it was appropriately varied in its religious habits. These new lower middle-class suburbs tended to have intermediate levels of churchgoing, with a fair mix of Anglicans and Nonconformists, and with Baptists and Wesleyan Methodists usually being most numerous on the chapel side. Here, more than in any other part of London, each household went its own way, so far as religion was concerned—and the resulting anarchy of individual allegiances pointed forward to twentieth-century trends more clearly than did the predictable patterns of observance or non-observance found in areas where the force of tradition was stronger.[10]

There were two religious groups which stood somewhat apart from the rest: the Roman Catholics and Jews. Both were heavily concentrated in certain areas of London, and both included a large element of first-and second-generation immigrants from overseas. In the case of the Catholics, who made up somewhere between 5 per cent and 10 per cent of the population of Greater London at the turn of the century, a very considerable proportion were of Irish descent. There were concentrated Catholic communities in central and west London and in the riverside boroughs; they were weak in the suburbs.[11] In 1880 there were only about 40,000 Jews in London, of whom, it is estimated, no more than a quarter were working class. By 1905, as a result of immigration from eastern Europe, the total had risen to around 144,000.[12] The historic focus of London Jewry was on the eastern edge of the City, and in Whitechapel and Aldgate in the East End.[13] Dutch Jews had settled there in the seventeenth century; German Jews went there in the eighteenth and early nineteenth centuries; and in the great exodus from Russia that started in 1881, a new generation of Jewish settlers established themselves in the same area, before gradually moving further east or northeast. The other area of London with a relatively large Jewish population was the northwest, where such districts as Bayswater, St John's Wood and Maida Vale housed many English-born Jews, belonging to the business and professional classes.[14]

II

In the later nineteenth century, the majority of adult Londoners were not regular attenders at a place of worship.[15] The 1886–7 religious census, which included attendances by children, indicated an attendance rate of 28.5 per cent of the whole population of Inner London on a given Sunday. By 1902–3, this had dropped to 22 per cent (see table 4). Frequency of church attendance was strongly related to social class. In a group of wealthy suburban districts, the median adult attendance rate was 37 per cent, and in the aristocratic West End it was 34 per cent; but in the middle-class districts it was 24 per cent, lower middle-class areas 18 per cent, in upper working-class districts 16 per cent, middle working-class districts 13 per cent, and poor districts 12 per cent.[16] What distinguished London from the majority of continental European capitals was the very large range of denominations from which the population could choose. By far the largest was the Church of England, which accounted for 43 per cent of all worshippers in 1902–3. However, the combined strength of the various Nonconformists almost equalled that of the Anglicans. Chief among them were the Baptists (11 per cent), Congregationalists (11 per cent), Wesleyan Methodists (8 per cent), Presbyterians (2 per cent) and Salvation Army (2 per cent). But there were many, many others, including four other branches of Methodism, the Brethren, the Unitarians and the Quakers. There were also the Roman Catholics (9 per cent) and the Jews (3 per cent).

Both Anglican and Nonconformist church attendance varied considerably according to the social character of the district, though the patterns were different. Anglican attendance, which averaged about 10 per cent of the adult population across the whole of Greater London, rose with the social status of the district. It averaged around 4–5 per cent in poorer working-class districts, 7 per cent in upper working-class districts, 9–11 per cent in lower middle-class and middle-class districts—but then rose very steeply to reach 20–30 per cent in many of the wealthiest suburbs and in the West End. Attendance at Nonconformist chapels also averaged around 10 per cent of the adult population. The peak of over 20 per cent was reached in the new lower middle-class suburbs on the northern and eastern fringes, such as Ilford and Wood Green; it was around 12–15 per cent in such wealthy suburbs as Blackheath and Hampstead, 7–10 per cent in more prosperous work-

TABLE 4

Church Attendance in Metropolitan London as a Percentage of Estimated Population, 1886–7 and 1902–3

1886–7	CofE[a]	RC[a]	OTHER[a]	TOTAL
City of London[b]	42.5	0.1	24.7	67.4
Elite areas[c]	21.3	5.5	9.5	36.3
White-collar suburbs[d]	16.9	1.4	14.9	33.3
Inner ring[e]	6.9	2.6	10.8	20.2
Other suburbs[f]	11.2	2.0	12.4	25.6
Metropolitan London	13.5	2.8	12.2	28.5
1902–3	COFE	RC	OTHER	TOTAL
City of London	41.6	—	47.3	88.9
Elite areas	14.1	3.8	8.4	26.3
White-collar suburbs	10.1	1.4	12.5	24.1
Inner ring	6.0	2.0	10.5	18.5
Other suburbs	8.2	1.6	10.5	19.1
Metropolitan London	9.4	2.1	10.5	22.0

SOURCE: Hugh McLeod, 'White Collar Values and the Role of Religion', Geoffrey Crossick, ed., *The Lower Middle Class in Britain 1870–1914* (London, 1977), pp. 86–7.

[a] CofE = Church of England; RC = Roman Catholic; 'Other' comprises all other religious denominations included in the censuses.

[b] The City of London was largely depopulated by the late nineteenth century, but still contained several major churches and chapels, including St Paul's Cathedral and the City Temple.

[c] Elite areas are those with more than 50 indoor domestic servants per 100 households in 1901, together with Holborn.

[d] White-collar suburbs are those where more than 8 per cent of occupied males were clerks in 1901 (except for Hampstead, which is counted as an elite district).

[e] Inner ring comprises the seven strongly working-class central boroughs of Stepney, Bethnal Green, Poplar, Shoreditch, Finsbury, Southwark and Bermondsey.

[f] "Other suburbs" comprises all the rest.

ing-class districts, 4–6 per cent in poorer working-class districts; and it fell to a minimum of around 3 per cent in the fashionable districts of inner west London.

Estimates by priests suggested that between 20 per cent and 30 per cent of Catholics went to mass on an average Sunday—which was lower than the figure for middle-class Protestants, but higher than that for Protestant members of the working class, to which the great majority of Catholics belonged.[17]

Attendance at synagogues was much more seasonal than that at churches, being high at the times of the major festivals, but much lower on the weekly Sabbath. The religious census of London in 1903 counted synagogue attendance on the first day of Passover. According to Gartner's estimate, no more than a quarter of London's Jews were present—but since adult males made up over half the attenders, the proportion of that group who were present must have been considerably larger. Furthermore, many of the smaller places of worship in the East End were missed by the census takers. However, attendances on the Sabbath were limited by the fact that many Jewish workers were required to work on that day—and, in any case, those who were not forced to work on the Sabbath frequently chose to spend the morning in bed rather than at the synagogue. Indeed there were many reports in the early twentieth century that religious observance was in serious decline in the East End. As one Jewish commentator wrote in 1903, 'It is a common saying among the foreign Jews that England is a "freie Medina"—a country where the restrictions of orthodoxy cease to apply.'[18]

Religious institutions and personnel were a pervasive presence in late Victorian London, which even the most indifferent could hardly escape altogether. The great range of religious bodies competing for the support of the people had led to a profusion of churches, chapels and halls. The Anglican church divided London into parishes which in working-class areas tended to contain about ten thousand people. Besides a vicar, most parishes employed one or more curates, and varying numbers of visitors, nurses or missionaries, paid or unpaid.[19] Anglican parish churches tended to be large and imposing buildings in prominent positions on major thoroughfares, in squares or beside parks. But, by the later nineteenth century, many parishes also ran a mission hall, situated in the back streets, and intended to attract those who would feel out of place in more exalted surroundings.

For every place of worship of the established church, there were several Nonconformist chapels of varying styles and sizes. The most prosperous Baptist and Congregational chapels were as prominently sited and as pretentious in appearance as their Anglican counterparts, and they too ran back-street missions. But there were also many autonomous congregations, who could manage nothing more conventionally ecclesiastical than a shed-like hall.

The Roman Catholics, on the other hand, who also were often desperately short of money, attached great importance to the sacredness and beauty of the church building, and they recognized the symbolic value of a conspicuous presence. So they preferred large parishes with large churches intensively used—four or five masses being held on a Sunday morning, rather than the one major service beginning around eleven o'clock, which was the normal Anglican and Nonconformist practice.

Even those who deliberately avoided religious buildings could still not entirely escape the many varieties of street preaching, most notably the Salvation Army, which had begun in 1865 as the East London Christian Mission and which, in the later 1870s, took to marching through the streets in uniform and bearing military titles.

The range of types of Jewish places of worship was rather similar to that which will be described in more detail in the chapter on New York: modern synagogues in the northwest, attended by middle-class and upper middle-class English-born Jews; historic synagogues in the City of London, once attended by the elite, but now largely used by immigrants; and a mass of small congregations meeting in the back streets of the East End, often in rented premises, and made up of Yiddish-speaking working-class and lower middle-class immigrants.[20] One major difference from New York was that Reform Judaism had made little headway in London, and most members of the Jewish elite were affiliated to Orthodox synagogues. However, this did not mean that relations between the elite and the immigrants were any better in London than in New York: the Chief Rabbi's claims to Orthodoxy cut little ice in the East End, where he was known as the 'West End goy'.[21]

As the distribution of church attendance suggests, those who occupied positions of power and status in Victorian London tended to have connections with church or chapel. The fashionable Anglican churches of the West End have already been mentioned. In wealthy suburbs like Hampstead, Highbury and Blackheath, both the Anglicans and the leading Nonconformist bodies had large and wealthy congregations of business and professional people. And in working-class districts like Stepney and Bethnal Green, the old parish churches and some of the larger Congregational and Baptist chapels were attended by the more modest local elite of workshop owners and larger shopkeepers.[22] Involvement in the synagogue by the Jewish elite was also fairly high.[23]

The religious census conducted by the *Daily News* in 1902–3 gives some indication of the number and variety of religious buildings in London. For instance, in the poor East End borough of Bethnal Green, with a population of 128,000, a total of sixty-six places of worship was recorded. These comprised forty churches, belonging to ten different denominations, seventeen missions, and nine 'other services', usually organized by groups of evangelical Christians operating independently of any denomination. In the adjoining borough of Poplar, with a population of 165,000 people, they counted attendance at sixty-seven churches belonging to eleven denominations, a synagogue, twenty missions and seventeen 'other services'.[24]

III

Our concern here is with what this pervasive middle- and upper-class religiosity meant for the religion of working-class Londoners. The effects were two-edged, but whether positive or negative, they were certainly important.

One consequence was that churches and chapels had a strong attraction for those working-class people who were in revolt against their own surroundings. A classic expression of this viewpoint is the autobiography of George Acorn, a Bethnal Green cabinet-maker, born about 1885, who complained of the 'mechanical lives' of the people among whom he grew up, who 'live, marry, produce children, fight, quarrel, all by rote, and never think'. From an early age, he had 'a leaning towards religion. Places of worship were so clean that I often felt the desire to go into a local church. The brooding feeling of peacefulness seemed to smooth one's turbulent desires.' Eventually he was persuaded to attend a Nonconformist chapel by a friend who told him: 'They don't preach at you much, no shouting about Jesus, or telling you what a wicked sinner you are. I believe they try to live good first and influence you like that.' This was 'probably the most important step I ever took in my life'. He valued both the intellectual stimulus and the more refined atmosphere, and he was influenced by the secretary of one of the chapel organizations, who 'wore down many of my jagged edges and shaped me into the image of an ordinary middle-class youth'.[25]

The same kinds of points were made more negatively by Alexander Paterson, a south London youth worker, who described the way in which the typical boy with whom he worked regarded 'the Christian life':

> He associates it with abstention from certain habits, and thinks of it as a path to almost certain prosperity. It is unfortunate, but perhaps inevitable, that the steady church-going fellow should work with greater diligence and gain promotion earlier than the rougher lad. This respectability of the church-going section robs Christianity of its old ideals. No longer in the garb of poverty, but in the glossiest of hats and the longest of frock coats does the typical Christian reveal the supremacy of his faith.[26]

The corollary of this was that churchgoers could sometimes be accused of snobbery or standoffishness, and that the many working-class people whose situation was not in any way improving could feel out of place in a church or chapel. Anglican churches, certainly, and possibly Nonconformist chapels too, were seen as part of the system of power. 'They had the authority and we didn't.'[27] In some people's eyes they were a benevolent authority; others saw them in a more sinister light; and some fatalistically accepted them as being part of the order of things. But for those at the bottom of a very hierarchical society there was inevitably at least some sense of distance from institutions that were seen to be associated with those at the top.

Anglican clergymen were often regarded as remote and even frightening figures: clergy and doctors were the 'two number one frighteners then'.[28] Alan Bartlett has analyzed some of the dimensions of the resulting distance between clergy and people in Bermondsey. There was education—the majority of incumbents in pre-1914 Bermondsey had taken degrees at Oxford or Cambridge; there was housing—vicarages tended to be large and comfortable buildings, with space for servants; there was lifestyle—where their parishioners were lucky to be able to afford a few day-trips, clergymen would take proper vacations, often in remote and exotic-sounding places which they would give talks about afterwards; there was even size—Anglican clergymen were often big, strong, healthy men, who towered above their half-fed parishioners. They were inclined to assume that the culture within which they had grown up was incomparably richer than that which they found in the poorer districts of London—indeed, this confidence provided one of the motives for their work. [29] McIlhiney notes that Canon Barnett and his wife, the founders of Toynbee Hall, believed that 'there was no genuine Cockney culture worthy of respect'. Anglican clergymen were thus in continual danger of becoming patronizing.[30]

Gillian Rose argues on the basis of her work on Poplar in the 1920s that the middle-class backgrounds of most church workers created a gulf 'which could only be bridged by exceptional individuals', and she notes that the memoirs written by East End church workers imply that 'Poplar people spoke oddly, dressed distinctively, behaved unusually'.[31] As one exceptional individual who transcended the class barrier, she notes the example of the Anglo-Catholic socialist, Fr St John Groser. In Bermondsey, Bartlett notes that some clergymen deliberately chose to live in a poor area near their church, rather than in a purpose-built vicarage, and that even within such a thoroughly working-class borough as Bermondsey there were differences in prestige between different parishes and between the social backgrounds of the clergy assigned to them. Celibate Anglo-Catholic clergy often gave the lead in the move toward a more modest clerical lifestyle and a more wholehearted identification with their parishes. These points are well illustrated in the account of Bethnal Green in the 1920s and 1930s in the memoirs of the East End criminal Arthur Harding. He made a distinction between St Paul's, the church where he was married, and various neighbouring churches, such as St Matthew's, the old parish church. The rector of St Matthew's was by implication accused of snobbery, and various of his churchgoing neighbours in the impoverished Gibraltar Walk area were presented as standoffish; on the other hand, references to Fr Jones of St Paul's were consistently eulogistic, and a Mr and Mrs Johnson 'were ordinary Bethnal Green folk and attended Father Jones's church on a Sunday'.[32]

To some extent this feeling of social resentment against the clergy and against members of Anglican congregations found expression in mainstream Nonconformity. Chapelgoers liked to contrast the 'simplicity' and 'heartiness' of their own services with the more formal and hierarchical atmosphere of the church. Interviews with elderly Nonconformists provide some good examples of the Nonconformist self-image. A man born in Cardiff in 1887, and brought up in Kentish Town, where his father worked as a horseman and his family attended a Methodist church, suggested that the Church of England was snobbish: it was 'the squire, the mayor, the doctor, the—some of the big shopkeepers would all have their own pew', whereas chapelgoers 'were all good working class people'.[33] The daughter, born in 1883, of an Edmonton basket-maker, felt that church people 'thought themselves somebodies. . . . We didn't have much to do with them', whereas Nonconformists were 'a very nice crowd'.[34] In the years around the turn of the century, the many Nonconformists who were active on the radical wing of the Liberal Party tended to see their religion and their politics as guided by common democratic principles.[35] From a later generation, but very much in the same tradition, a woman born in Walworth in 1927, whose father worked as a fitter and was a Primitive Methodist local preacher, made these comments:

> the Church of England ties up with the King and the state and the Conservative Party. I mean we knew that the people who were church were usually more classy than we were. . . . We were ordinary people. I suspect that everybody thinks that whoever they are, they are the ordinary people, but we were ordinary people, and ordinary people, if they went anywhere, went to chapel. And we rather suspected that people went to church in order to look good. We rather suspected that you didn't have to believe, all you had to do was to go through the motions. Have all the ritual and so on.[36]

But, for many of the working class, even the chapels were too much dominated by an atmosphere of prosperity and respectability. One consequence of this situation was the Pleasant Sunday Afternoon movement, which started in the Black Country in 1875 and reached London in 1888.[37] The P.S.A. provided an informal style of service, held in a hall, rather than a church. It seems to have had some success in attracting working-class men who would not go to more conventional services, and by 1913 there were 329 branches of the movement in London with 55,000 members.[38] Some of the poorer working class preferred to go to one of the small mission halls, sometimes associated with a larger church, sometimes undenominational. As the manager of a small Baptist mission in Hackney told a researcher for Charles Booth's *Life and Labour of the People in London*, they got people who wanted a 'plain, simple gospel service' but would not attend a formal church service. The manager of a Congregational mission in Islington said that 'It is the poorest who are touched—the better off do not like to come to "a mission"', though he admitted that of the poor, they only succeeded in attracting a small proportion.[39]

To outsiders, areas like the East End often appeared as an undifferentiated mass of poverty. Charles Booth's social map of London, published in 1902–3, showed that the reality was much more complex: in some working-class districts there would be concentrated blocks of pink ('fairly comfortable'), purple ('mixed'), light blue ('moderate poverty'), dark blue ('very poor') or black ('the lowest class'); but elsewhere, there would be a complete mixture—for instance, the parish of St John the Divine in Kennington contained streets in each of the five colours, and two predominantly middle-class streets as well.[40] And those who actually lived in such areas were highly sensitive to even more subtle distinctions between the social tone of different ends or different sides of the same street.[41]

Similarly, outsiders were inclined to make fairly sweeping claims about the 'heathenism' or 'irreligion' of huge zones of London—and historians have sometimes been prepared to echo them—whereas the testimony of locals suggests a much more differentiated picture. Thus a woman brought up in the early years of this century in Waite Street, Peckham (coloured purple on Booth's map), said 'I don't know. . . anybody round where I lived. . . that went to church, it was all the children'; and a slightly older man from Donald Street in Bromley-by-Bow (marked dark blue) thought there were three churchgoing families in the street, who kept themselves to themselves.[42] Church attendance was also said to be low in the 1890s on the Shaftesbury Estate in Battersea—a very different area, since it was a stronghold of working-class respectability; but here respectability seems to have found expression more through radical politics, and indeed Secularism, than religion. One special local factor may have been the influence of John Burns, elected Labour M.P. for Battersea in 1892, who had been brought up on the estate, and was a Secularist.[43]

On the other hand, in strongly Catholic areas like Butchers Road in Canning Town or Rook Street in Poplar, the religious allegiance of the majority of the population was highly visible at least on the days of Marian festivals, when altars were erected on the pavements, and banners hanging across the street declared 'Hail, Queen of Heaven' or 'God Bless Our Pope'.[44]

In mainly Protestant areas, religious allegiances tended to be less visible. But a woman born in Spitalfields in 1895 recalled that in Blackwall Buildings, where she lived, there was a mission that held services for children in the morning and adults in the evening: 'People in the Buildings used to flock in. We had crowds in.'[45] And Charles Booth commented on the upper working-class district of Southwark Park that 'Anyone walking through the district cannot but be conscious of the extent to which public attention is called to the affairs of the Churches. In every street there are bills—sometimes half the houses have them in their windows—bearing announcements of special services, or lectures or entertainments of one kind or another connected with the Churches.'[46] A similar area was the Queen's Park estate in Paddington, with its railway and post office workers, and a flourishing Congregational chapel, where Booth claimed that the majority of the population were churchgoers: 'The gulf that lies between these people and the cadging poor south of the canal is not easily bridged. Both may be accounted members of the working classes, but how far apart!'[47] And a woman born in North Place, Mile End New Town (marked purple and pink on Booth's map), conveys some of the flavour of life in one of these strongholds of working-class respectability. Her mother, a strong Anglican, had been a cook and was married to a brewery horseman. 'She was a very strict woman. Yes. Very strict woman. Never used bad language, nothing like. Or made any rude remarks. Or made any fun of anybody.' On Sunday evenings, when the family went to church together, 'you always 'ad gloves on, your shoes cleaned and a hat on your head'. The children were allowed to play with all the neighbouring children, 'but they were all nice children like ourselves—because they nearly all worked at Truman's Brewery [a bastion of regular employment amid the chronic insecurity of many areas of the East End economy]. . . . Or they was a policeman.'[48]

IV

The major oral history survey carried out by Thompson and Vigne, as well as a number of smaller surveys carried out in various parts of London, make it possible to reconstruct in considerable detail aspects of working-class religious life that are largely missing from the documentary sources.[49] Thompson and Vigne's nation-wide survey, which aimed to provide a regionally and socially representative cross-section of Britain in 1911, included interviews with forty-five men and women who had been brought up in working-class families in Greater London. The oldest of these respondents was born in 1878 and the youngest in 1908. The interviews were based on a standard list of questions, which covered, among other things, whether they had as a child attended Sunday school or participated in other religious organizations, whether their parents had attended church, whether prayers were said in the home, what kind of people went to local churches and chapels and how the clergy fitted into the local social hierarchy. Respondents were not specifically questioned about their own religious beliefs or those of their parents, though information on this sometimes emerged in the course of the interview, especially in response to questions about the things their parents emphasized in bringing them up.

The Thompson-Vigne interviews indicate that a wide spectrum of religious beliefs and practices was to be found in working-class London in the period from the 1880s to the First World War. I have divided the interviews into three roughly equal groups, according to the kind of religious ethos prevailing in the family in which the respondent was brought up. Admittedly, not all interviews fall clearly into one category: inevitably there are borderline cases. More seriously, there were a number of families that were religiously divided. For instance, mothers were often more religiously committed than fathers. In most such cases I have taken the mother as defining the family ethos, as this seems to reflect the balance of influence. However, in one case I have taken the irreligious father as the dominant influence. In a few cases, more devout grandparents or elder siblings acted as countervailing influences to religiously indifferent parents: in such cases I have assumed that the parents exercised the principal influence, though in doing so, I may be underestimating the religious dimension of the home atmosphere.

According to my classification, thirteen of the forty-five households had a strongly religious ethos, and fourteen an ethos of indifference or antagonism to religion, while eighteen fell somewhere between these extremes.

The first group includes the ten families where one or both parents attended church services or religious meetings regularly, together with three others where the parents engaged in no religious activity outside the home, but where the teaching of religion seems to have played a major role in the upbringing of the children, or where prayer, Bible-reading or hymn-singing had an important part in daily life. This group includes several families whose life revolved around a place of worship. For instance, a Kings Cross woman, whose father was a painter and her mother a seamstress, commented that the Baptist chapel was 'our life'. The parents received help from the chapel when they had little money, and when they were more prosperous they participated in a scheme organized by their chapel whereby they rented a room to a man recently released from prison.[50] In eight of the ten churchgoing families, both husband and wife were to some degree involved with a place of worship, and in a number of cases shared religion seems to have led to an unusual degree of sharing of lives between spouses. For instance, they would tend either both to be teetotallers or, if they went for a drink, to do it together; or they would join together in church socials or in musical evenings at home.[51]

However, in a number of cases where a strongly religious mother was married to a father who was much less interested, there would be a definite religious atmosphere at home, without the parents having much connection with a place of worship. For instance, a Stepney man, whose father was a docker and his mother an office cleaner, recalls that on Sunday evenings his mother would always read to him from the Bible. A Wapping pub cook, married to a docker, told her son: 'As long as you . . . lead a good life and . . . say your own prayers—that's good enough. As long as you attend your own church when you can when you're working'.[52]

Every one of the forty-five interviewees from working-class London attended Sunday school in childhood. What seems to have distinguished the strongly religious families was the degree to which they regarded Sunday school not just as an established custom, or an opportunity for some cheap treats, or a means of getting the children out of the way, but as an essential part of their growing up into decent adults. For instance, the Stepney docker's son, mentioned above, attributed the fact that his children had 'never caused us . . . not a day's trouble', and that he himself had 'thank God . . . never been in a police court' to the religious education which he had received and which he had given his children.[53] Respondents in this group frequently mentioned Sunday school or church among the things their parents regarded as 'particularly important'.[54]

On the other hand, respondents brought up by less religious parents often took a more cynical view of their parents' motives in sending them. There were fourteen households which I have described as indifferent or antagonistic to religion. In such families children were sent to Sunday school, and sometimes there were restrictions on Sunday activity, though there is no evidence that these were a result of religious conviction rather than social custom. Adults in these households tended to have little or no contact with churches and clergy. Only in one case does a respondent specifically state that one of his parents was an atheist,[55] though quite possibly there were other parents who simply did not discuss their anti-religious views with their children. One may speculate that a Hackney shoemaker who was an active member of the Radical Club and 'wasn't a bit interested in religion at all' may have had positively anti-religious views, but there is no direct evidence of that.[56] Generally speaking, respondents in this group emphasize apathy rather than antagonism.

In some cases, where the father was an active trade unionist or radical, lack of interest in religion may have had its roots in a politically based hostility to the churches and clergy.[57] However, parents were often as uninterested in politics as in religion, and this lack of interest seems to have been part of a pattern of life where the wife was ground down by the tasks of caring for an overlarge family, and had no interests outside the home, while her husband spent what little free time he had at the pub. A typical example was that of an Islington carpenter and his wife. Their son, when asked if his father ever helped in the home, replied 'Help himself to pints of beer, that's what his favourite pastime was. . . . Great drinkers them days you know, well—the homelife, they wanted to get out and escape from it. And the mother was—the mother with children was—handcuffed. No emancipation at all, no.' His parents were 'not unkind' but 'apathetic'. He went on to say that 'I assume they were Protestants but I don't know. As father never spoke about religion, or never talked to me. There was never a Bible in the house.' As for Sunday school, 'They just sent me there. It was the accepted thing to do them days. The result of going—whether you became religious—never entered my father's mind, no. It was . . . traditional and it was a—a kind of a must. Now go on, get dressed, go to Sunday school, you see.'[58] Respondents in this group sometimes had a rather cynical view of the motives of clergy and churchgoers, though often they simply professed ignorance of the subject. For instance, a Hackney man, whose widowed mother worked in a collar factory, claimed that 'half the working class who went to church only went for what they could get'— they were 'mumpers and cadgers'.[59] And the Islingon carpenter's son, mentioned above, felt that the clergy were 'very cosy and very snug' because 'their bread was buttered': 'I couldn't preach to a man if he was—belly was hungry. I would feed him first.'[60]

There remained a large group of families where the religious ethos was less easily defined. Children were often taught to say their prayers, grace was usually said at meals, and Sunday was in some sense recognized as a special day by restrictions on work and/or leisure, as well as the wearing of 'Sunday best'. Parents often attended church occasionally, or on a few selected occasions during the year. The attitudes toward the churches and clergy, whether distant or more intimate, was usually characterized as one of 'respect'. One respondent, born in Poplar, described his stevedore father and washerwoman mother as 'hundred per cent christians but not churchgoers', and the daughter of a Greenwich waterman described her mother as 'a christian woman you know in her own way'.[61] But the meaning of this Christianity is harder to penetrate than in the case of those who had a strong institutional commitment. Again, 'leading a good life' and 'saying your prayers' were probably major components. In this environment, a religious view of the world was taken for granted, but God remained rather further in the background than was the case for families in the first group. Children brought up in such families quite often became actively involved in a church or chapel in their teens, sometimes carrying the commitment through into adulthood—so that a number of the respondents were more religiously active than their parents had been.[62]

The relationships of non-churchgoers with the clergy were very varied. Relatively few people expressed hostility, though there were several who said they had little contact with the clergy. A revealing comment was that made by a Stepney man who had been active in the choir at St John's, Wapping, but gave up when the family moved to Stepney, opposite historic St Dunstan's, the mother church of the East End: 'I never . . . entered Stepney church, because I found that when I went to Stepney the church boys at the parish church there, St Dunstan's, were quite lofty, they were somebody. They were the sons of local businessmen.'[63] It may be that in solidly working-class areas the Anglican church made greater efforts to meet the needs of working-class parishioners, and equally important, working-class churchgoers were less likely to be put off by a wealthy lay elite. Certainly, those respondents who were enthusiastic about individual clergy or about the clergy in general tended to come from strongly working-class areas, such as Spitalfields, Wapping, Poplar and Canning Town.[64]

V

In 1897, the rector of West Hackney explained to Charles Booth's representative what he saw as the different motivations of the three main social groups attending his church. The largest element was the lower middle class: 'clerks are very sociable: they want a social centre and the church gives them one'. Then there was the working class, for whom:

it is more the personality of the 'man' that matters. The church is not for them so much the natural centre as the clergyman. If I or one of my curates make a point of going to see them and they like us as *men*, then they like to support us by coming to church. Then below this class of poor which is the best class, there is the class that comes merely for the loaves and fishes. Of course, there are plenty of them and always will be as long as there is anything to give. They are the camp followers of the church army.[65]

The interviews provide a good deal of support for the view that personal relationships with clergy had a big influence on the attitude to the church, whether positive or negative, of many working-class people. There were clearly some teenagers who hero-worshipped a particular clergyman, and there were adults too who admired or even revered a minister or priest. On the other hand, disillusion with a particular clergyman was quite frequently the precipitant for a break with the church or with religion in general. Here is an example from Bermondsey in the early 1900s:

Harry was well away on the altar and all that, he done very well and he was patrol leader in the Scouts until one year . . . he went [camping with the Sea Scouts]. . . and he saw too much of what the priests were up to and— finished. I don't know he went to church hardly after. 'Cos we're like that, . . . you're either all right or else you're all wrong with us lot, and evidently this Father— forget his name—he caught him, they'd got the bottles of Bass, I know it was Bass, and he said, 'Don't ever take on with this, Harry'. And Harry done with him. That was it.[66]

Popular Christianity as understood by working-class Londoners was a practical religion, and the great test of its worth was a practical one. Professing Christians, and clergymen in particular, were expected to live in a way consistent with their beliefs. If they did not, the beliefs were worthless. It is not clear, in the above story, whether the clergy were convicted of hypocrisy because they had been preaching temperance, or whether it was that all clergymen were expected by their parishioners to be teetotallers. Either way, they had failed the consistency test, and they and their church were thus condemned in the eyes of Harry. Similarly, a man brought up in Hackney Wick, a very poor part of the East End, said he became an atheist because of watching two or three neighbours: 'These women used to row and fight and swear at each other, and then they'd go to church on Sunday. And there was me mother, never went to church, never swore, never got into trouble.'[67]

Occasionally, disillusionment with particular churches or clergy developed into a systematic rejection of religion in general. Besides its many religious traditions, London also had its own secular tradition, which went back to the time of Tom Paine in the 1790s, and enjoyed some influence on the working class.[68] Paine's work was carried on by such figures as Richard Carlile, George Jacob Holyoake and Charles Bradlaugh who, as president of the National Secular Society from 1866 until his death in 1891, made Secularism an inescapable part of the London scene.

The roots of this tradition were in the eighteenth-century Enlightenment. Paine, like Voltaire, believed in God, but he rejected all revealed religions, insisting that God speaks to all humanity through nature and reason. Paine's attack on organized religion was associated with his attack on monarchical government and aristocratic privilege—and this combination of anticlericalism with political radicalism remained characteristic of London Secularism, though Bradlaugh introduced an element of explicit atheism that had been lacking before. Bradlaugh's main purpose was destructive: to undermine the credibility of the Bible, which was the foundation of English Protestantism, and literal adherence to the contents of which was the mainstay of popular belief. The stock in trade, therefore, of Secularist propaganda was the attempt to show that the Bible was full of absurdities, atrocities and inconsistencies. As the President of the National Secular Society put it in 1912: 'The Bible is, at least in parts, an obscene book.'[69] But Bradlaugh also offered an alternative. His headquarters was known as the Hall of Science, and the growth of scientific knowledge during the nineteenth century appeared to offer the basis for an understanding of the world that would supersede revealed religion.

The number of paid-up Secularists was always small. In the peak year of 1886 there were twenty-nine free thought societies in Greater London.[70] The movement's significance lay not so much in the total of its committed adherents, as in the number of those who were sympathetic toward it and to some degree influenced by its ideas. In the 1870s, lectures by Bradlaugh in the Hall of Science could attract audiences of a thousand.[71] In the 1880s, when Bradlaugh's campaign to take his seat in the House of Commons—which required him to take a religious oath—gave the movement its highest profile, Secularist ideas circulated quite widely in workshops and pubs, and especially in the Radical Clubs, many of which seem to have had a secular tone.[72] The Social Democratic Federation, which was formed in 1884, and remained for three decades the most important socialist organization in London, recruited many Secularists.[73]

In 1887, William Rossiter wrote an article on 'Artisan Atheism', in which he argued that 'the great body of artisans' was characterized by a 'a very deep and very bitter antipathy to teachers and professors of religion'.[74] Though Rossiter, who had been an artisan himself, and was later a Christian champion in public debates, should be regarded as a well-informed observer, it is difficult to find other evidence to substantiate such sweeping claims. Moreover, his account of Secularist meetings illustrates two factors that limited the movement's influence: one was the fact that it attracted very little support from women; and the other was that the Secularist appeal was largely negative. As long as the churches seemed both powerful and a barrier to social progress, there clearly was a place for an organization whose main purpose was to oppose them. But any diminution either of the power or of the apparent harmfulness of the churches made organized free thought seem less relevant. In its later nineteenth-century heyday, Secularism provided some working-class Londoners with the basis for a distinctive view of the world and way of life. So much was admitted by Alexander Paterson who, after offering a pessimistic account of the lives of working men in Bermondsey, concluded:

There are in every quarter men who do not fall into this mechanical animalism. Undaunted by the stiffness of an unused mind and the handicap of time, they set their faces toward knowledge. They read and think, attend classes at working men's colleges, fiercely dissect the arguments of the demagogue, quote from Spencer and Darwin with a flourish, and become oracles among their fellows. Such men live temperate and economical lives, dress in dark clothes, and wear badges at all corners of their coats. They may grow cranky and cantankerous . . . .[75]

In view of the references to Spencer and Darwin, one may assume that Paterson intended to portray this identikit working-class intellectual as a Secularist—for whom he offered no more than a grudging respect.

For a more sympathetic view, we might turn to the collective portrait of London Secularists in the 1870s offered by Stan Shipley in his study of working men's Radical Clubs. Most of these clubs were not explicitly Secularist, and not all their members were Secularists. But Shipley stresses the popularity of Secularist speakers, and the frequency with which Secularism was seen as interchangeable with other progressive causes, such as republicanism, parliamentary reform and opposition to coercion in Ireland. Furthermore, the fact that the favourite meeting time for the clubs, Sunday evening,[76] was also the time preferred by working-class and lower middle-class people for attending church meant that the club constituency and the church and chapel constituencies were likely to be mutually exclusive. While the educational and entertainment facilities provided at these clubs were not very different from those available at many church clubs (and, in fact, a number of the clubs listed by Shipley in the appendix to his book appear to have been church-based), one important cultural difference was the fact that most Radical Clubs provided beer,[77] at a time when support for temperance was fairly strong in Anglican churches and overwhelmingly so in Nonconformist chapels.

The salient characteristic of the clubmen described by Shipley seems to have been a passion for knowledge, which focused especially on science, but was very wide-ranging in its concerns: though science, politics and attacks on religion were the main attractions, they also took an interest in literary classics, especially Shelley, 'The Poet of Democracy', and Shakespeare. They judged their authors, like most things, by an instinctive radicalism, which directed itself against 'tyrants' and 'oppressors' of every kind. They also seem to have been highly combative: debates were a popular feature of the clubs, and when not directing their wit and invective against religion or the churches, Secularists seem to have been very prone to internal disputes.[78]

All the evidence suggests that both working-class churchgoers and Secularists were drawn disproportionately from the skilled workers. For Secularism, the evidence tends to be impressionistic, but both the distribution of branches and descriptions of those attending them suggest a mainly artisan constituency.[79] So far as churchgoers are concerned, the evidence is incomplete, but it all points in the same direction. Both Anglicans and Nonconformists did better in artisan districts than in very poor areas, though the churchgoing level in the poorer areas was boosted by the strength of Roman Catholicism in some of these districts.[80]

There is more evidence on the social composition of Nonconformist than of Anglican or Roman Catholic congregations. For instance, Nonconformist marriage and baptismal registers give a clearer indication of who was committed to the congregation than do those of the Anglican and Roman Catholic churches, which include large numbers of entirely nominal adherents.[81] My analysis of marriage registers in Bethnal Green between 1880 and 1901 shows that although about 80 per cent of men marrying were in manual occupations, only 49 per cent of those marrying in chapel were manual workers. Skilled manual workers were in fact about as numerous in the chapels (about a third) as in the general population of those marrying. The discrepancy was caused by a huge shortfall of unskilled workers, who made up 31 per cent of those marrying in church, and 23 per cent of those marrying in the registry office, but only 3 per cent of those marrying in chapel. There was also a less dramatic deficit of semi-skilled and service workers among those marrying in chapel.[82]

Cox's study of Nonconformist weddings in Lambeth shows a less unbalanced occupational pattern—though the difference may be explained by the fact that he took the occupation of the bride's father, rather than that of the bridegroom. Over the period 1880–1910, 53 per cent of the former were in manual occupations, whereas the proportion for all weddings fluctuated between 61 per cent and 68 per cent during that period.[83] Bartlett has undertaken an intensive analysis of the membership of Drummond Road Baptist Church in Bermondsey, which has unusually good records. By identifying members in the manuscript schedules of the 1881 census, he showed that 60–70 per cent of those joining the church in the early 1880s were in manual occupations, and that there was a fairly representative spread of different levels of skill. However, recruitment was skewed by the fact that far more members came from the more 'respectable' streets south of Jamaica Road than from the 'rougher' riverside area.[84] Similar results are produced when the addresses of members of two Peckham chapels are compared with Booth's social map of London, drawn up at about the same time. In a sample of 59 members from the Baptist South London Tabernacle, 11 lived in streets marked red (middle class), 29 in streets marked pink (upper working class), and 17 in streets marked red and pink (which meant a mixture, and probably reflected a mainly lower middle-class population); but only one lived in a street marked purple (middle working class) and one in a blue street (poor). In a sample of 55 from Hanover Congregational Church, there were 1 yellow (wealthy), 14 red, 11 pink and red, 25 pink, 1 pink and purple, 1 purple, 1 purple and blue, and 1 blue.[85]

The similarity in social backgrounds of Secularists and of working-class churchgoers is not surprising. There was a certain amount of traffic between the two groups,[86] and in terms of lifestyle they often had a good deal in common—for instance, an interest in education, and temperate or even puritanical habits. Both groups recruited well among members of skilled trades, with traditions of discussions during meal breaks, and sometimes of reading from newspapers during work. Higher incomes meant that skilled workers and their wives could more readily afford to pay seat rent at a church or chapel or a subscription to a club; they could afford better clothes, and so were less likely to feel ashamed to appear in public places. Two of the churchgoing wives of skilled workers in the Thompson-Vigne sample were even able to afford some help in the home, so that they enjoyed more leisure than the wives of lower-paid workers. The one major difference between the two groups was that Secularists were overwhelmingly male, while churchgoers were predominantly female.[87] I shall return to this theme in chapter 7.

On one other important point, the evidence is unclear. In view of the fact that the national religious census of 1851 had shown that the level of churchgoing in London was considerably below the national average, one would predict that immigrants to London would be more inclined to churchgoing than those born in the metropolis. The evidence of the Thompson-Vigne survey suggests this may be so. In the 10 churchgoing families, 10 out of 20 parents (50 per cent) had been born outside London, whereas, among 58 parents in non-churchgoing families whose place of birth is known, only 16 (28 per cent) came from outside the capital. On the other hand, Bartlett's study of recruits to a Bermondsey Baptist church in the 1880s showed that the proportion of Londoners (58 per cent) was more or less the same as in the general adult population of the borough.[88]

VI

From about the 1880s the churches began to decline in middle- and upper-class areas of London. Between 1886–7 and 1902–3 there was a sharp drop in the level of churchgoing in such West End and wealthy suburban boroughs as Kensington and Hampstead. At first, however, the effect on working-class areas of the city was relatively small. Although across the city as a whole the church attendance rate fell by about 30 per cent between the dates of the two censuses, two working-class boroughs, Finsbury and Bermondsey, registered an increase in that period, and in Bethnal Green there was only a tiny drop. The larger drops in, for instance, Poplar may have been due to middle-class residents leaving for the suburbs, rather than a decline in the number of working-class attenders.[89] Some repercussions of this decline in middle-class and upper-class religiosity were already being felt in working-class boroughs in the early twentieth century. For instance, Anglican ordinations peaked in 1886.[90] In Bermondsey the early twentieth century saw a slight drop in the number of Anglican clergy, and a rather larger drop in the number of voluntary church workers, after a high point in the 1890s.[91] Cox suggests that there was also a drop in the number of voluntary church workers in Lambeth, though he does not have precise figures.[92] Local studies by Cox, Bartlett and Morris in various parts of London have all shown how the role of the churches in education and welfare was contracting in the early twentieth century because of increasing activity by state and by local government in these areas.[93] There was probably also some growth in the number of agnostics and atheists. Secularism as an organized movement was in decline by the early twentieth century, but popular unbelief received a boost from the publication in 1904 by the leading socialist journalist, Robert Blatchford, of *God and My Neighbour*, probably the most widely read critique of Christianity since Tom Paine's *Age of Reason*. Blatchford was one of the first popular writers to emphasize arguments drawn from Darwinism, which had been influencing the development of middle-class agnosticism since the 1860s.[94]

Nonetheless, it was in the churches' suburban strongholds that the religious crisis of these years was experienced most acutely (see table 4, p. 33). In the East End, or in inner south London, where organized religion had always been relatively weak, the mood of the churches in these years was more optimistic: though they started from a low base, they seemed to be making progress.[95]

CHAPTER 3

New York

THE GREATNESS OF the island city of New York was built upon its port. The construction of the Erie Canal in the 1820s gave New York a vital advantage over its rivals, Boston and Philadelphia, in the form of better communications with the interior. In the years immediately following, the port of New York established itself as by far the largest in the United States. Already in the 1830s, over two-thirds of the immigrants entering the United States came through New York, and by 1850 the port was handling over half of the nation's foreign trade. Everything else rested on this foundation: New York's position as America's financial and commercial capital; the concentration there of characteristically metropolitan industries; its status as the nation's main intellectual and cultural centre.

In 1898 New York became the first of the world cities to adopt reasonably realistic boundaries. The new city of Greater New York contained nearly three million people, and ranked second only to London in the world. It comprised the old city of New York on Manhattan Island (henceforth Manhattan borough) and the areas already annexed on the mainland, together with some other parts of Westchester County (now Bronx borough); Brooklyn, which had been the nation's fourth city; and two areas that were still largely rural, Queens County on Long Island (now the borough of Queens) and Staten Island (known as Richmond borough).

I

In 1791 the First Amendment to the United States Constitution prohibited the setting up of an established religion. Some states continued to privilege a particular church, the last to end such arrangements being Massachusetts in 1833. In

49

New York City the final stage in the separation of church and state was the conflict in the 1840s over the management and syllabus of the city's schools. This
culminated with control of the public elementary schools being given to elected
boards, and sectarian teaching being prohibited.[1] But in many ways, an informal
religious establishment remained for many years thereafter. In the second half of
the nineteenth century, two of the city's innumerable religious denominations
were clearly pre-eminent in terms of the social status of their members, namely
the Episcopalians and Presbyterians. A city guide published in 1882 picked out
the Episcopalian Grace Church as presenting the greatest 'display of wealth and
fashion', while Fifth Avenue Presbyterian Church was 'large and enormously
wealthy, numbering more bank presidents and insurance men than any similar
body in the Union'.[2]

Hammack argues that by the 1890s it was no longer possible to speak of a
unified elite in the city. By now there were five elites, of which three (divided
from one another by crucial cultural differences) were still dominated by Protestants of British descent, and there were also two newer elites, consisting respectively of German Jews and German gentiles. Most of the bigger firms were still
controlled by Protestants of British descent,[3] and as late as 1914, when at least
three-quarters of the population were Catholics, Lutherans or Jews, a sample of
those living or working in New York City and included in *Who's Who in New York
City and State* showed that 50 per cent of those stating their religion were Episcopalians or Presbyterians, and a further 28 per cent were Methodists, Congregationalists or Baptists.[4]

In the wealthier districts of the city, church membership was high, and most
of the city's elite were at least nominally attached to a Protestant congregation. In
1901, Protestant church membership as a percentage of total population reached
a peak of 54 per cent in Brooklyn's 1st Ward, which included the wealthy Brooklyn Heights district. The other major concentrations of wealth in the city were
found in the Fifth Avenue districts of Manhattan (the 25th, 27th and 29th Assembly Districts) where Protestant church members were respectively 38 per cent,
36 per cent and 32 per cent of total population, and in the 20th, 23rd and 24th
wards of Brooklyn, including such strongholds of the nouveaux riches as Clinton
Hill, where membership was respectively 44 per cent, 26 per cent and 9 per cent.
The average for the whole city was 9 per cent (see table 5).

McCabe's city guide of 1868 had noted the high rates of churchgoing in wealthy
districts:

> Strangers have observed with surprise the quietness which reigns within
> the city limits on the Sabbath day. . . . In the morning the churches are well
> filled, for New Yorkers consider it a matter of principle to attend morning
> service. The streets are filled with persons hastening to church, the cars are
> crowded, and handsome carriages dash by, conveying their owners to their
> only hour of prayer.[5]

McCabe implied that much of this piety was rather superficial. However, there
were many wealthy and influential New Yorkers who were very actively involved in

TABLE 5

Church and Synagogue Membership in New York City, 1901

	ESTIMATED POPULATION	PERCENTAGE
Manhattan	1,898,238	
Roman Catholic	523,090	27.6
Protestant	157,390	8.3
Jewish	16,063	0.8
Brooklyn	1,213,359	
Roman Catholic	324,800	26.8
Protestant	137,060	11.3
Jewish	2,177	0.2
The Bronx	223,554	
Roman Catholic	44,450	19.9
Protestant	14,465	6.5
Jewish	?	
Queens	166,103	
Roman Catholic	41,950	25.3
Protestant	15,809	9.5
Jewish	26	
Staten Island	68,816	
Roman Catholic	11,412	16.6
Protestant	7,808	11.3
Jewish	?	
New York City	3,570,170	
Roman Catholic	945,702	26.5
Protestant	332,532	9.3
Jewish	18,266	0.5

SOURCE: Membership totals taken from *Federation*, 2 (1902). The population of each borough has been taken as that shown in the 1900 census, plus one-tenth of the increase between 1900 and 1910.

their place of worship. Churches often enjoyed the rather mixed blessing of the patronage of leading businessmen. For instance, the banker J. Pierpont Morgan was closely involved in the affairs of St George's Episcopal Church, where he did long service as warden, and provided a large part of the funding for the ambitious schemes initiated by the rector, W. G. Rainsford, a pioneer of the Institutional Church.[6] In the later nineteenth and early twentieth centuries, a large proportion of the charitable provision in the city was still Protestant-inspired. Within the Protestant elite, the strongly evangelical tone of the early and mid-nineteenth century was giving way to more liberal versions of the faith, as, for instance, in the Settlement movement, which represented the strongest current of middle-class reforming thinking at this time.[7] They were nonetheless 'Protestant' in the eyes of the Catholic and Jewish communities, which tried to make their own alternative provision, though with fewer resources available to them than the Protestants enjoyed.[8]

The Protestantism of the New York elite also had important implications for the city's politics. The rise of Tammany Hall, which was the dominant force for most of the period from the 1870s to the 1930s, was based on very strong support from Irish Catholics, together with more variable support from German, east European Jewish and Italian immigrants.[9] Ranged against Tammany in the years around 1900, whether as Republicans, anti-Tammany Democrats, Reformers or Progressives, were most of the Protestant elite, supported by the city's most influential newspapers and magazines, its most prominent educationalists, and its most famous preachers.[10] All were agreed in portraying Tammany as corrupt and self-interested, and in presenting their own men as superior in moral qualities as well as abilities. Nonetheless, Tammany kept on winning elections, and it did so in large measure because its candidates were men of the people whom ordinary voters could relate to.[11] Conversely, the lawyers, doctors, businessmen and professors who stood as Republicans and Reformers were written off as 'the silk stocking brigade'. And this was a good indication of both the strength and the weakness of the Protestant churches, to which most of them belonged. These churches enjoyed considerable prestige, influence and resources, but their constituency was considerably skewed, and they enjoyed only very limited success in winning the support of the masses.[12]

In the later nineteenth and early twentieth centuries, New York was a city of immigrants, and ethnic divisions influenced all areas of its life.[13] In 1870, approximately 45 per cent of the population of New York and 36 per cent of those living in Brooklyn had been born in other countries. By 1900 the proportion for Greater New York was 38 per cent and in 1910 it was 41 per cent. From 1830 to 1880, immigration to the city was dominated by the Irish and the Germans, in that order, with the British a poor third. The 1880s saw a last great wave of German immigration, as a result of which they overtook the Irish. That decade also saw a substantial growth in immigration from Russia and Austria-Hungary, and a smaller rise in the number of Italians. This immigration from southern and eastern Europe grew in the 1890s, and more especially in the years after 1900. By 1910, Russians and Italians constituted by far the largest bodies of foreign-born in the city, with Germans relegated to third, and the Irish to fifth, behind the natives of Austria-Hungary. First- and second-generation immigrants thus made up the great majority of the population throughout this period. By 1900 four groups—the Irish, the Germans, the Italians, and Jews from various east European countries—had emerged as by far the most numerous. Among the other immigrant groups, the most significant were the British, the Scandinavians, and the Catholic Bohemians, Hungarians and Poles, who settled in different parts of the city from their Jewish compatriots. If New York was a city of immigrants, this was even more true of the working class. In 1900, when only 18 per cent of occupied males were American-born whites with American parents, this group accounted for 45 per cent of those in high white-collar employment, 30 per cent of the semi-professional and managerial workers, and 33 per cent of clerical workers—but only 16 per cent of skilled manual workers, 14 per cent of the semi-skilled, 7 per cent of labourers and 1 per cent of garment workers. Among the immigrants, the British, Canadians and Germans included a substantial middle-class element, but all other groups were heavily working-class.[14]

These immigrants brought many different religious traditions to America with them, and the religious make-up of New York City at the turn of the century was correspondingly complex. A wealth of statistical material is available as a result of the efforts of the Federation of Churches and Christian Workers in New York City, which carried out surveys of religious affiliation and practice in various parts of the city.[15] In five districts they compared the religious affiliation of the head of household with his or her country of birth. From this evidence it is clear that Italians and Irish were overwhelmingly Catholic, and Russians overwhelmingly Jewish. Taking the five districts surveyed, the mean percentages were 97 per cent, 91 per cent and 85 per cent respectively. For Germans and those born in the United States the picture was more complicated, as there were significant differences in distribution between one district and another. For Germans the means were Protestant 65 per cent, Roman Catholic 23 per cent, Jewish 9 per cent, none or not stated 3 per cent; and for white Americans, Protestant 54 per cent, Roman Catholic 40 per cent, Jewish 3 per cent, none or not stated 3 per cent. As for the other significant groups, it is clear that Scandinavians and black Americans were overwhelmingly Protestant, and the British predominantly Protestant. However, the biggest problems of obtaining a representative sample relate to immigrants from Austria-Hungary. In some parts of the city, these were heavily Jewish and in some heavily Roman Catholic, and in a few areas they included a substantial mi-

TABLE 6

Religious Affiliation of Household Heads in New York City, c. 1900

	(Per cent)			
PLACE OF BIRTH	RC	PROT.	JEWISH	NONE OR NOT STATED
U.S.A. (white)	39.7	54.2	3.3	2.8
U.S.A. (black)	4.0	94.5	—	1.5
Germany	23.4	65.2	8.8	2.6
Ireland	91.6	7.7	0.1	0.6
Russia	6.2	4.5	84.7	4.6
Italy	96.9	1.4	0.5	1.2
Austria–Hungary	41.9	10.0	43.1	5.0
Great Britain	21.1	72.6	4.2	2.1
Scandinavia	3.0	93.7	0.3	3.0
Poland	81.7	3.0	12.9	2.4
France	74.8	13.4	2.5	9.3
Other countries	31.9	55.1	2.6	10.4

SOURCE: Surveys of religious affiliation in the 11th and 13th, the 14th, and the 21st Assembly Districts of Manhattan, and in the 1st and the 17th Wards of Brooklyn, published in Federation of Churches and Christian Workers in New York City, *Sociological Canvass*, 3 vols. (New York, 1897–1901), and in their journal, *Federation*. The figures for each ethnic group are the mean of those reported in the five surveys.

nority of Protestants. The mean for the five areas surveyed was Jewish 43 per cent, Roman Catholic 42 per cent, Protestant 10 per cent, none or not stated 5 per cent (see table 6).

Extrapolating from this data, I have estimated that in Manhattan borough in 1900, 45 per cent of heads of household were Roman Catholic, 37 per cent were Protestant, 15 per cent were Jewish, and 3 per cent were of no religion or unknown religion. Over the city as a whole, Protestants were certainly more numerous, Catholics slightly less so, and Jews much less so. If the ratio of church members to the nominally affiliated was the same in the other boroughs as in Manhattan, the figures for the city as a whole would be Roman Catholics 43 per cent and Protestants 42 per cent; if no religion still accounts for 3 per cent, that would mean that 12 per cent were Jewish.[16]

The Irish and Italians both showed very high rates of Roman Catholic affiliation, and very few whose religion was unstated, or who declared themselves to have no religion. The Americans, Germans, British and Scandinavians, all predominantly Protestant, showed a very varied pattern of denominational allegiances. It is notable here that although the Lutherans tend to account for the majority of Scandinavians and a substantial proportion of Germans, many immigrants whose religious background is likely to have been Lutheran moved into another denomination in New York.[17] The proportion of those of no religion was slightly higher among these predominantly Protestant groups than for the Irish and Italians. It tended to be highest among those east European nationalities that were substantially or predominantly Jewish. However, the great majority in all immigrant groups claimed some kind of religious affiliation.

There have been four main approaches to interpreting the role of religion in immigrant life. The best-known view is that of Oscar Handlin, who argued that the role of religion was both important, and essentially conservative and backward-looking.[18] It was important, because religious traditions gave the uprooted one point of continuity in their disoriented lives; it was conservative, because immigrants tried as far as possible to retain the forms of worship and the church structures that they had known in their homeland, and they were reluctant to adapt them to American conditions. A second view, of which Timothy Smith is the leading exponent, places more stress on the creative and innovative aspects of immigrant religion.[19] Smith and his school have also looked at the religious backgrounds of various immigrant groups, and have argued that the process of adapting religious beliefs and institutions to modernizing forces often began before they left Europe. A third view, which received its classic statement in the various writings of the Chicago School of urban sociologists in the 1920s and 1930s, stresses the secularizing effect of migration to America, or, at least, to American cities.[20] Writers in this tradition especially emphasize the effects of American pluralism in undermining taken-for-granted religious beliefs and customs, and of American freedom in prompting each individual to go his or her own way religiously. They also tend to attach special importance to the religiously neutral public school system, with its mission of training homogenized American citizens, for whom a commitment to 'American values' would override all loyalty to ancestral tradition.[21]

Examples can be found to illustrate the validity of each of these models. But when ethnic groups are compared, it becomes clear that experiences that are typical in one group are often exceptional in another. A fourth school of interpretation has therefore emerged, which emphasizes how widely the religious histories of the various ethnic groups in America varied.[22]

One example of this diversity has already been mentioned: the contrast between those ethnic groups whose members remained overwhelmingly loyal to one religious tradition, and those which were readier to experiment. Another example is the big variation between ethnic groups in levels of religious practice. We have at least one major source here, namely the religious census of the borough of Manhattan conducted by the Church News Association in 1902.[23] This only counted attendances at church, and not at synagogue. The results suggested an adult attendance rate among the gentile population of the borough of 37 per cent[24] (see table 7). When the distribution of attendances is compared with the distribution of religious affiliation, as shown in the surveys that were being carried out at about the same time, it becomes clear that there were considerable variations among the churchgoing habits of members of different churches. In fact, the four leading denominations fall into three main groups. At the top are the Roman Catholics, with an estimated attendance level of 50 per cent; in the middle are the Presbyterians with 33 per cent and the Episcopalians with 28 per cent; and at the bottom the Lutherans with 5 per cent. This suggests considerable differences among the levels of practice in different ethnic groups, and the sur-

TABLE 7

Church Attendance by Adults in Manhattan Borough, 1902

	ESTIMATED POPULATION[a]	CHURCH MEMBERS	PER CENT	ATTENDANCES	PER CENT
All Christians	1,169,840	695,872	59.4	451,810	38.6
Roman Catholics	639,518	522,130	81.6	317,454	49.6
Other Christians	530,332	173,742	32.8	134,356	25.3
Lutherans	143,785	18,868	13.1	7,542	5.2
Episcopalians	119,112	56,050	47.1	33,137	27.8
Presbyterians	57,287	25,742	44.9	18,929	33.0
Methodists	39,988	14,749	37.0	20,191	50.5
Baptists	34,457	27,263	79.1	27,225	79.0
Other[b]	135,703	31,070	22.9	27,330	20.1

SOURCE: Church attendance and membership and estimated adult population, (1,418,000) taken from *New York Times*, 24 Nov. 1902.

[a]Total nominal adherents of each denomination calculated by same methods as in table 8. Jews (14.9 per cent) and those of no religion or unknown religion (2.6 per cent) have been deducted from the adult population before calculating the church attendance rate. If, however, all of the latter were included, the church attendance rate for the non-Jewish population would be 37.4 per cent.

[b]Includes Protestants of no specified denomination.

TABLE 8

Church Attendance in the 21st Assembly District of Manhattan (Upper West Side), 1900

(Percentages in various categories reported to be church attenders)

COUNTRY OF BIRTH	MARRIED WOMEN IN TENEMENTS	MARRIED WOMEN IN PRIVATE HOUSES	MARRIED MEN
All countries	36.1	48.3	33.1
Canada	47.3	52.6	48.7
Scotland	45.5	46.6	41.1
England	43.3	48.9	38.4
Ireland	39.8	46.4	37.2
United States	37.0	50.2	34.2
Cuba	31.7	35.0	26.3
France	31.5	16.6	25.9
Sweden	28.7	—	26.7
Germany	28.5	38.6	25.6
Italy	27.1	—	25.0

SOURCE: Survey of religious affiliation and practice published in *Sociological Canvass*, 3.

veys carried out by the Federation of Churches confirm this. The most detailed of these surveys covered the 21st Assembly District of Manhattan (the Upper West Side). This found that churchgoing was highest among immigrants from Canada, Britain and Ireland, and lowest among Italians, with Germans and Swedes ranking only slightly higher. Respondents born in the United States were marginally above average[25] (see table 8). It will be noted that the immigrant groups with high levels of churchgoing were all predominantly English-speaking. The most likely explanation for this is simply that the English-speaking immigrant had a far better chance of finding a service in a language that he or she could understand—indeed, in most parts of Greater New York they were spoilt for choice.

Thus, immigrants as such were not more or less likely to be active in the church than those born in America. But it is likely that for the first generation, and probably for the second, too, traditions and experiences specific to each immigrant group had a decisive influence on their patterns of religious affiliation and practice. This point emerges still more clearly from the experience of three major immigrant groups, the Irish, the Germans and the east European Jews.

II

In 1900, 22 per cent of the city's population was of 'Irish stock', according to the census definition. Their strength lay in their dominant influence within the Democratic Party, as a result of which the Irish were well represented in all areas of public employment, and wherever jobs were filled through Tammany patronage.

They remained, however, a predominantly working-class community. Only about a quarter of occupied males of Irish descent were in middle-class jobs, and nearly half were semi-skilled or unskilled manual workers.[26] However, in the second generation there was considerable movement into white-collar employment and the professions. The 1900 census showed that over the country as a whole second-generation Irish were overrepresented not only as government officials, but also as lawyers, journalists, actors and salesmen.[27] The Irish were found all over the city, but the densest concentrations at the beginning of this century were along the West Side and the Middle East Side of Manhattan, and in a wide swathe of inner Brooklyn, stretching down the waterfront from the Navy Yard to Red Hook, and then inland to Prospect Park.[28]

The great majority of Irish New Yorkers had at least some connection with a Catholic parish. Approximately 91 per cent of the Irish-born said they were Catholics; of these, 90 per cent claimed membership of a specific parish. Comparison with church records suggests that in strongly Irish areas like the Middle West Side of Manhattan about 70 per cent of those identifying themselves as Catholics were regarded as parishioners by the clergy.[29] Wherever the Irish went in New York, the building of Catholic churches signalled their arrival. The biggest of them all, St Patrick's Cathedral on Fifth Avenue, which opened in 1878, may be said to have symbolized the collective arrival of the Irish as a central and inescapable force in the city's life. As an expensive souvenir, the Catholic historian John Gilmary Shea prepared a volume entitled *The Catholic Churches of New York City*, which was bound in red and gold with a picture of the new cathedral on the front, and the words 'New York's Cathedral, Peerless in our land, Tribute of Faith to Erin's Saint shall stand'. The mood of the book was one of self-congratulation—satisfaction that the years of struggle were over:

> The work here presented to the public shows perhaps more strikingly than any ordinary conception would picture the actual position of the Catholic body in New York City. The churches which are the sanctuaries of more than half the population of the great commercial city of the Western World, the churches which are each Sunday crowded by fully three-quarters of all church-goers in our metropolis. . . . The parochial schools created instinctively by these churches, where by the self-sacrifice of this one denomination a perfect army of their children receive a gratuitous education . . . ; academies for higher and the highest education of both sexes; three incorporated colleges; hospitals; asylums for orphans, the uncared for babe, the aged and forsaken; homes for the neglected and shelterless; communities devoting their lives and energies to works of mercy—are all presented here. . . .[30]

The cathedral belonged, of course, to all the city's Catholics, but it is hardly surprising that the Irish saw it as a distinctly Irish achievement, and that many non-Irish Catholics felt themselves marginalized by the Hibernian hegemony.[31] In 1842 the Irish-born John Hughes had become Bishop of New York, and in 1850 he became the first Archbishop. Every one of his successors, down to O'Connor at the present day, has been Irish by birth or descent. In 1878 the archbishop was Cardinal McCloskey, born in Brooklyn of Irish parents. He was assisted by an Irish-born vicar-general. Out of New York's fifty-four parishes, seventeen had Irish-born pastors, and probably another twelve had pastors of Irish descent.[32] McCloskey was succeeded in 1885 by Corrigan, born in Newark of Irish parentage, and on his death in 1902 there followed the Irish-born Farley: 'In 1908 Archbishop Farley made the centennial of the New York diocese a national event, the Irish atmosphere intensified by the presence of Cardinal Logue of Ireland. Four years later, after his return from Rome as Cardinal, he received a welcome comparable with the Lindbergh reception fifteen years later.'[33]

Many Irish at the end of the nineteenth century still kept painful memories of the days when 'No Irish need apply',[34] even if it was now newer immigrants from Italy and eastern Europe who bore the main brunt of America's scorn. All the elements in New York's uniquely heterogeneous population were victims of hostile stereotyping. But according to Elsa Herzfeld, whose study of West Side working-class life was published in 1905, it was still the Irish who suffered most among the longer-established white ethnic groups. 'The German and American element,' she wrote, 'have a distinct contempt for the Irish as a class. The Irish are always low, coarse and vulgar, or they are "dirty", . . . "They drink and fight continually".'[35]

In this situation Catholic churches and priests became symbols of Catholic identity cherished even by those who were far from devout. On 12 July 1870, when a body of Irish Catholics attacked an Orange family picnic in a riverside park, killing several people, the attack was said to have been provoked by the rumour that the Orangemen had fired on a Catholic church en route to the picnic spot.[36] The grandiose churches, which so horrified Catholicism's critics, were a source of pride to the Irish.[37] And indeed their pride was enhanced by the fact that it was they who had built the churches: financial reports from the years 1880–1920 show that about half the parish income typically came from the dimes and nickels collected as seat money at mass, with most of the rest coming from special collections and parish fairs, and only relatively small proportions from large donations by wealthy individuals. During the McGlynn controversy in 1887, when Mgr Donnelly, who had been foisted on St Stephen's parish by the Archbishop, tried to break up a protest meeting with the words 'I am the pastor of this parish', the protesters replied 'No, you are not, it is our church, paid for with our money'.[38] Similarly with the Catholic clergy: Irish New Yorkers were proud of their priests. 'If the priest be a man of sympathy and ability, he becomes an object of admiration. Indeed he may share a place with the other idols of the people—the successful athlete and the influential politician.' They particularly appreciated those priests who used their churches to support the Irish national cause. For instance, at the time of Queen Victoria's jubilee, the *Irish World*, the leading Irish radical paper in the city, devoted most of its front page to describing the contributions to the celebrations made by a New York priest who attracted large crowds to a Requiem Mass for 'the souls of the millions of the Irish race who have been done to death during that desolating reign by British law'.[39]

In the 1930s, a projected history of the 'Irish in New York', to be produced as part of the Federal Writers' Project, intended to stress the 'intimate part played by priest, politician and saloon-keeper in neighborhood life'.[40] The familiarity and taken-for-grantedness of the church in Irish New York are well conveyed in the memoirs, also written in the 1930s, of Dick Butler, a former docker, trade union organizer and West Side local politician, who had briefly been a State Assembly-man, and seems to have embodied those features of New York politics that critics of Tammany Hall found most objectionable. On the West Side about 1900, as Butler describes it, being a Catholic was first of all a sign that you were 'one of us'. He faced a good deal of hostility, not least from his intended in-laws, because he had been born in England: 'Only the fact that I was a right-hander in religion saved me from extinction.'[41] There were Catholic politicians noted for their overt piety or their strict moral principles,[42] but Butler was not one of them. For him, going to mass was simply what everyone did:

> All the folks from Twentieth to Thirtieth Street, west of Ninth Avenue, attended Guardian Angels, with the exception of a few neighbors of St Columba's parish on West Twenty-Fifth Street. The folks were of the labor-ing class and, as it has always been, they wanted to outshine each other. I, as a natty dresser, was sure to be there with my patent-leather shoes—and how they would hurt, but I had to be the dude.[43]

There are no suggestions that Butler tried to adhere to the letter of Catholic morality—and indeed accounts of chicanery of one kind or another take up large parts of the book. But the terms in which he describes his escapades again reflect the way in which churches and priests were an integral part of the local landscape. Harking back to the time when 'grafting used to be open and above board', he recalled how 'In the olden days you paid the ward man in his saloon or right out on the street corner or on the church steps, wherever you happened to meet him.' Similarly, during the freight handlers' strike in 1882, the boycotting of strike break-ers was organized by circulating lists of names during mass.[44]

If the Catholic Church was a popular institution in New York, it was also a very powerful one. There were two sides to this power. Irish loyalty to the church gave the clergy very considerable potential influence. At the same time, the con-nections that they had with other powerful figures in the Irish community, nota-bly politicians, meant that the clergy were respected even by those who had no love for them.[45] In the 1870s and 1880s political and trade union issues were a frequent source of tension between many Catholic bishops and clergy on the one side, and a large section of their Irish parishioners on the other. One problem was that of Ireland itself. In the eyes of many Irish New Yorkers the nationalism of most of their bishops and clergy was too narrowly constitutional. Clerical con-demnations of Fenianism and of the Land League's 'No Rent' policy provoked bitter criticism from many lay Catholics.[46] The other problem area was the labour militancy of these years. Reactions by the clergy to specific industrial disputes varied; but Archbishop Corrigan of New York, like many of his more conservative episcopal colleagues, was strongly opposed to the Knights of Labor and to the United Labor Party.[47] At the time it seemed possible that the Labor Party, the

Knights, the Irish-American press, and the various nationalist organizations might provide the focus for an alternative Irish-American culture, free of clerical influence, and largely antagonistic to the church.[48] But the crisis was short-lived. The Labor Party split in 1887, and from 1888 Tammany Hall exercised a firm grip over New York politics; the Knights of Labor were already in decline by then, and the American Federation of Labor craft unions that became the characteristic preserve of the Irish favoured a 'pure and simple' unionism which was acceptable to most clergy; the activities of the anti-Catholic American Protective Association in the later 1880s helped to revive the latent Catholicism of those Irish nationalists who had become somewhat detached from the church. So, by the later 1890s, the church no longer had any major rivals within the New York Irish community; and the dominant form of politics, that associated with the Democratic Party machine, complemented, rather than contested, the influence of the church.[49]

The Manhattan church census suggested that about half the adult Catholics in the city went to mass on the day of the census. Church records sometimes give even higher figures, though these may be slightly inflated by the fact that completely lapsed Catholics were likely to be left out of the base population from which the attendance rates were calculated. A survey, in which children were also included, was carried out by the pastor of Epiphany parish on the East Side in 1885. This suggested that 50–60 per cent of the whole parish attended on a typical Sunday.[50]

The clergy tried to draw this enormous population of those recognizing some kind of Catholic identity into an all-embracing 'parish life' (termed by the Catholic reformers of the 1960s 'the Catholic ghetto') which was intended to protect them from the contamination of a Protestant or pagan environment. A history of the archdiocese published in 1905 described the great network of organizations that characterized the modern parish, and which was 'aimed to meet every need of the parishioner and to deal with every condition'.[51] And a study of New York priests, partly based on interviews with a group of those ordained in the 1920s, refers to the 'Catholic culture', still flourishing at that time, in which the priest was 'cult leader, confessor, teacher, counsellor, social director for young and old, and social worker' and where 'hundreds went to mass each week, went to confession every Saturday, were members of parish organizations, . . . enjoyed the parish dances, plays, card parties and athletic teams, packed the parish mission for weeks as their children did the parochial school or Sunday School of religion, were attended at baptisms and marriages, in illness and death'.[52] Similarly, a former parishioner, born in 1904, of Sacred Heart on the West Side of Manhattan, wrote: 'My recollection of Sacred Heart is a very happy one, of my own family, my friends and neighbors. Our lives were centered round Sacred Heart church and one another.' Among their numerous parish activities, she mentioned that her family went to mass daily, her father belonged to the Holy Name Society, her mother to the Altar and Rosary societies, and she herself belonged to the Dramatic Club and collected door to door for parish funds. She also remembered trips to Rockaway Beach and the May Processions, when the various church organizations packed West 51st Street.[53]

Even by comparison with other loyal Catholics, this family's degree of parish-centredness seems to have been exceptional. But the parish was a basic reference point for large numbers of less pious Irish Catholics. In the later nineteenth century, priests in many parts of Europe, worried by the growing strength of secularist movements, and by the increasing contacts with non-Catholics that resulted from the migration of Catholic peasants to the cities, were making similar efforts to enclose their parishioners within a Catholic subculture.[54] In the United States these efforts were unusually successful, because sectarian exclusiveness was reinforced by ethnic exclusiveness.

The period around the turn of the century saw the emergence of a formidable generation of pastors of large and wealthy parishes who were as much businessmen as priests, managing an extensive network of schools and charitable institutions and a large team of assistant clergy.[55] Their status within the Irish community, often reinforced by the title of 'Monsignor', was such that their condemnations and pronouncements carried great weight. A typical comment on this pastoral influence is that by Dick Butler, who noted that his hard-drinking longshoreman father went to mass every week as a result of the combined efforts of his wife and the priest: 'Father was big enough to lick all the priests in the country, but he feared them more than he feared God.'[56]

Henry J. Browne, in his superb history of Sacred Heart parish, gives a vivid account of two alternative models of priest in the shape of Mgr Joseph Mooney, pastor from 1890 to 1923, and Fr William Scully, who was an assistant from 1921 to 1936 before himself becoming pastor.[57] Scully embodied a 'friendly, open, street-strolling type of charisma'. He is remembered by elderly parishioners as 'the most human priest', who did not 'push religion down your throat', but 'when he knew you were hungry and shoeless, he fed you and put shoes on you'. Mooney is also well remembered—and admired—but for very different qualities. His parish school, with 3,500 pupils, was one of the largest in the United States, but he only appeared there in person twice in the year. Nor were parishioners likely to see him preside at their weddings and christenings—unless they were prominent Democratic politicians. However, they were well aware of his prohibitions:

> He forbade the use of even the swimming pool of the YMCA on 10th Avenue and 50th Street for fear of Protestant proselytizing, and threatened excommunication to anyone who boxed at Hartley House on West 46th Street. He gave expression, in short, to the Catholic orthodoxy of the day. His influence in that respect was conservative and turned the parish inward as the self-sufficient total community. But the positive effects of this should not be lost. The parishioners' self-image seemed to improve as they viewed their pastor as a man of church power, a man who could also be called upon in 1918 to administer the archdiocese in the interim between John Cardinal Farley's death and Patrick Hayes' appointment as archbishop.[58]

George Kelly, in his history of St Monica's on the Upper East Side, gives a somewhat similar account of Arthur Kenny, pastor 1913–43:

. . . a public figure conscious of his position as a leader of men. His stately bearing, his richly pleasant voice, his pince-nez glasses, made him the personification of dignity. He was all that was good in the old-fashioned understanding of the word 'Father'. Whether he walked, talked or entertained, it was all done in the grand manner. He was probably one of the best preachers of his time, and had few equals in the art of persuading people to part with generous sums of their money for the support of various causes, parish and otherwise.

With Kenny parishioners seem to have got the best of both worlds. He 'had the capacity to blend regality with neighborliness and athleticism', presiding at the monthly bingo nights organized by the Rosary Society, and engaging in 'playful boxing with some of the young men of the parish'.[59]

As Catholic parishes prospered, and a growing section of their members entered the middle class, many pastors showed an increasing concern with questions of respectability and decorum. The *Calendar* of Holy Name parish on the Upper West Side included in 1916 advice on the correct way to receive communion: 'The mouth should be well opened; the tongue extended; the eyes modestly closed; the hands joined or clasped together, kept close to the body, and not thrust forward beyond the altar rail.'[60] Also in 1916, the church of Our Lady of Lourdes, Washington Heights, regarded at the time as a 'model parish',[61] published a *Year Book and Custom Book*, which is a remarkable expression of the prevailing concerns. The book included a lengthy section on 'The Etiquette of the Church': 'The purpose of the Church in prescribing this elaborate etiquette is to impress on us the dignity of her services, and especially to make us understand that we are in the Real Presence of God and that we should not for a moment be unmindful of the decorum that should characterize those worshipping at the court of the King.'[62]

A long section on funeral customs was directed against a dual target—'remnants of paganism' and the undue influence of the church's Protestant or secular environment. The pastor appealed to 'the leaders of our people, the better educated, the more wealthy', 'to be the first to comply *ad unguem*, to the very letter, with every part of the Church's ceremonial'. The 'Regulations for Lent', stretching over four pages, were so complex that they could fairly be described as an exercise in keeping the laity in their place by tying them up in knots. The section on the parish schools enthused about the uniform, introduced in 1905, which facilitated 'more rigid insistence upon cleanliness, neatness, personal appearance, etc.'.[63] It was all a far cry from St Stephen's in the 1880s, where parishioners were said to receive communion while carrying bundles and tin cans.[64]

IV

In 1900 those of German stock made up 28 per cent of the city's population. While the Germans were as residentially scattered as the Irish by the early twentieth century, they differed from the Irish in the fact that their major ethnic institutions were concentrated in a small area of the city. Until the 1880s the focus was clearly the Lower East Side. But from about that time a large-scale uptown migration set in. By the early twentieth century, the focus of organized German life was the area round East 86th Street, known as Yorkville. In 1910 a newspaper supplement listed over a hundred German organizations meeting in the square mile bounded by Central Park, the East River, 79th Street and 96th Street.[65] Each of the major German subcultures was represented by one of its leading institutions. On 88th Street stood Immanuel Church, with the largest German Lutheran congregation in Manhattan, numbering over two thousand in 1901, and on 87th Street was St Joseph's Catholic Church with an associated community of fifty-five hundred, the second largest German Catholic parish in Manhattan. On 83rd and 84th Streets were two other major Lutheran churches, Immanuel and Zion.[66] Close by were two of the most important German secular institutions: the Labor Temple on 84th Street, a centre for trade union and socialist meetings, and the *Turnhalle* on 85th Street, headquarters of the leading German sporting organization. (In the 1930s the American Nazis would also have their headquarters on 85th Street.)[67] Singing clubs, which were more ideologically neutral, typically met in such places as the Bismarck and Mozart Halls on 86th Street, which was also a major site for dancehalls.

In Brooklyn the first major German settlement was in Williamsburg. But by the end of the century, Germans had spread to most of the northern and eastern parts of the borough, and over the border into Queens, and they were particularly numerous in the Bushwick-Ridgewood section along the Brooklyn-Queens boundary. Although the period of German mass migration more or less coincided with that of the Irish, the level of prosperity was considerably higher among the Germans. In 1900 rather over a third of occupied males of German stock were in middle-class occupations, and slightly under a third were semi-skilled or unskilled manual workers.[68] Next to the British, the Germans were the most favourably placed of the foreign-stock groups, though still a considerable way behind those born of American parents. Their strengths lay in manufacturing industry, in retailing and in skilled labour. The relative prosperity of the Germans was graphically demonstrated by a study published in 1893 that compared the death rates of Germans and Irish in New York and Brooklyn. With the exception of cancer and suicide, nearly every form of death claimed Irish victims at a faster rate.[69]

There was no church that enjoyed an influence among the Germans in any way comparable to that of the Catholic Church among the Irish. Conversely, irreligious influences were much stronger. In 1856 the *Staats-Zeitung* had stated that no more than a fifth of the Germans in New York attended church with any regularity, and a few years later it suggested that half of them had no religious affiliation at all.[70] Similar comments were being made twenty or thirty years later. In 1888 a series of magazine articles on New York immigrant communities noted that 'it is frankly admitted by German clergymen that a large number of their countrymen in the great metropolis do not attend church' and that 'while some of them may be infidels and agnostics', 'most of them are simply indifferent'.[71] Both Catholic priests and Lutheran pastors were apt to see themselves as leaders of a beleaguered minority of church people. The pastor of St Luke's Lutheran Church on the Middle West Side at the turn of the century frequently returned to the theme that the godless were setting the dominant standards of thought and behaviour. The very first issue of his magazine in May 1902 included an article entitled 'Do you go to church?' which asked: 'Perhaps you are ashamed to go to church? . . .You think everyone will be looking at you when you are seen in church. You do not want to become an object of ridicule.' In 1903 the annual report of his church noted 'how impudently and generally, especially in a world city like this, unbelief has raised its head in our time,' and in 1906 it began by stating: 'We live in a city where Jews and unbelievers and those who belong to no particular church, form the great majority of the population.'[72] The parish regulations of St Joseph's Catholic parish reflect a similar suspicion of the world around. These began: 'As a German you should belong to a German parish', and not 'for reasons of prestige, convenience or business considerations' to an English parish. Parishioners were also told to protect their faith by choosing a Catholic spouse, to avoid contact with irreligious or immoral people, to read only good books and newspapers and to keep clear of any organization that could bring about close contact with non-Catholics. Mixed marriages were not permitted, and Protestants and freemasons could not be chosen as godparents. These rules were printed in a jubilee history of the parish published in 1932. The book ends with a section of jokes, equally revealing of the self-image of many German-speaking Catholics in New York: typically they take the form of a sturdy but unsophisticated Catholic, often a Bavarian or Tyrolean villager, outwitting some self-important Protestant or freethinker.[73]

Levels of church membership were much lower than among the Irish or, indeed, many other sections of the population. In 1901 Protestant church membership reached its lowest level in the city in the strongly German Upper East Side of Manhattan, where only about 6 per cent of the Protestant population were church members—as against 50 per cent or more in some of the middle-class 'American' districts of Brooklyn. In Brooklyn, the average ratio of Protestant church members to total population was 11.3 per cent; the nine wards in which Germans were the largest ethnic group all had ratios below that average, in spite of the fact that most Germans were Protestants. The level of church membership among Catholics was a good deal higher, though admittedly the criteria for membership were laxer; even so, the 46 per cent or so of Catholics who were counted as parish members on the Upper East Side was well below the 70 per cent that was common in mainly Irish districts.[74] German Jews were mainly adherents of Reform synagogues, but attendance at the Reform synagogues seems to have been low.[75]

In New York the German Protestant churches had little power. Both the patriotic religiosity and the fierce anticlericalism bred in the home country were inappropriate. But religious indifference was widespread. It also affected the Catholic minority, which in Germany tended to be more attached to its churches than were the Protestants. In New York the Catholic Church found it harder to protect its members from hostile influences, as they no longer lived in distinct regions or enclaves, and there was no longer a Protestant state to keep alive their sense of group identity. The separation between the various German subcultures was less rigid than ideological purists of all kinds would have wished: many Catholic men defied the church's prohibition by joining the masons and other lodges—and in consequence were excluded from the sacraments.[76]

In contrast to the situation in many other sections of the New York population, religious indifference was widespread in the German elite. Both among the New York Irish and among white or black Americans, clergymen were prestigious figures, whose pronouncements were prominently reported by the press; politicians, lawyers and businessmen tended to be at least nominally church members. By contrast, church affairs attracted little attention either from the middle-class *Staats-Zeitung*, the socialist *Volkszeitung*, or the mass-circulation *Morgen Journal*—and in fact German-language journalism in the United States had an anti-clerical tradition, since the founders and many of the contributors to these papers were so often liberal refugees from the 'restoration' of the 1850s or socialist refugees from the repression of 1878–90.[77] Similarly, a directory of New York's German elite in 1913 showed that only 21 per cent of those listed mentioned a religious affiliation,[78] whereas in *Who's Who in New York City and State, 1914*, 52 per cent of those living or working in New York City did so.

But if the churches were relatively weak in German New York, there was *no* German institution of any kind with an influence in any way comparable to that enjoyed by, for instance, the Roman Catholic Church among the Irish and the Poles. A major characteristic of the Germans, by comparison with most other immigrant groups in later nineteenth-century America, was an extreme degree of cultural fragmentation. A history of German America written during the Third Reich by an advocate of the unification of the world's *Deutschtum* ignored one major component, the Jews, but identified five main subcommunities, each substantially separated from the others: Catholics, conservative Lutherans, liberal Protestants, socialists and members of the *Vereine* (the mass of lodges, choirs and gymnastic and shooting clubs, which were a conspicuous feature of German city life in the nineteenth century, both in the fatherland and overseas). While there was some overlap in membership between the *Vereine* and the more liberal Protestant denominations, Catholic, strict Lutheran and socialist leaders encouraged their members to keep clear of the *Vereine*, both because they were competitors and because they did not like the distinctive ethos associated with these organizations. This ethos was spelled out most clearly by the *Turnerbund*, the influential gymnastic organization, which the socialists disliked because it was liberal and bourgeois, and the more conservative Christians disliked because they saw its devotion to individual freedom, science and culture as a rival religion.[79] The fact that the *Vereine* often acted as direct alternatives to the churches was also emphasized by their tendency to meet on Sundays, and to expect attendance at the funerals of fellow members.[80] The same was more obviously true of the socialists who, by the 1880s, were a large and highly organized element in the German districts of American cities, with their own newspapers, libraries, theatres, schools and choirs.[81]

Because there were so many German organizations, it is easy to forget that there were also many German immigrants who had little to do with any of them. The daily rhythms of life in the long-established German neighbourhoods of the

Lower East Side were well described in a series of short stories first published in the *New Yorker Staats-Zeitung* and collected in 1886 under the title *Klein-Deutschland: Bilder aus dem New Yorker Alltagsleben*. A first chapter, called 'Our House', sets the scene: the crowded five-storey tenements, in which everything that one family did could be seen or heard by the other nineteen households in the building; the plaster falling from walls and ceiling; the piles of rubbish in the streets; the taps that were always running dry. The stories, quiet and mildly ironical in tone, are never melodramatic, but the picture they present is often a sombre one. They tell of the recent immigrant, unable to find a job, and without a friend to whom he could turn, reduced to begging; of dying children; of evictions; of feuds between neighbours in adjoining apartments; of a young wife waiting up all Saturday night for her husband to return from a drinking bout, only to find that he has spent the night in the cells. Occasionally, the brighter side of tenement life is stressed—for instance, the Sunday evenings spent visiting friends and drinking beer, the kindness of neighbours in time of need. The church gets a few mentions in passing, but never is at the centre of the story. Nor do *Vereine*, trade unions or political parties receive much attention. The world described is focused on the tenement, the street, the saloon and the work group.[82] It is also a world in which loneliness and homesickness play an important part—a fact reflected in the very high suicide rate among German-born New Yorkers.[83]

In spite of all the weaknesses of the churches, the Lutheran pastor had a role in immigrant neighbourhoods that extended far beyond the circle of regular churchgoers. Lutheran churches, like those of other denominations, were centres for a wide range of organizations, some of which attracted those not otherwise connected with the church. The ubiquitous *Frauenverein*, or Ladies Aid as it was known in English-speaking parishes, was particularly important, as many women had few other opportunities to relax and socialize outside the home. The *Frauenverein* was usually one of the first organizations to appear in a new parish, and in some cases it maintained a semi-independent existence.[84] Many Lutheran parishes also maintained a day school, though these often struggled to survive, as most Lutheran parents preferred to send their children to a public school.[85]

In 1918 a well-known New York Lutheran minister, G. U. Wenner, wrote a study of *The Lutherans of New York*, in which he suggested that, beside the 150,000 'souls' counted by the city's churches, there were a further 400,000 'lapsed Lutherans': 'We meet them at weddings and funerals. We baptize their children and we bury their dead. Once in a while some of them even come to church. In spite of all their wanderings and intellectual idiosyncrasies they still claim to be Christians. And whatever their own attitude to Christianity may be, there are few who do not desire to have their children brought up in the Christian faith.'[86]

Some idea of the proportion of Lutherans in different categories can be got by comparing the surveys of church membership carried out around 1900 by the Federation of Protestant Churches with the records of individual parishes. For instance, the Federation survey of the Middle West Side of Manhattan suggested that about 7 per cent of the population, or about eight thousand people, regarded themselves as Lutherans. The records of St Luke's, the only Lutheran church in this area, show that in 1901 there were 843 communicants, equalling about 10 per cent of all the Lutherans in the area—or maybe 15 per cent, if only those old enough to be communicants are counted. However, it is clear that there were much larger numbers who had been confirmed at St Luke's, married and baptized their children there, and would eventually be buried by the pastor. In 1901, there were 154 baptisms, 98 confirmations, 97 weddings and 74 burials in the church, suggesting that it was providing the rites of passage to a community of around six thousand people.[87]

Regional differences seem to have been more important among the Germans than they were among the Irish. For instance, St Luke's Lutheran Church seems to have been dominated by immigrants from Hanover in the later nineteenth century, while natives of Bremen were very prominent in the Schermerhorn Evangelical Church in Brooklyn.[88] Differences in dialect were clearly a major practical reason for German organizations splitting on regional lines. But clearly other factors were also at work, including the recency of German unification and the ambivalence with which the new state was widely regarded; and differences between the religious traditions of the various predominantly Protestant states. However, it is possible that the depth of these divisions has been exaggerated. Analysis of membership records at St Luke's in 1880, when the census frequently recorded the state of origin of German immigrants, suggests that although natives of Hanover made up about a third of those who did name their state of origin, the remaining two-thirds included people from most other regions of Germany. Though Hanoverians were somewhat overrepresented, the church was in no sense exclusive.[89]

However, internal divisions caused by differences over theology, lifestyle and language perhaps plagued the Lutherans more than any other denomination in New York. The tensions within Roman Catholicism were certainly bad enough, but these were to some extent modified by that church's extremely hierarchical structures, which meant that in the last resort there were generally recognized authorities who could impose a solution on matters of dispute. American Lutheranism had no such accepted authorities, and it accordingly split into numerous rival synods, which congregations and individual pastors moved in and out of as a result of further splits. Matters at issue included degrees of Lutheran orthodoxy, relations between synods and individual congregations, attitudes to the lodges, and attitudes to American religious practices such as revivalism and teetotalism.[90] In New York there were three main groups of congregations. The Missouri Synod stood for strict Lutheran orthodoxy and the autonomy of individual congregations. The General Synod was less rigid on matters of belief, and attracted most of the English-speaking congregations. The General Council occupied an intermediate position.[91] As in Germany, hymn-books were particularly productive of controversy, because of demands that they contain nothing that conflicted with Lutheran doctrine.[92] And of course there were the inevitable power struggles between pastors and leading laymen. Maybe Lutheran quarrelsomeness was a tribute to the emotional hold on many Germans that Lutheranism still possessed. In most other Protestant churches, the discontented simply left and joined a different denomination—the prevailing American orthodoxy was an interdenominational Evangelicalism, which saw nothing sacred in the distinctive tenets and practices of any one church. By contrast, many Lutherans were inclined to make special claims for their own branch of Christianity. To quote the charming analogy proposed by one West Side pastor in 1912: Lutheranism was like a pure stream; Calvinism was like a stream that was two-thirds pure water, and one-third sewage; Roman Catholicism was one-third pure water and two-thirds sewage.[93]

'The language of Luther' was a source of endless disputes. Most churches came sooner or later to the realization that the younger generation was being lost because most or all services were being held in German.[94] In church after church the verdict of hindsight was that action had been taken too late. Sometimes the problem may have been mainly financial. For instance, Wilhelm Busse, pastor of St Luke's from 1874 to 1900, could not preach in English, and constantly urged the congregation to employ a full-time English-speaking assistant. They refused, apparently because of the cost, but in 1900 he was succeeded by an American-born pastor, who spoke both languages.[95] However, some conservative Lutherans saw an intrinsic virtue in the German language, arguing that the use of English correlated with a loss of faith, or with an Americanized form of Christianity that was a betrayal of Lutheran orthodoxy. The leading exponent of this view in the 1860s and 1870s was Friedrich Steimle, pastor of Zion Church in Brooklyn Heights, who from 1866 to 1872 was leader of his own 'Steimle Synod', many of whose members later joined the Missourians. Steimle ran a German-language school and encouraged the use of German in the home. Besides his staunch defence of the Augsburg Confession, he was also a vigorous critic of such manifestations of Americanization as revivalism, temperance, Calvinism and religious enthusiasm of all kinds.[96] Though Steimle died in 1880, the language issue remained a subject of dispute right up to the time of World War I. For instance, St Peter's-in-the-Bronx was founded in 1890, but its first American-born pastor was not appointed until 1912:

> Up to this point it had been a truly German church. The young were expected to learn German and worship in German. . . . But the young people here, as in hundreds of other congregations, could not help being American in language and spirit and in many cases did not feel at home in their own church. Many drifted away and were lost to the Lutheran church before those responsible were willing to face the facts and take steps to remedy the conditions.[97]

World War I gave a big boost to the use of English, and in the 1920s a fresh generation of German immigrants found that they were the ones who were now being neglected.[98]

The language problem was a major factor in the loss of many of the second generation to other denominations. But surveys around 1900 showed that although Lutherans were certainly the largest section of German immigrant Protestantism, the percentage of German-born Protestants claiming to be Lutherans varied in different parts of the city from four-fifths to less than half. The Episcopalians,

Presbyterians and Reformed all had a fair number of German adherents. And there were always considerable numbers of Germans who were Protestants but did not identify themselves with any specific denomination.[99]

Approximately a quarter of the German-born in New York were Catholics. There were also considerable numbers of German-speaking Catholics from Austria and Hungary. From an early stage they showed a desire for their own parishes. The first specifically German Catholic parish in the city, St Nicholas on the Lower East Side, came in 1833. The neighbouring parish of Most Holy Redeemer, which was for long the best-known German church in the city, followed in 1842.[100] The desire of German-born Catholics for their own churches and priests was a constant theme at least until the time of World War I. Whenever a new settlement of Germans was formed further uptown, a committee of laymen would soon be formed to collect money for the building of a church, and to press the archbishop for the assignment of a German-speaking priest. For instance, in early 1903 a committee claiming to represent 'the German people of the Bronx borough' called on the archbishop to ask for the formation of a new parish, and a month later they were thanking him for the formation of St Anthony of Padua parish, and asking a priest to be assigned speedily, preferably a Father Strack, 'the choice of all': 'as Lent is coming on, they are very anxious to have their own priest. Lenten sermons, and devotions in German, are a source of great spiritual good even for the cold and lukewarm.'[101]

Nonetheless, there clearly were many German Catholics who were not joining German parishes, whether because of a preference for English-language parishes, or because they were joining no church at all. By 1901, when there were about 250,000 Catholics of German stock in the five boroughs, the combined membership of the twenty-five German parishes was 69,300. In Brooklyn, the combined membership of the German parishes was only 18,800.[102]

The signs are that German Catholics were less involved in their church than their Irish coreligionists, but more so than their Protestant compatriots. Because the Irish had a reputation as more generous givers to parish funds, one German parish in the 1860s made deliberate attempts to attract the local Irish through English-language sermons, as they believed that a Germans-only parish would not be financially viable. The result of these endeavours was constant conflict between the two sections of parishioners.[103] The theory that different sections of the Catholic community differed considerably in their willingness or ability to contribute to church funds gains some support from the financial records of five parishes. Comparing receipts from seat money, pew rents and collections in 1901 with the estimated membership, we find that the members of an Italian parish (Our Lady of Mount Carmel) gave 78 cents per head during the year; in a German parish (St Joseph's) they gave $2.11; and in three predominantly Irish parishes (Holy Cross, St Paul's and Holy Name) they gave $2.56, $3.23 and $3.68 respectively.[104]

When the Germans got their own priests, relations were not necessarily smooth. Conflicts between the clergy and the various parish organizations are a frequent theme in the records of German parishes. At Most Holy Redeemer, for instance, the clergy seem to have been in constant dispute with the *St.-Liborius-Verein* for young men, and in 1891, after members of the *Verein* had 'acted and spoken most disgracefully' to one of the clergy, the latter announced that this organization was 'no longer considered as a society of the church'.[105] There is less sign than among the Irish of any generalized pride in the clergy. However, the Redemptorists commented on the strength of devotion to Mary and the popularity of Corpus Christi celebrations—'The German people are still heart and soul in this holiday,' they noted in 1885.[106] Parish societies often had a large membership, many of whom would turn out to parade through the streets on special occasions, like the May Day processions in honour of Mary or the parish fair in October. And whenever miracles were expected, there were also likely to be crowds. In summarizing events during 1890 at the Immaculate Conception Church in the Bronx, the Redemptorists referred to 'the niche containing the picture of Our Lady of Perpetual Help. This picture fully deserves the title of miraculous. . . . After every Mass and service numbers flock to the little shrine and God alone knows the spiritual graces meted out at this hallowed spot. Countless novenas are made to Our Lady of Perpetual Help, and various tokens of gratitude are brought to the altar by those who experienced her assistance.'[107]

For the year 1910 information can be obtained about the social composition of three of the major German subcultures in Yorkville: the *New Yorker Staats-Zeitung* published an extensive list of *Vereine*, together with names and addresses of officials, many of whom can be identified in the manuscript schedules of the federal census held in that year; the Socialist Party kept a list of recruits joining in that year, from which I have selected those giving Yorkville addresses; and Zion Lutheran Church kept a list of members who took communion at Easter (see tables 9–10). All three groups consisted very largely of persons who were either born in Germany or had German parents. This applied even to the Socialist Party, which contained a great mix of nationalities, but was in Yorkville two-thirds German. Of 97 recruits to the party whom I was able to identify, 63 were of German stock, and there were also eight German speakers from other countries, such as Austria. My analysis is limited to the 63 who were of German stock. The Socialist recruits and the *Verein* officials had two main points in common: they consisted very largely of immigrant males. Only 9 per cent of the *Verein* officials and 23 per cent of the Socialists were women; 9 per cent of the former and 6 per cent of the latter had been born in the United States. They differed in generation, and to some extent in social class. The officials were mainly middle-aged: 74 per cent were aged forty and over; and they were mainly drawn from the lower middle class or skilled working class, each of which accounted for about a third of the officials. The Socialists attracted some recruits from all age groups and social classes, but their appeal was predominantly to young manual workers. Of these, 59 per cent were aged under forty, and 83 per cent came from a household headed by a manual worker.

The main difference between these two groups and the communicants at Zion was that the latter were predominantly female. Out of 246 communicants whom I have identified, 78 per cent were women. They included a far higher proportion of the American-born (54 per cent), and they were more youthful even than the

TABLE 9

Social Composition of Heads of a Random Sample of Households with Members of German Stock, and of Heads of Households Members of Which Were Associated with Various Local Institutions, Yorkville, 1910

	(Per cent)			
	RANDOM SAMPLE (N = 217)	LUTHERAN CHURCH (N = 180)	SOCIALIST PARTY (N = 63)	*VEREINE* (N = 46)
High white-collar	7.8	6.6	1.6	10.9
Low white-collar	28.1	31.5	14.3	32.6
Skilled manual	28.1	35.9	65.1	32.6
Semi-skilled manual	26.2	20.4	9.5	17.4
Unskilled manual	8.3	3.9	7.9	6.5
No occupation	1.4	1.7	1.6	—

SOURCE: Manuscript schedules of U.S. census, 1910; 'Lutheran' households are those with members who took communion at Easter 1910 at Zion Lutheran Church, as listed in the communicant register at the church; Socialist households are those with members who joined the Socialist Party in 1910, as listed in party records in the Tamiment Collection at New York University Library; *Verein* households are those with members who held office in one of the organizations listed in a supplement to the *New Yorker Staats-Zeitung*, 24 April 1910. Out of 247 households containing communicants at Zion, which were in the Yorkville area, 180 (70.9 per cent) could be identified in the census. (In 47 cases no person of the name given in the communicant register was listed at the address given in the census; in 20 cases, the address given was either omitted by the census, or else I failed to find it.) The classification of occupations is taken from Stephan Thernstrom, *The Other Bostonians* (Cambridge, Mass., 1973).

TABLE 10

Age and Sex Composition and Place of Birth of Members of Yorkville Organizations, 1910

	(Per cent)		
	LUTHERAN COMMUNICANTS (N = 247)	SOCIALIST PARTY MEMBERS (N = 63)	*VEREINE* OFFICIALS (N = 46)
Male	21.9	76.2	91.3
Female	78.1	23.8	8.7
Aged 14–19	36.2	6.3	—
Aged 20–39	29.3	52.4	26.2
Aged 40–59	28.9	33.4	69.0
Aged 60+	5.7	7.9	4.8
Foreign-born	46.3	93.7	91.1
Foreign-born (aged 20+ only)	68.2	98.3	91.1

SOURCE: As in Table 9.

Socialists (70 per cent were aged under forty). But where the younger Socialists were predominantly immigrants, the younger Lutherans were largely the American-born children of German immigrants. In terms of social class, the communicants at Zion were nearer to being a cross-section of the local population than the other two groups: 38 per cent of the heads of households containing communicants were in middle-class jobs, as against 36 per cent in a random sample of households in the area containing members of German stock. As with the *Verein* officials, skilled manual workers and the lower middle class were somewhat over-represented, and semi-skilled and unskilled manual workers somewhat underrepresented. But the discrepancy was not dramatic.

In the immigrant generation, some churches seem to have attracted a cross-section of the local population. The encouraging point from the church's point of view was the relatively high proportion of the young and the American-born among their communicants. In part, this was a matter of life-cycle variations in religious practice. As in London at that time, churchgoing was relatively high among adolescents, and especially female adolescents. It is also possible that higher levels of churchgoing among the American-born may have been an aspect of Americanization. However, it would be premature to reach any firm conclusion on this subject, as the evidence from Immanuel Church, to be discussed in a moment, suggests a more complicated picture, with American-born men being communicants more often than foreign-born men, but the reverse being true for women.

Not all Lutheran churches attracted such a mix of social groups as Zion did. Two other Manhattan churches have retained extensive membership records from this period, and they reflect two further possibilities[108] (see tables 11–12). St Luke's on the Middle West Side was as much a church of immigrants in the later nineteenth century as Zion was, but its membership was biased toward the middle class, and especially toward shopkeepers. In 1880, 95 per cent of the heads of pew-holding families had been born in Germany, and 51 per cent were in middle-class occupations. Grocers and saloon-keepers were by far the most numerous occupations—no wonder that Lutherans did not see eye to eye with 'American' Protestants on the subject of drink. In 1900, 76 per cent of members were German-born, and 50 per cent were in middle-class occupations. (The middle-class element was probably actually larger, as the church had a rather elderly membership, including 16 per cent who were retired, and for whom no occupation was given.) St Luke's was predominantly a church of immigrant shopkeepers and artisans, which was slow to adapt to the needs of the American-born generation. By contrast, Immanuel on East 88th Street introduced English-language services at an early stage and tried to cater for both young and old. In the early twentieth century it had the largest membership of any Lutheran church in Manhattan, and its communicants included a balanced mix of the German- and American-born, with the latter in a slight majority. Among the American-born, the church was especially attracting those in white-collar occupations, and clearly not all of the older generation were happy with the way things were moving.

In 1911, a former elder and parish collector published an account of his dispute with the pastor. The main precipitant of the conflict had been the funeral of

TABLE 11

Social Composition of Members of St Luke's Lutheran Church, New York, 1880 and 1900

	(Per cent)	
	PEW HOLDERS 1880 (N = 68)	MEMBERS 1900 (N = 50)
High white-collar	10.3	8.0
Low white-collar	41.2	42.0
Skilled manual	33.8	24.0
Semi-skilled manual	5.9	4.0
Unskilled manual	4.4	6.0
No occupation	4.4	16.0

SOURCE: Record books kept at St Luke's Church. In 1880, there were 116 pew-holding households, out of which 13 that were at a distance were excluded. Of the remaining 103, 68 (66.0 per cent) can be identified in the census. In 1900, out of 93 members listed as living in the vicinity of the church, 50 (53.8 per cent) were identified in the census.

TABLE 12

Social Characteristics of Easter Communicants at Immanuel Lutheran Church, East 88th Street, New York, 1898

SOCIAL COMPOSITION OF HEADS OF HOUSEHOLDS CONTAINING COMMUNICANTS (PER CENT: N = 110)	
High white-collar	5.5
Low white-collar	34.5
Skilled manual	25.5
Semi-skilled manual	20.0
Unskilled manual	7.3
No occupation	7.3

COMMUNICANTS COMPARED WITH NON-COMMUNICANTS IN THE SAME HOUSEHOLDS

76.7 per cent of communicants, but only 42.3 per cent of non-communicants were female.

55.9 per cent of those communicants who were employed had white-collar jobs, but only 42.9 per cent of the non-communicants.

Communicants were slightly more youthful: 66.7 per cent, as against 60.4 per cent, were aged 39 or under.

Women communicants were slightly more likely to state an occupation than women non-communicants: 29.2 per cent, as against 19.3 per cent.

Women immigrants were more likely to be communicants than American-born women, whereas for men the pattern was reversed: 46.9 per cent of women communicants were Americanborn, but 67.0 per cent of the non-communicants. 64.7 per cent of male communicants were American-born, but 44.0 per cent of non-communicants.

SOURCE: Communicant register at Immanuel Church; manuscript schedules of 1900 federal census. Out of 612 communicants, a sample of 391 was taken. Of these, 149 communicants (38.1 per cent) were identified in the census.

a church member who had also been a member of a lodge, in spite of the Missouri Synod's ban. The rebel condemned the pastor's tolerant attitude, and wanted all lodge members expelled from the church. But many other areas of difference came up: class—the pastor was said to hobnob with more educated members of the church and to neglect the poor; styles of preaching—sermons were alleged to be excessively long, to include too many long words, and also too many jokes and stories; differences between German and American styles of Protestantism—the pastor was alleged to have got mixed up with things that 'have nothing to do with the church', including politics and support for prohibition, and his style was said to be too moralistic; and the decoration of the church—'of what use to us are beautiful churches with high altars and showy organs?' In conclusion the author stated that the Bible and Luther were good enough for him, and he reinforced his points by frequent quotation from both.[109]

V

I shall conclude this chapter with a briefer discussion of the east European Jews. In 1880 there were only about 5,000 natives of Russia living in Greater New York; by 1900 this had risen to 182,000 and by 1910 to 484,000.[110] The great majority of them were Jews and they formed the core of a huge east European Jewish community, which by 1915 made up approximately a quarter of the city's population and constituted by far the greatest concentration of Jews anywhere on earth.[111] The great majority of them initially settled on the Lower East Side of Manhattan, the centre of the garment industry. In the early twentieth century, the heavily overcrowded 'ghetto' included a number of 'sub-ghettos' of Jews from Hungary, Romania, Galicia, and elsewhere.[112] By 1903 the proportion of the city's Jews living on the Lower East Side had fallen to half. Major new settlements had now been established in the Brownsville section of Brooklyn and in Harlem, and soon many other Jewish neighborhoods developed, notably in Brooklyn and the Bronx.[113] Nor was it only the prosperous 'alrightniks' who were escaping; many working-class Jews joined the exodus, whether to take advantage of new job opportunities in what were then suburbs, or because of the appalling housing shortage downtown.[114]

Brownsville, Harlem and the Lower East Side had their showpiece synagogues, sometimes in converted churches, and sometimes purpose-built. But far more numerous were the *chevrot*—small congregations formed by immigrants from a particular town, who banded together for the combined purposes of worship, socializing, and ensuring that deceased members had a decent burial and their families were looked after. The *chevrot* tended to meet in rented premises, and most were too small to employ their own rabbi. A survey of 1905 estimated that there were 350 congregations on the Lower East Side, of which only 60 had their own premises. Most of the small congregations were strictly Orthodox, and despised the larger synagogues for their compromises.[115] There were also small synagogues started by unemployed rabbis, and there was sharp competition between congregations.[116]

Among New York's many religious communities, the Jews were similar to the Italian Catholics in the fact that their celebrations and observances were highly visible—and audible. At the New Year, crowds of men and women stood on Brooklyn Bridge, or beside the lakes in Central Park, shaking the sins of the old year into the waters. At the Feast of Tabernacles they ate under fir trees, which had been erected in the tenement courtyards. In December the windows of Jewish shops would fill with Hanukkah lamps and candles. As the High Holy Days approached, the streets were full of synagogue members selling tickets for their services, and the walls were plastered with placards advertising the cantors who would be appearing. According to a newspaper article of 1897, a typical handbill read: 'The world-renowned cantor Rabbi Meyer Goldstein of the city of Ponevesh, recently arrived from the Old Country, will conduct the services at the Synagogue of the Men of Ponevesh. He will be assisted by a choir of five excellent men. The best singing in the city at the lowest prices. Make haste to secure a ticket or the seats will be sold.' And throughout the period of the Holy Days the early morning air was thick with the sound of the ram's horn.[117]

Yet in spite of the highly visible presence of religion in the Jewish districts of New York, most observers were agreed that Judaism was in a state of crisis in the years around 1900.[118] There was a vocal minority of militant freethinkers, most of whom were active socialists or anarchists, and some of whom specialized in shock tactics, such as the staging of Yom Kippur balls.[119] But there were also many people who had made no such open break, but had largely given up religious observance. Surveys of various districts of New York by the Protestant journal, *Federation*, in the early twentieth century consistently showed that the proportion of Jewish families claiming affiliation with a synagogue was much lower than the proportion of Catholic or Protestant families claiming to belong to a church. For instance, in the eastern wards of Brooklyn in 1909, 26 per cent of Jewish households claimed an affiliation, as against 72 per cent of Protestant households and 88 per cent of Catholic households; in Harlem in the same year, the figures were 21 per cent, 63 per cent and 89 per cent.[120]

When in 1899 the strike by the Pantsmakers' Union ended with the employers submitting on a Friday morning, it was decided, because of the imminence of the Sabbath, that work would not resume until Monday. A journalist commented that some of the workers were themselves quite willing to work on the Sabbath, but their employers closed on that day, while others 'are kept from violating it by their fathers, wives or mothers-in-law':

A minority declared this morning that they would not start work on Saturday, lest they should forfeit the fruit of their victory. It would not do to celebrate their triumph with sin, they said, and while they expect to desecrate many a Sabbath to come, they have decided to become pious tomorrow. By far the greater part of the union, particularly the younger fellows, have no such scruples to stand between them and their machines. They wear four-in-hand neckties of the latest cut, smoke cigarettes, read newspapers—Yiddish or even yellow English—and generally consider themselves Americans.[121]

Frequently the break with religious tradition was bound up with the conflict of generations. Samuel Chotzinoff, who was brought up on the Lower East Side in the early years of this century, recalls that the plays performed in the Yiddish theatres on Grand Street typically focused on the conflict between 'Jewish Orthodoxy in the person of a pious old grandfather' and 'rebellion and Americanization' as represented by the teenage son and daughter: 'In scene after scene the young people scoffed at religion, at parental and grandparental authority, and at old-fashioned decorum, proclaiming the advantages of nonconformity and insisting on the individual's unobstructed pursuit of happiness as guaranteed by the Declaration of Independence.' The daughter would often wind up her defence with 'This is the *United States of America after all*'—though at the end of the play some sort of reconciliation between new and old was usually achieved. In Chotzinoff's own life there is not much evidence of reconciliation. He rejected the faith of his father, and in spite of a temporary revival of religious interest at the time of his bar mitzvah, he soon realized that his real interest was 'not in ritual, which everlastingly complimented God, but in "goyish" books, music and the expression of life in art'. He also became a socialist, though the impression given is that this was a temporary phase. The book ends with the author full of hope, and starting on his career as a musician.[122]

Though the pious Jews in the years around 1900 were mainly the foreign-born, it by no means followed that all of the foreign-born were pious. Many had already rebelled before emigration, and there were many more who had largely given up the practice of their religion after settling in America. This is, for instance, a common theme in the novels and short stories of Abraham Cahan, the most famous chronicler of the 'ghetto'. The protagonists are frequently men who came to New York as strictly Orthodox Jews, but soon found themselves compromising in all directions, as they pursued the twin goals of economic success and Americanization.[123] There also seem to have been some Jewish immigrants who welcomed the freedom to disregard observances and prohibitions that they had found burdensome in Russia or Poland, but had then seen no way of evading.[124]

It appears then that migration to New York had a more markedly secularizing effect for the east European Jews than for any other major immigrant community. Why was this? The explanation seems to me to lie in a combination of the previous history of the Jews in eastern Europe in the later nineteenth century, with the nature of the encounter between Orthodox Judaism and the New York environment.

The erosion of loyalty to the Jewish faith had already begun in eastern Europe in the period after 1870, partly because of the attraction of the culture of secularized Russian intellectuals, which many educated Jews aspired to share, and partly because of the appeal of socialism, which became a secular faith for many of the Jewish working class. By the time of the 1905 Revolution, Jews were heavily over-represented among those active in the various forms of radical and revolutionary politics in the Russian Empire—and to a very large degree these radical Jews were those who had broken away from the Jewish religion.[125] The political radicalism that was such a prominent feature of New York Jewish life in the period from the 1880s to the First World War was largely an inheritance from eastern

Europe. In New York the Jewish districts were the main bases of Socialist Party support—and in 1914 the Lower East Side elected the Socialist Meyer London to Congress. Such organizations as the Workmen's Circle took on for radical Jews many of the educational, social and insurance functions that synagogues fulfilled for their more religious neighbours.[126] Jewish immigrants certainly did not learn to be socialists in New York, a city dominated by the Democrats where other forms of politics were open to charges of irrelevance. But for a time, New York provided an environment in which ideas originally generated in Russia could grow freely, and in which a whole range of supporting institutions could develop. Trade union struggles also played an important role here. By far the biggest area of employment for the first and second generation of Jewish immigrants was the garment industry, which in the early twentieth century was the scene of several major strikes and which became highly unionized. These unions became major agents of recruitment to the socialist cause.[127]

In the early twentieth century, the Jews were the most radical of America's immigrants, with the possible exception of the Finns,[128] who mainly settled in the Midwest and West, and were not numerous in New York. But life in New York could have a secularizing effect even on Jews who had no interest in politics. Some of the threats posed by New York to Jewish religious life were no different from the threats that any great city might pose to the religious traditions of any immigrant group: for instance, the city offered endless possibilities for entertainment—not least on Friday evenings, when the Jewish theatres did some of their best business—and for crime and vice.[129] Similarly, the problem of the transition from the immigrant to the American-born generation faced Jewish religious institutions in much the same way that it faced, for instance, the German Lutheran church: the *chevra* was dominated by Yiddish speakers, who made a virtue of changing as little as possible in the ways of worship they had brought over from eastern Europe.[130]

However, life in New York posed specific problems for Orthodox Jews that it did not pose for most other immigrant groups. Of these, one of the biggest was the difficulty of observing the Sabbath, which was a requirement for membership of many of the small Orthodox synagogues that dominated the religious landscape of the immigrant districts.[131] While some Jewish-owned firms did stop work on Friday evening and Saturday, there were necessarily many Jews who worked for gentile employers, and there were also many Jewish firms that felt constrained to do business at the same times as their rivals. Surveys of 1912 and 1913 suggested that 75 per cent of Jewish workmen were working on the Sabbath, and that in a strongly Jewish area of the Lower East Side nearly 60 per cent of retailers were open on that day.[132] As one Russian-born Brooklyn factory worker observed, she did not like working on the Sabbath, but she eventually got used to it, because 'If you don't work on Saturday, you can't work on Monday.' However, she continued to carry out Jewish practices in the home, and to ensure that her children received a religious education.[133]

Questions of dress and appearance also posed problems that did not arise for Catholic or Protestant immigrants. Orthodox men wore beards and their wives wore wigs: in American eyes they looked spectacularly outlandish, and one of the first aims of those immigrants who aspired to an accepted place in American society was to look like an American.[134]

Life in New York was profoundly demoralizing for many men who had enjoyed an influence or a degree of respect in eastern Europe, founded on their religious status, which was denied to them in America. Rabbis who had been figures of power and who had made a good living in their *shtetl* found that their efforts to lay down the law in matters such as kosher food were widely ignored in New York, and that they were reduced to an undignified struggle for survival. Men who had studied the Talmud while their wives supported the family found that such a way of life was no longer respected, and was perhaps not even financially viable.[135] The efforts of Christian missionaries caused some anxiety, but were, in fact, among the least of the problems facing Orthodox Judaism—however little they practised their ancestral faith, most Jews retained a deep suspicion of Christians.[136] This meant that the great majority married Jews and lived in a Jewish neighbourhood, so that a strong sense of Jewish identity survived, even where religious practice was very irregular. A foundation thus existed on the basis of which more distinctively American forms of Judaism might be built.[137]

In the years around World War I, Conservative Judaism was emerging as an attractive third way between the extremes of Orthodoxy and Reform. It deviated from Orthodoxy at certain points, such as the mixing of the sexes during services and the greater use of English, but in most respects it adhered to traditional forms of worship.[138] Many of the new synagogues formed in this period followed a well-established Protestant lead by providing a wide range of social and educational facilities—so that cynics referred to the Synagogue Centers of the 1920s as 'a pool with a school and a *shul*'.[139] A typical example was the Temple Petach Tikvah, built in East Flatbush in 1914. Its services were traditional, and 'did not jar the sensitivities of those who were brought up on the traditional services in the Brownsville synagogues.' At the same time, however, it moved away from the heavily adult male character of the *chevra*: at a very early stage, organizations were formed for women and for young people, and a large programme of activities was instituted, ranging from evening classes to dances.[140]

These innovations were only partly successful in giving the Jewish community a generally acceptable focus, for by now Jewish culture was highly fragmented. In the first generation, there were very important divisions between Jews who had come from different parts of eastern Europe, and most synagogues were formed by immigrants from a particular town. The Synagogue Centers, on the other hand, tried to attract Jews from a mixture of national backgrounds.[141] The major divisions were now ideological. The tendency toward cultural fragmentation was accentuated by selective migration. As Jews moved from the Lower East Side, their choice of destination was influenced by their own ideological predilections. While Brownsville attracted working-class Jews of all persuasions, the Bronx became a stronghold of Jewish radicalism—partly because of the huge cooperative housing projects sponsored by such bodies as the Workmen's Circle and the International Ladies Garment Workers' Union, which parallelled the Social Democratic, Communist and Protestant ghettos established by similar means in Berlin. Williamsburg became a stronghold of Orthodoxy, and Borough Park of Zionism. The newly predominant Conservative Judaism was strong in Brooklyn generally, but especially in middle-class districts, such as Flatbush. The end result of the conflicts that had so deeply divided New York Jews in the years around 1900 was a highly pluralistic Jewry, in which a series of discrete Jewish subcultures existed side by side, partly protected by concentration in specific districts of the city.[142]

VI

Patterns of immigrant religiosity were thus very varied. Influences derived from their country of origin, collective experiences in the United States, factors specific to their own religious tradition—all of these played a role. In the first generation, it is difficult to detect any archetypal 'immigrant experience'. The east European Jews certainly provide many striking examples of the potentially secularizing effects of emigration to America. On the other hand, in the case of the Germans, it is the continuities between religious life in the fatherland and in New York that are most evident. The New York Irish were much less divided in matters of religion and politics than their German or east European Jewish neighbours. One reason for this was that the secularist challenges to religious tradition were already a major fact of life in Germany and in many parts of eastern Europe, whereas in most parts of Ireland Catholicism was a unifying force. But it is also important to note that the Irish derived certain advantages from the fact that they were the first of the major immigrant communities in New York. They were able to establish a dominant position within both the Democratic Party and the Catholic Church, and these strongholds were the foundations of Irish power in the city for several generations. The mutually reinforcing loyalties to church and party provided a double focus for New York Irish life. Those Irish New Yorkers who supported other political parties, or who openly rejected the church, were thus outsiders in a sense that had no equivalent in other immigrant groups.

Differences between immigrant groups in their patterns of religious practice persisted over several generations. Returns by priests in the Catholic diocese of Brooklyn in 1943 suggested that attendance at mass in predominantly Irish parishes was still very high, and still much higher than in Italian parishes. In twenty Brooklyn parishes where the pastor had an Irish name, the median attendance level reported was 63 per cent, whereas in fourteen parishes where the pastor had an Italian name the median was 33 per cent. Attendance in parishes where the pastor had a German or Polish name also averaged around 60 per cent (which, in the case of the Germans, probably represented an increase since the days of mass immigration), whereas the figure for Lithuanian parishes was around 20 per cent.[143] These religious differences were one reflection of the central role still played by ethnic divisions and conflicts in New York life.[144]

In part II, I shall be comparing the religious histories of Berlin, London and New York and attempting to explain some of the differences. One question that will frequently occur is why the level of working-class involvement in organized religion was relatively high in New York—and this, of course, relates to the wider question of why levels of religious practice have tended to be higher in the United States than in Europe during this century. It should be clear from what has been said in this chapter that there is no simple answer to that question. Certainly, the common argument that immigrants as such were more likely to be attached to their churches, and that the United States has inherited this predisposition, is clearly erroneous.

PART TWO

THE CITIES COMPARED

CHAPTER 4

Religion in the City

COMPARISON BETWEEN BERLIN, London and New York at the end of the nineteenth and the beginning of the twentieth century shows some striking differences in patterns of religious belief and practice, and in the part played by religious institutions in the life of the city. Thus it will be recalled that adult church attendance in New York's Manhattan borough on a Sunday in 1902 was equal to 37 per cent of the non-Jewish adults living in the borough, and that in the County of London the rate of adult attendance at church or synagogue in 1902–3 was 22 per cent. No such detailed figures are available for Berlin; but a count of attendance at churches of the Evangelical *Landeskirche* on one Sunday in 1913 found that approximately 0.6 per cent of the Protestant population were present at morning service.[1] If that figure is doubled to allow for those attending in the evening;[2] if another 1 per cent is added for those attending free churches;[3] and if we make the (possibly generous) estimate that 30 per cent of Roman Catholics went to church on that day,[4] we arrive at an attendance rate for the whole Christian population of the city of around 6 per cent.[5] A second comparison is of the ratio of ministers of religion to total population in 1910 or 1911. In New York the ratio was 1:1,318; in London 1:1,358; in Berlin 1:5,064.[6]

Clearly, the differences between the three cities were far more complex than can be conveyed through such statistics. Nonetheless, the figures help to bring out the fact that the religious situations in these three giant cities differed in major ways, and that historians' preoccupation with the connection or lack of connection between urbanization and secularization has led them to neglect the huge differences between the religious histories of the various metropolitan centres of Europe and North America.

Rather than looking for a consistent relationship between urban growth and religious growth or decline, we should be looking at the specific context in which urban growth took place and the social forces that urbanization brought to the

83

fore. A first point to note is that there were qualitative differences between rural and urban religious patterns. Second, there is the importance in nineteenth-century cities of religious conflict: rather than being homogeneously secular or generally devout, they tended to be deeply divided. Third, one should note the crucial influence of the bourgeoisie on the religious patterns in nineteenth-century cities.

I

Extremes of both collective religious practice and collective non-practice were a rural phenomenon. The various nineteenth-century religious censuses always showed rural areas both at the top and the bottom, with the cities somewhere in between. The widest differences were found in France, where the proportion of men receiving Easter Communion in the years around 1900 varied from 90 per cent in the arrondissement of Cholet to less than 1 per cent in eight cantons of the Creuse department.[7] In England the ratio of total church attendance (including some people who attended more than one service) to total attendance varied from about 100 per cent in Bedfordshire and Huntingdonshire, the two most churchgoing, and both mainly rural counties, to a minimum of 16 per cent in the very rural Longtown district, next to the Scottish border. In Scotland, where average attendance levels were higher in urban than in rural areas, the minimum ratio of total attendances to population was 14 per cent in the rural areas of Selkirkshire, and the maximum was 132 per cent in the tiny burgh of Dingwall, where there were clearly many people who attended more than one service.[8] Even in Germany, where average levels of Protestant religious practice were considerably higher in the countryside than in the towns, it was still a rural district, the Jeverland in Oldenburg, that appears to hold the record for the lowest communicant rate around the beginning of the twentieth century.[9]

Rural areas, then, were sometimes able to maintain some kind of religious or irreligious consensus; cities were by their nature more pluralistic. This aspect of great city life was noted in 1846 by the radical journalist Friedrich Sass, who declared that in Berlin a complete range of religious possibilities, from Pietism to atheism, was available.[10] In the same year, another journalist, Ernst Dronke, enumerated in more graphic terms some of the contemporary images of the Prussian capital. For Pietists, it was a 'Babel', where all ties were broken, and nothing was sacred—'neither God nor church, nor fatherland, not even the holiest family bonds, not marriage or the sense of duty'. For liberals, on the other hand, it was a citadel of reaction, swarming with police spies and arrogant aristocrats, 'where the government pampers the Pietists and suppresses the free pursuit of knowledge'. Rhinelanders saw it principally as the seat of their unloved rulers, while south Germans dismissed it as 'a city without a heart', archetypally Prussian. Some claimed that an exaggerated religiosity held sway in the city, and that attempts were being made to introduce a Sabbath of 'English severity', while others accused the press of holding believers up to ridicule, and alleged that the drinking places were full of blasphemers singing irreligious songs. Dronke concluded that it was precisely this many-sidedness that was of the essence of the great city: 'It is, it is, it is—yes, it is many things, it is the great city. There everyone can live as he wishes, because everything is to be found there. . . . In the great city no one cares what anyone else is up to.'[11]

The image of Berlin as a city of endless complexity, where any sense of moral community had broken down, was well reflected in a series of fifty volumes, inaugurated in 1905, and entitled *Grossstadt-Dokumente* (metropolitan documents). Though some other cities, notably Vienna, also found a place, most of the volume related to Berlin. The first promised that the series would act as a guide through the 'urban labyrinth'.[12] Crime and prostitution each merited several volumes, and most contributors gave ample space to the sleazier and more sensational aspects of their subject. But they also showed an enthusiastic savouring of the rich variety of urban life, which they found reflected in areas ranging from 'Berlin's Bohemia', and the prevalence of clairvoyants and exorcists in the city, to the many sects which also found a home there.[13] The series might also have investigated the city's large subcultures of conservative Protestants, Roman Catholics, or militant freethinkers—though probably none of these was considered sufficiently exotic to be of interest.

In 1874–5 a famous series written by a London clergyman did try to depict the complete range of forms of public religion and irreligion operating in the capital. The first two volumes concentrated on the various forms of Anglicanism and Nonconformity. But the third went on to look at the many smaller bodies that fell outside the bounds of religious respectability. They included groups of mystical, fundamentalist and rationalist tendencies. The one point they had in common was that each was far enough removed from conventional forms of belief and practice to require city surroundings in order to find toleration and an adequate constituency of potential supporters.[14]

This emphasis on the bewildering variety of religious life in the city could sometimes be extended to suggest that urbanites had a tolerant and relativistic outlook. A guide to Berlin published in 1905 concluded with a section entitled 'Why we love Berlin,' in which the authors commented that 'In this shop full of wonders there is room for everything—except prejudices.'[15] But this was in some ways misleading. There certainly were many small groups which flourished in the city but made relatively little general impact. But there were also major communities of conservative Protestants, liberal Protestants, Roman Catholics, Jews and unbelievers, and relations among these five groups were far from being free of prejudices. Moreover, the conflicts that divided them were intensified by the fact that religious differences were often partly bound up with other differences, such as those of politics or class.

Nineteenth-century cities were nearly always religiously divided. Sometimes, as in most parts of Britain, the crucial dividing lines were those of class. Horace Mann, in his famous commentary on the 1851 religious census, drew a sweeping distinction between, on the one hand, the middle class, with its long-standing traditions of religiosity, and the upper class, where interest in religion had recently revived; and on the other hand, the urban working class, which was largely absent from the churches.[16] Recent research has shown that Mann presented the picture in oversimplified terms and that, in particular, he exaggerated the extent of working-class alienation from the churches.[17] Nonetheless, the census did show quite sharp differences between the levels of churchgoing in the riverside and workshop districts of central London and those in prosperous suburbs. Total attendance as a percentage of population varied between 18 per cent in Shoreditch and 69 per cent in Hampstead. There is also a wealth of other evidence to suggest that, although Mann overstated his case, he was right to emphasize the fundamental importance of class differences in nineteenth-century British religion.[18]

In Berlin the most important dividing line was political: the Protestant church was relatively strong in those social groups, such as the aristocracy, army, state employees and the self-employed, where conservatism was relatively strong; it was much weaker in the business and professional classes, which were predominantly liberal; and weaker still in the industrial working class, which was strongly Social Democratic. In spite of Berlin's reputation for irreligion, there were thus important sections of the population that provided an exception to the rule. The lower middle class of master artisans and shopkeepers had included the most fervent champions of Lutheran orthodoxy in the later eighteenth and early nineteenth centuries, and this had led to conflict with the rationalist preachers who occupied the city's most prestigious pulpits.[19] In the later nineteenth century, this group provided much of the lay leadership of Protestant parishes in poor areas of the city, and Adolf Stoecker drew much of his support from them.[20]

Since the 1820s and 1830s there had also been a lively religious tradition in aristocratic, military and official circles in the city. For much of the century the main focus of elite religiosity was St Matthew's in the Tiergarten, erected in 1846, though in the 1890s, the relatively modest St Matthew's was partly superseded by the Kaiser Wilhelm Memorial Church, built on a scale and with a decorative extravagance that better reflected the mood of the times. In the early twentieth century, the area between the Potsdamer Platz and the Zoo was still identified as the only part of the city where the churches were full: 'Only in the New West, where officers and bureaucrats and their families lead their lives in quiet streets, untouched by great-city strollers, does the parish crowd in to hear the word of the Bible.'[21] Nor was this religiosity entirely a matter of Sunday display. It also found expression in small circles meeting for prayer and Bible reading and in the traditions of charity that were especially strong among aristocratic women in Berlin.[22]

Sometimes, as in Belfast or Liverpool, or in some of the towns on the Ruhr, the deepest division was that between Protestants and Catholics.[23] Sometimes, as in most American cities, the major divisions were ethnic. As we have seen in the case of New York, Irish, German and east European Jewish immigrants differed widely, not only in the religious denominations to which they belonged, but also in the role and importance of organized religion in their collective lives; all differed considerably from the native-born Protestant population; and there were also sharp religious conflicts between ethnic groups that, superficially, seemed to have more in common—for instance, Irish and Italian Catholics.[24]

By the later nineteenth century there were few European or American cities that could be described as religiously homogeneous. In most cities the religious practices of the various sections of the population were strongly differentiated, and in many cases there was a significant degree of antagonism between organized blocs of Christians and secularists, Christians and Jews, or rival branches of Christianity. In a number of cities this antagonism took violent forms. The most notorious examples were such cities as Nîmes, Belfast and Liverpool, with their recurrent warfare between Protestant and Catholic. But antagonisms between Catholics and secularists could sometimes take equally bloody forms. In Paris in 1871 the Communards seized priests as hostages, and shot twenty-four of them for the sole crime of being priests and accessible when most of the ruling class had fled. In Barcelona's 'Tragic Week' in 1909, anticlerical mobs toured the city setting fire to religious buildings, the favourite targets being monasteries and convents.[25]

This high level of antagonism between rival sects and between believers and unbelievers was perhaps the most distinctive feature of nineteenth-century urban religion. By comparison with the eighteenth century, nineteenth-century cities were much more religiously heterogeneous: rather than bringing the urban community together, religion had become a major source of internal division. By comparison with the twentieth century, religion or irreligion was far more closely bound up with the identity of social classes or ethnic groups—religious convictions were far more of a collective phenomenon, and less a matter of individual choice.[26]

II

The earlier stages of rapid urban growth in the nineteenth century were generally associated with the growing influence of the commercial, industrial and professional middle class. Newly rich factory owners, merchants and so on, together with members of the more prestigious professions such as law, medicine or (in Germany) university professors, frequently exercised a wide-ranging influence over the culture and politics of nineteenth-century cities, and this could have important consequences for religion, as for much else. Patterns of bourgeois religiosity varied considerably from country to country in nineteenth-century Europe and America, so that the ways in which this influence was exercised varied considerably.

Clearly, in every city the bourgeoisie was to some degree religiously divided. In the nineteenth century the unanimity that still existed in some country areas was no longer possible in the city. Nonetheless, the weight of bourgeois opinion and practice generally fell in a particular direction. I am going to suggest five kinds of religious situation that were characteristic of nineteenth-century cities, and I shall argue that the preponderant religious stance of the bourgeoisie varied accordingly.

1. Cities with a dominant church, closely linked with traditional elites and conservative political parties

2. Cities with a pluralistic religious structure but where ethnicity was relatively unimportant

3. Those with a pluralistic structure, where ethnicity was the main determinant of religious affiliation

4. Those where the population was polarized between two antagonistic religious communities

5. Cities where the dominant church had become the major symbol of national identity in the face of alien rule

In practice, the situation in many cities was more complicated than this typology might suggest. Take, for instance, Liverpool: it had elements of type 1, as it had an established church, linked with traditional elites and with the Conservative Party; it had elements of 2 and 3, since it also contained several other major religious groups, and affiliation was partly, though not wholly, determined by ethnicity; and it had elements of 4, since there was a considerable degree of polarization between Protestant and Catholic. It is apparent, therefore, that many cities do not fit clearly into a single category. Nonetheless, it would not be oversimplifying too drastically to say that Berlin comes closest to type 1, London to type 2 and New York to type 3.

It was in the cities that conformed most closely to the first type that the secularizing role of the bourgeoisie was most important. Cities with a dominant church, closely linked with traditional elites and conservative political parties, were typical both of Protestant north Germany and of many parts of Catholic southern Europe. In such situations there was a growing tension between clergy and bourgeoisie in the first half of the nineteenth century.[27] The main reasons for this were political. In the eyes of the official clergy of most European countries, the French Revolution, with its Reign of Terror and its religious persecutions, had discredited all experiments in liberty, equality and fraternity. In the years after 1815, the majority of the clergy saw the best hope for the future in the alliance of throne and altar, and they had little sympathy for the liberal agenda of representative institutions, restrictions on the power of monarchs and free trade in goods and ideas. They often disliked what they saw of early factory industry, a major bone of contention being the prevalence of Sunday labour.

Theological changes exacerbated the tensions. In Prussian Protestantism, eighteenth-century rationalism was giving way to Pietism. The new theological trends may have increased the church's appeal to many peasants and artisans, but they tended to repel the educated middle class.[28] In Berlin, the preaching of Schleiermacher exercised an enormous influence on the latter section of the population. After his death in 1834, as the Berlin religious scene came increasingly to be dominated by theological conservatives, the educated middle class became increasingly receptive to deism and atheism and to completely privatized forms of religion. In the 1830s and 1840s, Ludwig Feuerbach, with his materialism, and D. F. Strauss, with his re-interpretation of the New Testament as myth, were winning numerous disciples. In the 1850s, Ludwig Büchner's scientific critique of religion, *Force and Matter*, was equally popular. By the 1870s, the vogue was for Darwin, who achieved a far bigger following among middle-class Germans than he did among his fellow-countrymen.[29]

An alternative path of religious revolt, which was particularly attractive to many middle-class women, was through the arts, and especially music: from the age of Beethoven to the age of Wagner, the religion of music had many devotees.[30] The turning point in Berlin was the 1840s. First, the Friends of Light, a movement of religious and political liberals enjoying considerable support among middle-class Berliners, were forced out of the Protestant church by the church authorities working in conjunction with the state.[31] Then the 1848 revolution, after initially being welcomed by some clergy, ran into widespread opposition from the church. In the reactionary 1850s, church and state worked hand in hand in Prussia as in many other parts of Germany.[32] But with the New Era, the Left Liberals rapidly became the dominant political force in Berlin. Though some leading members of the party were Jewish, most were Protestants. However, their attitude to the church was at best wary, and in some cases openly antagonistic.[33]

This had important consequences for the character of the Berlin press. In the new atmosphere of relative freedom from the 1860s onwards, old newspapers became more adventurous, and many new ones were started. Berlin became famous for the number of its papers and the influence they enjoyed. Gradually a distinct 'Newspaper Quarter' developed in the southern part of Friedrichstadt.[34] The most widely read papers, such as the *Berliner Zeitung*, the *Berliner Morgenpost* and the *Berliner Tageblatt*, were Left Liberal in politics, and while not explicitly anti-religious in the manner of the Social Democratic press, were inclined to treat the Protestant church as a stronghold of reaction and obscurantism, and most overt manifestations of religious zeal as fanaticism and superstition. This applied particularly to their view of Adolf Stoecker and his allies on the church's theologically orthodox and politically conservative wing. Religious liberals received more sympathetic treatment—though in a spirit of tolerance more than of positive encouragement.

Comments by the *Freisinnige Zeitung* on the big programme of Protestant church building in the 1890s, and by the *Berliner Zeitung* on the City Mission, provide a good indication of the characteristic tone of an influential section of the press. In an article of 1896, the former paper commented that the provision of new churches in the city had gone far beyond what was really needed: 'The Berliner is in general thoroughly averse to the external aspects of church life. . . . The effort to increase the number of churches is in Berlin merely something called forth from outside and from above. . . . The Kaiser Wilhelm Memorial church, recently built for four million marks, is a beautiful piece of architecture, but in the place where it now stands, it is a hindrance to traffic.' The article went on to argue that the real need was for more parks, and that any empty space that was used for a church could be better used as a park: 'At all times of the week and of the day, these parks offer the whole population, big and small, poor and rich, the opportunity for refreshment in God's open air and for strengthening and revitalization of heart and spirits.'[35]

This was one side of the journalistic assault on the churches: the voice of robust common sense, mixed with a little bit of idealism, and a few non sequiturs— a favourite method of cutting the church down to size was to suggest that money being spent on churches was thereby being withheld from some self-evidently worthy object, such as better working-class housing. The other side was the name-calling and sneering tone which some papers habitually adopted when dealing with such institutions as the City Mission. Here, for instance, is how the *Berliner Zeitung* commented on the practice whereby the *Kurrende*, a boys' choir run by the City Mission, would sing hymns in tenement courts, and those who appreciated their efforts would throw them coins: 'The "quiet in the land", our sweet religious people, have of late not been quiet, as everyone knows, and they are especially noisy when it comes to complaining about the plague of beggars and vagabonds. But nobody talks about the way in which the pious people train growing youth in begging, and do their best to destroy all self-respect in the hearts of children.'[36]

Among conservative Protestants a fear and resentment of the press developed in the later nineteenth century, reaching its highest point in the Weimar period. Because a number of prominent newspaper proprietors and editors were Jewish it became common to refer to 'the Jewish press' and to imply that journalistic attacks on the church were part of a Jewish plot to discredit Christianity.[37]

Financial support for churches and religious activities ranked as a low priority for wealthy middle-class Berliners. There certainly were some 'Christian employers', of the kind so familiar in London and other British cities, but they were a relative rarity. The best-known examples in the later nineteenth century were probably Louis Schwartzkopff, head of a big Wedding engineering firm and patron of many Protestant churches, and Carl 'Milk' Bolle, the proprietor of a large dairy in Moabit, who provided a works chapel and chaplain, as well as extensive welfare facilities for the use of his employees, and was also a generous supporter of foreign missions. However, Wendland, in his standard history, notes that the liberal bourgeoisie generally avoided 'Christian charitable work that was Conservative-influenced and supported by the Court'. Instead they preferred to direct their charitable energies into the educational field, where they could put into practice their ideas concerning 'the full development of the personality'.[38]

In Berlin, as in other part of Germany and Switzerland, members of the liberal bourgeoisie founded *Arbeiterbildungsvereine* (evening classes for workers) in the 1850s and 1860s. The 'modern knowledge' provided in these classes was dominated by scientific-materialist writers like Büchner and Jakob Moleschott, who were self-consciously continuing the work of the 1848–9 revolutions, and who saw their atheism as undermining the hold of the reactionary forces that had defeated the revolutions. Later, Darwin's ideas would spread in a similar way and would for similar reasons be enthusiastically received. The first great work in popularizing Darwin was undertaken by bourgeois liberals, who were attracted by the anti-Christian implications of Darwin's theory. The most notable example was the Jena zoologist Ernst Haeckel, whose *History of Creation* (1868) was the first German work to present Darwinism as the basis for a whole world-view, based on the supremacy of science, faith in progress and rejection of all existing forms of religion. The future socialist leader August Bebel was converted to atheism as a result of his studies in the *Arbeiterbildungsvereine*, and when he was imprisoned in the 1870s, he spent much of his time reading Darwin, Haeckel and Büchner.[39] Soon Darwinism was being enthusiastically adopted and combined with Marxism by large numbers of German socialists as the basis for a view of life that may not have been orthodoxly Marxist, but certainly put paid to any lingering faith they had in Christianity.[40] Many Social Democrats of this period were also influenced by a characteristically German phenomenon that has no British or U.S. counterpart, namely the tendency for the classics of German literature (particularly Goethe and Schiller) to become the basis for a secular faith, built round such values as freedom, the endless pursuit of knowledge and reverence for nature.[41]

One other point that distinguished the Berlin bourgeoisie from their counterparts in London or New York was that they showed little interest in restricting either work or leisure on Sundays. Sunday was the great day for outings of all kinds. But it was also a day of work for many more besides those in the leisure industries. In 1885, it was estimated that 30 per cent of workers in factories and 42 per cent of those in workshops were working on Sundays.[42] Stores were legally required to close during the hours of Sunday worship, but in practice they frequently put up their shutters while continuing to do business. In the period before Christmas 1878, Berlin went through a controversy rather similar to that which hit England and Wales in 1991: the Berlin police decided to permit all-Sunday opening of stores, which led to some protests from religious groups. One of the leading city papers, the *Berliner Tagesspiegel*, replied with an editorial supporting Sunday opening in the name of 'freedom' and adding: 'Although this explanation does not come directly from Mount Sinai, but from the editorial office of the *Tagesspiegel*, please give it a friendly hearing, dear police, in the interests of many hard-pressed people.'[43]

By the end of the nineteenth century, the development of autonomous working-class institutions was making middle-class religion or irreligion less relevant to the majority of the Berlin population. The period from the dropping of the Anti-Socialist Law in 1890 until Hitler's coming to power in 1933 saw the proliferation of Socialist political organizations, trade unions, cooperatives, libraries, choirs and so on.[44] During this period the urban working class was better insulated from bourgeois influences than at any time before or since. I would argue, however, that the alienation from the church of large sections of the middle class in the middle decades of the nineteenth century prepared the way in important respects for the subsequent, more thoroughgoing, alienation of the working class.

III

The biggest religious difference between Berlin and London was the importance in the latter city of the Protestant free churches. Admittedly, they were weaker in London than in many parts of northern England, but they still made an essential contribution to the middle-class religiosity that was one of the distinctive features of life in the British capital during the nineteenth century. The relatively loose-knit denominational structure of nineteenth-century London provided a context in which it was possible to be religious in many different ways, from Anglican to Quaker, and from Calvinist to Unitarian. (Some denominations, such as the Anglicans, and increasingly, from about the 1860s, the Congregationalists and Baptists too, also allowed for very considerable internal variations.)[45] In the early nineteenth century, middle-class Londoners were under increasing pressure to adopt one of these ways. In an atmosphere where seriousness, hard work and strict moral principles were becoming prerequisites for social acceptability, regular religious practice came to be accepted as the best guarantee of a person's credentials. Throughout the nineteenth century there were middle-class sceptics, some of them quite prominent as writers, scientists or social reformers, but not before the 1880s did they win any substantial middle-class following. Up to that time, secularism was a working-class and lower middle-class phenomenon, regarded by the established middle class as socially disreputable.[46]

This had important implications for the character of British politics. Liberalism, the characteristic ideology of the middle class in nineteenth-century Europe, took a secular form in most continental countries, but in Britain it was strongly coloured by religion, and especially by Nonconformity. And this was true of London too—although the metropolis was far from being one of the strongholds of Dissent. London certainly had its secular radicals, but equally conspicuous, and more electorally significant, were the Nonconformist radicals both clerical and lay.[47] They played a particularly big part in the Progressive Party, which ran the London County Council from 1889 to 1907, providing a mixture of puritanism and municipal socialism that Nonconformists found very attractive.[48]

In Victorian Britain there were often close associations between employers and particular denominations or places of worship. Jobs would be given by preference to people who belonged to the same denomination as the employer or foreman; or those seeking work at a factory might be told that they were expected to attend a particular church or chapel.[49] In London, this seems to have been rare, though it was claimed that one foreman at the docks would only take on church-going Catholics.[50] Some employers offered encouragement to religious activity among their work force. For instance, at Peak and Freen, the big biscuit firm in Bermondsey, employees were given paid leave to attend an Anglican mission in 1875,[51] and in the 1890s the Barclay and Perkins brewery in Southwark paid a city missionary to work among their seven hundred employees.[52] Numerous employers held prominent positions in church, chapel or synagogue,[53] which may have meant that ambitious employees were encouraged to curry favour by attending the same place of worship; but overt pressure to do so seems to have been much less common than in some parts of Wales or northern England.

However, the religiosity of a large section of the middle class meant that a great deal of money was available for religious purposes in London and, indeed, that many employers and professional men devoted much of their own free time to religious work. This had important consequences for the distinctive pattern of religious provision. Jeffrey Cox, in his study of the south London borough of Lambeth, distinguishes what he calls the 'plebeian' from the 'liberal' form of Non-conformity.[54] Chapels of the former kind were small, often lacked a paid minister, tended to be relatively conservative in their theology, and had a membership drawn mainly from the skilled working class. Thus they had a good deal in common with the free churches in Berlin, except for the fact that many of their members were politically active. What was completely lacking in Berlin was an equivalent of 'liberal' Nonconformity. Chapels of this kind had a large and predominantly middle-class membership. Apart from the sine qua non of being a good preacher, their ministers were also expected to be well educated, and well read not only in theology, but also in literature and in contemporary social and political problems. (Clearly there was no rigid distinction between the chapels of the two kinds: if the Railway Mission stood at one end of the spectrum and Brixton Independent Church at the other, there were many points in between.) These large, prosperous and predominantly middle-class chapels were a very important element in the London religious scene. They combined intellectual liveliness and progressive politics in a way that made the kind of anti-religious polemic that was familiar in Berlin harder to sustain in London. (Their Achilles heel was rather different—the puritanism which, by the 1890s, was leading many of the younger generation of Nonconformists to revolt.)[55]

The one point I would add to Cox's valuable analysis is that these chapels often included a significant working-class element. For instance, Christ Church, Westminster Bridge Road, one of the 'liberal' chapels discussed by Cox, was said by the church secretary to be one-third working-class—which was a minority, but in view of the fact that seventeen hundred adults attended services there on census Sunday in 1902, it was still a large group of people.[56] A church of this kind would have less to offer in the way of friendship and mutual support than one of the small 'plebeian' chapels; but it could offer outstanding preaching, at a time when the pulpit was a major source both of new ideas and of entertainment. Thus, as a young man in the first decade of the twentieth century, London's future Labour boss, Herbert Morrison, spent his Sunday mornings at the Marxist-inclined Brixton Forum, and the evening at any church or chapel where there was a famous preacher (F. B. Meyer of Christ Church being among those whom he mentions).[57] Although there are no indications that Morrison had any religious convictions of his own, his experience overlaps in this respect with that of many socialists of his generation for whom active membership in a Nonconformist chapel was the first step toward thinking about the world for themselves.

In late Victorian London, both churches and chapels bristled with educational activities of various kinds, whether sponsored by the clergy and other leaders, or organized on the initiative of the users themselves.[58] There were also many religiously inspired educational initiatives that were independent of any specific congregation. The most powerful influence on adult education in London was liberal Anglican—through the Working Men's College, founded by F. D. Maurice in 1854, the University Extension Movement and such institutions as Toynbee Hall, to the Workers' Educational Association at the beginning of the twentieth century, under the leadership of such Christian Socialists as Albert Mansbridge, William Temple and R. H. Tawney.[59]

Many future leaders of the London labour movement gained an important part of their intellectual training in a church or chapel. Here one can compare August Bebel with Tom Mann or George Lansbury, who belonged to a slightly younger generation than the German Socialist leader, and came to maturity in the later 1870s and early 1880s. The biggest influence on Lansbury's early years was the rector of Whitechapel, the Rev. J. F. Kitto. Tom Mann, who spent his youth in Birmingham before coming to London at twenty-one, claimed to have got most of his education from Anglican and Quaker evening classes.[60]

There were also evening classes provided by Secular Societies, and the more informal educational activities associated with the Radical Clubs. But they seem to have influenced fewer people. Only with the formation of the Central Labour Colleges on the eve of the First World War did Londoners have access to the kind of Marxist education that had been available for many years in Berlin.[61]

The religiosity of middle-class Londoners was certainly double-edged so far as its influence on the working class was concerned. Any example of hypocrisy or injustice by employers or landlords could be blamed on their religion. The south London youth worker Alexander Paterson referred to boys who had 'many a story to illustrate the inconsistency of some notorious "Christian" employer'.[62] Equally, the wider inequalities and injustices of the social system could be seen as illustrating the religious hypocrisy of those in positions of power, most of whom had some kind of connection with the churches. Differences of class constantly bedeviled relations between clergy and their working-class parishioners, and between middle-class and working-class people belonging to the same church or chapel.

In spite of all this, the religiosity of middle-class Londoners also had some favourable effects on the religious attitudes of their working-class fellow citizens—and this contrasted with the overwhelmingly negative effects on working-class religion of the more secular approach adopted by the Berlin bourgeoisie. For one thing, the relatively small, well-staffed Anglican parishes in London, not to mention the existence of numerous other churches, made it possible for the clergy to make contact with a far higher proportion of the population than was the case in Berlin. Furthermore, the employer or manager who combined piety with success in business provided a role model that some working-class people found impressive: it was a matter for constant comment in late Victorian London, by friend and foe alike, that working-class individuals or families with a passion for self-improvement tended to be involved in church or chapel. This was equally true of many working-class idealists, whose concern was with changing society, rather than simply improving their own position: some of the latter became Secularists, but they were equally likely to find the focus for their idealism in some form of Christianity—and here the role of liberal Nonconformity was particularly important, because it made it possible to combine Christianity with progressive politics.

In the late nineteenth and early twentieth centuries this had important implications for the character of Socialism in London, as elsewhere in Britain. Socialism grew out of Liberalism, and if Berlin Social Democracy inherited much of its secularism from Berlin Liberalism, London Labour, like London Liberalism, was more religiously pluralistic. Admittedly, the Nonconformist component that was vitally important in many other parts of Britain was relatively weak in London, and the Secularist component was relatively strong; there was also a significant element of London socialists who belonged to Ethical Societies, or other forms of humanist or 'New Life' movements. But there were also significant Nonconformist, Roman Catholic, Jewish and, indeed, Anglican elements in London Labour; and as the movement grew in the years immediately before and after World War I, this diversity became increasingly apparent. In spite of its sometimes secular image—which in the British context may be partly justified—London Labour was in no way comparable in religious terms to Berlin Social Democracy.

IV

In nineteenth-century New York, which had no monarchy, aristocracy, all-powerful bureaucracy or established church, many of the issues that were of burning concern to European Liberals were of no relevance. On the other hand, the moral crusades mounted by the Protestant churches won the support of many of the city's elite, who saw in evangelical Christianity the foundation for a moral, industrious and socially harmonious community. The period from the 1820s, which saw a very rapid growth in the city's population, also saw a series of religious revivals in the city, the first coming in 1829, and others in the winters of 1834–5 and 1857–8. The revivals were mainly based on Presbyterian and Methodist churches, and merchants and their clerks seem to have been the social group most strongly affected.[63] In the 1890s there was still an important section of the city's business and professional elite that was actively involved in one or other of the Protestant churches, and in associated charitable work. They were often attracted to a style of independent politics that had some spectacular, though short-lived, successes in the city in the years around the turn of the century: it combined crusades against prostitution and alcohol with an interest in municipal ownership and housing reform, a relatively sympathetic attitude toward labour unions, and an insistence on the overriding importance of voting for candidates of proven moral probity.[64]

In the latter part of the nineteenth century the religious situation in the city was rapidly changing because of large-scale immigration, first from Ireland and Germany, and then from Italy, Russia, Scandinavia, and many other countries. These immigrants came to a city that in religious terms had a certain amount in common with nineteenth-century London. It was indeed Brooklyn that prided itself on being 'The City of Churches'. But in spite of Brooklynite aspersions on metropolitan vice and laxity, the sobriquet was equally applicable to New York. The twin cities facing one another across the East River both abounded in large and prosperous Protestant churches, with a mainly middle-class membership, and a massive machinery of charitable and social reforming agencies. As in London, they were less successful in attracting the working class, and missionary efforts were consequently high on the agenda. As in London, the multiplicity of denominations partly served the purpose of meeting the needs of different social constituencies: among the leading Protestant denominations there was a clear status hierarchy, with Presbyterians and Episcopalians at the top, Baptists and Dutch Reformed in the middle, and Methodists at the bottom.[65]

For immigrants, concerned with such questions as how to obtain jobs, secure political representation and retain some form of national identity, ethnic churches were potential allies. There was a psychological dimension to this, defined by the daughter of an Irish-born janitor. 'The immigrants,' she wrote, 'of the years 1914, etc., were insecure, unknowledgeable, frightened, and the only thing that kept them going was their faith, which they passed on to the next generation.'[66] There was a practical dimension, described by the daughter of a Lutheran pastor, who recalls her father's wide-ranging social role in the German immigrant community, helping people to find jobs, advising them on personal problems, lending money from the parish poor fund, and so on.[67] There was a symbolic dimension reflected in the importance attached by each Catholic nationality to having its own church, dedicated to one of its own saints: indeed, among some immigrant nationalities, such as the Italians, among whom regional differences were of major importance, the national parish could become the site for contests between rival groups of immigrants from the same country, each wishing to assert the honour of its own region, town or village.[68]

The tendency for the immigrant church to take on a many-sided role perhaps went furthest among the Poles: many of these points are made—though in less sympathetic terms—by John Bukowczyk in his account of St Stanislaus Kostka Catholic Church, Greenpoint. In the years around the turn of the century, this parish was, according to Bukowczyk, the largest Polish-owned business in the district. The giant church (still a neighbourhood landmark) towered above the streets of working-class housing, proclaiming that the Poles were a force to be reckoned with—and also proclaiming the importance of the pastor, Fr Wysiecki. Bukowczyk portrays Wysiecki as a uniquely powerful figure in the Polish community—not only because of the influence exercised directly through the church, but also because he was president of Greenpoint's Polish bank, and had close links with local Polish businessmen. Since he was apparently in the habit of staying up to 1 a.m. hearing confessions, some of his local influence was hard-earned. He seems to have shown great energy in founding parish organizations, to meet the social as well as the spiritual needs of parishioners. Bukowczyk presents him as a relentless empire-builder, who may have been feared, and even admired, but was unlikely to have been loved. In a community where wages were low, unemployment high, and knowledge of English frequently poor, pastors like Wysiecki occupied a strategic position, with a combination of status, skills and contacts that potentially gave them a commanding influence. This influence was challenged, but only with limited success, by nationalist and socialist organizations.[69]

Some immigrant groups, such as the Germans, often brought anticlerical or irreligious traditions with them. But these were an inheritance from Europe that had much less relevance to the American situation. Admittedly, German anticlerical traditions gained some continuing nourishment from American puritanism: German immigrants were doughty opponents of the so-called 'blue laws', which tried to stop Sunday drinking.[70] Generally speaking, however, these anticlerical traditions were being undermined from two directions. On the one hand, most of the social and political factors that had nourished them were no longer present. On the other hand, America's flourishing churches exercised a positive attraction for those Protestant immigrants who wanted to adapt themselves fully to the American way of life.

This certainly applied to some of the German elite. A biographical guide published in 1913 showed that of those declaring a religious affiliation, 33 per cent were Jewish, 16 per cent Lutheran, and 4 per cent Roman Catholic, but 28 per cent belonged to one of the 'American' Protestant denominations.[71] However, the latter were also active in immigrant districts—where they sometimes attracted newcomers by providing 'Institutional Churches'. A good example would be Holy Trinity Episcopalian Church in Yorkville. In 1909 the parish magazine declared that 'Jesus came to save the whole man—Body, Mind and Soul', and in this spirit, the parish provided a day nursery, a gymnasium, a club, a library, lectures and dances, though it still claimed that 'saving the soul' was its first priority. In 1912 it announced its support for Christian Socialism and in 1915 it reported that one of the clergy was starting a discussion group for the consideration of labour questions. The clergy of the parish were also keen advocates of Prohibition. Considerable numbers of first- and second- generation German immigrants were attracted to the church, and it would appear that most of these were working-class. A list of eighty-four families connected with the church in 1894 shows that about half had German names; among those heads of household who could be identified in the City Directory, just over half were manual workers. Teenagers confirmed in the church frequently came from a Lutheran background—for instance, 23 per cent in 1900, 44 per cent in 1910, and 21 per cent in 1920 had been baptized as Lutherans. The church also attracted smaller numbers of German Catholics, the peak being 9 per cent in 1900.[72]

For Catholic immigrants, the Irish offered a model of Americanized religion that was objectionable to many of the first generation, but had a good deal of influence on their children and grandchildren. Components of the Irish model included regular attendance at mass and confession, support for the parish schools, respect for the clergy, relatively restrained devotional styles, active support for the Democratic Party, and American patriotism. For those groups, such as Germans, Italians and Czechs, where anticlericalism had been quite important in the first generation, one sign of Americanization was its increasing marginality.[73]

There was thus a combination of factors which made for a very different religious situation from that in Berlin. In the first place, many of the things that contributed to the growth of secularism and anticlericalism in Berlin—for instance, the ties between church and state—did not exist in New York. Secondly, the homogeneity of the Berlin working class, in which ethnic and religious differences played a very minor role, contrasted with the very fragmented condition of the working class in New York, where ethnic and religious differences were of fundamental importance: for a brief period in the 1880s, it seemed that workers of different ethnic backgrounds might unite on the ground of class, but this degree of unity was never achieved again. And third, in this situation of ethnic diversity and inter-ethnic competition, churches and religious practices *potentially* took on an important role as symbols of identity, and priests were *potentially* ethnic leaders: this contrasted with the situation in Berlin, where the majority of working-class people did not readily identify themselves with their churches or clergy.

In the last sentence I stress the word 'potentially', as the extent to which this actually happened varied between ethnic groups and religious denominations, and varied over time. Also the role of class conflict in New York must not be underestimated. In spite of the difficulties of working-class action across ethnic lines, there were times when it was achieved—most notably in the 1880s, a time of unprecedented labour militancy, when New York's Central Labor Union succeeded in bringing the city's Irish and German workers together.[74] Bukowczyk notes that the big strikes in Brooklyn's sugar refineries and jute mills in 1907 and 1910 brought Polish immigrants together in common action with immigrants from other countries. This led both to a stronger sense of working-class identity and to a weakening of ties with the church, which was seen by many strikers as being too close to the companies.[75]

It should also be noted that intense class conflict sometimes took place *within* particular ethnic communities. The best-known example would be the garment industry, scene of numerous strikes in the later nineteenth and early twentieth centuries, where east European Jewish socialists initially confronted German Reform Jewish owners, but in the early twentieth century increasingly faced owners drawn from among their own Orthodox Jewish fellow-countrymen.[76]

Before the period of Jewish hegemony, the mainstay of New York socialism was the Germans, who had their strength in industries like brewing and baking, where German unions confronted German employers.[77] The potential religious significance of such conflicts has been highlighted by David Feldman in his study of Jewish immigrants in the East End of London. He shows that the many small synagogues were an important means of bringing workers and small employers together—though to the exclusion both of the richest Jews, who affiliated to more prestigious congregations, and the poorest, who could not afford to belong to any at all. However, when strikes took place this unity was inevitably threatened. And the situation was particularly exploited by some Jewish radicals who used the fact that employers often had prominent positions in synagogues as an argument to persuade working-class Jews to break with their religion.[78] On the other hand, there were also situations where shared religion provided the basis for an eventual solution to the conflict. In the 1912 strike of New York fur workers, when a largely Jewish work force confronted largely Jewish employers, Rabbi Magnes of Emanu-el Reform Temple successfully mediated.[79]

However, the extreme heterogeneity of the New York population often made for complex forms of social conflict, in which loyalties were divided, and the role of particular denominations, let alone of religion in general, was hard to pin down. Even the Roman Catholic Church, in spite of its hierarchical structure and relatively coherent, centrally defined teachings, was deeply divided along the lines of ethnicity, and although on occasions the archbishop tried to impose a common political line on the clergy, he was only partly successful. Episcopalian bishops did not even try. In 1886, when Archbishop Corrigan was trying to steer Catholics away from the United Labor Party, the Episcopalian Bishop Potter tolerated a wide diversity of clerical politics in his diocese, including some active supporters of Henry George.[80] Many Protestant denominations, as well as the various branches of Judaism, were organized on congregational lines, so that any attempt to impose a common line would have been impossible anyway.

The general political and social positions adopted by Protestant ministers in this period, as well as their stance in specific crisis situations, tended therefore to be very varied. A whole series of factors might influence the attitude they took, including their own general understanding of Christianity and the views of their congregation, as well as their assessment of the needs of the neighbourhood within which they worked,[81] and their estimate of how the interests of the church might best be served. The second point was clearly very important, not least because the congregation paid the minister's salary. This point was made very clearly in a *cause célèbre* of 1887, when a Newark Congregationalist, Rev. Hugh Pentecost, was forced to resign: his political radicalism, though acceptable to the majority of his congregation, was opposed by a wealthy minority. In 1916, the future Socialist presidential candidate Norman Thomas was converted to socialism as a result of his encounters with poverty through his work as pastor of East Harlem Presbyterian church, and he consequently got involved in Morris Hillquit's campaign for mayor of New York: he was forced to resign by wealthy patrons of the church.[82] But theological factors could be important too. Conservative evangelicals tended to remain committed to economic individualism and political conservatism, whereas a significant number of more liberal Protestants, together with High Church Episcopalians, argued that the church's mission included the redemption of society, as well as of the individual, and stressed the virtues of cooperation, common ownership and greater social equality.[83] There was also an important current of opinion, according to which the Christian response to situations of conflict should be reconciliation, and the minister's prime duty was to mediate without identifying too closely with one side or the other.

One example will illustrate the variety of Protestant responses in a temporary situation of communal crisis, the Brooklyn trolley strike of 1895. The strike ended in defeat for the workers after a month; during that time up to seventy-five hundred militia had been deployed to protect strikebreakers, and two men had been killed. In Sarah Henry's account of the strike, four types of ministerial response can be identified. In the working-class district of Greenpoint, where support for the strike was strong, the predominant response seems to have been one of solidarity with the local people. Both a Baptist minister and a Roman Catholic priest lent their support to demands that the trolleys be boycotted until the strike had been won. In the central part of Brooklyn, with its large and often wealthy congregations, the predominant note was mediatory, with criticism of the low wages paid by the companies being balanced against criticism of the use of violence by strikers. However, several ministers came down clearly on the side of the strikers, like the Rev. Dr Arthur Goodenough of Nostrand Avenue Methodist Episcopal church, who denounced the companies, declaring that 'God's curse will rest on all money made in such a way'. On the other hand, a smaller group joined the Rev. Dr A. J. F. Behrends of Central Congregationalist church in denouncing the strikers.[84]

V

In the introduction, I outlined two models of religious development in the nineteenth-century city, one of which stressed the connection between urbanization and secularization, while the other stressed the religious vitality of nineteenth-century cities. I also briefly referred to a third, more sceptical view, according to which the religious significance of nineteenth-century urbanization has been exaggerated, and the most important religious changes in the modern world happened either earlier or later. There is clearly a good deal of truth in this latter argument. For instance, three of the crucial turning points of modern religious history—the introduction of toleration, the Enlightenment, and the French Revolution of 1789—all happened long before the massive demographic shifts of the nineteenth century. On the other hand, the cities of the nineteenth century provided an environment in which the possibilities inherent in these momentous developments could be realized to a far greater degree than ever before. For instance, it was cities like Berlin, London and New York in the second half of the nineteenth century that saw the birth of the popular press, with a readership running into tens, or even hundreds, of thousands, which for the first time rivalled the pulpit as a disseminator of ideas. In Berlin, though not in London or New York, the press had a very important role in undermining the authority of the pulpit, by presenting in an accessible form alternative ways of looking at the world.

But, as this example indicates, the possibilities inherent in the nineteenth-century city were realized in very different ways in the varied contexts of the metropolitan centres of Europe and North America. For this reason, both of the models mentioned above are too rigid, and take insufficient account of the range of social, political and religious factors influencing the situation in each city. In their more extreme forms both models tend to become excessively abstract, and to lose their grounding in empirical research and the complex realities revealed thereby. For instance, the claim that the strength of organized religion in nineteenth-century American cities arose from the existence of a religious 'free market' in which every 'customer' was able to select the religious 'brand' best suited to his or her taste ignores two important facts: first, in New York, at least, the majority of the population remained loyal to the denomination inherited from their parents; and second, Jews, who could choose between several rival varieties of Judaism, and Protestants, who were faced with a plethora of choices, were less likely to be attached to a place of worship than Roman Catholics, who only had one 'brand' available to them. Equally unconvincing is the claim by proponents of the secularization thesis that industrialization and urbanization brought about a mental revolution, as a result of which mechanistic and rationalistic ways of looking at the world became predominant. Granted that some movement in that direction took place, recent research[85] (and, indeed, observation of present-day New York or London) suggests that the extent of this mental revolution has been greatly exaggerated.

In fact both models point to important possibilities which were realized in varying degrees in different nineteenth-century cities. So far as the first model is concerned, it is certainly true that the very rapid growth of cities in the nineteenth century presented established churches with enormous logistical problems that were seldom adequately solved; it is equally true that the giant cities of the nineteenth century, with their numerous discrete sub-cultures, were so heterogeneous that it was impossible for established churches to exercise the degree of cultural dominance that they sometimes enjoyed in the countryside. On the other hand, it was equally impossible for secularism to gain the degree of dominance that it enjoyed in some rural areas. Nineteenth-century cities were pluralistic. Proponents of the second model are right in arguing that this pluralism was potentially conducive to the growth and prosperity of organized religion, and that favourable factors included the absence of an established church, the presence of a wide and varied range of denominations, and links between religion and ethnic and/or national identity. Neither model, however, takes sufficient account of the wide variations within the same city in the nature and importance of religious involvement between different ethnic groups and between different social classes.

In the next chapter, I shall look in greater detail at the relationship between religion and the working class, and in the latter part I shall return to considering the particularly complex form that this relationship took in New York.

CHAPTER 5

Religion and the Working Class

THE WORKING-CLASS alienation from the church that was so common in the industrializing nations of Europe and North America in the nineteenth and early twentieth centuries developed in at least three stages.[1] The first was the loosening of ties with the church that was usually associated with rapid urbanization, or with the establishment of mines or factories in areas previously dominated by agriculture or domestic industry. The second stage was the growth of a sense of separate working-class identity and revulsion from the intimate contacts with members of other classes that active church membership might require. The third was an explicit rejection of Christianity, usually following the adoption of some form of socialism.

In the first stage, the loosening of ties with the church tended to be reflected in the fact that working-class attendance at church services and participation in church organizations was lower than for other sections of the population. In the second stage there tended to be a much more marked decline of attendance at regular services, but the great majority of working-class people retained some links with the church, and in particular they observed the Christian rites of passage. In the third stage, a significant section of the working class had broken with the churches entirely, and to some extent secular rites of passage had been devised to replace those of the churches.

There was no inevitable progression from the first stage to the second and the third. The extent of working-class alienation from the church varied greatly from one city or region to another, and within some cities there were major differences among ethnic and religious communities. Of course, within every city there were also significant minorities of working-class people whose religious outlook differed from the prevailing pattern.

Around 1900, Berlin could be said to be at the third stage, in that a significant minority within the working class had come to reject Christianity altogether, and to break all their ties with their churches. London was at the second stage, in that the participation of working-class people in the churches was markedly lower than that of other social classes, and there was a widespread tendency to regard the churches as middle-class institutions, but the number of convinced secularists was small. And the position in New York was one of complete confusion, because of the wide differences among ethnic groups.

I shall begin by looking at Berlin, where working-class alienation from the church had gone furthest, before considering to what extent and for what reasons London and New York were different.

I

In Berlin the first distinctively proletarian suburbs had developed in the 1830s and 1840s. These areas experienced to the full the conditions that led to the loosening of ties with the church in many working-class communities at this time. They were literally on the margins of the city, and for long they remained on the margins in ecclesiastical terms. The best-known of these suburbs was the Voigtland, the area around the Hamburg Gate on the northern edge of the city.[2] Like the rest of north Berlin it was originally in St Sophia parish, the population of which had grown to around sixty thousand by 1835. In that year it was chosen as the site for St Elizabeth, one of the four Schinkel churches. On the south side of the city, the Luisenstadt parish only began to be split up in the 1840s, and on the east St George's remained the only church until the 1850s.[3]

These new churches were not always very successful in attracting the local working-class population. A report of 1837 claimed that at two of the Schinkel churches (Nazareth and St John's) Sunday congregations were often limited to about fifteen people. Congregations at St Elizabeth were larger, but mainly because of the fame of the preacher, the Pietist Otto von Gerlach, who attracted hearers from a distance.[4] From at least the 1860s onwards, numerous observers commented on the sparseness of congregations in poorer areas of the city and the alienation of many working-class people from the church.

I shall quote four examples of such comments, the first two being from outside, and the third and fourth from within the Berlin working class. The first is a report by the deacon of St Elizabeth parish, writing in 1862, on the religious situation in his parish:

> Especially since 1848, church life has been in shocking decline. For eighty years until 1835 this part of the city was without a church; at the moment it contains nearly fifty thousand people, and has a church that will hold two thousand people when overfull, and two to three clergymen! But only on some festivals is the space insufficient: on ordinary Sundays attendance is occasionally good, but mostly only fair. The person who goes to church is ridiculed as 'backward' or 'someone who has been left far behind'. At the start of the main Sunday service, the throng of people returning from the Sunday market chokes all efforts to remind people that it is Sunday. There

are tens of thousands who enter a place of worship only on the occasion of baptisms and weddings. When this happens, some of them would rather wait for the end of the service outside the church door, instead of going in. Sometimes that means standing through storm and rain. Or else people will finally accede to the friendly and pressing request to come in, but will then disturb the worshippers by talking in loud whispers, mocking or laughing—so that things end up even worse than they started. The presence of a clergyman at funerals is only asked for in very exceptional circumstances, although it is offered to the bereaved free of charge. The majority of those inhabitants of the Voigtland who get any intellectual nourishment at all receive it from anti-Christian publications, which mix revolutionary ideas with scandal. . . . These papers will not let any high festival go by without getting on the high horse of 'modern knowledge' in order superciliously to dismiss the things of salvation as ingenious fairy tales, which no rational person any longer believes in.[5]

Thirty years later, in 1891, much the same verdict was rendered in a series of newspaper articles on Berlin published by a Cologne journalist, Otto von Leixner, who was evidently hostile to Social Democracy and sympathetic toward Christianity. Von Leixner described the circumstances in which many a young worker gave up going to church:

In the rest periods at work, or in the pub, or often also at home, he hears only ridicule or the hard word of hatred; he notices perhaps how a non-Social Democratic worker is treated with scorn because it is known that he attends religious meetings or church services, or how people will even make fun of those who attend lectures given by the Free Parishes, although their standpoint is basically atheistic.

Von Leixner felt that religious indifference was more widespread than militant atheism. Nonetheless, books that popularized a materialist and determinist view of the world, and claimed to present the findings of modern science, had a wide readership, especially among the more committed Social Democrats. He noted that many pastors blamed popular irreligion on socialist influence, but in his view the causes lay deeper. The most fundamental cause, he suggested, lay in the effects of *laissez-faire* economics, which he saw as an abdication of responsibility by the state. The result was a decline in working-class living standards, a growing sense of insecurity, and consequently an increasing sense of alienation from the rest of society. Perhaps for this reason, workers who saved money were treated with ridicule—such as a building worker, known as 'Capitalist-Fritze with the big wallet'. The failure of the churches to speak out on behalf of the workers had led to a loss of respect for the clergy. This was exacerbated by 'the unequal treatment of rich and poor in the administration of the sacraments'—mass baptisms and weddings for the poor, and personal service for the rich.[6]

These views from the outside are confirmed by the results of a questionnaire sent to members of the Social Democratic Free Trade Unions between 1907 and 1911 by a sociologist sympathetic to Social Democracy, Adolf Levenstein. Respondents included a considerable number of metal and textile workers from Berlin. When asked if they believed in God, 96 per cent of those answering the question (a considerable number did not answer) replied 'No'. From the few examples given by Levenstein it is difficult to deduce the reasons for this unbelief. But a distinctive feature of the replies was the fact that several mentioned the influence of scientific-materialist writers, such as Arnold Dodel and Ernst Haeckel, or of classic authors such as Goethe and Heine.[7]

Finally, light is thrown on the Berlin working-class attitude to religion by the autobiography of Erich Schmidt, who was born in the Rosenthaler Vorstadt in 1910, and was a leader of the Social Democratic youth movement before going into exile in 1933. Schmidt's father was a glove-maker from Silesia; his mother came from a village on the outskirts of Berlin; both were active in Socialist politics. The notable point here is the degree to which socialism had become a complete way of life for his parents, giving them a sense of purpose and a vision of the future. For such people the way toward the socialist state of the future was not through fighting on the barricades, but by making ever stronger the vast network of institutions through which the Socialists built up the independence of the working class and propagated their own alternative values:

> The way to get there was to strengthen the organizations, trade unions, party, cooperatives; the freethinkers against the reactionary churches, the workers' sports clubs against their bourgeois counterparts, the workers' choirs as part of an autonomous proletarian culture over against bourgeois culture, the party newspaper over against the reactionary and the boulevard papers. . . . [Schmidt's father] was present at countless meetings and talks; he took part in election campaigns and strikes, whether it was a case of improving living conditions or of hitting back at reactionary attacks on the weak republic. And he was on the committee of the local cooperative. Wherever the movement needed him, you could rely on him.

Schmidt went on to note that scholars later accused the Socialists of this period of 'organizational fetishism'. This, however, was a misunderstanding:

> For those who had been robbed of their humanity, who were alienated from the goods which they had created, there was only one way to emancipation: union. In the solidaristic identification of the individual with the whole, they built their powerful organizations and communities which, like great religions, placed people under their spell. They gave them a view of the world, a country and a home. Here people did not only take part in politics: they also sang and drank, celebrated, and made friendships. What was impossible elsewhere was possible here: you could be a human being.

Though the church does not feature much in Schmidt's account, he mentions his parents' approval when he refused an invitation to join the cathedral choir, saying 'I'm not even baptized'. He interpreted his parents' approval as another expression of the need for solidarity in the face of class enemies—'proletarian pride in front of the church door!'[8]

The picture suggested in these documents is of an extensive and deep alienation, not only from the church, but from Christianity in general—at least on the part of working-class males (while the deacon of St Elizabeth did not distinguish between men and women, and Schmidt presented his parents as being of one voice so far as politics and religion were concerned, von Leixner and Levenstein were referring exclusively to men). Apart from very low rates of church attendance—something already apparent from the statistical evidence—these sources suggest that atheism was widespread, that religious believers were frequently ridiculed, that the church and clergy were regarded with considerable hostility, that works of popular science written in refutation of religion had considerable influence, and that Socialism had been adopted by many workers as a new faith. On the other hand, there was little sign of the kind of Christian Socialism derived from the Bible that was popular in some other parts of Europe at this time: Berlin socialism was overwhelmingly secular.[9] As I shall show in Chapter 8, the picture of Berlin as a stronghold of militant irreligion was a considerable oversimplification. However, this picture still had quite a lot of truth in it. For instance, many Berlin Social Democrats were active in the Free Parishes or the Freethinkers' League. Admittedly, some were religiously indifferent and saw attacks on religion or the church as a tactical mistake. But there were others—including such prominent figures as Johann Most in the 1870s and in the early twentieth century Karl Liebknecht and Adolf Hoffmann—who were fervently opposed to the church, or to religion in general, and were willing to give these attacks a high priority. And although the official policy remained that religion was 'a private matter of the individual', and that the party was not therefore to be identified with any specific religious position, there were in fact huge numbers of party members who had adopted Socialism as a *Weltanschauung*, in which Marxism was mixed with Darwinism, atheism and determinism.[10]

II

To what extent do the same observations occur in contemporary accounts of London and New York? Certainly complaints of low working-class church attendance were echoed many times in comments by London churchmen and social commentators. To take one example, Charles Booth's *Life and Labour* is full of comments of this kind, and in this he was echoing the complaints of many of the clergymen he had interviewed.[11] One can find some similar comments in New York too. A number of the pioneering social surveys from the early years of this century made the assumption that organized religion was in general decline in the tenement districts. For instance, T. J. Jones, in a study published in 1904 of a mainly Catholic and Jewish area on Manhattan's Upper East Side, suggested that emigration to America was itself a cause of falling religious involvement:

> A majority of the people are so occupied with efforts to obtain food, clothing and shelter that they have no energy for religious interests. Many of

them, moreover, manifest a desire to shirk social responsibilities to which they have been subject in their native lands. . . . The religious life of the Italian is spasmodic. . . . The Hebrew devotion to his church is intermittent. . . . The American Catholic and the American Protestant are irregular both in their church attendance and in their religious interest.[12]

However, the London and New York sources refer less frequently to ridicule of religion. Certainly there were reports from later nineteenth-century London that men who were known to be actively religious might face mockery from some of their workmates. In workshops, and to a lesser extent in pubs, city missionaries could face a barrage of hostile arguments.[13] On the other hand, there is little evidence of the obsessive and bitter quality that distinguishes much of the criticism of religion by Berliners. The religious attitudes of working-class Londoners seem often to have been more complex and ambivalent.[14] It is a striking feature of oral history interviews with Londoners brought up in the late Victorian and Edwardian periods that there seem to have been very few who were brought up in avowedly Secularist homes: in the few cases where the father was a Secularist, his influence was usually to some extent counterbalanced by that of his wife or of another adult member of the family.[15] It would also appear that those religious people who were known to be sincere and consistent in their beliefs enjoyed considerable respect. Hence, for instance, the popularity of such Christian Socialist politicians as George Lansbury in Bow and Bromley or Dr Salter in Bermondsey.[16]

In New York, references to ridicule of religion cannot be detached from a specific ethnic context. Particularly in the 1880s, when there were still large numbers of recent German immigrants in New York, one finds comments on Little Germany, on the Lower East Side, that might as easily have come out of Berlin or Hamburg. A typical remark was that by the Redemptorist fathers at Most Holy Redeemer parish in 1885: 'The Germans delight in readings that have fallen lower than Lucifer and are not fit fuel for hell; some have little good to shout about 'Pfaffen' [a derogatory word for priests]; in the midst of our own parish live families who despise baptism, Communion, Mass. No wonder that some speak of "Dutch [i.e., German] infidel" and "Irish papist"'.[17]

But as this quotation suggests, piety was as much a part of the Irish immigrant stereotype as irreligion was part of the German stereotype. There were certainly many Irish New Yorkers who were too busy with simple survival to give much thought to the Catholic faith, and there were a few who hated the Catholic Church as a bastion of political reaction.[18] But the one thing Irish New Yorkers did not do was mock the church. Thus, unlike the situation in most other Catholic cultures, there is little tradition either in Ireland or among the Irish in New York of jokes about clerical sex lives.[19] Among the New York Italians, by contrast, priestly unchastity was a popular subject for humour, and this reflected a strong current of male anticlericalism. However, ridicule was directed at the clergy rather than at the Catholic faith as such. In particular, the Virgin Mary was sacrosanct.[20]

Two stories will convey something of the flavour of the differences in attitudes to the clergy among the various sections of the New York Catholic population.[21] Here is the first story, as told by a Mrs O'Callahan:

'The father was just afther going t' give a dyin' woman th' Holy Communion. He was stheppin' down the street when these fellows set in upon him.
"B'ys," he sez, throwin' back his coat and takin' an' showin' thim th' Sacra-
ment which he had in his pocket, "d'ye see what I'm carryin' here? For yer
own good," he sez. An' with that they hit him an' took what money he had—
twenty-six dollars he was carryin', so they say. Oi can't understand why the
fire from above didn't sthrike thim down dead. In Ireland, a priest there
has only t' stamp with his foot and they'd ha' been sthruck down where they
stood. But America is a bad place, it ain't like th' owld counthrey.'

This story was reported by the manager of a girls' club in a poor West Side
district, who described it as 'the most thrilling gossip of the entire year'. Since the
principal figure in the story, Fr Langan, denied that it ever happened, she classi-
fied it as a piece of 'modernized Irish folklore'.

The second story is much briefer and consists of actual events, recorded in
their parish chronicles by the Redemptorist fathers in the German parish of the
Most Holy Redeemer. The Redemptorists were plagued by burglars, and one night
in 1897, a man called Meyer set off the burglar alarm while stealing from the
poor-box. In escaping, he shot a policeman. He was subsequently overpowered by
another officer and taken to the police station, where he said that 'he had not
intended to kill the policeman, that he would rather have shot down three priests'.

The first story reflected a sense that priests had lost some of their authority,
and that there were aspects of New York life that they were powerless to influence—though their image as men of substance was reflected in the quite considerable sum that Fr Langan was thought to be carrying in his pocket. Yet it was the
very rarity of such acts of open defiance that gave the story its piquancy; and it
was because Irish New Yorkers understood the drama and solemnity of the priest
hurrying to the deathbed that the story was both horrifying and exciting. In Mrs
O'Callahan's version of the story, Fr Langan is unmistakably the hero; but one
gets the feeling that Sadie Fleming, who was telling the story to the girls at the
club, had more mixed feelings, in which admiration for the heaven-defying daring
of the 'Gopher' gangsters played a part. Nonetheless it is unlikely that she would
have openly admitted to such ambivalence; and indeed it is hard to imagine that
the Gophers themselves would have echoed Meyer's sentiments. On the German
Lower East Side, by contrast, it would seem that churches and priests had lost a
good deal of their aura. Burglaries at churches were too frequent to cause any
special excitement—though the fact that Meyer showed such interest in killing
priests suggests that the figure of the priest still retained some of its power and
fascination, even if for many people it did so in a purely negative way.

The largest concentration of militant atheists in New York was found among
the east European Jews. Joseph Jablonower, who was born in Austria in 1888 and
came over to the Lower East Side in 1896, described 'the clash between the Orthodox and the "emancipated" Jew':

There was a group of younger Jews known as the Bundists. . . . [They] were

avowed atheists who saw it as their obligation to discredit the orthodox. They
had all kinds of ribald songs about the miracles the rabbis would perform. . . .
They would defy every prohibition that the book contained. . . . The Bundists
on the Day of Atonement, when the Orthodox Jew was fasting . . . would
foregather in front of the synagogue and take out baloney sandwiches—everything that would just make these people outrageously hungry. Sometimes
these behaviors were resented and you had physical combat. It was a time of
great turmoil and conflict, not exclusively intellectual.[22]

However, this deep divide within the Jewish community had little impact on
the Christian majority, who were ignorant of the specific issues, and had only very
limited contacts with the Jewish population.

III

A characteristic feature of the criticism of religion by working-class Berliners was
the claim that it was 'unscientific'. Reports by city missionaries on the objections
they encountered provide many examples: 'I have studied science and can prove
that the world has come into existence without any Creator'. The director of the
Mission, Adolf Stoecker, said that 'The dogma of Berlin unbelief is very instructive. The first chapter could be called "Religion is nonsense". . . . People call the
Bible a book of fairy stories, etc. . . . Who is God? People reply: he is nothing. A
worker said: "I believe everything which is in the introduction to Humboldt's Cosmos."'[23] While these scientific criticisms often consisted simply of a generalized
objection to anything miraculous, supernatural, unprovable or 'mystical' (a favourite
Berlin term of abuse), there was also a widespread interest in works of popular
science written from an anti-religious standpoint. Levenstein's material on the
reading habits of trade unionists is instructive here. A fair number read nothing at
all, or only what Levenstein referred to as 'trash' (*Schundliteratur*). Among those
who read more serious works, four distinct categories were apparent: religious
books; socialism (mainly Bebel, Marx, Engels and Lassalle); German classics (especially Goethe, Schiller and Heine); and scientific or anti-religious writers (including, in order of popularity, Nietzsche, Haeckel, Darwin, Büchner and Dodel).
The interesting point is that while those who read religious books seldom read
anything else, books in other categories were often intermixed, so that reading of
Marx and Bebel often went hand in hand with reading books like Dodel's *Moses
or Darwin?*, which had no overt connection with Socialism but became an integral part of the socialist world-view as it was understood in Germany at that time.[24]

One can certainly find parallels in London. The fusion of Marx and Darwin that
was so typical of the working-class intelligentsia in Germany about 1900 sometimes
took place in Britain too. For instance, Thomas Jackson, a Clerkenwell printer, born
in 1879, who was converted to socialism by reading Robert Blatchford and later
became an ardent disciple of Marx, recalled that he had already had the 'last shreds'
of supernaturalism in him killed by his reading of Darwin, Huxley and Tyndall.

Jackson's reading of Marx completed a process that began with his study of Darwin—the search for a coherent world-view. His reading of the *Communist Manifesto* gave him 'as in a flash of blazing revelation, a completely inter-related Universe, in which mankind and human society and their history were details in an endlessly developing whole'. He went on, however, to complain that 'religionists' were gaining 'an insidious prominence in the socialist and labour movement' in the period immediately before the First World War, and to comment that 'It says much for the astuteness with which the ruling-class manage things in Britain that the great Darwinian battle which had been long-since fought and won for the educated classes, was a thing known only vaguely to the generality of the working class'.[25]

London Secularism was in fact dominated by the tradition of biblical criticism going back to Tom Paine, and scientists were very late recruits to the cause of irreligion.[26] Secularist criticisms of the Bible had quite a widespread impact in later Victorian London, going far beyond the relatively small circles of those belonging to Secular Societies. A characteristic example is this entry in the diary for 1897 of an Islington scripture reader: 'Had conversation with man here who professes not to believe in the Scriptures. Says one part contradicts another but he could not point to me the parts. He declined to continue the conversation, saying that religion was all rubbish.'[27] It may be guessed that the man had read or listened to Secularist criticism of inconsistencies in the Bible, and a few of the other Islington people to whom the scripture reader spoke made similar points. However, most of the religious objections cited were of the instinctive kind that are more likely to have arisen from private reflection than from reading or attending meetings. For instance, two people declared that 'when we die that is the end of us'.[28] But this appeared to be simply something that they felt, rather than something they wished to argue. In fact none of the people quoted in this diary made any reference to scientists or to arguments derived from a knowledge of science.

If the Bible played a bigger part in London Secularism than it did in Berlin, it also played a bigger part in London Socialism. No doubt this role was smaller than in most other parts of Britain;[29] but besides the well-known secular element in the London socialist movement, there were also various forms of Christian Socialists, as well as Ethical Socialists, who rejected both Secularism and orthodox Christianity.[30] Thus if one characteristic route toward active participation in the Social Democratic Federation (SDF) or Independent Labour Party (ILP) was via the Secular Societies or Radical Clubs,[31] another was via bible classes and church discussion groups.[32]

America, too, had its traditions of Christian social radicalism, many of which closely paralleled those found in Britain. For instance, in some parts of the United States many trade union leaders came from a strongly Protestant background, and habitually drew on the Bible in their advocacy of the labour cause.[33] However, as with everything in turn-of-the-century America, distinctive ethnic and regional traditions had a decisive influence on the local development of the working-class movement. Although a significant proportion of Episcopalian, Presbyterian, Methodist, Baptist and Congregationalist clergymen in New York were followers of the Social Gospel, and on various occasions ministers of these denomi-

nations gave support to strikers, their influence on the New York labour movement was limited by the fact that the great majority of working-class New Yorkers
were Catholics, Lutherans or Jews.[34] In religious terms, the two major strains in
the New York labour movement in the late nineteenth and early twentieth centuries were a secularism, prevalent among east European Jewish and German socialists, and an Irish radicalism with roots in Irish nationalism and the Land League,
which tended to be Catholic, but often rather anticlerical.[35] The high point of
Christian radicalism in New York was Henry George's campaign for mayor in
1886, when the Protestant George joined hands with Irish Catholics like Fr Edward McGlynn, and biblical rhetoric resounded through the campaign.

In New York, Socialism was very unevenly distributed among ethnic groups.
Socialism as a *Weltanschauung* was especially characteristic of the east European
Jewish communities, and tended to be associated with the rejection of Orthodoxy,
or even a total rejection of Judaism. Those who came to Socialism from a Catholic
background also tended to reject their ancestral faith, because of the strong and
explicit anti-socialist teaching of their church at that time. On the other hand, the
Protestant churches were more politically pluralistic.[36] The link between Socialism and attacks on Orthodoxy had already been developing among the Jews in
Russia since the 1880s, and many people continued under the shadow of the Statue
of Liberty with ideas and activities that they had begun in the land of the tsars.[37]
One woman who settled in New York in 1912 and found work in a garment factory recalled that she had already been converted to Socialism while at school in
Russia: she came to America to enjoy the political freedom and the educational
opportunities that Russia denied her. The most important thing to do on arrival
was 'to join the Socialist Party'; the other great part of her life was the union.
When the Russian Revolution took place, she felt that it was her dream come
true, and she soon joined the Communist Party. Her father, as a religious man,
thanked God for the fall of the tsar. But while she and her father had some political ideas in common, they continually quarrelled over religion.[38] One immigrant
garment worker, who combined political radicalism with passionate pursuit of
knowledge, recalled that 'everybody I knew was either an anarchist or a socialist':

> It came to me in a flash that this social idealism was the soul that stirred
> within everything that was going on about and within me. I remembered
> that all our meetings and lectures were colored by it. And I understood that
> every intelligent [i.e., *intelligent*—the Russian word for a member of the
> intelligentsia] was an atheist partly because every clodpate was a believer
> and partly because the established creeds were cluttering the road to social
> and political progress. When I asked myself why we studied the abstruse
> principles of physics, the answer was that it helped us to disprove the argu-
> ments of the religious. Our enthusiasm for evolution, I saw, was due to that
> doctrine's implied denial of the biblical story of creation. And if we loved
> the poets, it was because they seemed to us to be pervaded by a lofty dis-
> content with the existing order of things. In short, I perceived that we were
> moved by a very vital religion of our own; although of course we would
> have scorned to call it by that hated name.[39]

IV

How can one explain the differences among the three cities in the forms and extent of working-class alienation from the church? I shall begin by looking at differences between Berlin and London, since the situation in New York is so much complicated by ethnic diversity.

In explaining the greater strength of militant secularism in Berlin, two kinds of factor seem to have been of paramount importance. The primary factor was political. In Germany, the Protestant *Landeskirchen* were emphatically anti-socialist in the period of the Empire, and the few clergymen who declared support for the Social Democrats were disciplined;[40] though some clergy were liberals, the majority were conservatives, and loyalty to king and fatherland were preached as Christian virtues that were above questioning.[41] For working-class Berliners who sympathized with Social Democracy—and in the later nineteenth and early twentieth centuries, that meant the great majority—the churches were seen as a major obstacle to the achievement of their aspirations.[42]

The monolithically anti-socialist character of the *Landeskirchen* in the period before the 1918 revolution arose from the closeness of the tie between church and state. A classic example of this relationship was the joint campaign against Socialism in the 1890s.[43] Following the lapse in 1890 of the anti-socialist law, the *Oberkirchenrat* of the Prussian church issued a decree urging the clergy to fight against Socialism. They were to do this both by direct attacks, and by themselves taking a more active part in the search for solutions to social problems. The Prussian government followed this with a circular to the provincial church authorities asking them to report on the measures being taken in their areas. Most of them had plenty to report, and in Prussian Saxony the Provincial Synod even sent a letter condemning Social Democracy to every Protestant home in the province. At the same time, many of the clergy were taking more literally than the *Oberkirchenrat* might have wished the second part of the decree. In particular, the Evangelical Social Congress, formed in 1890, soon became a major forum for Protestant social reformers. The leaders of the Congress varied widely in ideology, ranging as they did from anti-Semitic conservatives, like Stoecker, to the future Social Democratic deputy Paul Göhre. But both wings soon found themselves in conflict with industrialists and landowners, especially following a report on the land question in 1894. In 1895 the *Oberkirchenrat* decided to turn off the tap that it had so carelessly turned on in 1890. A decree was now issued which told the clergy to keep out of 'social-political agitation'. This was followed by a general clampdown on social radicals within the church: suspect organizations were ordered to be dissolved, or pastors were prohibited from attending their meetings; disciplinary proceedings were instituted against the more outspoken pastors.

The fact that the Prussian church authorities were willing to identify themselves so closely with the interests of the state was due primarily to the direct control over the church exercised by the king as 'supreme bishop'; the fact that they were able to impose this policy so effectively on the clergy was mainly due to the system of church discipline, whereby pastors could be, and quite frequently were, dismissed for political, theological or moral offences.[44] But for this intervention by the church authorities, the radicalization of the clergy would no doubt have continued, and a few would probably have gone so far as to join the Social Democrats. This did in fact happen in the 1920s. But even then, the number was small, and their position was somewhat embattled. For instance, 'red' Dehn felt that his efforts to provide a bridge between the world of the church and the world of the worker in Moabit were almost entirely unsuccessful. The nature of the problem was underlined when he managed to secure the election of a number of Social Democrats to the Church Council: they attended a few meetings, but soon felt so out of place that they dropped out.[45]

This suggests that there were also other factors, besides the external constraints, that were pushing the majority of the Berlin clergy in a conservative direction. One of these factors was the tradition going back to the 1820s, whereby conservative politics went hand in hand with doctrinal orthodoxy, while liberal politics were associated with doctrinal innovation, or at least with a wider toleration within the Prussian church. By the 1830s there was a tendency toward religious polarization in Berlin that continued over several generations. The predominance of theological and political conservatism in the church encouraged the trend toward militant irreligion, and the growing extremism of those at the liberal end of the theological spectrum encouraged many clergymen to argue that the only genuine Christianity was rigidly orthodox.[46] Liberal Protestants were thus fighting a war on two fronts, and by the later nineteenth century they seemed to be losing both battles, as religious sceptics had a predominant influence on the political Left, and political conservatives were on top in the church.

The relationship between religion and politics in London differed from that in Berlin in several ways. The important political role of the free churches in London, right up to the time of World War I, has been mentioned already, and need not be discussed again. By contrast, the last examples of religious sectarianism carrying political significance in Germany were the German Catholic and Friends of Light movements of the 1840s, many of whose members were active in the revolutions of 1848–9.[47] In the late nineteenth century several Protestant sects were active in working-class areas of Berlin, but there is no evidence that they took any part in politics.[48]

Although there were some parallels between the political stance of the Church of the Old Prussian Union and that of the Church of England, there were also important differences. First, the involvement of the Crown in church affairs was much more limited in England than in Prussia. Although Queen Victoria took a keen interest in the appointment of bishops,[49] the principal voice was that of the prime minister. The alternation of Liberal and Conservative governments made it unlikely that the bench of bishops would be politically homogeneous. In any case, by the later nineteenth century the political affiliations of episcopal candidates were far from being the only criterion of their appointment: these affiliations often carried less weight than, for instance, their theological and liturgical sympathies, or their reputation as preachers.[50] Parliamentary interventions in church affairs were infrequent, except for the various (unavailing) efforts to stop the spread of High

Church ritual.[51] Furthermore, the German church authorities had the means of whipping the clergy into line, which the highly decentralized Church of England did not. By the 1890s the Church of England was beginning to take on a chameleon-like quality; in rural and suburban areas it still tended to be strongly Conservative, but in working-class areas the loudest voices among the clergy were beginning to be those arguing for some kind of Christian Socialism. Moreover, the church authorities connived at this trend, believing that the church's ability to survive in working-class areas depended on some degree of adaptation to local opinion.[52]

In time, labour organizations would outgrow the need for clerical support, but for a fledgling trade union or Labour Party, the respectability and skills that clerical supporters brought could be valuable. According to Paul Thompson, areas of London where independent Labour candidates had early successes tended to have a significant element of Labour sympathizers among the local clergy or ministers. He cites the examples of West Ham, which in 1898 elected Britain's first Labour council, with the warden of the Congregationalist Mansfield House Settlement as deputy mayor, and of Poplar and Woolwich, where several clergymen were Labour supporters.[53] During the London gas workers' strike in 1890, the strike headquarters was the workmen's club attached to St Peter's, Vauxhall, where the curate, Rev. W. A. Morris, was a trustee of the union.[54]

The political role of Roman Catholicism also differed between the two cities. In Prussia, the Roman Catholic Church was closely associated with the Centre Party, so that the church was not only opposed to Socialism in principle, but actively supported one of the Social Democratic Party's major rivals. This conflict also extended into the field of trade unionism, where the predominantly Catholic 'Christian' unions confronted the socialist 'Free' unions.[55] In London, by contrast, the Catholic Church had no fixed political loyalties. In local elections there were sometimes Catholic candidates in the later nineteenth and early twentieth centuries,[56] but there was never a national Catholic party. Most laypeople were Liberals before 1914, though there was a growing body of Labour voters.[57] The clergy were completely divided, some voting Conservative, because of Conservative support for church schools, some Liberal because the Liberals offered Home Rule for Ireland, and a few Labour because Labour promised a better deal for the working class, to which most of their congregation belonged. The strong Irish Nationalist sympathies of many clergy prepared the way for the shift to Labour that they often made in the 1920s.[58]

The huge variety of forms of organized religion flourishing in London meant that it was far less easy to reject 'the church' as a reactionary bloc in the way that often happened in Berlin, where Levenstein's enquiry into the religious attitudes of trade unionists produced replies like:

> The church has lost its influence because its servants have abased themselves to become unscrupulous tools of the class state.

> I do not believe in the God of the present state church. I do not know if there is a God.

If there were a God, as we are taught in school and church, his representatives the *Pfaffen* would not survive for one hour.[59]

The relative strength of atheism among Berlin workers also has to be understood in the context of the whole intellectual history of the Prussian capital which was discussed earlier—especially the traditions of rationalism and scepticism among the liberal bourgeoisie, which were an important part of Social Democracy's inheritance from Liberalism.

V
_____

Two major differences between New York and the other cities were the strength of Roman Catholicism and the central role of ethnicity. Both of these facts are relevant to the relatively high level of working-class religious involvement in New York—though they did not contribute quite as directly as is sometimes suggested.

One point that was common to all three cities was the fact that working-class Catholics were more frequent churchgoers than working-class Protestants and were less likely to be secularists. Since Catholics made up over 40 per cent of the population of Greater New York in the early twentieth century but only around 10 per cent in London and Berlin, this clearly provides one explanation for the higher rates of churchgoing in New York. It does not, however, provide the whole explanation, as New York Catholics attended church in greater numbers than those in the other two cities, and New York Protestants were slightly more churchgoing than those in London, and much more so than those in Berlin. In the period around 1900, levels of Catholic practice were generally rather high in countries where Catholics were in a minority and Protestants controlled most positions of power. In countries where Catholics were in a majority, the position was more complex. Where, as in Poland or Ireland, Catholics were subject to foreign rule, the church tended to become the major focus of national identity, and levels of Catholic religious practice were exceptionally high. In other nations, where Catholicism was the majority faith, the population tended to polarize along regional or class lines, with some areas and groups remaining strongly Catholic and others becoming highly anticlerical. The latter situation obtained in such countries as France, Belgium and Spain. Overall, the Catholic Church had more successes than the Protestants in its efforts to retain working-class loyalty in this period, but it also suffered some spectacular failures.[60] These very varied results can be related to the high-risk strategy adopted by the Catholic authorities in the later nineteenth and early twentieth centuries in their approach to the working class. Key elements in this were the attempt to form a Catholic subculture, the promotion of certain forms of popular religion, and the pivotal role of priests and nuns.

In the years following the Vatican Council of 1869–70 the Catholic Church felt itself on the defensive in most parts of Europe and North America.[61] The faith of Catholics was threatened both by the anticlerical or anti-Catholic policies pursued by governments, and by the fact that many Catholics had migrated to find work in cities or industrial districts where most employers were Protestants. The characteristic response by the church to these dangers was the establishment of networks of Catholic organizations. Most important of all was the Catholic school. But this period also saw the formation of numerous Catholic workers' associations, friendly societies, youth clubs, football teams and so on. In some countries, Catholic political parties and trade unions were set up, and Catholic daily papers were published. Germany, with its so-called *Vereinskatholizismus*, provides one of the best examples of this phenomenon. German Social Democrats and, to a lesser extent, German Protestants tried to do the same thing in the years between 1871 and 1933. Socialist and Protestant subcultures also developed during this period in the Netherlands. But by comparison with both Protestants and socialists, Catholic subcultures tended to benefit from greater internal cohesion. The socialists split disastrously into Social Democratic and Communist wings in the 1920s, and Protestants were generally split between liberal and conservative factions, and between those belonging to the state church and those belonging to free churches. The accepted position of leadership enjoyed by the clergy within the Catholic community was an advantage here: Catholic organizations usually had a priest as president, and though clerical authoritarianism could lead to resentment, the dangers of schism were much less than in a Protestant or socialist organization. By comparison with clergy of the Protestant state churches, Catholic clergy also had the advantage of being relatively classless.[62] And the fact that in religiously mixed societies in the nineteenth and early twentieth centuries Protestants tended to be more socially mobile than Catholics meant that Catholic congregations were less likely to be under the control of an elite of successful businessmen.[63] All this did not mean that the attempt to create a Catholic subculture was always successful. But the prospects were much more favourable than they were for Protestants who tried to do the same.

Catholicism also had two unique advantages. One was the success with which the church had inculcated its members with a sense of their separate identity, founded on the claim that the Catholic Church was the only true church. The other was the status enjoyed by the clergy, whose task it was to whip backsliders into line. In London and New York they were assisted in their efforts by the concentration of large numbers of Catholics in particular districts, and by the facts that religious identity was intermeshed with ethnic identity, and the two were mutually reinforcing. Catholic areas of London were famous in the years around 1900 for priests who specialized in marching into pubs in order to break up fights. New York also had its fair share of priests of this type, like Fr Bergen of St Raphael's in Hell's Kitchen, who was said to be equally adept with a horse-whip or with his fists when dealing with delinquent parishioners.[64] Clerical authoritarianism would not work unless there were enough priests and nuns to keep fingers in every pie. But in London and New York recruitment of clergy was high enough to permit well-staffed parishes.

Catholic styles of popular devotion also contributed to the church's ability to retain the loyalty of its working-class members. The biggest difference between

Catholic and Protestant popular religion was the highly personal relationship be-tween Catholics and the saints.[65] Unlike God, the saints could be portrayed in statues or paintings in church or home, or in little pictures that devotees carried around. Unlike Jesus, they represented ideals of humanity that were in principle attainable. Because they were fully human, they appreciated the temptations and difficulties to which ordinary people were subject, and they could identify with their devotees in their time of trouble. Yet, because they were saints, they could intercede effectively with God on behalf of those less holy than themselves. At the same time, an important attraction of the relationship between Catholics and their saints lay in its conditionality—the reverse of the unconditional faith in God taught by orthodox theology. The saints offered help in return for the perfor-mance of tasks that were often onerous, but were nonetheless limited and clearly defined. If the saint failed to keep his or her part of the bargain, the trust would be broken, and the devotee would turn elsewhere. Orsi, in his outstanding history of the cult of Our Lady of Mount Carmel in East Harlem, refers to one of his informants who made great sacrifices in caring for her severely disabled mother: 'Anna bitterly resented St Anthony, however. The saint had been her mother's favorite, her special protector. Anna had prayed to him to heal her mother—but the saint had done nothing. She was surprised at his cruelty and now wanted nothing more to do with him.'[66]

Thus, while many of the clergy presented the saints primarily as exemplars, it was above all as miracle-workers that they were honoured by the people. Catho-lics believed that God intervenes continually in everyday life, to heal the sick, to bring peace to divided families, to change the hearts of drunkards and thieves, to convert heretics and unbelievers. These miracles could ultimately be traced back to the prayers of the faithful, who entreated the saints to intervene with God. The records of New York churches during this period include many examples. For instance, the Redemptorists kept a chronicle of notable events in Most Holy Re-deemer parish. The pages from the 1880s and 1890s are full of accounts of miracles. In October 1893 a Solemn Triduum was held in honour of Blessed Gerard Majella, a giant picture of whom was placed above the High Altar. Small copies were given to everyone going to confession, and the fathers subsequently recorded the favours won through Brother Gerard's intercession. As one example, a woman in the im-mediate neighbourhood of the church was in childbirth, and both she and the child were apparently in great danger. 'By simply applying the picture of Blessed Gerard, and saying a prayer to him with confidence, she was almost instantly out of danger, and had a safe delivery.'[67] Some New York churches won such formi-dable reputations as places of miracles that they attracted the sick from all over the city, or from all parts of the northeastern United States.[68] The search for cures was the most visible aspect of these shrines, for those visiting them were often obviously disabled, and some churches displayed wax arms and legs, given by the grateful recipients of favours, in order to show the parts of their body that had been cured. But a much wider range of problems was also brought to the saints. They were seen as friends with whom problems could be shared.[69]

The saints also had an important presence within the Catholic home. A New York social worker, Elsa Herzfeld, described a 'typical' Irish tenement flat on the West Side of Manhattan, with its family shrine (a brown wooden box with a slanting roof, in which there was an image of the Virgin, over which was hung a rosary). Other decorations included a crucifix, a plaster image of Mary holding the Infant Jesus, pictures of Christ healing the sick and of Saints Benedict and Anthony.[70] In Italian East Harlem, the most cherished images of the saints were those that depicted them in family roles: Mary holding her infant, St Ann as mother of Mary, Saints Cosmos and Damian as brothers who died together.[71] The presence of the saints in the household was particularly important in Italian immigrant families, where ties with the church tended to be fairly loose, and household religion played a big part in the transmission of Catholic tradition.

All this would not have been enough in itself to maintain Catholicism's popular appeal, if it had not been for the fact that most of the factors that led to popular anticlericalism in Europe were missing in New York. Occupational analysis of the active membership of New York parishes shows that churches with a mainly immigrant constituency were sometimes socially well-balanced, and without the marked overrepresentation of particular occupational groups that was common in European churches and in those American churches with a mainly native-born membership. A first example is the strongly Irish Sacred Heart Roman Catholic Church on the West Side of Manhattan (see table 13). A collectors' book is available for the year 1882, listing subscribers to parish funds, and it is possible to identify slightly over half the subscribers through the manuscript schedules from the 1880 census. Eighty-seven per cent of the heads of subscribing households had been born in Ireland, and they made up a remarkably representative cross-section of the local population of Irish stock. Seventy-six per cent of the heads of subscribing households were manual workers, as against 79 per cent of the heads of a random sample of local households with members of Irish stock. Fifteen per cent of the parish sample and 16 per cent of the random sample included members who were illiterate; 9 per cent of the parish sample and 11 per cent of the random sample included members who had suffered unemployment during the previous twelve months. The age distribution was also very similar: 55 per cent of the heads of household in the parish sample, and 56 per cent in the random sample, were aged forty and over. The one significant difference was that 19 per cent of households in the random sample, but only 11 per cent in the parish sample, were headed by a woman. Since most of these women were widows, their below-average level of financial support for the parish may reflect the severe poverty that many of them suffered.

A second example is that of Zion Lutheran Church in Yorkville, which was discussed in chapter 3. Although the proportion of Yorkville Germans attending Lutheran churches was far smaller than the proportion of West Side Irish attending Catholic churches, there too the churchgoers seem, in terms of social class, remarkably representative of the local German population. However, as the example of St Luke's Lutheran Church (also discussed in chapter 3) shows, not all immigrant churches were so evenly balanced (see tables 9, 11).

TABLE 13

Social Composition of Heads of Households Subscribing to Sacred Heart Roman Catholic Parish, New York, 1882, Compared with a Random Sample of Households in the Parish with Members of Irish stock, 1880

(Per cent)		
	SACRED HEART (*N* = 237)	RANDOM SAMPLE (*N* = 161)
High white-collar	3.4	1.3
Low white-collar	16.9	16.3
Skilled manual	20.3	28.8
Semi-skilled manual	21.9	23.1
Unskilled manual	34.2	27.5
No occupation	3.4	3.8
Households with illiterate adult members	14.8	15.6
Households with members who experienced unemployment in past 12 months	8.9	11.3

SOURCE: Collectors book, dated 1882, at Sacred Heart rectory, New York City; manuscript schedules of 1880 U.S. census. Out of approximately 1,400 households listed, a sample of 448 was taken, of which 237 (52.9 per cent) were identified in the census.

VI

I shall conclude this chapter with a discussion of the McGlynn affair, which dominated the history of New York Catholicism in the later 1880s and 1890s, and which provides a dramatic illustration of the complexities of the interrelationship between ethnicity, class, religion and politics in New York.[72]

In 1886 the newly formed United Labor Party nominated Henry George for mayor of New York. With 32 per cent of the vote, he ran a good second to the victorious Democrat, winning support from both the Irish and the Germans, the two main sections of the city's working class, and proving that there was considerable potential for a class-based party.[73] At the time it seemed the start of a new era. But in the hundred years since, no subsequent Labor or Socialist candidate for mayor has polled so well, and class-based parties have always been weakened by an over-narrow ethnic base.[74] Among George's most prominent supporters was Fr Edward McGlynn, pastor of St Stephen's Roman Catholic parish on the Middle East Side. McGlynn was already widely popular because of his speeches in support of the Irish Land League. His outspoken views on a wide range of issues had brought him into conflict with the archdiocesan authorities, with other bishops, with more conservative colleagues in the Archdiocese and with the Vatican authorities.

Michael Corrigan, who became Archbishop of New York in 1885, was leader of the conservative faction in the bitterly divided American hierarchy, and he felt that the archdiocese had suffered from the cautious style of leadership exercised by his predecessor, Cardinal McCloskey, who had avoided any open breach with McGlynn. Corrigan believed that bishops were meant to 'rule' their dioceses. He told McGlynn to keep out of George's campaign, and when McGlynn insisted on delivering a speech which, he said, he had already promised to make, Corrigan seized the opportunity of suspending him. In January 1887, McGlynn was dismissed from his position as pastor of St Stephen's, and when he refused to go to Rome to explain his allegedly erroneous teaching on the land question, he was excommunicated.

From the moment that McGlynn was thrown out of his parish, a large movement in his support developed among New York Catholics, but the fervent advocacy of thousands of lay people apparently achieved nothing. However, McGlynn had more discreet friends in high places who eventually came to his rescue. They did not necessarily think that McGlynn was right, but they thought that Corrigan was wrong and that, in particular, his handling of the dispute threatened to alienate working-class Catholics from the church. Corrigan's critics included the papal secretary of state—the social reformer Cardinal Rampolla—and many members of the American hierarchy, most notably Cardinal Gibbons. In 1892 the balance of power at Rome favoured Rampolla, and McGlynn was restored to the church. However, Corrigan waited two years to give him a new parish, and then he sent him to a small town up the Hudson—where McGlynn at least had congenial neighbours, as the archbishop had for long been using the area as a dumping ground for clerical dissidents.

This was the kind of episode that acted as a catalyst for the estrangement of church and workers in many parts of Europe. But in New York this mass alienation of workers from the church, which was familiar in Europe, never quite happened. Certainly, in the short term, the impact of the 'affair' was enormous. Within St Stephen's parish, McGlynn's dismissal was followed by a widespread revolt that made life impossible for his successor, Mgr Donnelly, who soon left, making way for the more subtle and tactful Fr Charles Colton, one of McGlynn's former assistants. Gradually Colton gained control of the situation within the parish, though at the cost of a fair number of defections. In April 1887, a press report stated that the church was only half full at Sunday services, and that some of those who were there left halfway through.[75] And in 1894, when the church was consecrated following the final clearing of its debts, another press report stated that 'St. Stephen's is a parish of the poor, and the payment of its many debts has been slow since Dr. McGlynn was removed. Its people sympathized with him, and when he was put under the ban, many of his parishioners went with him. Consequently the work of payment was retarded, for even those who remained in the church had full faith in their rector.'[76]

Nor was support for McGlynn limited to his own parishioners. Shortly before his excommunication, an estimated seventy-five thousand people marched through St Stephen's parish in support of the exiled pastor, and one observer claimed that no public demonstration in the city had ever attracted the support of so many women. In April 1887, when McGlynn formed the Anti-Poverty Society and started giving Sunday evening addresses to its supporters, audiences initially averaged between two thousand and three thousand. Though numbers later declined, the

society was a source of continuing anxiety to Archbishop Corrigan, who eventually prohibited Catholics from attending. The archbishop's stringent policy resulted in a number of *causes célèbres*, like that of John Maguire, who was refused
Catholic burial after dying at an Anti-Poverty meeting. The problem of what to do
with Anti-Poverty parishioners continued to plague loyal Corriganite clergy for
years: it would seem that there were quite a few John Maguires around, who
regarded themselves as Catholics, but who were willing to defy their archbishop.[77]

While contemporary accounts frequently identify McGlynn's supporters as
'the poor',[78] patterns of support and opposition seem to have been more complex.
On the one hand, by no means all working-class voters backed the Labor Party: in
particular, many first-generation Irish immigrants voted for the Democrats.[79] And,
on the other hand, McGlynn had the support of considerable numbers of
middle-class Catholics, who sympathized with his plea for a more 'American' church
and his defence of the rights of laypeople and parish priests *vis-à-vis* the hierarchy.[80] So the Catholic community did not simply split on class lines.

There were also certain factors telling against McGlynn, even among those
who had joined him in the George campaign. Of these, the biggest was the sense
of Catholic solidarity, which was embodied above all in loyalty to the pope. Defy-
ing the archbishop was quite acceptable to many Catholics. After all, archbishops
were not infallible, and they clearly differed among themselves on social and political matters. The conservatism of Corrigan could always be contrasted with the
views of more enlightened prelates such as Cardinal Manning of Westminster
and Bishop Nulty of Meath.[81] But when McGlynn refused to accept the summons
to Rome, he broke one of the most powerful of the taboos that surrounded later
nineteenth-century Catholics—that which protected the person of the pope from
any direct criticism. The case was put most tellingly by Patrick Ford, editor of the
influential radical paper *The Irish World*, and one of McGlynn's strongest advocates in the early stages of the 'affair': 'Whilst he confined himself to the discussion of that question [the land] I was with him, but when he went beyond that—
when he began to traduce the church and insult and defy the Pope amid the
applause of scoffing infidels and avowed enemies of the entire Christian system—
then I halted and drew the line.'[82]

With his 'Americanism' and his philo-Protestantism, McGlynn was indeed row-
ing against the tide. For the later nineteenth century was a period when emphasis
in the teaching and practice of the church on the cohesion and separate identity of
Catholics reached unprecedented heights.[83] In the case of the New York Irish, this
sense of Catholic identity was reinforced by the fact that it was intertwined with
their sense of national identity, and both were fortified by a mixture of pride in the
achievements of church and nation, and resentment at discrimination inflicted by
the dominant Anglo-Saxon Protestants. In the later 1870s and 1880s, a period of
increasing working-class organization and severe industrial conflict in which the
Irish played a prominent part, a third form of identity, that of class, was increasingly important for many Irish-American workers.[84] Sometimes, Catholic, Irish and
working-class identities were mutually reinforcing; sometimes there were signs of
tension between them, as for instance, when priests took the side of employers

during strikes, or when Irish workers made common cause with German or American Protestant workers, or when priests opposed the more violent or socially radical manifestations of Irish nationalism.[85] Again, Patrick Ford illustrates some of the tensions. Born in Ireland, he came to Boston as a boy. Among his formative experiences was the struggle to find a job at the time when 'No Irish need apply'. His paper, *The Irish World*, founded in Brooklyn in 1870, initially combined strong support for the national cause in Ireland with the labour and Catholic causes in America. From the late 1870s to 1886, Ford's labour radicalism became more pronounced, and he became much more critical of the clergy, because of their friendship with Tammany Hall and the undue influence of the richer laity within the church. But in 1887, he began to modify his radicalism, while returning to greater emphasis on Catholicism. According to Rodechko, the revival of nativism and its associated Protestant bigotry 'forced Ford once again to recognize and accept the basic identity between the Irish-American community and Catholicism'.[86]

Meanwhile, in the later 1880s, the United Labor Party fell apart, while Tammany Hall revived and entered one of its periods of greatest prosperity.[87] For several decades thereafter the Irish remained safely within the Democratic camp, and the revolt of 1886, when Irish and Germans came together on the common basis of working-class unity, was never repeated. In the years around World War I, the Socialist Party won substantial support in German and especially in Jewish areas of the city, and the Lower East Side even sent a Socialist to Congress; but the Socialists got nowhere in Irish districts.[88] An Irish-dominated Tammany, with plenty of jobs to offer, and led by men with whom the average Irish voter could identify, offered a powerful pole of attraction that no more radical class-based party could effectively rival.[89] Political, religious and national identity were mutually reinforcing, and though the Irish continued to be active in the labour movement, the American Federation of Labor craft unions in which they were prominent tended to be suspicious of radicals and of newer immigrants.[90] Especially in the years immediately before World War I, when the Democrats began to take a greater interest in social reform issues, trade union and Democratic loyalties were able to mesh reasonably well.[91]

Irish-American folklore would hold that many Catholics left the church as a result of the 'affair'. Stephen Bell, in his hagiography of McGlynn, refers to such people without naming names. The Communist leader Elizabeth Gurley Flynn repeated the claim in her memoirs, naming her father, an Irish-born Bronx building worker, as one of those who left. An Irish-American Catholic writing in 1952 stated that there were Protestant families in his home town who had been Catholic until the McGlynn affair.[92] On the other hand, the 20 per cent increase in contributions by New Yorkers to Peter's Pence in 1893, the year after McGlynn's restoration, suggests that there may have been quite a few Catholics who followed McGlynn's own line of action by staying with the church, while giving public expression to their disapproval of its contemporary line of action.[93] The number of outright defections must have been small, in view of the fact, already mentioned, that surveys in the early twentieth century showed that over 90 per cent of household heads of Irish birth declared themselves to be Catholic. Neither, in the long run, was there any mass desertion of the churches.

In any case, the end result of the battle between Corrigan and McGlynn had been a draw: the future shape of the church in New York remained an open question. As McGlynn was eager to point out, his restoration to the church meant that the orthodoxy of his social teachings had been accepted, and the way was open for any priest who wished to follow in his footsteps. Under Cardinal Farley, Corrigan's successor, McGlynn underwent a posthumous rehabilitation.[94]

However, analysis of lists of subscribers to Irish parishes suggests that the Catholic Church was undergoing gradual changes of a kind that made it less likely that future McGlynns would emerge. One change was that middle-class occupations were not only increasing as a proportion of the whole—which was to be expected as the Irish community increased in prosperity—but were beginning to be overrepresented. This change was associated with the rise of the second generation of New York Irish. Whereas in the immigrant generation huge numbers of working-class Irish, including many unskilled labourers, had been active parishioners, in the second generation those who moved into white-collar jobs were more likely to be active parishioners than those who stayed in the working class. The other important development was the increasing prominence of those in public employment. Thus in 1901, when St Stephen's published a list of subscribers to parish funds, 43 per cent of those heads of contributing households who could be identified in the census schedules were in middle-class jobs, and only 22 per cent were in semi-skilled or unskilled manual jobs; in a random sample of households in the parish with members of Irish stock these proportions were reversed—only 25 per cent of heads were in middle class jobs, and 50 per cent were semi-skilled or unskilled manual workers. Thirteen per cent of the heads of contributing households worked in the police, the fire department, the post office, the courts or other city offices, as against 1 per cent in the random sample (see table 14). These were all areas in which Tammany patronage was an important factor in finding jobs. The fact that many Tammany politicians were closely involved with Catholic parishes makes it unsurprising that those working-class and lower middle-class Irish who were most closely involved with the Tammany patronage networks were also likely to be closely identified with their parish. The situation at St Stephen's may well have been exceptional, because of the legacy of internal feuding going back to the McGlynn affair. However, the same tendencies can be seen in less pronounced form at St Paul's on the Middle West Side. A list of contributors from 1904 shows an overrepresentation of the upper middle class and of public employees (especially policemen), and an underrepresentation of unskilled workers (see table 15). There was no mass alienation of poorer Catholics from the church, and there was no rival institution that arose to challenge the place of the church in New York Irish life. But in New York, too, the long-term trend seems to have been toward a predominantly middle-class church.

Another important difference, then, between New York on the one hand, and Berlin and London on the other, would seem to be the relative lack in New York of a hereditary working class. Leinenweber has shown the importance of this fac-

TABLE 14

Social Composition of Heads of Households Subscribing to St Stephen's Roman Catholic Parish, New York, 1901, Compared with a Random Sample of Households in the Parish with Members of Irish Stock, 1900

	(Per cent)	
	ST STEPHEN'S ($N = 118$)	RANDOM SAMPLE ($N = 182$)
High white-collar	12.7	3.8
Low white-collar	30.5	21.4
Skilled manual	22.0	22.5
Semi-skilled manual	22.0	31.7
Unskilled manual	8.5	18.1
No occupation	4.2	2.7

SOURCE: List of contributors in St Stephen's *Church Bulletin* (1901) (available in New York Public Library); manuscript schedules of 1900 U.S. census. Out of 278 subscribing households, there were 12 cases where no address was given, and 25 where the subscriber lived at a distance from the church; out of the remaining 241, 142 (58.9 per cent) were identified in the census.

tor in the decline of New York City socialism: the Socialists attracted the immigrants in considerable numbers, but failed to keep their socially mobile children.[95] The churches, on the other hand, tended to benefit from this situation, because of their appeal to the socially mobile.

VII

In most parts of Europe and North America, at some point in the nineteenth century, the working class came to be seen by the churches as a religious problem area. As has been shown in this chapter and in the earlier chapters on Berlin, London and New York, the actual nature and extent of the 'problem' varied considerably among the three cities, and among different ethnic groups within the same city. This chapter has shown that at least three factors had a major bearing on these variations, namely differences in social structure, in ecclesiastical structure and in the political role of the churches; at least two others were also relevant, namely differences in the distinctive traditions of particular religious denominations, and in the intellectual atmosphere of different cities. For instance, working-class religious involvement tended to be higher where the most important social dividing lines were those of ethnicity than in situations where class was all-important; it tended to be higher where there was a well-developed system of free churches; and in these cities at this time some religious denominations were far more successful than others in mobilizing working-class support—for instance, Roman Catholics were much more successful than Lutherans. On the other hand, the kind of militant secularism that was widespread in Berlin, but less common in the other two cities, depended crucially on political factors, with some admixture

TABLE 15

Social Composition of Heads of Households Subscribing to St Paul's Roman Catholic Parish, New York, 1904, Compared with a Random Sample of Households in the Parish with Members of Irish Stock, 1905

	ST PAUL'S (N = 104)	RANDOM SAMPLE (N = 102)
High white-collar	15.4	2.9
Low white-collar	27.9	36.3
Skilled manual	21.2	22.5
Semi-skilled manual	19.2	16.7
Unskilled manual	11.5	20.6
No occupation	4.8	1.0

SOURCE: List of contributors in St Paul's *Calendar* (1904) (available in Archives of the Paulist Fathers, St Paul's rectory, New York City); manuscript schedules of 1905 New York State census (available at New York County Court House). Out of approximately 500 subscribing households a sample of 180 was taken; 22 that were at a distance from the church were excluded; of the remaining 158, 104 (65.8 per cent) were identified in the census.

of intellectual factors. The most important influence on working-class secularism was the link between the major churches and conservative political parties, and the outspoken opposition of both Protestant and Catholic clergy to the Socialism which was widely popular among working-class Berliners; however, it was also relevant that intellectual criticism of religion was much further developed in Berlin than in the other cities, and provided working-class secularists with a pool of arguments to justify an unbelief that had its genesis mainly in politics.

In chapters 4 and 5, the emphasis has been on the factors affecting the overall religious situation in the three world cities and the contrasting relationship between church and working class. The considerable differences between London, New York and Berlin have been frequently highlighted. In chapters 6–8, the focus will be on the role of religion in the life of the individual, the household and the neighbourhood. Once again, some important differences among the cities will appear. In particular, a small but significant minority of Berliners had adopted a completely secular way of life, whereas that situation was rare in New York, and even rarer in London. On the whole, however, it will be the similarities among the three cities which are most apparent in the remaining chapters.

PART THREE

RELIGION IN EVERYDAY LIFE

CHAPTER 6

Heart of a Heartless World?

IT WAS A SWELTERING night on Manhattan's Lower East Side, and in one Chrystie Street tenement, the young Michael Gold, a child of Romanian Jewish immigrants, was lying in his bed, battling with the bedbugs:

> They crawl slowly and pompously, bloated with blood, and the touch and smell of these parasites wakens every nerve to disgust. . . .
>
> It wasn't a lack of cleanliness in our home. My mother was as clean as any German housewife; she slaved, she worked herself to the bone, keeping us fresh and neat. The bedbugs were a torment to her. She doused the beds with kerosene, changed the sheets, sprayed the mattresses in an endless frantic war with the bedbugs. . . .
>
> I cried softly. My mother woke and lit the gas. She renewed her futile battle with the bedbugs. The kerosene smell choked me. . . .
>
> 'Momma,' I asked, 'why did God make bedbugs?'

Gold gave other examples of what life meant in the slums of New York, which would have been equally true of London or Berlin. For instance, there were the filthy streets, the crumbling buildings, the familiarity of crime and prostitution, and the accidents—his sister was killed in a street accident, and a fall at work crippled his father. Like Gold's mother, many poor people were engaged in a constant struggle to maintain standards of cleanliness and order—to stay 'decent' and 'respectable'—in the face of the dirt and decay, the smells, the noise. And like Gold himself they sometimes asked questions about what it all meant. Gold's pious mother 'laughed at her little boy's quaint question'. For her it was enough to know that 'God made everything in the world'. Her face 'darkened solemnly and mysteriously when she talked about her God'—but she did not attempt to argue about the rights and wrongs of what God had done. Michael, on the other hand, like many Lower East Siders of his generation, rejected God, becoming an active radical, and eventually a Communist. Not that the piety of Gold's mother made her passive—it gave her a strong sense of justice, and of God as the avenger of wrong. And she made effective use of these beliefs in order to intimidate the equally pious landlord during a rent strike.[1]

I

As a result of Charles Booth's researches, we have very detailed knowledge of the map of poverty in late Victorian London, and of its incidence in each occupational group. Booth's research, carried out between 1886 and 1889, showed that 31 per cent of the population of Inner London, and 40 per cent of the working-class population, were living, according to his definition, 'in poverty'. The densest concentration of poor families was in a long narrow band along the south bank of the Thames, stretching six miles from Vauxhall to Greenwich, with the poorest area of all being the northern part of Southwark, where 68 per cent of the population was estimated to be living in poverty. There were also several districts in the East End and in north central London where the poor made up the majority of the population. More intensive local studies, such as that by Maud Pember Reeves in Lambeth, provide many details of the ways in which families living around the poverty line used their resources. Food, rent, heating, cleaning materials and burial insurance were the priority items, and when these were accounted for, very little was left. Most men spent something on beer and tobacco, but they seldom enjoyed any other luxuries, and most women did not even have those.[2]

While no studies of Berlin or New York were carried out on a scale comparable to Booth's work on London, there are plenty of indications that the incidence of poverty was at least as high in those cities. A study of working-class living standards in New York, published in 1909, estimated that $800 a year was the minimum family income required for a 'normal' standard of living; yet the report of the Immigration Commission published two years later found that in the several thousand households surveyed in New York City the average household income was $775 where the household head was foreign-born and $753 where the head was native-born (the probable explanation for this discrepancy being the poverty prevailing in native-born black families).[3] Infant mortality, one of the starkest indicators of poverty, was higher in Berlin than in London, and the differential between richer and poorer districts was greater. Thus in London the average infant mortality rate for the years 1891–1900 was 152 per thousand, with the Strand (248), Stepney (242) and the City (225) being the only three districts where the rate exceeded 200, out of a total of twenty-nine. In Berlin in 1900–2 the worst rate was 329 in inner Luisenstadt; and in thirteen out of eighteen districts the rate exceeded

200.[4] Crowding was another indicator of the level of poverty in Berlin. In ten out of eighteen districts more than 45 per cent of the population lived in one- or two-room apartments, the proportion reaching a maximum of 70 per cent in outer Luisenstadt. The average for the whole of Greater Berlin was 42 per cent. The figure for the County of London in 1901 was 22 per cent.[5]

How did the experience of poverty affect people's religious beliefs and allegiances? And how did their religion affect the ways in which they coped with poverty? The most famous answer probably is that religion was 'The heart of a heartless world, . . . the spirit of spiritless conditions. . . the opium of the people.'[6] But this formulation probably owes most of its fame to the person who said it and the characteristic eloquence with which it was expressed. On the other hand, there were those who claimed that religion was a luxury that the poor could not afford—either in financial terms, or in terms of time and energy.[7] A third view was that of Horace Mann, who in his commentary on the 1851 Religious Census in England and Wales, shared Marx's assumptions as to what religion should have been doing, but reached very different conclusions as to what it actually was doing. He declared that the majority of working-class people were 'unconscious secularists—engrossed by the demands, the trials or the pleasures of the passing hour, and ignorant or careless of the future', and he felt forced to accept the 'melancholy fact' that 'the classes which are most in need of the restraints and consolations of religion are the classes which are most without them'.[8]

Marx's famous aphorism was wrong in several ways. In the first place, there is plenty of evidence from nineteenth-century cities to suggest that the experience of poverty nourished doubt and despair as much as religious faith. Secondly, religious commitment was more often found among those working-class people whose situation was improving than among those who were in the direst poverty. Thirdly, religious belief, rather than inducing passivity, more often provided a stimulus to action.

II

So far as the association between poverty and religious alienation is concerned, a characteristic comment is that published in the journal of the Berlin City Mission in 1880:

> It is a sad experience in Berlin that in times of trouble many people move ever further away from God, instead of letting themselves draw closer to Him. Thus one woman said to a City Missionary: 'Because fate has dealt so hard with me, I am not letting my child be confirmed; I have finished with all those things.' In her home everything was thick with dust and dirt and she said with sharp self-knowledge: 'It looks like that inside me!'[9]

In more active mood, a London working-class autobiographer in 1911 expressed similar feelings of revolt against an unjust world: 'we felt sure that there was a God, but that he was no friend of ours, that it was of no use to depend on Him for anything, and that it behoved us to sharpen our wits and fight the world for what we could get'.[10] And Charles Stelzle, who came from Manhattan's Lower East Side, and had worked as a machinist before becoming a Presbyterian minister, wrote as follows in 1907:

> More dangerous than any opposing religious system is the Church's apparent failure to recognize the influence of the social and political conditions which affect many of those whom we are seeking to win to Christ. These conditions have more to do with their alienation from the Church than is generally supposed. The filthy slum, the dark tenement, the unsanitary factory, the long hours of toil, the lack of a living wage, the backbreaking labor, the inability to pay necessary doctor's bills in times of sickness, the poor and insufficient food, the lack of leisure, the swift approach of old age, the dismal future—these weigh down the hearts and lives of vast multitudes in our cities. Many have almost forgotten how to smile. . . . What meaning have the Fatherhood of God and the Brotherhood of Man? Where is God? they ask; and what cares man? they say.[11]

The relationship between poverty and religious apathy was analysed with particular care by certain observers of working-class life in New York, including both Catholic priests and some more detached commentators. Typical were the comments of the Paulist fathers, who ran parish missions with a special emphasis on temperance, and who reported in their unpublished mission chronicles on the conditions of life and the response to their efforts in the various parishes they visited. At St Veronica's in Greenwich Village, where they conducted a mission in 1894, they admitted that the improvement in the quality of Catholic life that they had hoped for after their last mission had only been partly realized: 'For, given the same conditions, poverty, desultory and irregular work, a superabundance of saloons, and other occasions of sin, it would take a miracle, or the most unremitting manifestations of zeal to work any notable change.' And the response to their mission in their own West Side parish of St Paul's in 1879 inspired an analysis of the connection between poverty and religious apathy. They saw this relationship as having several dimensions: poverty tempted some to seek escape by routes condemned by the church, including crime and prostitution; the enforced idleness caused by unemployment sucked others into the saloon subculture, which in practice acted as one of the church's greatest rivals; the poor found it difficult to achieve the standards of respectability expected of churchgoers; and frequent moves led to a 'lack of attachment to any particular church or priest'. Each of these points gains some corroboration from other sources.[12]

In so far as poverty led to the strengthening of ties between neighbours it could contribute to the base of community feeling on which an institution like the church could build. But poverty kept some families continually on the move, in search of work. Moves of a few blocks or within the same street, whenever a family could not pay the rent, were very common. But frequent moves over longer distances had a disruptive effect on the social life of the poor, who could not afford, and had little energy for, travel. One woman, who had, in her fourteen years of marriage, lived at eleven addresses, including Harlem, the Bronx, New Jersey and a few months in New Hampshire, as well as many parts of the West Side, asked Elsa Herzfeld: 'What's the use of going to church when you don't know the people as comes there' or 'don't know how long you will stay in the neighborhood?'[13]

There are also some indications in Herzfeld's study that some very poor families may have stayed away from church through feeling that they would fail a respectability test. One possible reflection of this was the fact that church membership was lowest in the area closest to the Hudson River, beyond Eleventh Avenue, popularly regarded as the roughest part of the West Side.[14] The explanation Herzfeld gave for this was simply that working-class people preferred a church within easy walking distance, and that few churches were sited in the riverside area. But she also mentioned that 'In several instances the family said, as an excuse for non-church attendance, that their clothes were too shabby, or that they did not have the proper clothes. They prefer to stay at home rather than have their old acquaintances talk about their poverty.' Apart from such feelings of shame, sheer exhaustion left many of the poorest with little surplus energy for anything but the struggle to bring up a family, and the release offered by an occasional drinking spree. 'Nobody cares now if we go or not,' one Irish wife told Herzfeld. Married at seventeen, she had given birth to ten children, six of whom still lived. Her husband, a tramway conductor, spent most of his spare time and some of his working time in the saloon, while she had not been out in years. Frequent moves in connection with her husband's work may have reinforced her isolation.[15]

In such poor and socially isolated families, even the ties of sectarian identity sometimes broke down. The case files of the Charity Organization Society are an interesting indicator here. Their summary sheets stated the religion of the adult members of the family applying for aid. But the society often found it hard to determine what that religion was. Many of the applicants had no settled allegiance, but were willing to make use of whatever benefits a church had to offer. The Roman Catholic Church was particularly vulnerable to the greater resources, and probably less stringent requirements in such matters as church attendance, of Protestant bodies. Mary Sweeney, Irish-born and described in 1889 as a Roman Catholic, sent her son to a Catholic day school 'on account of its convenience', but her children went to a Protestant Sunday school. John Tighe, an Irish-born hod carrier, and his wife, described as Roman Catholics (the wife was in fact given a Catholic burial with High Mass) also sent their children to a Protestant Sunday school. Francis Berry, an Irish-born coachman, converted from Catholicism to Methodism, but seems to have been as poorly regarded by his new church as by the old. Bridget Buckley, the wife of an Irish-born stonemason, had received help from an Episcopal church, although she was a Roman Catholic—'she could not apply to priest for assistance, as she never goes to church'. The German-born Storm family were attached at various points in their travels round New York to Lutheran, Reformed and Roman Catholic parishes.[16]

Interesting evidence concerning the range of religious attitudes in a very poor area of London is provided by the diary of Joseph Oppenheimer, a missionary, who in 1861–2 went from door to door in the St Giles district, preaching Christianity and sometimes assisting people with financial and other problems.[17] The St Giles area contained at that time one of the heaviest concentrations of Irish immigrants in London, many of them living in the direst poverty. A considerable proportion of the native-born population of the area were also living in one-room apartments, and they included several prostitutes. Oppenheimer noted the conversations that he had. He probably did least justice to those Protestants who did not share his own strongly Evangelical standpoint: the nuances of their beliefs tend to get lost in Oppenheimer's account. On the other hand, with those who were unequivocally outside the fold, such as Roman Catholics, Jews and sceptics, he knew where he was, and he was sometimes willing to record their statements in some detail.

Articulate religious scepticism was rather rare; on the other hand, there were several homes where Oppenheimer met violence or abuse, and rather more where the predominant note was one of religious apathy. In about a third of the households where definite information is available, Oppenheimer encountered hostility or indifference to religion in general. There certainly were other places where he encountered opposition, but in those cases it was because the people held to some form of religion different from Oppenheimer's. In slightly under half of the households where there is explicit information about the religious attitudes of the occupants, the people with whom Oppenheimer spoke appear to have been committed to some form of religion or other. Most of these were Catholics, but there were also a few Jews, and a rather larger number of pious Protestants. There remains a smaller group of those the precise nature of whose religious beliefs is less clear, but who did not meet Oppenheimer's stringent requirements. They include a few who argued that God only requires that we live a good life, and who rejected the specifically Evangelical doctrines preached by Oppenheimer. There were also several people who were said by Oppenheimer to be 'indifferent about the one thing needful'. One may surmise that some of these were simply uninterested in religion, whereas others had beliefs of their own that did not tally with Oppenheimer's. But the diary does not provide any definite information.

It is clear that for many people, poverty was certainly an obstacle to religious practice, and sometimes to any kind of religious belief. As Mrs Terry of the back room on the second floor of 28 Dudley Street said, 'poor people can't do what they ought'. The small traders tended to say that they would like to be sabbatarians, but could not afford it. Several prostitutes said that they would prefer to be doing something else, but could not see what alternatives were open. For instance, at 1 Monmouth Court he spoke to two prostitutes, one of whom was in tears: 'I know, sir, I am ruining body and soul, but what shall I do. I have been seduced whilst in service, and by degrees I have become what you see me now. I could not now get any place, my character and all is gone and I must put up with it there is no chance left.' More generally, many of the very poor had no surplus time or energy for anything that did not relate directly to the struggle for survival. For instance, in the back room on the second floor of 17 Dudley Street, Oppenheimer spoke to 'An old woman named Collins. Complained very much of poverty, so much so that I found it extremely difficult to avert the subject from things temporal to things spiritual.'

In some cases the experience of suffering led to feelings of bitterness toward God. Thus, in the front room on the top floor at 19 Dudley Street, Oppenheimer found

> An Irish family extremely poor, no Scriptures, attend occasionally St Patrick's chapel. Their children five in number are not going to school at all, for they are all but naked, two of them were running about the room with nothing about them but rags in the shape of a shirt. 'I wish we were all dead,' said the mother, 'I don't care, we could not be worse off than we are now. I don't believe there is a God at all. If there is, He don't care much for us, I know. Maybe we haven't tried him, but I don't think it would be any use. I wish he would send us a loaf of Bread now.'

These feelings of bitterness could find expression in occasional threats of violence against the missionary or in the abusive language of those like the 'miserable looking old Irishman, in extreme poverty and almost in a state of idiocy' who said '"I don't want no religious talking, don't care a "" [Oppenheimer does not record the expression used] farthing for no religion at all."'

A similar mood of resentful defiance of God and man is also suggested in the comments of the old woman at 1 Monmouth Court, who was one of the more articulate sceptics encountered by Oppenheimer:

> I don't care for nobody and you need not trouble yourself with me. I am old enough to know all about it; it's nothing to nobody else as I have a soul or not; what of that, I am not such a fool that I don't know I will have to die. Of course I must die and so must you. I never bother myself with heaven or hell, my old man when he was alive always said it was all parsons' tricks and no more and I believe so too.

She refused a tract because, she said, she could not read. Perhaps the most eloquent expression of despair was from an Irish woman on the top floor back of 72 Dudley Street: 'I could wish I was dead if it was not for this little Baby and he would be much better off if he was dead too; don't know as I would be better off, but I could not be much worse; well I heard a great deal about heaven and hell, but I am sure I have got my hell here. I need not have another. I am sure if anyone ought to go to heaven I ought.'

Certainly one can find examples of people in the direst poverty, whose religion enabled them to keep going and to accept their sufferings. At 25 Dudley Street, 'poor Mrs Oldham' said: 'Its very hard for me, but God knows best what is for our good. I pray to him & he gives me strength to bear any trial, &c.' And in the top front at 55 Dudley Street, there was an old couple who 'always pray for their daily bread & always get it'. Unfortunately, the more pious households often receive no more than brief notes of approval in the diary, whereas the sceptical are quoted at length, so that the reasons for belief remain more obscure than the reasons for unbelief. But explicit comments on the poverty of the households are more often associated with accounts of religious indifference or hostility than with reports of exemplary devotion.

The association between the experience of poverty and religious alienation was equally marked in Berlin, though here outright scepticism was probably more common and more explicit than in London or New York. In a typical encounter, one of the agents of the City Mission told how he had spoken to a young man suffering from tuberculosis and living in great poverty, who was very bitter against the authorities, ridiculed 'the religious people' ('die Frommen'), and declared that 'if there is a God in heaven, he could not treat him so unjustly'.[18] Indeed Max Weber referred to a survey which found that a sense of the injustice of the world was the most common reason given by working-class people for religious unbelief, and Günther Dehn drew the same conclusion from his study of the religious beliefs of working-class youth in the 1920s.[19] However, it is a frequent theme in the writings of the City Mission that those suffering acute poverty or illness were often immensely grateful for the interest that the city missionaries took in them and the material help they were sometimes able to offer. A long account in the City Mission journal of a conversion achieved by one of the missionaries is worth quoting in some detail, because so many features are characteristic.

He first visited the couple on a bitterly cold day in February 1876. Their conditions were very bad, as the man had long been out of work, but the missionary took to the couple as he was impressed by their cleanliness and 'air of honesty'. The man was reading 'a bad novel' and the missionary told him 'You will get no comfort from that', to which he replied 'I don't want comfort, but distraction'. The missionary suggested he try reading the Bible instead, to which the man replied that he had read it twice, and did not believe in it. However, he invited the missionary to call again, which he did. On a third visit, the missionary told him that he must not trust in his own powers, but in God. The man asked him to prove that there is a God. The missionary replied that the existence of God could not be proved by argument, but that if he were willing to trust in God, he would soon know through experience that God was a living reality. The man asked to borrow some books, and under the influence of these, he began to change his ideas. He also returned to reading the Bible, and eventually he was converted. He came to believe that the missionary had been sent to him by God at a time when he had lost hope and was close to suicide. What apparently had impressed him about the missionary was the fact that he was willing to take him seriously, and that he had returned for a second visit, even though he had got nowhere on the first visit. The story ends happily in a material, as well as a spiritual sense, as the man helped the missionary run a Sunday school, and the missionary found the man a job.[20]

III

Religion did more than help people to accept their suffering: it frequently led into one or more of three ways of ameliorating the situation, which could be mutually exclusive, but were not necessarily so—individual self-help, neighbourly support, and political action.

The association between religion and self-improvement is a very familiar theme in accounts of working-class London during this period. The interviews by Thompson and Vigne with working-class Londoners from churchgoing families usually revealed that their religion was closely bound up with ideas of respectability and pride. Admittedly, some of these families were reasonably well off. But the majority had to struggle. A typical comment was that of a Tottenham cabinet-maker's son, when asked if his family had ever sought help from the Guardians. He replied: 'No, no, no. Lots of people used to. . . starve rather than go to the R.O. [Relieving Officer]. . . They'd sooner go without than go belittle themselves.'[21] Clergymen in poor areas frequently complained that they were continually losing members, as they moved to 'better' neighbourhoods, further out in the suburbs. For instance, in 1897 a Congregational minister in the southern part of Islington, with a congregation he described as 'all working class'—'people earning a weekly wage, but not the irregular labouring people'—noted that in the past eighteen months they had lost fifty members by transfers out, but only gained one by a transfer in: members were moving out to new working-class and lower middle-class suburbs, like Wood Green, and joining chapels there.[22]

Inevitably such restless self-improvers might be suspected of snobbery and standoffishness. The hostile view was given graphic expression in an interview with a man born in 1891 in a very poor part of the East End—Donald Street, Bromley:

> In your street, were there social differences—were some more respectable?
>
> Oh yes, you had one or two churchgoers, you know. They'd never mix with anybody else. They'd pass the time of day with you, but they never mixed in any shape or form.
>
> Would their kids mix with you?
>
> No, they sent 'em to play the violin and all that stuff. They wasn't— we was too rough for them.
>
> Did they go to the same school?
>
> No. They 'ad private schools somewhere. There's about three of them lived down 'ere.

He went on to say that the churchgoers lived 'at the top end of the street', 'up the posh end', that their children were better dressed than anyone else's, and that they were 'escorted to school, to church', whereas 'we ran wild'.[23]

In Berlin, as in London, pastors preached the virtues of thrift and many parishes ran savings banks. The deacon of the St Elizabeth parish in the proletarian north wrote in 1880 that although there was a lot of work involved, it was worth it, because of the 'moral gains': 'How else can one effectively and lastingly overcome the carelessness of poverty, but by educating people in thrift?' His savings bank was initially intended for the children of the Sunday school, but it was soon being used by many adults too. Under his direction saving took on a ritual character, and the correct performance of every detail of the rite reminded the savers of the solemnity of what they were doing. Everyone had their own savings book, and transactions could only be made if the book were clean and equipped with blotting paper: 'Thrift is a virtue, and virtues must not go around in dirty clothes.'[24] There are signs that this gospel of self-improvement was winning a following among churchgoers in Berlin, as it did in London. Here too we find an analysis of household budgets in 1891 that included a section on a churchgoing Moabit building worker and his wife, who were saving fifty or sixty marks a year and buying furniture and a sewing machine on installments: 'With what joyful smiles and gleaming eyes the people showed their savings book'. And a city missionary, in an article of 1886 on household decorations, noted that the homes of churchgoing workers were distinguished by 'the greatest possible cleanliness'.[25]

In New York the proportion of working-class people who were regular churchgoers was higher than in London or Berlin. Nonetheless, speakers at a Protestant conference in 1888 on 'The Religious Condition of New York City' described the gulf between the churches and the poor in terms rather similar to those that might have been used in London—with the difference that in New York the ethnic dimension to the problem was far more important. Most speakers deplored this separation and suggested ways of overcoming it. But two Presbyterian speakers seemed to be rather proud of the fact that few members of their denomination were poor. Rev. Charles Parkhurst, the famous crusading preacher from Madison Square church, declared:

> The immediate effect of pure Christianity is to improve the condition of a man. I tell you that a bank account is one of the fruits of the Spirit. Change and purify the heart of a man and his circumstances instantly begin to improve. A great many of those that are here have climbed the ladder of Christianity and have attained to some of the affluence and comfort and luxury of living that naturally goes with it.

And another Presbyterian speaker thought it was natural that those who had been converted would want to move away 'from the vicinities in which vice and drunkenness and open sin are continually showing themselves'.[26]

Similar themes of industry, thrift, sobriety, a passion for cleanliness and order, etc., emerge in accounts of strongly churchgoing Catholic families. A good example of this is a questionnaire completed in the 1970s by elderly members of Sacred Heart parish on the West Side of Manhattan. Sacred Heart was in a mainly working-class district close to the Hudson River piers, and within the area popularly known as Hell's Kitchen. The daughter, born in 1904, of a worker in the Sanitation Department remembers that her parents had 'a nice home', though they had to be careful: they and their friends were 'all very hard-working, religious, trying to give their neighbors, their church, all they could'. Like many others, she ridiculed the 'Hell's Kitchen' tag. Another respondent, the daughter, born in 1906, of a trolley-car conductor says that she objected 'furiously' to that title:

hers was a poor, but emphatically self-sufficient family. 'We never needed financial help—nor did we think the Church was over-demanding in asking our financial help.' Another woman, whose father drove a trolley-car, and who grew up in the parish in the 1920s and 1930s, insisted: 'we lived in a good neighborhood. If there were toughness around we did not know it or see it, we were brought up in our home not on the street. No-one stole or hurt anyone that I ever knew. All my friends grew up very nice. . . . There were five children in our family. My parents worked hard to bring them up. They never had to accept charity from anyone or any place. . . . They always supported their church and school. Then if there was money left over they bought a well-needed pair of shoes.' A longshoreman's daughter praised her school for giving her 'a sense of dedication to my own job. A desire to do my best at all times and keep high standards', and she recalled that her parents and teachers 'worked hard to keep us away from bad influences'. Another longshoreman's daughter was indignant at the name given to her beloved neighbourhood, and equally indignant at the way her father's profession was portrayed in the film *On the Waterfront*. She wanted to shout: 'Hey, my father's nothing like that, a more honest hard-working man you'll never find'; and she defined the outstanding personalities in the parish as 'My parents and other parents that sacrificed to put their children through Sacred Heart school and with the help of the parish have taught them certain ideals and lived life as best they can'. It is significant that although most of the respondents in the Sacred Heart questionnaire had come from poor families, few of them had lived in the roughest part of the parish close to the river: thirty-four of the forty-one addresses at which respondents had remembered living were east of Tenth Avenue.[27]

III

While this militant respectability could take the form of every family for itself, this was not necessarily so. One of the Sacred Heart members just quoted remembered her parents and friends 'trying to give their neighbors...all they could', and we know from other sources that neighbourly ties were often strong on the West Side. Elsa Herzfeld, in her account of West Side tenement life, published in 1905, gave examples, from incidents she had observed, of the kinds of things that were expected of the good neighbour:

> The readiness to give and share seems to be one of the chief traits in the relation of neighbor to neighbor. The aid given is of a simple kind. It satisfies an immediate need. Above all it is spontaneous. Your neighbor, no matter how cold the night, runs across the street to help nurse your neighbor's dying child. Or she washes the dead child in preparation for burial. If she lives on the floor above she sends her own children to a relative for quiet. She helps watch all night. She comes to the wake, attends the funeral and if she knows the family at all well she goes out to the cemetery with the bereaved. . . . As a rule all the families in the house know one another inti-

mately or at least by sight. They know one another's needs to the most
intimate details. There is little privacy in the house.[28]

A very similar note is struck in a London woman's account of her upbringing
in Mile End in the 1880s and 1890s: 'But she was very good, my mother. If anyone
is sick, she'd go and 'elp them, always, always. If anyone was ill or say anyone had
passed away and they want to lay someone out, run and fetch Mrs Carter.'[29] Mrs
Carter was a churchgoing Anglican, who combined neighbourliness with a strong
emphasis on respectability and on decent behaviour. A Canning Town woman,
born in 1895, has rather similar memories of her washerwoman mother, a devout
Roman Catholic, who had stringent standards of honesty, cleanliness and polite-
ness, and would also do anything to help her neighbours and gave her last halfpenny
to a beggarman.[30] It seems likely, though it is not explicitly stated by their daughters, that both women saw neighbourliness as 'practical Christianity'. Certainly
other working-class Londoners of her generation did so—though sometimes 'practical Christianity', which was the essence of true religion, was contrasted with
mere formalism, such as regular churchgoing. As a Bermondsey woman said of
her mother, who was also a good neighbour, 'I wouldn't say she was religious, but
she *practised* religion.'[31]

The relationship between being a good neighbour and being a practical Christian was made explicitly by the *Calendar* of St Paul's Catholic parish on the West
Side of Manhattan. In the years around 1900 one of the consistent themes in the
magazine was an attack on contemporary individualism, and the inculcation of an
ethos of community and mutual support. An article entitled 'Be Neighborly' called
for more friendliness and help and less gossip:

> In this age of congested tenements, particularly in a city like ours, it is very
> difficult to fulfil the precept of loving one's neighbor. We have such neigh-
> bors! They come and go so frequently that we think it no harm to act just as
> we please towards them. We have to listen to their gramophone all day, and
> their baby all night. Mrs Gabby is always on the front stoop, and Mr Stag-
> gers falls up the stairs regularly at one a.m. . . . Then the janitor is forever
> raising a rumpus. . . . Resolve for the New Year to make every family who
> moves in know by your actions that you are a Christian and a Catholic.

Other articles in this period criticized rich Catholics who shunned their poorer
co-religionists, and insisted that 'loving our neighbor' meant that Catholics must
be active in campaigns to improve the quality of working-class housing and re-
duce infant mortality. Similar thinking lay behind the frequent stress on the family. The good family member was someone who subordinated the desire for a
purely individual happiness or success to the needs of the family as a whole, and
their reward lay in the fact that a good family life offered the greatest happiness
that life can afford. An article entitled 'Heroism in Family Life' declared that
priests learned in the confessional to respect human nature. The article was in
praise of 'The man—many millions of him', who 'goes on year after year, fulfilling
a contract the exactions of which he did not realize in the days when he went

a-wooing', the wives who care for their husband and children although 'the duty is oftentimes hard, very hard' and the 'poor widow, without proper training in any pursuit, who brings up her family of little ones to be self-respecting maidens and youths.' It would be understandable if more husbands and wives deserted their families, like Nora in Ibsen's *Doll's House*, but few do it.[32]

Ideas of community and mutual responsibility were particularly strong and explicit in the Judaism of this period. Not only were there numerous charities supported by the more prosperous members of the Jewish communities of New York, London and Berlin—the principle of mutual aid was integral to the small synagogues formed by groups of immigrants in areas like London's East End or New York's Lower East Side. These communities were based not so much on the fact that the members were all Jews, or that they were neighbours, as on the fact that they were Jews coming from the same town in Europe. In this way the community of mutual obligation was narrowed down—but the sense of obligation to those within this community was very strong. In particular, the newly arrived immigrant could expect a bed in the home of a *landsman*, and sometimes he or she was helped by a collection. As Landesman comments, with regard to Brownsville, 'the Jerusalem of America', the small synagogues 'were of great assistance in time of distress, offering sick benefits, free loans, cemetery rights, insurance, and a variety of other advantages. Above all, these associations gave the newcomers in a strange land a sense of security, a feeling that behind them was a group ready to be helpful and to respond to a call in time of need.'[33]

There is less evidence about the extent and nature of neighbourhood ties in Berlin during this period. The early and rapid rise of Social Democracy, and later of the Communist Party, set the agenda both for contemporary discussion of Berlin working-class life and for most work by historians. Research has focused on the organizations, the ideology and the political activity of the working class. In spite of the recent fashion for *Alltagsgeschichte*, historians have continued to show much more interest in the ways that working-class people related to one another as fellow members of the working-class movement rather than simply as neighbours. The only two historians who have shown much interest in the kind of issues that are so familiar to writers on London and New York are the American Hsi-Huey Liang, whose Yale thesis of 1959 has never been published and remains little known, and Dietrich Mühlberg, who led a team of East German researchers in a pioneering reconstruction of Berlin working-class life around 1900. Mühlberg's vivid and imaginative, but highly generalized portrait, which makes few direct references to primary sources, provides plenty of discussion of pubs, allotments and the movies, but says little about relations with neighbours, apart from a passing reference to the fact that a large part of the life of working-class women was concentrated on the immediate vicinity of their homes—'the court, the shops in the street, and often too the church'. Liang is somewhat more explicit: placing as he does overriding emphasis on the family, he stresses the tendency for each household to keep itself to itself and the consequent superficiality of contacts with neighbours. He gives a few examples of situations where neighbours failed to be of much help to those in need.[34] Liang's study contains unique and valuable material derived from extensive interviewing. However, in wishing to challenge over-romanticized accounts of working-class solidarity and popular commitment to the Socialist cause, he has gone rather far in the opposite direction by stressing the extent of working-class individualism. It may be that in this instance, the interpretation of his limited data is predetermined by the explanatory framework that he has adopted.

For the time being, the question of how far neighbourly relations in Berlin took different forms from those obtaining in working-class districts of London or New York will have to remain open. The tendency of the literature is to emphasize high rates of mobility and lack of emotional ties to the place of residence,[35] together with high levels of involvement in clubs and political organizations and/ or participation in public amusements, such as pubs and theatres. Accounts of family leisure focus on trips out to allotments, parks, concerts or the surrounding countryside.[36] Only very occasionally do we find hints that the tenement itself was an important social unit. Accounts of life in Berlin's impoverished northern suburbs around the middle of the century reported that neighbourly help played a vital part in the survival strategy of the Voigtlanders; and an oral historian studying women home workers in the early part of this century found that strong neighbourly ties sometimes existed between them—even to the extent of the adoption of a neighbour's orphaned child.[37] An account of Berlin life in the 1890s noted the role of the court as a focus for life in the tenement—a place where people might sit out in summer or where musicians would play and children would dance.[38] On the other hand, a wartime reference to the mutual support shown by tenement dwellers when a neighbour's son was killed seemed to imply that this was part of a 'new spirit', which was unknown in peacetime.[39]

The ethos of neighbourly solidarity fed into a kind of politics that took its classic form in working-class areas of New York, but which found expression in other working-class areas too. Among the congregation at Sacred Heart was the well-known Tammany Hall politician George Washington Plunkitt, who, like many of his colleagues, had been born into poverty, but had achieved prosperity as well as power through a successful career in local politics. Plunkitt's style of politics resembled a gigantic system of neighbourly assistance, which very effectively reflected the local ethos.[40] Mary Simkhovitch, director of the Greenwich House Settlement on the Lower West Side, gave this account of the attractions of boss politics to the urban working class around the time of the First World War:

> The loyalty which makes of the industrial family the strongest type of family we possess, the limited number of relationships which vastly intensifies those that do exist, apply of course to political life as well. . . . The political ideal that appeals to the mass of city voters is that of an organization of like-minded loyal friends who will all work for one another. . . . Friendship, if really practical, connotes helpfulness. Friendship in power means help to supporters.[41]

Plunkitt expressed his friendship by obtaining jobs for his supporters, getting their sons out of jail, attending their funerals, making substantial charitable donations whenever a fire, blizzard or some other natural catastrophe took place, giving money to their churches, and so on. They showed their friendship by voting him back to the state Senate, and rejecting those middle-class advocates of 'good government' who condemned the 'corrupt' nature of Plunkitt's influence.

One of the most interesting aspects of New York politics, from our present point of view, was the mutually supportive, if sometimes ambivalent, relationship between the Democratic Party and the Catholic Church.[42] The ambivalence about the relationship was mainly on the side of the clergy, who suspected the motives of Democratic politicians, and feared that their corrupt reputation could rebound on the church, if the relationship ever became too close. In a typical comment entitled 'After the Election', the *Calendar* of St Paul's parish in 1888 stated: 'We trust that all our politicians who are now so loud-mouthed about their Catholicity will, after the elections are over, devote a little time to approach the Sacraments and attend Mass on Sunday. The "shock" might be a good thing for them.'[43]

In spite of their reservations about the ethical credentials of some Democratic politicians, there were all sorts of factors that bound the majority of Catholic priests to the Democratic Party. Personal ties were important: Cardinal McCloskey was related through marriage to the then Tammany leader, 'Honest' John Kelly; Archbishop Corrigan had contacts with many of the leading Democratic politicians of the 1880s and 1890s through the Catholic Club, an organization for wealthy Catholics, which gave the Archbishop fervent support during his controversy with Fr McGlynn; in some parishes the most prominent layman was a Democratic politician.[44] There were also affinities of style between church and party that assisted mutual understanding:[45] hierarchical organization; an overriding stress on the virtue of loyalty, and preference for the good organization man rather than the unpredictable individualist; and a pragmatism far removed from the moral crusading style favoured by many politically minded Protestants, who in this period might become Republicans, Progressives or Socialists, but were unlikely to feel at home as Democrats. In the later nineteenth century, the Democrats periodically courted Catholic support by offering public funding for Catholic institutions. But there were also good negative reasons for sticking with the Democrats: the strongly Protestant tone of the Republican Party, and its associations with the anti-Catholic American Protective Association, ruled out Republicanism so far as most Catholic priests were concerned, and the hierarchy (as opposed to some individual priests) had no sympathy with labor or socialist politics. Twice the dangers from one side or the other seemed great enough to justify an explicit intervention by a section of the clergy: in the 1886 mayoral election; and in the 1894 state elections, when the Republicans were denounced from several New York pulpits, and Catholics were urged to 'vote the straight Democratic ticket'.[46]

At first sight this is completely different from the type of politics that operated in London, where both before and after World War I there were major ideological differences between the parties. But Gillian Rose in her study of Poplar has suggested that by the later 1920s the dominant Labour Party was taking on characteristics rather like those of the Democratic Party in New York, and that these characteristics were similarly well rooted in local values. It was said of one leading councillor that 'he never in any circumstances deserted [a] pal', and this loyalty was reflected in the fact that Labour Party supporters were found jobs as relieving officers, husbands and sons of councillors got places in the Electricity Department, and the Catholic councillor, Peter Hubbart, found jobs for members of the Knights of St Columba.[47]

IV

But religion could also nourish a more radical form of working-class politics, which challenged the existing economic and social system. A questionnaire-based survey of the religious background of Labour M.P.s in the 1929–31 Parliament gave numerous examples of how this happened. Admittedly the connection between religion and political radicalism tended to be strongest among M.P.s from the mining and textile districts. But there were several examples among those who came from London.

Here, for instance, is the summary of his career given by Fred Messer, M.P. for South Tottenham. Born in 1886, he had left school at twelve. At sixteen he joined a Wesleyan Bible class; at nineteen he became a Sunday school teacher; at twenty-one he became an open-air preacher; and at twenty-two secretary of a Baptist mission. Meanwhile, he became active in the French Polishers' union, becoming general secretary at twenty-nine. A few years earlier he had joined the ILP, and after the war, which he had strongly opposed, he was chairman of his local Labour Party for several years. He summed up the connection between his religion and his politics as follows: 'The teacher or preacher sees how social life conflicts with all that he has been teaching or preaching and he attempts to relate that to religion and has to show that there should be a connection between actual life and religion.' Charles Ammon, a former Wesleyan Sunday school teacher, who was a leader of the postal workers and M.P. for Camberwell North, was more explicit: 'My interpretation of Socialism is that it is the practical expression of Christianity. I identify Christianity and Socialism. . . . The Book of Socialism is the Bible.' Ammon claimed to have got his original political education through his religious activities.[48]

A more detailed account of how this might happen comes from the biography of Charles Jenkinson, who was born in 1887 in Poplar, where his father was a craftsman employed irregularly in the docks. Jenkinson sang in the choir at St Stephen's Anglican Church, became a Sunday school teacher, and then was an active lay member of the largest Anglican congregation in the East End, St James the Less, Bethnal Green. His first political experience was the successful leadership of a campaign to end seat rents at that church. He also became active in the Church Socialist League, after he 'became a Socialist at exactly twenty minutes past six one evening while sitting in the church'. He then worked as an organizer for the Agricultural Labourers' Union in north Essex, where, in a statement of faith to the local deanery conference, he declared: 'A Christian must believe in the salvation of the whole man, body, mind and spirit. . . . The Church's duty is to proclaim that the agricultural labourer as well as everybody else, is entitled to fullness of life and that all men are equal in the sight of God.' After World War I he was ordained, and in keeping with his principle of working for 'the whole man', he combined his work as a Leeds vicar with chairmanship of the city's Housing Committee, where he became a famous and controversial figure through his big programme of slum clearance and his masterminding of the building of the Quarry Bank apartments (recently demolished in a new wave of slum clearance).[49]

While, then, political radicalism often had its roots in religion, it is important to note that the relationship between them tended to be complex, and that tensions sometimes developed. Take the example of Bill Brinson, who was chairman of the Poplar Labour Party in the 1930s. Born on the Isle of Dogs in 1894, Brinson moved to Poplar with his family when he was fourteen and stayed there the rest of his life. In his childhood, he regularly attended All Hallows' Anglican Church with his mother and he continued as a young man to be active in the church. The Brinson family lived a life of constant struggle because of the father's frequent unemployment and heavy drinking. They were consequently forced to rely on what the mother could earn by working appalling hours at the sewing machine. Brinson was strongly influenced by a group of radical clergy at All Hallows': 'They had some very enthusiastic parsons up there—they preached the Gospel as to my mind it should be preached.' His first experience of politics came during the 1912 dock strike when his bible class ran a soup kitchen. But eventually he left the church—apparently (though the reasons are not explicitly stated) because he felt that it did not give enough support to its more radical members.[50] Similarly, Fred Messer resigned his church membership during World War I, because of the lack of support from fellow church members for his anti-war stand—though he later returned.

There were also, of course, some socialists who came to reject Christianity or Judaism on intellectual grounds. More significant, however, than any direct conflict between religion and radicalism was the tendency for socialist and labour organizations to become a complete way of life, which simply crowded out any other commitment. Religion and politics, while in theory often complementary, were in practice competitors for the limited time and energy at the individual's disposal. The point is well made in an interview by Alan Bartlett with a woman brought up in inner south London in the 1920s and 1930s. Her father was a Primitive Methodist local preacher; she stated that most members of the chapel voted Labour and that her father and his friends 'very much preached socialist ideas when they preached: the people's needs for homes and housing and jobs as well as salvation'. But she noted that few members were active in the Labour Party—for them it was their religious work that came first, and absorbed most of what free time they had. Conversely, for many of those who became active in the ILP or SDF in the pre-war period, involvement in propaganda work on Sundays and in weeknight meetings left little time for the chapel, no matter how deep their sense of Christian identity remained.[51]

In London, as in most other parts of Britain, working-class Nonconformists and Roman Catholics were moving from Liberal to Labour—slowly in the pre-war

years, and then very rapidly in the 1920s. But, among the relatively small proportion of working men who were active Anglicans, a considerable proportion stayed
with the Conservatives. One Stepney vicar told Charles Booth in 1898 that all the
working men in his congregation were Conservatives—'Further east they get hold
of radicals and socialists, but not here.' A Greenwich vicar even complained to
Booth that his churchwarden was 'the gas-works spy'.[52] However, the association
between established religion and Conservative politics was still much less close
than in Berlin.

In Berlin, the Protestant worker who wanted to get organized faced a stark
choice. On the one hand there were the Free Trade Unions and the numerous
other organizations associated with the Social Democratic Party. However, a Berlin printing worker who regularly took part in meetings of the Evangelical-Social
Congress complained that he had left the Free Trade Union, because it 'tolerates
convinced nationalist and Christian workers only as silent paying members; as
soon as such workers gain any spiritual influence they are eliminated'.[53] Similarly,
three labour movement veterans told an oral historian who interviewed them in
the 1950s that there had been an unwritten rule in Berlin Social Democratic circles
before the First World War that no churchgoing worker could hold office in the
movement. Some trade union branches made assistance with burial costs for bereaved members conditional on no clergyman being present.[54]

On the other hand, the Protestant Workers' Associations in Berlin were strongly
Conservative. They were clearly stamped by the dominant personality of their
president, Adolf Stoecker. They declared in their statutes their 'loyalty to the
Emperor and the Empire', and their objectives included 'the cultivation and maintenance of peaceful relations between workers and employers' and of 'love for the
fatherland and its hereditary ruling house'. About half the members of the Protestant Workers' Associations also belonged to the Christian Trade Unions. In their
strongholds on the Rhine and Ruhr these unions were formidable competitors to
the Social Democratic unions, and provided a base for an alternative (usually
Catholic) form of radicalism. But in Berlin, there was no contest. In 1905 the
Christian unions had only four thousand members in the capital, of whom more
than half belonged to three sections, these being, in order of strength, women
home workers, bricklayers and builder's labourers.[55] In factories where the great
majority of workers belonged to the Free Unions, members of the Christian Unions
were under constant pressure to transfer.[56]

In the German Catholic world, Berlin, and indeed the Archdiocese of Breslau
generally, were strongholds of conservatism. Successive archbishops combined
Ultramontanism in ecclesiastical matters with conservatism in political and social
matters. Archbishop Kopp, who occupied the see from 1886 to 1914, called, in
successive pastoral letters, for submission to authority in church and state, and
counselled workers to be content with their lot. Until after World War I there is
no evidence that any of Berlin's Catholic clergy challenged this teaching.[57] There
was a section of the Catholic laity who did, and in the early twentieth century
parish council elections were fiercely fought between supporters of the Christian
Unions and those who supported the more conservative social-political approach

of their archbishop and clergy.[58] However, the Catholics were not sufficiently numerous overall to make a major impact in Berlin politics. Nor were they sufficiently concentrated in particular districts to make the important local impact that they had in certain areas of London.[59] And in any case the Social Democratic movement was exercising a strong counter-attraction that pulled many Catholic workers altogether away from the church's influence.[60]

Of course, in Germany (as in Britain and the United States) the electorate in the period before World War I was exclusively male. When women did vote for the first time in 1919, the main beneficiaries were the Catholic Centre Party; on the other hand, the Social Democrats proved much less successful in attracting women voters than they had been in attracting men.[61] Up to now, examples have been given of the religious attitudes and activities both of women and of men, but (except to some extent in the chapter on London), the possibility has not been considered that these may have been essentially different. The next chapter looks both at the differences between male and female patterns of religiosity, and at the interrelationships between them.

CHAPTER 7

Male and Female

IN LONDON, NEW YORK and Berlin, the working-class districts were full of drinking places. The London pub was often a Gothic palace, rivalling the parish church as the most conspicuous local landmark, whereas the New York saloon or the Berlin *Kneipe* tended to lie at the bottom of a block of tenements, and was often reached by descending a flight of stairs. All alike were strongholds of the working-class male. 'There were so many pubs in Berlin in earlier times,' one elderly woman recalls, 'there was a pub in every building. And when things perhaps got too boring for father upstairs, he would pop downstairs to play the fool. There were always people down there.'[1] Mother, meanwhile, would be left upstairs with the children and the sewing-machine.

The pub was the most vivid symbol of the separation of male and female worlds. It represented a freedom that most men could enjoy, at least for a few hours in the evening, but which was much less often available to married women. The atmosphere of the pub tended to be aggressively masculine—though, admittedly, there were men who had a drink with their wife on Saturday or Sunday, and some pubs had a corner reserved for women drinking with other women. Apart from the usual card-playing, chatting, storytelling and joking, pubs could also provide a meeting-place for all-male friendly societies, trade unions, political organizations or singing clubs.

But if men saw their evening in the pub as well-earned relaxation after a long day's toil, their wives often saw it as money squandered that was desperately needed for food and clothing. Observers of working-class life in all three cities noted the tendency for husband and wife to grow apart under the strain of life on very tight budgets.[2] Ellen Ross has described the sexual division of labour operating in working-class families in London. Nearly all tasks were the exclusive province of one sex or the other—the only area of overlap being the upbringing of children. This was primarily a job for the women, but some men also made a significant contri-

149

bution by playing with children, talking to them, taking them out or disciplining them. Men and women socialized separately, and often knew different people in the street. Women had sole responsibility for feeding and clothing the children, and men often knew little of how this was done. Pawnings, borrowing money or food, relations with rent collectors, also belonged to the female sphere, as did neighbourhood gossip.[3]

Clearly, there were some households in which husband and wife spent a lot of time together, and many in which they at least came together on Sundays. In Berlin, for instance, Sunday was often the day when the whole family went to work on their allotment. But when the time came to stop work, the tendency was for the men to sit in one group drinking beer, while the women sat at a slight distance drinking coffee.[4]

I

The distance between women and men was also apparent in religious matters. Indeed, at one stage, Charles Booth, who generally analysed differences in religious practice in terms of class, seemed to imply that gender differences were even more fundamental. He described in the following terms the characteristic religious outlook of working men in Hackney:

> They like their club with its pot of beer, its entertainments, its game of cards or billiards, or the 'pub' and its associates and a bet on to-morrow's race, but they look on these things as inconsistent with a religious profession, and every form of religious association thus becomes (if they think about the matter at all) something from which, in honesty, they must hold themselves aloof. They are unwilling to accept a restraint that would deprive them of these everyday pleasures, and the step to denounce as hypocrites those members of religious bodies who lead mundane lives is thus easily made. . . . Coupled with this there is some class feeling against joining churches which are supposed to side with the rich, so that to go to church may even be regarded as disloyalty to class. Thus there springs up a public opinion among themselves which in their workshops may make a favourite, if not a hero, of the man who most defies religious restraints; who is even most reckless in his life and conversation.

Booth immediately went on to say that working-class women and girls were much keener churchgoers than men. Elsewhere, without explicitly contrasting men and women, he drew a distinction between the workshop and the home: 'The attitude of the workshop indeed is contemptuous, but not that of the home. In family life religion has a certain recognition, as for instance we are told in the habit of private prayer among the women, though how far this really is common I do not know.'[5]

The implication of Booth's argument is that working-class separation from the churches was a specifically male phenomenon, a product partly of the class solidarity generated in the workplace, and partly of the pub- and club-based culture, in which wives had little part. Gillian Rose advances a similar argument rather more explicitly in her study of Poplar in the 1920s. Noting the 'masculinism' that developed in such all-male environments as the docks, railways and engineering workshops, she argues that 'male bravado precluded anything as effeminate as going to church'. On the other hand, there were many churches, chapels and mothers' meetings which acted as 'women's spaces' and 'centres of female conviviality'.[6] There is a good deal in these arguments, though as I shall explain later, I think they overstate the sharpnesss of the division between the religion of women and men. There is also an ambiguity in Booth's argument: was the home more religious than the workshop because it was part of women's sphere, or because men behaved differently at home from the way they did at work?

The idea that patterns of employment affected the division of labour between women and men, and that this in turn affected patterns of religious practice, gains some support from the findings of the Thompson-Vigne oral history project. I have looked at transcripts of all the interviews with respondents brought up in working-class families in industrial regions of England. Answers to the questions about the churchgoing habits of the respondent's parents suggest three regional patterns. In all areas the proportion of mothers attending church regularly was higher than the proportion of fathers doing so, but the ratio of male to female attendance varied considerably. In Lancashire and West Yorkshire the gap was fairly narrow, attendance by both sexes being high; in the northeast and the north Midlands, the gap was wider, attendance by women being high and that by men low; in London the gap was narrow again, with attendance by both women and men being low. Until more research has been done on this subject, any explanations must be very tentative. In particular, I would stress that while the relatively large numbers of interviews with Londoners and Lancastrians make me fairly confident in asserting both that the level of churchgoing was considerably higher in Lancashire than in London, and that the gender gap was relatively narrow in both instances,[7] the number of interviews conducted in some other areas was too low to permit such confidence.

However, I would suggest that the regional differences indicated by the interviews may at least partly be explained by differences in regional economies. Here I would refer in particular to Elizabeth Roberts' comment that the sexual division of labour within the family was much less rigidly defined in textile towns, where a high proportion of married women worked in factories, than in towns dominated by engineering, where women tended to be limited to such home-based jobs as taking in washing.[8] It is particularly interesting to note that whereas churchgoing by women was no lower in Lancashire than in other regions of England, that by men was higher. The greater interchangeability of roles included, for instance, the possibility that the husband would take the children to church while the wife stayed at home—something that does not seem to have happened in any of the northeastern families whose habits were recorded in the Thompson and Vigne interviews. In areas like the northeast, dominated by mining and heavy engineering, there seems to have been a much sharper division between male and female worlds. The relatively high earnings enjoyed by an important section of the labour force in these two industries opened the way for two possibilities: first, the development of a strong culture of exclusively male institutions, including trade unions, friendly societies and pubs; and second, wives who were not required to earn money, and who thus had more time to devote not only to their children, but also to the church and/or the co-op.[9]

In London the combination of a large middle- and upper-class presence with the prevalence of industries where earnings were low and/or irregular, including docking, building and tailoring, meant that there were both plenty of opportunities for part-time female employment, and often an acute need to supplement the inadequate earnings of their husbands.[10] Working-class London women were accustomed to spend a large part of their day at the sewing-machine or the washtub, and many of them had little life at all outside the home. On the other hand, for those who did get out, churches and chapels were in competition with numerous music-halls and theatres. While mothers' meetings, in particular, attracted large numbers in London too, churches and chapels did not enjoy the degree of cultural dominance that they had in many parts of the north, where they were the only alternative to the pubs.

II

Although by national standards churchgoing in London was low, places of worship were among the few environments in which the sexes did to some extent mix—and indeed some people went to church precisely for that reason. Nonetheless there were plenty of religious activities that were organized on a single-sex basis. Organizations or events for women tended to attract a larger participation than those for men; but where men did take an interest in religion, the aspects that interested them were often different from those which interested women.

Charles Booth claimed that 'The London working man is great in all forms of discussion . . . religious subjects are the most popular.'[11] At first sight this looks surprising, in view of the reputation of working-class Londoners for religious indifference. However, there is a good deal of evidence to support his contention. For instance, park oratory was a well-known feature of nineteenth-century London, going back at least to the 1790s,[12] and still flourishing at the time of Charles Booth's survey of London around 1900. Every Sunday, the open spaces of the metropolis were full of Christians and Secularists, Protestants and Catholics, not to mention occasional exponents of more exotic creeds, propounding the truth of their own doctrines and refuting crowds of hecklers. While the Salvation Army attracted special interest by the fact that many of their preachers and musicians were women, both speakers and audience were usually predominantly male.[13]

A popular attraction in the 1860s and 1870s was the set-piece debate between Christian and Secularist champions—a religious equivalent of prizefighting, which sometimes went on for many rounds, as in the marathon contests between the champion bare-knuckle heavyweights, Charles Bradlaugh and the Rev. Brewin

'Boanerges' Grant.[14] The East End Settlements found that combats of this kind were a big popular draw—though in keeping with the general civilizing trend, the style was now more that of a short sharp bout with gloves on. For instance, in 1888 Oxford House in Bethnal Green staged a debate between the then warden, Hensley Henson (later Bishop of Durham), and a well-known Secularist on 'The Historical Origins of Christianity', which was attended by '800 men'.[15] And Toynbee Hall in Whitechapel provided similar fare at its Sunday afternoon discussions, where the audiences were 'male, large, uncouth, inclined to be irreverent'.[16]

While the special attraction of these events arose, no doubt, from the similarity to a sporting contest,[17] and the fact that each side was given an equal opportunity to state its case, working men would sometimes attend religious meetings in considerable numbers if the emphasis was on preaching and the preaching was expected to be good. P.S.A.s (Pleasant Sunday Afternoons), Men's Owns, and the like depended for their popularity on the quality of the speaker. One of Booth's assistants gave an account of the crowded Men's Own at New Court Congregational chapel in Islington in 1898, which brought out well the popularity of good preaching even with men who did not attend conventional services:

I made for New Court Chapel where Mr Morgan was billed to address his 'Men's Own' on 'The paralysis of Impurity'. Mr M. began his address at 3.15. I arrived at 4.15 and he was still speaking: almost as I came in he said 'I have been speaking for more than an hour and I must stop' but here he was saluted with a tremendous burst of applause telling him to go on: he then spoke for about another 15 minutes with tremendous passion and eloquence. That for the time being at all events he profoundly moved his audience, there can be no question. The whole body of the chapel was filled with men, I suppose about 600 or 700 in all: a large number were young men of the upper artisan class.[18]

Supporters of P.S.A.s and Men's Owns sometimes argued that it was an essential part of the appeal of such meetings that the audience was entirely male:

The men have come to feel 'at home' in their P.S.A., and regard it as their own meeting. There is an 'atmosphere' in the P.S.A. quite different from that at an orthodox service or mixed meeting. There can be theoretic objections to sectional gatherings, but facts prove that men who are untouched by ordinary religious agencies may be got to a men's service, when nothing will induce them to attend a 'mixed' service.[19]

While the writer does not attempt to define what it was that made men more at home in such meetings, it probably was a combination of the fact that they relaxed more easily in the company of members of their own sex, and that in attending such an all-male gathering they were not placing their masculinity in question. A third factor was probably equally important: these meetings were directed specifically at working men, and so were much less likely than conventional church services to involve close proximity to members of other social classes.[20]

Nonetheless popular preachers were sometimes able to attract quite large congregations of both sexes to conventional church services in working-class areas.
Notable examples would be St James the Less, Bethnal Green, the best-attended
Anglican church in the East End in 1903, where men slightly exceeded women,
and the Wesleyan Central Hall in Bermondsey, said to be the only Protestant
church in south London attended by 'the poor in bulk'.[21]

Sectarian conflict, though much less important in London than in northwest
England or the west of Scotland, was also an area of religion in which men came
to the fore. Certainly in Lancashire fathers were accustomed to make life hell for
those of their children who chose a marriage partner from the wrong faith: Protestants tended to feel degraded by the admission of a Catholic into the family, and
Catholics felt betrayed when one of their number married a Protestant.[22] In London, where Catholics only made up about 10 per cent of the population, mixed
marriages were much less frequent than in Lancashire. But most parts of London, especially those close to the river, had concentrated Catholic communities,
and London experienced on a much more limited scale some of the same tensions
that troubled Liverpool and Glasgow in this period. For instance, there were a
number of sectarian brawls in the 1890s, usually in association with lectures by
Catholic or Protestant propagandists. In 1893, a Protestant lecture in Victoria
Park was broken up by a group of three hundred Catholics, said to be members of
the same guild.[23] In 1850, at the time of the restoration of the Catholic hierarchy,
Catholic men had formed guards to protect their churches from Protestant attack; and at the end of the century there were still Catholic men who had little to
do with the church for most of the time, but were ready to step forward whenever
defenders of the faith were needed. In 1900 Charles Booth's representative spent
an afternoon with a group of priests in Bermondsey:

> They appeared to think that the rougher and more neglectful of his reli-
> gious duties a man was, the more stalwart a defender he would prove in
> case of real or imaginary need. Let the Church or a priest be insulted in the
> bar of the public house, in a club, or on the wharf, and fisticuffs would soon
> be flying about. And Fr Mostyn gave an amusing instance of what hap-
> pened to him lately. Owing to a complete misunderstanding, a man was
> supposed to have insulted him. The next day, going down Tooley Street, he
> was met by one of his flock: 'Mornin', F'thurr, I've bin waitin' for you. Two
> ov us 'ave got 'im down there by the river all right, the chap that insulted
> you, and we want to know wot we shall do to 'im.' The men were quite
> strangers to Fr Mostyn. . . . [24]

The generation of Anglican clergymen ordained in the 1880s and 1890s seemed
to be especially productive of 'men's men', who had imbibed a passion for games,
and sometimes for imperial adventuring at their public schools, and then discov-
ered a vocation to work with urban working-class youth while at a Settlement or
college mission. The attempt to show that Christianity is manly went back at least
to Charles Kingsley in the 1850s, though the 'muscular Christians' of the Kingsley

type were mainly concerned with affirming what they saw as good in the culture and value-system of upper-class and upper middle-class males.[25]

In the parishes of east and south London in the 1880s and 1890s there were clergymen of many different denominations who were trying to do the same with working-class men and boys. They were eager to disprove the idea that Christianity appealed only to women. Accordingly they took a keen interest in anything of a sporting and/or violent nature, especially boxing, which had the advantage of being both;[26] they expressed their feelings of comradeship with the members of their men's club by smoking pipes or cigarettes. One of the best-known examples of the breed was the Rev A. Osborne Jay, vicar of Holy Trinity, Shoreditch. He was described by Booth's representative as 'a stout, plain, coarse-looking fellow, with the appearance of a prize-fighter out of training',[27] and he was indeed known as a boxing enthusiast. Jay had a band of teenage followers who formed a gang called 'Father Jay's Boys',[28] and his main interest was in his men's and boys' clubs. He told Booth's representative that he had always got on better with men than women, and that men made up over half his congregation.[29] He provided the model for the heroic 'Father Sturt' in Arthur Morrison's *A Child of the Jago*, the best-known novel written about the late Victorian East End: no doubt this reflected a widespread feeling that the church needed to build up its support among men and that Jay was the kind of man to do it.

Tom Collings, a curate in nearby Spitalfields in the mid 1890s, was of a similar type. In 1896 he was dismissed from his curacy. His subsequent comments to a meeting at a Nonconformist chapel convey something of the style of studied informality cultivated by clergymen of this kind:

> Well, I shall have to clear out. It's like this: with a parish of 30,000 souls the rector has had to give up like the one before him, and the new one and I don't hit it. I'm glad your parson won't have Reverend in front of his name. I'm never known as Rev., but always as Parson Collings, or the smoking Parson. Yes, we've had some fine times with our smokers and baked 'tater feeds. What shall I do? Well, I don't know. Perhaps some other church will take me in—or I shall put up for Parliament or go a-scavenging; or if the worst comes I shall have to do my bit of work for 'a reasonable amount of food' (a little gruel) [i.e., in the workhouse, where this was the food provided]. I'm not afraid. With God's help and a strong arm, I can do a bit of work yet. Yesterday I preached in a Baptist chapel in the morning. In the afternoon I spoke to 2000 railway men, and at night I preached a Socialistic-independent-labour-party-up-to-date sort of sermon in a church, and they asked me to come again.

Subsequently, in his farewell to Hanbury Street P.S.A., Collings protested against the vicar-curate relationship, the Establishment, church unfriendliness to Dissent and the Anglican liturgy; accused 'the brewers, the capitalists and the landlords' of having captured the church; said he was a socialist; and declared that he was proud to be known as 'the dossers' parson'. A year later, he was in fact taken on by an Anglican mission in Edmonton.[30] It is probably characteristic that

Collings combined his crusade against formality with radical political views: radical politics, as much as smoking and boxing, could be seen as a means of getting closer to working men.

Gillian Rose's research on Poplar in the 1920s suggests that, whereas there were several clergymen who attracted large numbers of women to their churches, there were only three who were known for their ability to attract men—Fr St John Groser (St Michael's, Anglican), Rev. William Dick (Trinity, Congregational), and Rev. Clapham (Bow Wesleyan Mission). They obviously differed in liturgical approach—Groser was a very high Anglican, whereas the other two were Nonconformists; and in important matters of lifestyle—Groser would have a drink with his parishioners in 'The Cherry Tree', while the other two were teetotallers. But the link between them was that all three were politically active socialists, and this, Rose argues, is what put them on the same wavelength as their working-class male parishioners.[31]

Rose also notes that many Poplar churches ran sports clubs.[32] Interviews with elderly East Enders suggest that a number of clergymen did succeed in forming quite close relationships with working-class boys and youths, in which a common love of sport and the open air usually played a part. For instance, a Canning Town man, born in 1900, recalled that an Anglican vicar, the Rev. Gardner, was the biggest influence on him when he was a boy. His parents, who were respectively a pipe-fitter and a ship's scrubber, never went to church, but he was sent to St Gabriel's, and there he got 'in with the parson'. He earned money by doing gardening for the vicar, and he also learnt to box at the church club and took part in gymnastics. 'He was a great man, he was.' More cryptically, a Wapping docker, born in 1899, who combined Anglicanism with large amounts of soccer-playing (the relationship between the two is not explicitly stated), comments, 'if we had a good clergyman, he was our skipper. We relied on him.'[33]

There was also an aspect of male religious practice that might relate to the father's status as 'head of the family'. In those fairly numerous working-class families where grace was said before meals, it was sometimes the father who said it; there also were familes where the father read the Bible to the assembled household. However, there seems to be no clear pattern: in some working-class families it was mother who did these things, and in other cases grace was said by the children.[34]

III

Otherwise it was women who took the leading role in those areas of religious life that related to the home, to the upbringing of children, and to rituals connected with the annual cycle or the life-cycle. Sometimes this was a matter of an accepted division of labour—for instance, mothers taught their children their prayers, because prayers were conventionally said before going to bed, and mothers generally put the younger children to bed.[35] On the other hand, prayers of all sorts

seem to have been said more frequently by women than by men.[36] This was probably because the help of God was frequently sought in those areas of life that
were least humanly controllable, and most of these fell within the sphere of female responsibility. It may also be that social conventions that tabooed any public
display of emotion by men would have made it much more difficult for men to
pray in front of others, except in a formalized way, as in a church service or a grace
before eating. Women also seem to have taken more interest in the baptism of
their children.[37] And, of course, one widely practised rite, that of churching or
thanksgiving for the birth of a child, was an exclusively female concern, which
women went through with no one else but the clergyman present.[38]

For poorer women, contacts with the churches as charitable agencies permitted a vital addition to precarious household resources. In this respect large numbers of women, whose husbands had little knowledge of organized religion, needed,
as a part of their responsibilities within the household economy, to be familiar with
clergymen, district visitors, parish nurses and such like. This did not necessarily
make for friendly relations with the church. Clearly an element of humiliation was
potentially present in this kind of relationship. Some charity workers were ob-
sessed with trying to root out 'charity mongers'—those who tried to make a living
from milking charities—and 'frauds', who misrepresented their circumstances; this
obsession could lead to insensitive treatment of those who were perfectly honest
in their claims, and only applied for charitable help when in desperate straits.

The evidence collected by Ellen Ross, in a very thorough study of the subject,
suggests that in London around the turn of the century most families earning less
than 31 shillings a week made at least some use of charity.[39] Since so much charity
was provided by religious bodies, this meant that large numbers of poor women
had to establish some kind of relationship with a church, chapel or mission. The
relationship took many different forms. Occasionally quite close friendships were
made between the charitable agents and the women they visited. For instance,
this seems to have been the case sometimes with the Bible Nurses—working-class
women who combined visiting the sick and dying with reading from the Bible and
preaching.[40] Partly because of the very traumatic circumstances in which their
visits were often made, and partly because they were relatively close socially to
those whom they visited, they seem to have been valued as individuals, rather
than being merely regarded as officials.

Sometimes the relationship between receivers and givers of charity was seen
in terms of reciprocity: the church provided help that was needed, and the recipi-
ent showed her gratitude by attending services.[41] Sometimes the response was
more manipulative: the feigning of piety in order to squeeze out the maximum. In
one family living in a very poor part of Islington, it was the father who turned this
into a fine art, converting to Roman Catholicism because he decided that the St
Vincent de Paul Society had the most to offer, and putting on a moving display of
deserving poverty whenever a charitable agent visited.[42] Another such family attended church together, deliberately picking an Anglican church where the vicar
was known to be on an important charitable committee. Some mothers felt great
bitternesss when they were denied help that they felt was due to them. The mother

of the family just mentioned had some fierce tussles with a charitable visitor nick-named 'The Ferret' because of her skill in winkling out information about people's financial circumstances.[43] And a Bethnal Green curate, whose diary was largely filled with details of requests for money, recorded that a Mrs Donald had asked him for money 'if it were only eighteen pence so as to get food to the end of the week'. When he refused, 'She said it would go hard with the poor if all the clergy were like me.' The curate replied that it would go better with them, as they would rely more on themselves, and Mrs Donald went away saying it was very hard.[44]

The female equivalent of the Men's Own was the Mothers' Meeting, which usually took place on a Monday afternoon or evening—sometimes known as 'Mother's Day'[45]—when women who spent all Sunday at home had their few hours of freedom. These meetings originated in London around 1850, flourished through-out the later Victorian period and began to decline in the early twentieth cen-tury.[46] They differed in various ways from the religious services that were directed exclusively at men. One was that the programme related directly to women's do-mestic concerns: typically the meeting was divided between 'business' (the sale of materials at cost price) and the more specifically religious part of the meeting, during which the women would sew. Singing, praying and readings played as big a part as preaching, and the address was in the form of a religious chat, rather than a piece of spellbinding pulpit oratory of the kind that guaranteed a large turnout at a meeting for men. The opportunity to socialize also seems to have been more important than it was in the meeting for men. In fact, letting off steam about husbands was said to be a significant aspect of the Mothers' Meeting.[47] Here it was no doubt a major factor that the Mothers' Meeting might be the only occasion in the week when the mother got out of the house for a prolonged pe-riod, whereas men had plenty of such opportunities. The attraction of a 'Men Only' service was thus more likely to lie in what was unique to it, namely the preaching. Charles Booth gave this description of a Mothers' Meeting in a Con-gregational mission in Islington in 1897:

> I attended the Monday evening meeting, coming in a little before seven & finding the building nearly full of working women all in a full buzz of talk & business. . . . No one left & by 7.15 much still remained, but Mr Smith stopped the business promising to make the service short so that they might all get home by 8 O'Clock. There could be no question that the women liked to come & liked to stay. The service was very simple—one hymn was tried and failed as no one knew the tune—so another was chosen—the singing was hearty. Mr Smith's address was very simple & his whole man-ner friendly and delightful.[48]

Although, in this instance, a man was in charge, it seems that the meetings were more frequently run by women, whether it were the vicar's wife, a middle-class 'District Visitor' or a working-class 'Bible Woman'.[49] Whereas the members of a P.S.A. were often akin to an audience, with all that this relationship implied in terms of distance between the man on the stage and the men on the chairs in front, the atmosphere of a Mothers' Meeting was more intimate. This was partly a matter of numbers: though some Mothers' Meetings were attended by hundreds, the typical size of a meeeting in late Victorian London was around sixty. But close ties would also develop between members, and between organizers and members, and this was reflected in such practices as prayers for individual members when they had experienced such tragedies as the loss of a child. The intimacy also had its obverse side: because an atmosphere of friendliness and mutual concern was so important to the success of these meetings, patronizing or insensitive organizers were more resented than they would have been in a more formal kind of meeting.[50]

One other distinctive aspect of the religious experience of working-class women was the fact that large numbers of London women spent several years before marriage in service in a middle- or upper-class family. Frequently this experience included compulsory attendance at church services or family prayers. No doubt this experience varied greatly according to both the nature of the employing family and the personality of the woman herself. On the whole the effect on the religion of the women who had been in service seems to have been negative, since it often led them to associate formal religious practice with hypocrisy and snobbery. For instance, a Bermondsey woman, born in 1893, who had gone to church when she lived with her parents, gave up when she was a servant in Brixton: 'We had a code between ourselves that you never went to work for anybody church or chapel people, because we didn't get much money anyway, but you got less with those. Yes. They got the name—the church and chapel people did not pay wages.'[51]

IV

The main Sunday services of each Christian denomination, held in midmorning and in the early evening, were of course attended by both women and men. The proportion of men tended to be higher at the morning service, because churchgoing women in the working and lower middle classes usually spent Sunday morning preparing for dinner, and so went to church in the evening. In spite of claims by some observers that congregations were overwhelmingly female, there was in fact a fairly even balance overall, with women in a clear, but far from overwhelming, majority. The 1902–3 religious census showed that total attendances by adult women equalled 24 per cent of the adult women in Inner London, and those by men equalled 18 per cent of the adult men.[52] There were, however, considerable variations in the distribution between individual places of worship and, indeed, denominations. The pattern is fairly clear. Overall, 61 per cent of churchgoers were women, whereas women made up only 54 per cent of the adult population. The overrepresentation was most marked in the case of the Anglicans (66 per cent women) and the Roman Catholics (64 per cent). In an intermediate position we find the Baptists (60 per cent), Presbyterians (59 per cent), Brethren (a small evangelical denomination)(59 per cent), and Congregationalists, Wesleyans and Salvation Army, bunched together on 57 per cent. Then we find two denominations where men were overrepresented, namely the Quakers and Primitive Meth-

TABLE 16

Women as a Percentage of Adults Attending Services of Various Denominations, London, 1902–3

Church of England	65.7
Roman Catholic	64.2
Unitarian	60.0
Baptist	59.8
Presbyterian	59.2
Brethren	58.5
United Methodist Free Churches	57.3
Bible Christian	57.1
Congregationalist	57.0
Wesleyan Methodist	57.0
Salvation Army	56.8
Catholic Apostolic	54.1
Quaker	52.0
Primitive Methodist	51.6

SOURCE: Richard Mudie–Smith, ed., *The Religious Life of London* (London, 1904).

odists (52 per cent women) (see table 16). (A study of ten Nonconformist congregations in Bradford in the 1880s showed that Quaker members were almost exactly equally divided between the two sexes, whereas all other congregations surveyed showed a female majority, In this instance, no information was available on Primitive Methodism.)[53] The pattern of attendance by Jews was completely different from that by Christians: only 22 per cent of the adults attending synagogue were women. Because they were so different I shall omit the Jews from the present discussion and return to them later.

Four factors influenced the degree to which the congregations of a given denomination tended toward approximate equality between the numbers of men and women, or toward a clear female majority. In the light of these four factors one can predict with a considerable degree of precision the sexual composition of the congregations of any given denomination in early twentieth-century London. First, the distribution tended to be more even in the more sectarian denominations. This reflected the fact that sectarian families had made a commitment to a way of life that to some extent set them apart from the wider society, and which was equally binding on male and female members. A second point, which is stressed by Rosemary Chadwick, whose thesis on Bradford contains the most thorough analysis so far available of the sexual composition of congregations, is that the gap between male and female religious practice was wider in the working class than in the middle class, so that other things being equal, a denomination with a largely working-class membership would be expected to show a greater imbalance than one with a mainly middle-class membership.[54] She relates this to the middle-class emphasis on the family unit, and the tendency of middle-class couples to spend their free hours together; working-class couples, when they had free time, often enjoyed it in different ways and in different places—and in any case many working men took the view that religion was 'women's work'. A third point is that the sharper the distinction between clergy and laity in a given denomination, the more likely it was that women would predominate in the congregation. One reason for this was the tendency of clericalism to provoke a corresponding anticlericalism, which in this period was a predominantly male phenomenon—probably because men saw clerical leadership as a threat to their manhood, whereas women were accustomed to the idea of the public sphere being dominated by men, and were less concerned as to whether leadership came from the clergy or from a lay elite. The fourth point is the interesting paradox that those denominations which most sharply separated male from female roles both within the church and in society generally also tended to have a marked preponderance of women in their congregations.[55]

The latter are related, as denominations that sharply separated clerical and lay roles within the church also tended to be those that separated most sharply male and female roles within the church and went furthest in positing essential differences between the nature of the two sexes. While Anglican and Roman Catholic women could, for instance, as members of religious orders, play a crucial part in church life in roles set aside for women, the positions of greatest status and power in the church were reserved for men.

The Salvation Army and the Quakers, on the other hand, by the early 1900s made no distinction between the roles within the church that were open to women and those open to men (which is not to say that practical equality had been achieved); and the Primitive Methodists, though since 1860 their ministers were all men, still had women local preachers.[56] One would expect, therefore, that these latter three denominations would especially attract women, and at first sight it is surprising to find that these were the three denominations where the sexes were most evenly balanced. There is indeed evidence that some of the early Salvation Army officers were converts from Anglicanism, attracted by the greater opportunities for women to use their talents in the Army.[57] However, within any church (or any other organization), the prospect of taking on a position of leadership is only likely to influence a minority consisting of the highly articulate and committed. Of more general significance was the fact that the less rigid segregation of sex roles within the Primitive Methodist, Quaker and Salvationist communities led to less sharp divisions between male and female patterns of behaviour, and undermined the idea prevalent in the wider society that churchgoing was a highly appropriate activity for women, but less so for men.

To sum up, the Anglican and Roman Catholic churches both scored high on three of the four relevant predictors, so it is not surprising to find that they had the highest proportions of women in their congregations. Thus the Catholics scored high on working-classness,[58] clericalism, and the rigidity with which sex roles were defined within the church; on the other hand, the relatively sectarian nature of London Catholicism at a time when a high proportion of Catholics were first- or second-generation Irish immigrants, living in Irish districts, was a factor modifying the female preponderance. The Anglicans scored high on all the relevant indicators, except that of working-classness—the Church of England had, of course, practising members in all social classes, but the proportion rose steeply with each step up the social scale. At the other end of the scale, the Quakers scored high on all the factors associated with a relatively even balance of the sexes, and the Primitive Methodists and Salvationists scored high on all except their strong working-classness. The larger Nonconformist bodies all had intermediate levels of female preponderance, and also had intermediate scores on the four predictors. Also with an intermediate level of female preponderance were the Brethren, though here the predictors show a balance of extremes. The Brethren scored high on sectarianism and low on clericalism. But unlike the Primitive Methodists or Quakers, whom they resembled in certain other respects, they also made sharp distinctions between the roles of men and women in the church.

Returning to the patterns of Jewish synagogue attendance, the relationship between male and female Jewish religiosity in this period has been discussed by Rickie Burman in a paper on the Manchester 'ghetto' in the early years of this century,[59] and by Marion Kaplan in various articles about middle-class German Jews. The pattern described by Burman seems to be equally applicable to London (or, indeed, New York).[60] She argued that the religious role of women, which had been relatively peripheral in the *shtetl*, became increasingly important in Manchester immigrant communities, and central in the second generation of Manchester Jews. This was because of the reduced role in Jewish life of the synagogue, which had belonged mainly to the male sphere, and the increasing importance of household observances, which were a mainly female responsibility. In Manchester around 1900 the male sphere of public religiosity was under pressure, both because of the need to work on the Sabbath, and because businessmen were replacing scholars as the role models that Jewish parents presented to their children: fathers who spent too much time at prayer were increasingly seen as failing in their duties to their family. Women also gave up the practice of wearing wigs, and more slowly gave up ritual bathing. But most of those religious practices which did continue fell within the female sphere: for instance, the Sabbath evening meal, the maintenance of a kosher kitchen, and ensuring that boys received a religious education. (By 1980, in one London suburb, 10 per cent of Jewish adults attended synagogue regularly, but 70 per cent of households lit candles on the Sabbath eve.)

While religious conflict was endemic in Jewish immigrant communities in this period, and spouses frequently found themselves at odds, there does not seem to have been a stereotyped pattern of male/female division of the kind found in some other working-class communities at this time. Weinberg's account of family relationships among Jewish immigrants in New York would suggest that where one partner was leading a flamboyant revolt against Orthodoxy, it was most likely to be the husband, influenced either by political idealism or by a desire to keep up with his more 'Americanized' colleagues at work. On the other hand, wives were sometimes undermining the Orthodoxy of the household in more subtle ways, either because of their preoccupation with scraping together a living, which the scholarly concerns of their hubands did not seem to be assisting, or else because of the desire to keep the peace with provocatively 'American' children.[61] There were also many households where spouses shared the same ideals.

Marion Kaplan's analysis of the role of religion in middle-class German Jewish families in the later nineteenth century suggests patterns that were closer to those of middle-class German Protestantism than those of the 'ghettos' of London or New York—or of Berlin's own miniature 'ghetto' in the Scheunenviertel. Here, too, the celebration of the Sabbath and of holidays at home and the maintenance of the kosher kitchen (where this continued) were all the responsibility of women. But Kaplan also stresses the crucial part played by mothers in the transmission of Judaism to the next generation, and the tendency for women to retain some kind of faith at a time when many middle-class men were losing all interest in religion. The importance of the religious role of women was further enhanced by the fact that the role of men had in many cases shrunk to vanishing-point.[62]

In London, where churchgoing by middle-class men was much higher than in German cities, synagogue attendance by middle-class men also seems to have remained relatively high. At the same time the growing importance of women's religious role was reflected in increasing attendance by women at synagogue. The London statistics show striking differences between the immigrant areas of the East End, where the majority of Jews lived, and the wealthy districts of northwest London, or the more middle-class districts in northeast London.[63] Over the whole of London, the proportion of women among adult participants in Jewish services was 22 per cent. However, in the borough of Stepney it was only 12 per cent, and in the City, where the historic Great Synagogue seems to have attracted a mainly immigrant congregation, it was 16 per cent.[64] On the other hand, it was 26 per cent in the northeastern borough of Hackney, which provided the first step out of the East End for more prosperous immigrants; in the northwestern boroughs of Paddington, St Marylebone and Hampstead it was 40 per cent; and it was 43 per cent in Islington, with its more distinctly middle-class Jewish community. It seems, therefore, that the very sharp sexual division of labour in religious matters that characterized Jewish immigrant communities was an inheritance from eastern Europe; in London it was gradually eroded, as a result both of changing conditions and, in the case of the economically successful, of English Christian influences.

V

In Berlin the Protestant *Landeskirche* published extensive statistics of religious practice. These showed that in the later nineteenth and early twentieth centuries, the proportion of communicants who were women hovered around two-thirds.[65] A survey of attendance at morning service in 1913 showed that women also made up about two-thirds of the congregations counted—though women may have made up a higher proportion of the total churchgoing population, as there are some indications that (as in London) evening congregations were more strongly female than those in the morning.[66] The disproportion between female and male churchgoers thus appears to have been slightly greater in Berlin Protestantism than in London Anglicanism, and considerably greater than in London Nonconformity.

Unfortunately, I have not been able to obtain relevant information about the Ro-man Catholics or free churches in Berlin.

Berlin, like London, had its religious organizations for women and those for men, and as in London, those for women tended to be more flourishing. Certainly, organizations for working-class men were relatively weak: the Evangelical Workers' Associations, with only sixteen branches and twelve hundred members in Greater Berlin in 1905, were much weaker than in some other parts of Germany, notably Westphalia and the Rhineland.[67] On the other hand, most parishes had an organization for young men (*Jünglingsverein*), and associations of supporters of the two main church parties, the Liberals and Positives, which were generally all-male, but occasionally had a special branch for women. Organizations for women multiplied: every parish had at least one, and many parishes had several. It was normal to have at least a *Frauenverein*, together with a *Jungfrauenverein* for young women; many parishes also had an organization for old women, and others specifically for mothers or for single women; Gethsemane parish had an organization for the daughters of men working at the Schultheiss brewery, and the Kaiser Friedrich Memorial Church had a *Damenverein*, which presumably reflected the higher status of its members. Many parishes simply had several *Frauenvereine*, the distinctions between them not always being evident.[68] The vitality of church organizations for women was reflected not only in their number, but in their ability to arise and to flourish, without being dependent on the impetus provided by one of the clergy.

As an example, Capernaum parish in Wedding, which was founded in 1903 in an area inhabited mainly by skilled workers and their families, has exceptionally good records, including minute-books of three parish organizations, one of which was exclusively female, and two of which were exclusively male. The women's organization was the *Frauenhilfsverein*. In many Berlin parishes the women's organizations were the longest-lived and enjoyed a certain degree of autonomy. They offered women their own sphere of power and responsibility, and they had their own alternative hierarchy. The *Frauenhilfsverein* at Capernaum was true to form in both respects, as it was founded in 1902 (shortly before the foundation of the parish) and remained active at least until 1936; it was also too independent for the pastor, who in 1919 founded a rival women's group, with himself as chairman. The main purpose of the *Frauenhilfsverein* was to care for the sick and poor of the parish. In 1908 it helped 134 families, usually by making garments to give them. Like the other parish organizations it was working in an area generally regarded as appropriate to the age and sex of its members: caring for those in distress was seen as a particularly appropriate concern for women—and when in 1908 the founder chairwoman of the society died, the eulogy by one of her colleagues stressed her compassion, love of neighbour and love of peace. The members also engaged in a good deal of socializing, especially in summer, when Sunday afternoon trips 'to admire the beauties of nature' were a frequent event. The leaders of *Frauenvereine* seem to have been mainly middle-class, and it is not clear how far the membership embraced a wider social range. An enthusiastic account by a city missionary of a similar women's group in another Wedding parish in 1900 suggested that the fifty members were socially very mixed, but I have not seen any other evidence.[69]

Of the other two parish organizations, the Men's and Young Men's Club was by definition all-male, and the Liberal Parochial Society seems in practice to have been so in the pre-1914 period, though it is likely that with the enfranchisement of women, by church as well as state, in 1919, women were admitted to organizations of this kind. The principal concern of the Liberal society, as with its conservative counterpart, was church politics, and politics, whether ecclesiastical or secular, belonged to the male sphere.[70] Not only could women not vote in Imperial Germany: until 1908 they were even legally prohibited from joining political organizations (though Social Democratic women found ways around the ban). While members of the society had a more general interest in questions of religious doctrine, their main purpose was to draw up lists of Liberal candidates for the thrice-yearly church elections, to campaign on their behalf, and possibly to call 'foul' if the rival party won. Berlin church elections were ruthless affairs and irregularities were frequently alleged.[71] The peace-loving qualities that were so much admired in the chairwoman of the *Frauenhilfsverein* would not have been much appreciated if exhibited by the chairman of one of these church-political societies. In the early twentieth century there were a number of *causes célèbres* in which Liberal pastors were dismissed or disciplined for allegedly heretical teaching: the Liberals felt that they were fighting for their ecclesiastical lives, and the conservatives argued that true Christianity would be lost if the Liberals were allowed to advance any further.[72] While most working-class male church members were eligible to take part in church elections, in practice relatively few did so, and the society was mainly an organization of middle-class men—out of twenty-four founder members, only one was a manual worker.[73]

The men's and young men's group—which was in practice a young men's group, since the great majority of members were teenagers—was a very different matter. The membership comprised a cross-section of the local teenage male population, including labourers, apprentices, and workers in shops and offices, with the latter probably slightly over-represented (out of sixty-six members from the years 1902–7 whose professions were listed, sixteen were in white-collar jobs). The club offered a mixture of Bible study, discussions, sport, singing, drama and hiking. By 1908, activities were taking place five nights a week. In 1913 it had fifty members, of whom thirty were said to be active, and the latter were the pride and joy of the parish helper, who ran the group in conjunction with an elected conmmittee. So the membership was enthusiastic, but it was small—which seems to have been the usual story so far as male religious activities in Berlin were concerned.[74]

Differences between male and female religiosity seem already to have been fairly marked at the age of confirmation, which was fourteen. According to one Berlin clergyman, writing in 1880, it was a popular saying that 'All the girls enthuse about their preacher'. And he in turn enthused about the girls in his confirmation class:

They have always become more faithful, more eager and warmer in the love of the Lord. With feminine tenderness they have used their talents and multiplied them a hundredfold. After the very trying boys' classes, it was like a breath of fresh air to experience the faithful application and the undiminshed tenderness and receptivity with which the girls of all social classes listen to the word of grace and truth. If every soul that burns with the love of faith works a magic all around it, that is exactly what the pure maidenly heart does which says 'Look, I am the Lord's handmaiden'.[75]

Similar points were made (in considerably less florid language) by Günther Dehn in the 1920s: girls were more likely than boys to have enjoyed religious education at school; they were more likely to have had a good relationship with the pastor during confirmation instruction; and they were more likely to be religious believers. In keeping with Dehn's mainly critical tone, and his mission to shatter the complacency of his clerical colleagues, he explained the difference mainly in negative terms: the girls were less likely to be interested in politics, and politics was one of the main sources of religious alienation; and they were more likely to hanker after the petit bourgeois respectability with which belonging to the church was associated.[76]

A south London youth worker, Alexander Paterson, summed up the attitude to organized religion of working-class boys as one of detachment: 'The boy is not naturally reflective. . . . He might see a church in every other street and a parson on every third doorstep, and yet never ask himself very pointedly what all this religion is about, and whether he could have any use for it. He is rarely or never hostile. . . but his point of view is normally that of a friendly looker-on.'

In terms rather similar to those used by Charles Booth in describing the religious outlook of working men in Hackney, Paterson saw the problem as being mainly one of lifestyle: active Christians were seen as self-improvers, who got ahead by a combination of hard work and puritanism. Most working-class youths respected such a way of life, but did not feel it was for them.[77]

A survey carried out around 1900 on the Upper West Side of Manhattan, an area with a predominantly Protestant and American-born population, traced the growing gap between male and female churchgoing. Between the ages of eight and thirteen the figures were almost identical: 51 per cent of girls and 50 per cent of boys were said to attend church. A narrow gap opened up at fourteen or fifteen, around the time when the majority of children left school. At this age, 51 per cent of girls and 45 per cent of boys were reported to be churchgoers. For both sexes there was a drop between the ages of sixteen and twenty-one, but the gap widened further: the rate fell to 38 per cent for girls and 30 per cent for boys. Thereafter the rate for women was more or less stable, whereas that for men continued to fluctuate. For unmarried women in their twenties the rate was still 38 per cent, but for unmarried men in their twenties it fell further to 26 per cent. Then for married women it rose to 39 per cent and for married men to 33 per cent.[78]

Zion Lutheran Church on Manhattan's Upper East Side provides even more detailed indications of the fluctuations in female religious practice (see table 17). The most important point to emerge is that the fluctuations were not very large. There were no very dramatic differences between young and old, married and unmarried. The second point, however, is that women who were in employment

TABLE 17

Women Communicants at Zion Lutheran Church, Yorkville, Easter 1910

In 217 households which included communicants the proportion of women in various categories who were communicants was:

	N=	COMMUNICANTS (PER CENT)
All females aged 14+	325	59.7
Single 14–19	89	67.4
Single 20+	61	54.1
Married with children under 10	42	64.3
Married without children under 10	85	52.9
Widows	48	60.4
Manual workers	67	65.7
White-collar workers	50	72.0

SOURCE: as in Table 9.

were more likely to be communicants than those who gave their occupation as 'keeping house' or 'at home'. One reason for this probably was that they were more independent of the men in their households, and thus less likely to be prevented from churchgoing by demands for meals or by anticlerical prejudice.

For some teenage girls, part of the attraction of the church may have lain in the fact that it offered an escape from home in a form to which even the most protective parents would have found it hard to object. A Bethnal Green woman remembers as a teenager regularly going to St James the Less Church with a gang of her old school friends.[79] And Orsi, describing the parish organization for young women in East Harlem, notes that 'the church was one of the few places where they could socialize and enjoy themselves away from parental scrutiny'.[80] In New York, young women's sodalities were responsible for 'Island Work', which meant visiting the Catholic inmates of the various city institutions on Blackwell's Island in the East River. Even today, after several changes of name, and major improvements in communications with Manhattan, 'The Island' has a somewhat remote feel. One can still sense some of the excitement with which respectable Catholic girls from across the water in Yorkville landed on its shores in the hope of bringing friendship and spiritual sustenance to the outcast inmates.[81]

While the patterns of male and female religiosity were in some respects fairly similar in London and Berlin, religious differences were more often a source of tension between men and women in the latter city. A Berlin city missionary commented in the 1870s that couples were often deeply divided on the question of whether their children should be baptized. While the husband was opposed to baptism, the wife would be 'deeply moved' when the missionary explained 'the blessing of baptism' and prayed for the child.[82] A pastor noted in 1880 the problems that sometimes arose when a believing woman married a godless man. Intending brides sometimes asked for his advice in such situations. If the man was an aggressive unbeliever, the pastor usually advised the woman against marrying him. But there were many cases where the man's unbelief was fairly superficial, or where he was ready to respect his wife's beliefs—in such cases 'the unbelieving husband is sanctified through the believing wife'.[83]

One such case was described by a city missionary in Wedding in 1900. A woman from Silesia was being maltreated by her drunken husband, who was a waiter. Since moving to Berlin, she had become estranged from the church, but under the influence of a missionary, she started attending a Bible class and sending her children to Sunday school. Soon after this the family went through a bad patch. The husband was ill, and the wife had to support the family, but then she lost her job: 'He ridicules her as she comes from the Bible class: "What good has praying done you? Have you found something to eat?" etc. But she takes no notice. "I had to put the four children to bed hungry," she recalled, "but I still prayed with them."' The story had a happy ending. She found work, and her husband's health improved. Gradually his attitude changed. He gave up his job as a waiter, and found work in the Humboldtshain park, and he also started attending the Bible class. The woman claimed that she owed the city mission 'the saving of her soul, the peace of the house and a happy family life'.

However, the story often ended less happily, and religious differences continued to plague many marriages. For instance, in 1886 a missionary reported that a woman who went to his Bible class, and whose son travelled some distance to Sunday school, 'was covered in scorn and ridicule by her husband because of her piety', and he added that 'this complaint is unfortunately not uncommon'.[84] The movement of mass resignation from the churches in the early twentieth century could also be a cause of domestic disharmony, as a significant proportion of those men who wanted to join faced resistance from their wives. Here, as elsewhere in Germany in this period, we have accounts of wives taking the baby secretly to the church to be baptized, in order to escape reprisals from their husbands.[85]

The extent of this religious divide between women and men must not be exaggerated. For instance, as was mentioned earlier, when husbands left the church, in most cases their wives left too. Similarly, while churchgoing by women was higher than that for men, it was still low, and by the early twentieth century the Social Democrats were having some success in appealing to women. So there were many working-class marriages where husband and wife shared the same political goals. It remains true, however, that there was a significant minority of working-class marriages where the partners had completely opposing standpoints on religion, and this sitution seems to have been much more frequent in Berlin that it was in London.

In France, as in some other Catholic countries, male jealousy of the priest, and his alleged misuse of the confessional, added richly to the repertoire of accusations that jealous husbands could level at their wives.[86] I have not seen any evidence that German Protestant clergy were subject to sexual accusations. The essence of the problem in Berlin was political. Hostility to the clergy derived mainly from the belief that they were tools of political reaction, and religiously minded wives were opposed by their husbands because they were thought to be weakening the Socialist cause. London clergymen were quite often accused of being snobs

TABLE 18

Women as a Percentage of Adults Attending Services of Various Denominations in Manhattan Borough, 1902

Roman Catholic	72.8
Christian Science	67.8
Episcopalian	66.4
Lutheran	59.3
Reformed	59.0
Disciples of Christ	58.7
Baptist	58.0
Presbyterian	57.9
Methodist Episcopal	55.0
Congregationalist	44.4

SOURCE: *New York Times*, 24 Nov. 1902

or of being too much attached to good eating and drinking, and in such accusations husband and wife could join together. But by the end of the nineteenth century outspokenly conservative clergymen were much less numerous in working-class areas of London than in equivalent districts of Berlin, and both the Anglican and the Nonconformist clergy in such areas included a significant element of radicals and socialists. Though there were tensions between working-class radicals and the churches in London too, the obsessive 'Le cléricalisme—voilà l'ennemi' form of politically based anticlericalism that was widespread both among French Catholics and German Protestants made little sense in the pluralistic London environment, with its many different clergies, each with a different mix of political loyalties.

VI

In New York, a religious census in 1902 showed that 69 per cent of Manhattan worshippers were women—which was significantly higher than in London, though nothing like the proportion in some parts of France.[87] In fact the proportion of Protestant churchgoers who were women (60 per cent) was little different from the figure in London. The difference was caused by the fact that Catholicism predominated in New York, and that the percentage of women among Catholic churchgoers in Manhattan (73 per cent) was somewhat higher than the figure for London Catholics (see table 18).

There seems to have been operating among Catholic New Yorkers a more pronounced sexual divison of labour in religious matters, such as that which I have noted in London. The most extreme form of this division of labour was found among the New York Italians, who, at the beginning of this century, comprised around a fifth of the city's Catholics.[88] About 97 per cent of New York Italians claimed to be Catholics, but in the early twentieth century levels of formal Catholic practice were low. This led to misunderstandings in many quarters. On the part of many Protestants it led to hopes that the Italians were ripe for conversion: as a result, evangelical missions were set up in areas like East Harlem and Little Italy, but with very meagre results. Both radicals and red-baiters believed that socialism, anarchism and anticlericalism were rife among Italian immigrants; this was one reason why the latter were looked upon with some suspicion by the immigration authorities and by some politicians. Yet the radical element in the Italian community was small, and indeed smaller than in a number of other immigrant groups. The heavily Irish Catholic hierarchy regarded the Italians as bad Catholics and frequently referred to what was called 'The Italian Problem'.[89]

Yet very few Italian New Yorkers left the church, and on certain select days in the year, areas like East Harlem gave the impression of a community united by a common and fervent Catholic faith. It was indeed a form of Catholicism that the Irish church authorities and those influenced by them did not accept as worthy of the name, and the separation of male and female forms of religiosity was an essential part of it. The sphere of male religious responsibility related to the community; that of female responsibility related to the home. Competition and tension among ethnic groups were endemic in early twentieth-century New York, and even when relations were more peaceful, there were few areas of life that did not have a significant ethnic dimension. Defining and defending the ethnic community was thus a matter of considerable importance, and religion was often closely bound up with it.

So far as the Italians were concerned, the saints had a crucial role here. Most Italian saints began their life in New York by being associated with immigrants from a particular town or village; but some went on to win the devotion of the whole Italian community in a particular section of the city. For instance, men from Polla who had settled in East Harlem formed a burial society on 1881 with Our Lady of Mount Carmel as patroness, and in 1882 they organized a *festa* in her honour. With the building of the church of that name in 1884, and the purchase by the pastor of the statue of the Virgin, the cult passed out of the control of its original sponsors, and it soon won general support among Italians living in that part of the city. This pattern of development was typical, though in a number of instances there are signs of conflict between the committees of immigrant men who had pioneered the public devotions in honour of a particular saint and the clergy who felt that the time had come for them to take control. For instance, in 1899 it was reported that one mutual benefit society preferred to have the statue of their patron in a saloon, where they could keep their eyes on it, rather than in the church.[90]

Immigrant men also formed committees to press for the formation of an Italian national parish in their neighbourhood, free from tutelage to an Irish pastor. It was an important matter of national pride to have a parish dedicated to an Italian saint and staffed by Italian clergy. But feelings toward the clergy themselves were ambivalent. Italian priests did not have a role as community leaders or symbols of ethnic identity in any way comparable to that of their Irish colleagues. They were frequently involved in disputes with their male parishioners over money: running a Catholic parish was an expensive business, and the clergy were handicapped by both the poverty of the Italian immigrant community, and the lack of any tradition of regular giving to the church. The clergy were also to some extent victims of the widespread feeling among Italian immigrants that any display of overt piety was inappropriate in a man: nuns thus enjoyed a general respect and acceptance that priests did not.[91] Interviews with elderly Italian-born New York men frequently reflect ambivalent feelings toward the church and the clergy—but an ambivalence that was seldom openly stated. If pressed to do so they would speak in such cryptic tones that very little would be revealed. Thus a Sicilian-born Williamsburg factory worker recalled that he had refused to confess before his wedding: 'I'm not too friendly with the churches. I'm a Catholic. I mean, don't get me wrong. But I've. . . I don't see eye to eye in certain things with the church.'[92]

In this tight-lipped culture, religious belief was a private matter, not suitable for public discussion, and pronounced piety or militant irreligion would both have seemed in poor taste. But the worker's wife was 'the religious one', and he does not seem to have done anything to discourage her from bringing up their children as Catholics. A Neapolitan, who had variously worked as a barber, elevator man and insurance agent in New York, stated that he did not like priests 'for the simple reason that they used to criticize all the Protestants'. If it had been left to him, their children would not have received any religious upbringing; but his wife was a 'fanatic', and their son became an altar boy.[93]

Likewise, a militant trade unionist, who was extremely hostile to the church because of its opposition to a strike that he had organized, nonetheless never openly stated his anti-religious views, because 'Religion is a very sensitive issue. To mention religion doesn't pay.'[94]

Attendance at the church's regular weekly services tended to be largely a matter for the women, both because of these tensions between the immigrant male and the clergy, and because going to mass every week seemed to smack of the overt piety that was acceptable, even admired in women, but suspect in men. Women also took responsibility for devotions practised in the home. They stuck up pictures of the saints or of the Sacred Heart, and burned candles before statues of the Virgin. They took charge of the religious upbringing of children and of matters relating to baptisms and weddings.

The one occasion when the male and female spheres substantially overlapped was the annual festival of the local saint.[95] Both women and men participated in large numbers, though roles were still differentiated. Men and women processed in separate groups. Men, with suitably solemn and impassive expressions, carried the statue of the saint, and marched at the front as guests of honour, or in the middle as representatives of Italian regional societies; but the most dramatic role, that of penitent, was largely filled by women, walking barefoot, or crawling on hands and knees, and giving free rein to the expression of the agonies and ecstasies associated with the openly emotional religiosity deemed appropriate to their sex. On these occasions the presiding figure was the saint, and a large part of the organizing was undertaken by committees of laymen, so that the clergy were to some degree marginalized. Male jealousy was thus less of a factor than on ordinary Sundays, when the priests unequivocally took the leading role.

Among the Irish in New York, contrasts between male and female religiosity were less dramatic. Certainly, women attended mass in greater numbers than men, and were more often known for conspicuous piety. It became something of a cliché for those Irish New Yorkers who had achieved distinction in disreputable ways to look back to a childhood home ruled by a saintly mother;[96] quite frequently her influence was ultimately undermined by a less pious father or uncle.[97] Yet there was also quite a strong tradition of male piety among Irish New Yorkers. It found expression in, for instance, the flourishing Holy Name societies that were attached not only to Catholic parishes, but to such Irish strongholds as the New York police. Sport and religion were also effectively mixed by some New York parishes in this period, in the same way that they were in London.[98] In the early twentieth century prowess at basketball was a useful asset for a young priest, and parish magazines devoted increasing space to results in the inter-parish league. In fact Catholicism was so much bound up with ideas of respectability, decency, etc., among the New York Irish that anyone who aspired to a position of public prominence as a politician, businessmen, doctor or trade union leader could find it helpful to be 'seen at mass'.[99] So the fact that such public roles were monopolized by men also meant that men were likely to be conspicuous in the main church services—even if they did not attend early morning masses or special devotions.

Nonetheless, while Catholic piety was an integral part of the prevailing ideal of Irish-American womanhood,[100] the church had some powerful competitors for the allegiance of the men. In particular, New York's numerous saloons were focal points of an alternative Irish-American culture, coexisting rather uneasily with the culture supported by the church. The church, with its aspirations to monopolize the public leisure of the faithful, would have been suspicious of any institution, however worthy, that took up so much of their time. But, in practice, the saloon often nurtured norms of conduct sharply at odds with those inculcated by the church, ranging from easygoing, broadly tolerant good fellowship to gambling, illicit sex and theft.[101] There were thus quite sharp cultural divisions among Irish Catholic men. As the Paulist fathers put it, after their mission to St Agnes' parish on the Middle East Side in 1889: 'The young men of the parish were clearly divided into two classes, a good one and a bad one. In the former, we found intelligence, regularity in attending to religious duties, and the many advantages derived from the sodalities of the parish. In the latter, tepidity, laxness, and the many evils resulting from neglect of the Holy Sacraments.'[102]

However, the depth of this divide should not be exaggerated. After all, many saloon-keepers were generous benefactors of Catholic parishes. They had a foot in each camp, and the same certainly applied to many of their customers. This tension is illustrated by the Casey and Finnegan stories transcribed by members of the Federal Writers' Project in the 1930s as part of a collection of jokes prevalent within the city's various ethnic communities.[103] In one of the stories, Casey and Finnegan spend Saturday night visiting just about every gin mill between the Battery and the Bronx, and around six o'clock they run into some people going to mass. Casey thinks they should join them, so that they can go home to sleep with a clear conscience, but Finnegan would rather go home and attend mass after they have had a sleep. Eventually Casey persuades Finnegan to go in, but on the understanding that he will wake Finnegan if he falls asleep. He does indeed fall asleep several times, and each time Casey wakens him. But when the sermon gets going, Finnegan falls asleep definitively, marking each of the priest's rhetorical flourishes with a loud snore. Finally the priest turns on Casey and yells, 'Wake that man up', to which Casey replies, 'Wake him yourself: you sent him to sleep.'

A first point to note is that Casey and Finnegan have been enjoying an extended evening of male freedom. No doubt, Mrs Casey and Mrs Finnegan are at home with the children, but they play no part in the story. Their job is to have a good breakfast ready for their husbands when they return home, but not to spoil their well-earned relaxation. By contrast, the kind of Catholic husband who was commended in sermons spent his Saturday evenings either at home with his family or out at a sodality.[104] So Casey and Finnegan were far from being model Catholics, as most priests understood the term. On the other hand, model or not, they are definitely Catholics, and they recognize their obligation to go to mass. Maybe if they had not stumbled across a church, they would have forgotten, but when they see a church, they know what their duty is. But then, on the other hand, that does not mean that they intend to sit back meekly and do what the priest tells them: priests are very holy men, but they are apt to get a bit full of their own importance, and it does no harm to take them down a peg or two occasionally.

In 1905 an article in a New York parish magazine, discussing the differences between male and female nature, referred to 'the devout female sex'.[105] This was in tune with a long tradition of American writing, Protestant as much as Catholic, on the greater religiosity of women than of men, which historians have traced back to New England in the later seventeenth century.[106] Yet it seems to me that such claims are only appropriate where, as in parts of Germany or France, we have evidence of antagonism in religious matters between the two sexes. In Italian New York we have two contrasted and complementary forms of religiosity, the more intense female form coexisting with, and indeed partly dependent on, its more restrained male counterpart. In working-class London, where the separation was in any case less complete, the male and female forms of religiosity also coexist with little apparent conflict. What we seem to have here is a single view of the place of religion in the world, but with different roles in its maintenance and practice allotted to the two sexes, rather than the collision of rival world-views that sometimes took place in Berlin.

CHAPTER 8

Religion in a Half-Secular Society

BERLIN IN THE 1920s was regarded by contemporaries as a very secular place. And within the city most people would probably have picked out such working-class boroughs as Wedding, Neukölln and Friedrichshain as the most secularized areas. Indeed, Wedding and Neukölln were the main strongholds of a new institution that symbolized Berlin's reputation for irreligion—the secular school, attended by those children who were not required to receive religious instruction, because their parents had left the church.[1] Instead of religious instruction, these schools had lessons in *Lebenskunde* (learning about life). Nor were the schools merely religiously neutral: most of the children received a form of secular confirmation, the *Jugendweihe*, which was explicitly provided as an alternative to the religious confirmation received by most adolescents at church. The *Jugendweihe* was originally devised by the humanist Free Parishes; but by the 1920s, there were also Social Democratic and Communist schemes of instruction.

The clergy took the challenge of secularism very seriously, though their analysis of its causes and possible remedies varied according to their own political and theological orientation. Conservative clergy were inclined to blame 'agitators', the secularizing policies of Social Democratic politicians, and criticism of the church by Liberal and Jewish journalists. Ideas of this sort were a major factor in the support that many Protestant pastors in Berlin gave, at least initially, to the German Christian movement and the Nazi Party.[2] On the other hand, Socialist pastors, like Paul Piechowski and Günther Dehn, tended to criticize the church for failing to respond to working-class needs, and Piechowski wrote a book in which he argued that the workers were converts to a new faith, with which Christians had got to come to terms.[3]

However, it may be that the religious situation in Weimar Berlin was more complex than it appeared on the surface. This, at any rate, is argued in a thesis by Jörg Kniffka in which he analyses the role of Protestantism in the east Berlin

175

borough of Friedrichshain. The picture that emerges is this: while a small minority of working-class Protestants were strongly committed church members (usually attending the services of one of the free churches or religious associations, rather than the *Landeskirche*), and a rather larger minority were convinced atheists, the majority had a less consistent relationship with religion and the churches. They remained members of the Protestant church, and thus paid their church taxes if their income warranted it; they baptized their children, had them confirmed and sent them to a school where religious instruction was provided, and often sent them to children's services at church; they gave their close relatives religious funerals. They were very unlikely to attend the main church services, which were widely regarded as an exclusively middle-class affair, but some working-class men and many working-class women attended other kinds of religious meeting, such as Bible classes, where the atmosphere was less formal, and there was much more social contact between participants. While tending to be critical of the clergy as a body, they were warmly appreciative of some individual clergy, especially those who appeared to be approachable and unpretentious, with a sense of humour and an ability to speak in simple and direct language. This was reflected in the fact that some clergy attracted much bigger confirmation classes than others, and that attendance at confirmation services and examinations also varied greatly—a refutation, in Kniffka's view, of the suggestion that parents and children saw participation in this rite as a purely routine matter. Kniffka also rejects the common view that east Berliners were indifferent to the church. On the contrary, he suggests, they had a high conception of what the church ought to be. They expected it to be, for instance, an active exponent of social equality and international peace and, at a more local level, ready to help individuals in a wide variety of crisis situations. Harsh criticism of the church often reflected not so much irreligion as disappointed expectations.[4]

Günther Dehn, who was a pastor in Moabit from 1911 to 1930, and wrote extensively on the religious outlook of working-class Berliners, made some of the same points. He, too, noted that 'The Confirmation Day is regarded by the people as a great and joyous festival, when even the poorest will put on something special. On such days, the church is still something like a popular power even in the working-class districts.' Dehn estimated that in the later 1920s, 88–90 per cent of teenagers were confirmed in Moabit, and 90–95 per cent of babies were baptized. Noting that only a very small proportion of children were sent to secular schools, he suggested that the majority of parents, even if they never went to church themselves, still believed that religion played a useful part in the upbringing of children. He also noted the predominantly friendly reception that he received on his visits to people's homes.[5]

These ambiguities in people's religious outlook were even more evident in the pre-war period. For instance, many of the points made by Dehn in the 1920s were made by Eugen Baumann, archdeacon of St Elizabeth parish from 1875 to 1882, who published a book in 1880 about pastoral work in Berlin. He stressed the importance of visits by the clergy, and how much these were appreciated by all but the most militant opponents of the church. When he went visiting, he was greeted most enthusiastically by the children. 'But adults, too, like it very much, when the time and place are right, to be spoken to by the clergyman, to give him their views, and to make him welcome in their own quarter of the city.' Baumann's assessment of the situation, though finely nuanced, was more optimistic than Dehn's. Writing at a time when the church appeared to be reviving after a long period of decline, he was very hopeful about the progress that might be made if the clergy went about it in the right way. He argued that 'a large part of the present estrangement between clergy and people is really the result of not knowing one another. That is why the home visit is such an exceptionally important element in the professional life of the Berlin clergyman.'[6]

Summing up, one could speak of a 'half-secular society', in which the social role of the churches was more restricted than in earlier times, and it was possible in principle to live one's life without any reference to religion, but where in practice the churches entered people's lives at many points, and few people had a wholly secular view of the world. Although London, New York and Berlin each had its own distinctive forms of religion and of secularity, the generalization can be applied to all three cities.

I

The ambiguities were particularly striking in predominantly Catholic cities, where vigorous anticlericalism and relatively low levels of formal religious practice often coincided with frequent recourse to supernatural aid and patterns of thought that distributed all areas of life into sacred and secular spheres. Herzfeld's study of working-class families on the West Side of Manhattan provides many examples of the pervasive influence of distinctively Catholic ways of thinking and behaving, even in areas where many people seldom went to church. The purpose of her volume was, in fact, to identify the distinguishing features of what was termed 'Tenement-House Man'. There is a tendency, therefore, to stress what is common to the families studied and to suggest a shared pattern of life. Time and again, though, there are hints that religion was a differentiating factor within this allegedly homogeneous culture. Here are some examples:

> In the Irish Catholic home the colored religious print is always found. . . . In every Catholic home there are crucifixes either of light wood, black ebony, enameled or white glass. There are frequently china figures representing the Virgin Mary and the Christ child, colored in bright reds and blues with golden halos.

> The Irish Catholic mother believes that praying over a sick child will cure it, and placing 'holy bones' on the body of a crippled child will make it whole.

> If the relative is dead, the Catholic will give his name [to a child] only if another is added for good luck.

There are also various references to beliefs and practices that are evidently distinctively Catholic, though this is not explicitly stated: for instance, the wearing of scapulars, or the claim that 'A child born in May is always lucky'. Equally revealing of the importance of religious identity are reports of anti-Catholic prejudice and of the ill-feeling caused by mixed marriages.[7]

In predominantly Protestant cities, there were fewer visible signs of people's religion, and so where churchgoing was low, it was easier to assume that simple indifference had taken its place. But appearances could be deceptive. As the references to Kniffka and Dehn have indicated, one of the areas in which secularization had made least progress was in the observance of the rites of passage. There were differences in the relative popularity of particular rites, which reflected differences in the meaning given to them both in particular cities and within particular religious traditions. The widest variations were in attitudes to the confirmation, bar mitzvah, or other equivalent rite of admission to full membership of the church. For instance, among German Protestants, confirmation marked the break between childhood and adolescence, much as the bar mitzvah did for the Jewish boy, and it thus had a festive importance that went beyond its religious significance.

The fact that there was a clearly established age for the Jewish boy's bar mitzvah and for the German Protestant child's confirmation (namely, thirteen and fourteen respectively), suggested that the relatively stable forces of social custom had a bigger influence than the much less predictable factor of individual religious conviction. A woman born in 1912 in Lichtenberg, a poor district in east Berlin, recalls some of the associated rituals, and her memories indicate how the specifically religious meaning was inseparably bound up with a more generalized desire for celebration. The pastor was 'very strict', and beat the boys 'because they had learnt nothing, but not us girls': 'About the confirmation itself he had already given us a sermon: There will be no bouquets, no veils! That was then the general custom—a little bouquet, then the veil and the hymn-book. But my mother said: You are taking a bouquet. And I had tea roses and got a veil. And what could we girls do? We had to wrap it all together in a handkerchief and hide it behind the hymn-book.' Dehn's enquiry in the 1920s into the religious views of Berlin youth suggested that confirmation was more popular than the *Jugendweihe*, because it was seen as more 'festive' (*feierlich*). Many of those questioned seemed to show little awareness of the differences in ideological content between the two forms of initiation into adulthood.[8]

The desire to celebrate also played a big part in the bar mitzvah. Rabbi Landesman, chronicler of the archetypally working-class Jewish district of Brownsville, recalls that these were 'joyous occasions in which the family, friends and neighbors joined'. For the socially mobile, the celebrations also provided a great opportunity for conspicuous display. In 1887, a sardonic critic of New York Jewish life commented on the 'enormous splendor and great show' and the 'wisdom-filled speeches' that characterized these events. And Sarna comments that the speeches seemed to contain as much about patriotism and being a good citizen as about the boy's new status as a full member of the religious community.[9]

In Berlin, Catholics generally took First Communion at fourteen—much to the regret of one priest, who saw this as a result of the 'Protestant spirit': in his view the Protestant confirmation was no more than a way of marking the termination of school.[10] The Catholic clergy hoped that by pushing forward the age of First Communion, they could turn it away from any association with a natural turning point in the child's life, and that they could thus establish habits of regular communion before the onset of adolescent rebellion. In doing this, they tried to stress the religious significance of the ceremony; on the other hand, it resembled the Lutheran confirmation in that it was a festive occasion, for which both the children and their parents dressed up, to which relatives and friends were invited, and which did not require any special degree of religious commitment on the part either of the child or of its parents.

For Anglicans, on the other hand, to be confirmed at all implied some degree of religious commitment; those who did so generally wished to stay on with the church after leaving Sunday school. Even further removed from Catholic or Lutheran practice were those Protestant churches with a free church tradition, such as the Methodists, Baptists and Congregationalists. Here the right to participate in communion depended on an experience of conversion followed by an application for church membership. Among the Baptists this was followed by a believer's baptism, the most memorable of all the rites of initiation into full membership—though, in view of Baptist disapproval of alcohol and of dressing up, the style of celebration was very different from a Catholic First Communion or a Lutheran confirmation. Among paedobaptist free churches, admission to church membership was a rather low-key affair. And in all of them, the strictness of criteria for admission to membership meant that many Baptists, Methodists, etc., went through their whole lives without taking part in communion.

The most widely practised of the rites of passage was the baptism of infants. Prussian bureaucracy provides the student of Berlin with a wealth of precise figures that are not available for the other cities. For instance, variations over time can be traced. The low point was the later 1870s, following the introduction of civil registration which, some people felt, obviated the need for any religious ceremony. As a city missionary reported in 1879: 'Many people regard the registration of the birth, together with the giving of a name, as a sufficient substitute for baptism. They refer to the May Laws, and say, "What's the need for a christening now?"'[11] However, there was a substantial revival of the baptismal ceremony in the 1880s and 1890s.[12]

In London, too, the later nineteenth and early twentieth centuries seem to be a peak period. Here, too, differences between religious traditions are important. The importance attached to infant baptism was greatest in Catholic cultures because of the traditional Catholic teaching that the unbaptized child who died in infancy would go to limbo. Consequently there was pressure on Catholic parents to have their children baptized within three days of birth. Failure to baptize one's child was regarded by Catholics as an act of extreme impiety, and there were few so indifferent or so resistant to the requirements of their church as to fail to comply. Herzfeld claimed that on the West Side of Manhattan babies were usually christened within a week of birth.[13]

Lutheran and Anglican views on infant baptism were a somewhat modified form of the Catholic attitude. The teaching of the clergy varied more widely than it did in Catholicism, because of the deep divisions between high, low and broad in Anglicanism, and between Pietists, orthodox Lutherans and liberals in the German Protestant churches.[14]

Some high Anglican clergy differed little from Roman Catholics in their teachings concerning baptism. Here from about 1890 in Edmonton, on the northern fringes of London, is an account by a woman whose parents were devout Christians, but did not belong to any church, of her experiences at an Anglican school:

> I got into trouble at school because the Vicar asked us if we had been christened. And of course Norah and I hadn't been christened. Because dad didn't believe in christening—he thought you should, you know, be christened when you knew what you were taking on. And this Vicar was terribly cross because we was at a church school, St Barnabas. And Norah got up and started screaming and rushed home 'cos he said we wouldn't go to heaven because we weren't christened.[15]

While not making such explicit threats as to the future of the unbaptized child, the pastor of St Sophia's in central Berlin strongly hinted that the consequences of such parental neglect might be dire. In 1905 he deplored the delays in the baptism of children, and noted that in the previous year fewer than one in ten had been baptized in their first month, 'as the good old Christian custom is'. Quoting various popular excuses, he was particularly scathing about those who mentioned the child's ill health. To this his reply was: 'then you had better not delay any longer.' The main reason for the frequent delays seems to have been that the christening was the occasion for a big celebration, and the parents were either saving up for it, or else waiting until they both felt strong enough to cope with the preparations. The pastor also encountered the view that early baptisms were 'no longer the custom', which perhaps reflected a feeling that such haste might reflect an exaggerated piety.[16]

Nonetheless, the overwhelming majority of parents did eventually have their children baptized, and it is clear that they regarded the matter in a less blasé fashion than might at first appear. The pastor referred to the fact that 'parents often reproach themselves bitterly after the event, when, through their own fault, the child dies without being baptized'. In 1880, another Berlin pastor reported that 'In summer, the number of emergency baptisms is large. Death knocks on the door of culpable negligence and causes terror. Post-haste they send for the clergyman. He must quickly—but immediately—make good what laziness has spoiled. They demand vehemently that, in spite of other urgent business, the emergency baptism should be carried out at once.'[17] Some of the anxieties associated with baptism are reflected in an encounter of a Berlin city missionary with an impoverished craftsman and his wife whose children included one who was four, but had not yet been baptized. 'Dear people,' declaimed the missionary, 'have you perhaps forgotten your God? Do you have him in your house or not? . . . For four years long you have left your child unbaptized, and yet things did not use to be as miserable for you as they are now. Make things go better in the future! . . .' The woman remained silent for some time. Finally she said: 'You are right. Every time I look at the child I feel uneasy.'[18] The missionary's anxiety, it would seem, was for the parents: they could not enjoy God's blessing if they wilfully ignored one of his ordinances. The parents' anxiety related to the child, whose life was surrounded with all kinds of dangers that the baptismal ceremony might help to keep at bay.

Thus the fears for the unbaptized child related not only to the future life, but also to the present life—such a child was likely to be unlucky. There were also a whole series of more specific beliefs relating various aspects of the baptismal ceremony to good or bad luck. A sick child could be cured through being baptized, and indeed so potent was the baptismal water that adults would sometimes try to procure some in order to relieve their own pains. On the other hand, if the ceremony were wrongly performed that meant bad luck: in particular, it was essential that it was a man who held the child at the time of the sprinkling of the water.[19] There was a more pragmatic side to all this: even parents who themselves saw little point in the ceremony feared that their children might be disadvantaged in some way if it were known that they were unbaptized. Indeed, the parents themselves might suffer disadvantages, such as the refusal of church charity.[20] Conversely, the small number of children whose parents had deliberately chosen not to have them baptized had a strong sense of their separate identity.[21]

The ceremony seems to have had a smaller hold on the popular imagination in London, and the proportion of children remaining unbaptized was probably slightly larger. Nonetheless, Bartlett's study of the strongly working-class riverside borough of Bermondsey suggests that the period 1880 to 1907 saw a substantial increase in the proportion of babies baptized in an Anglican church. The peak may have come as late as the 1920s. Bartlett associates this increase with increasing stabilization in the local community, as more and more Bermondsey people had lived for long periods, or indeed their whole life, in the borough, and in the process had formed links with local churches. One woman he interviewed attributed the large number of christenings to 'just rules and regulations'—which might seem an appropriate way of understanding a ceremony prescribed by a state church. Yet clearly the matter was not as routine as might appear. Bartlett has found that christenings were heavily concentrated on particular churches: rather than just going anywhere, parents went back to the church where they had been married, or they went to the historic parish church of the district, or for other more mysterious reasons they selected a particular church or parson, passing over others nearer to home. The same point was noted in 1858 by the rector of St Matthew's, Bethnal Green, where babies would be brought in from surrounding parishes, and there were often thirty or forty christenings on a Sunday:

The first incumbent, the Reverend Joseph Brown, was a very active and energetic man, and he rendered himself very popular among the poor by taking them out into the country on excursions, and I attribute the number in great measure to that circumstance; they have become attached to the church and it is a popular church for baptisms. In London there are churches popular for different things; this is for baptisms.

In keeping with the strong idea of locality that was typical of working-class Londoners, they often had a keen sense of the different characteristics of the various local churches. Gillian Rose, in her study of early twentieth-century Poplar, sees this in terms of the personalities of the various clergymen—churches were known as 'Lax's', 'Green's', and so on. But the vicar of St Philip's, Stepney, in his evidence to the parliamentary enquiry of 1858, suggested that the building itself may also have had a role: some of his parishioners would ask him to conduct their wedding, but wanted the ceremony to take place in St Dunstan's, 'because the prestige of the old mother church is so very strong; it is one of the most ancient churches in London'.[22]

In the various free church traditions, infant baptism had a relatively minor place, and of course there were some, such as the Baptists, Quakers and Salvationists, for whom it had no place at all.

In the extremely pluralistic atmosphere of New York, where there was no predominant religious tradition, customs varied according to ethnicity and religious background, and the baptismal ceremony did not have the normative character that it had in Berlin. A survey on the Upper West Side of Manhattan around 1900 reported that 62 per cent of those aged between sixteen and twenty-one had been baptized. Among the major nationalities, the proportion was highest for those with Irish mothers (85 per cent), and lowest for those with German mothers (51 per cent), those with American mothers being average (61 per cent). However, Herzfeld's study of the West Side suggests that many of the beliefs prevalent in Berlin were also widely held in New York. The child 'is not safe from harm' until it is baptized—the dangers apparently including both illness and death, and also trouble in the world to come, since an Irish-born wife whose child was born dead nonetheless baptized it, and prayed over its body. A multiplicity of beliefs and rituals surrounded the ceremony itself: the child might wear a family christening robe, but it must not be borrowed; before being taken to the church, the child must be carried through the house, and it must cry during the ceremony; and so on. The constant theme was luck: the infant was surrounded by dangers, and only with the aid of all the luck that was available would it survive them. Indeed, big question marks hung over the life ahead: in poor West Side families, the possibilities of accident, illness and sudden death were a permanent reality. Moreover, there was no reason to be confident about the way that the child would grow up: crime was a a major fact of New York life, and no matter how carefully children were brought up, a certain proportion would, for reasons that were often mysterious, go to the bad. The christening was a turning point in life, at which all available sources of supernatural aid were summoned on the child's behalf.[23]

The equivalent rite in the Jewish community was the circumcision of male infants. But, while baptism, as it was popularly understood, had an individualistic character—the emphasis being on the benefits of the ceremony to the child, and possibly to the parents too—the emphasis in circumcision was on entry into the Jewish community. Perhaps for this reason, those who had no religious faith, but still had a sense of Jewish identity, did not want their child to be considered a goy, and accordingly had him circumcised.[24]

In Berlin, unlike London or New York, there was a regular flow of Jewish converts to Christianity. For them baptism took on a role very similar to that of circumcision within Judaism, becoming the supreme symbolic moment that signalled the passage from one community to the other. The 'baptized Jew' was a characteristic figure of Berlin life throughout the period from the later eighteenth century to the mass deportations and murders perpetrated by the Nazis.[25] The cynicism with which both Jewish and Christian observers frequently regarded these conversions was reflected in the nickname given to the Kaiser Wilhelm Memorial Church, a frequent site for the baptism of the wealthier converts. This most ostentatious and fashionable of Berlin churches was known, with reference to the nearby department store, 'Das Kaufhaus des Westens' ('The Store in the West'), as 'Das Taufhaus des Westens' ('The House of Baptism in the West'), the implication being that the church too was a place for making purchases (in this case for buying social acceptability), and that a visit to the font might be as casual as a visit to the department store.[26]

Church weddings in Berlin dipped furthest in numbers during the 1870s, and they never fully recovered their popularity.[27] As Kniffka comments, with regard to the 1920s, they were seen as 'a beautiful, but overexpensive, duplication'.[28] The civil ceremony which, since 1875, had been legally required, was seen by many couples as sufficient. Dehn came to a similar conclusion: poorer couples were put off marrying in church by the cost of paying for the organist, the decorations, etc.[29] An oral historian, reporting one elderly woman's account of her wedding in the early days of the century, noted that she 'dispensed with a church wedding in order to save (in her estimate) fifty to sixty marks. Like so many other working-class women she believed that the church ceremony would require her to have a bridal gown, a bridal carriage and other luxuries she could not afford'.[30] So the type of wedding became to quite a large degree a matter of social class. In London and New York the duplication argument did not apply, as a religious wedding was a legally acceptable alternative to the civil ceremony. In London certainly, and probably in New York too, the great majority of couples did choose a church wedding—though in London the proportion of civil ceremonies steadily grew, rising from 5 per cent in 1874 to 14 per cent in 1894 and 27 per cent in 1913.[31] It is difficult to detect any clear pattern to this increase. In some districts civil weddings were more often chosen by working-class couples, and in some by middle-class couples; in the 1880s the highest proportion of religious ceremonies was in the ultra-proletarian district of Bethnal Green, but the highest proportion of civil ceremonies was in another mainly working-class district, Woolwich, notable for its arsenal and barracks. Bethnal Green had the largest proportion of

London-born in its population of any metropolitan district, and the very high proportion of religious weddings may be because the great majority of Bethnal Green families had lived in London long enough to have formed some kind of link with one or more local church.[32]

Whether solemnized by priest or by registrar, working-class weddings were, in the opinion of many observers, frequently hurried and rather casual affairs. Here is a characteristic comment in a book published in 1911, which described life in a poor district of south London: 'The ceremony of marriage has curiously little emphasis set upon it by custom in these parts. A funeral demands special clothes and carriages, very considerable expense, and to attend such an event second cousins will take a day off work, and think it but dutifully spent. Yet a marriage is by comparison almost unnoticed.' Few people attended the ceremony, except for 'a small circle of lady friends', though afterwards they would adjourn to a nearby pub, and more friends would turn up. At Christmas and Easter many churches had so many weddings that the service would be shortened and the couples married in batches.[33]

In contrast with this view through the eyes of a middle-class observer, a story published in New York in 1886 described a working-class wedding from the point of view of the participants. The story comes from the *Klein-Deutschland* collection, which recorded scenes from everyday life on the German Lower East Side. It tells how a laundress named Emma married a porter called John in her sister's tenement flat. At first John, who 'was a bit of a freethinker', suggested marrying at City Hall, and using the money saved on a trip to the theatre. But Emma was not very keen on the idea, and her sister quashed it with the words: 'You shall not be disgraced on your day of honour, my child. What's the Mayor got to do with your wedding? No, you will be married here in my house, and by a pastor, as is fitting for Christian people, and that's enough of that.' On the day of the wedding, the guests arrived at the bride's sister's flat, and immediately separated into male and female sections. At the very moment arranged, the 'Herr Pastor' arrived, greeting everyone with 'an unctuous "Good evening to you all"'. After taking off his overcoat, 'this very conscientious man of business in the service of God got ready the pen which he always had with him on his visits to customers, so that he could ensure that the prescribed entries were made in the register'. The ceremony began with the pastor 'repeating mechanically one of the little talks that he had learnt by heart many years before'. When he finally asked the couple to make their promises, the bride's sister started sobbing, 'which was the signal to the other ladies that they should take out their handkerchiefs'. But, soon after, 'the priest's "Amen" lifted the spell of earnestness that had fallen on all present'. The pastor was invited in a friendly way to stay on, but replied in an equally friendly way that he could not. He gave the bride her certificate; the bridegroom paid the pastor his fee; and with 'the obligatory "Good Night to you all"', the pastor was gone. Only then did the main business of the evening get under way— an enormous meal, with singing of German songs.[34]

The picture which the wedding story suggests is that of the pastor as an important and respected official, but one with whom an intimate relationship is hardly expected. He is kept busy performing weddings and similar rites because of the prevailing ideas concerning the proper way of doing things. But the specifically religious dimension of his duties is not highlighted in the story—for instance, the chief symbol of his office appears to be his pen, rather than the Bible that he presumably also had with him.

There were no doubt many reasons for the relatively casual attitude toward the wedding ceremony. The point that concerns us here is that the religious dimension seems to have been less important than in the other rites surrounding the great turning points of life—ironically so, since marriage involves a choice, and possibly the most fateful that many people are ever called upon to make, whereas the events celebrated by the other rites of passage are ones over which the individual has no control. (It is worth noting that in recent years, Soviet attempts to displace religious weddings by instituting 'wedding palaces' enjoyed considerable success, whereas attempts to supersede the other Christian rites of passage made little progress.)[35]

The following factors may be relevant here. First, it should be noted that most people married in their twenties at a time when, some evidence would suggest, religious interest tends to be lower than at other points in the life-cycle. Second, it is worth noting that the other life-cycle rituals involve doing something for someone else—whether it is ensuring that one's child is baptized and confirmed, or that one's deceased relatives receive a proper funeral. The need to do the right thing, either by the child or by the deceased, may lead people to insist on a religious ceremony that they may be prepared to risk doing without where only their own welfare is involved. Third, the other life-cycle rituals relate more clearly to situations in which many people either experience religious feelings or feel that the church has an evident role. This is most obviously the case with regard to bereavement, where religious faith and religious personnel have often been among the principal sources of comfort. The same applies to birth, with its associations of danger and of feelings both of gratitude for safe delivery and of the need for protection and support in the times ahead. Confirmation relates to the widespread belief that some instruction in religion is a necessary part of the upbringing of the younger generation and the training of 'decent' adults. Clearly the religious dimension of a wedding was potentially important—and sometimes it actually was. But it does not seem often to have been the case. A major factor, perhaps, was that weddings were so often hurried affairs, prompted either by the bride's pregnancy or by the urgent desire of one or both partners to get away from living with their parents.[36]

Funerals, as already indicated, had a very important role in working-class life in London, and except in very rare cases they took a religious form. The same was true in New York. Tragic bereavement was part of the normal experience of working-class New Yorkers, and the great majority of families prepared for the death of their members by carrying burial insurance policies. Funerals became the ultimate test of a family's respectability: to fail to show proper respect for the dead was a kind of sacrilege, and even more shameful in the eyes of neighbours than being frequently seen drunk, or failing to clothe the children properly. So, no matter what the family's feeling toward the deceased, they found themselves bound for their own sakes to give him or her a 'decent' burial. In a typical incident cited by Herzfeld, a deserted wife, who felt well rid of her drunken husband, continued paying his insurance premiums, since 'the father of her children should not end in Potter's Field'. Where the deceased was really missed, an elaborate funeral, like the one the same woman gave her favourite son, was a last expression of love ('While I'm alive and can work,' another woman told Herzfeld, after the death of her husband, 'I'll give him a fitting lay-out'), a last opportunity to atone for wrongs done, and perhaps some help in coming to terms with the loss. And if the bereaved family felt itself under the eyes of neighbours when one of them was to be buried, this was also an occasion when they could assert their own dignity, and their refusal to accept the judgement on them of the 'successful'. Any perceived slight at this time by a relative or neighbour was likely to lead to a permanent estrangement.[37]

In Berlin, a relatively high proportion of working-class funerals took place without a clergyman being present,[38] though it is not entirely clear how far this was due to shortage of money, how far to the shortage of clergy, and how far to people not wishing to have a clergyman present. The financial argument no longer applied after 1881 when fees for the performance of baptisms, weddings and funerals were abolished.[39] Before that time, poor families could apply for exemption, but may have preferred not to do so, either because of pride or because it was too much trouble. After 1881, the proportion of funerals with clergymen participating increased, though in the early twentieth century the number dipped again, because of the increasing popularity of cremations, which were not approved by the Prussian Protestant church until 1925.[40] The main duty of the clergyman was to deliver a graveside sermon. The significance attached to these is reflected in the fact that the Social Democrats and Free Parishes had 'speakers' who took on this role at secular funerals,[41] and also in the fact that two women in Capernaum parish who resigned from the church in 1908 did so because of disputes over these orations. In one case the pastor refused to give an address by the grave of a dead child, and in the other the woman objected to the contents of the sermon delivered at her husband's grave.[42] An article published in 1889 in the journal of the City Mission deplored the frequency of funerals in which no pastor took part: 'Such funerals make a very sad impression—lots of mourners and plenty of money spent on wreathes and flowers, but without God's Word, and without a prayer or a blessing.' The author mentioned many factors, ranging from unbelief and indifference to the fact that funerals tended to be concentrated on Sunday afternoons and that, in view of the shortage of clergy, none might be available at that time. The latter probably was a major factor: mass baptisms and mass weddings had long been a familiar feature of Berlin life,[43] and there were certain exceptional situations, notably the funeral of the 183 barricade fighters during the 1848 revolution, when mass burial seemed appropriate. But no one considered the presence of a clergyman at the funeral so essential that they were prepared to advocate mass burials as a normal practice. The City Mission prepared a leaflet entitled 'To Those Who Mourn', which they distributed at funerals where no clergyman was present. Another solution was to instruct the coffin carriers to read verses from the Bible at the graveside if no clergyman was available.[44] However, the author of the City Mission article felt that a general secularization of attitudes was reflected in the decline of Christian symbolism in the cemeteries over the previous twenty years. Crosses were giving way to 'stone tablets, fat granite obelisks, cracked pillars or tree trunks', and biblical texts and pious sayings were giving way to short and religiously neutral inscriptions like 'Irreplaceable! Unforgettable!' or 'Rest in Peace!', or to poetry that expressed sorrow without offering any religious hope, or gave voice to feelings of revolt in a way that the author found blasphemous.[45]

II

Working class city-dwellers also had their holy days, which called for special observances within the weekly and annual cycles. For Jews and Protestants, the weekly Sabbath was an observance of fundamental importance. The Catholic observance of Sunday was less rigorous than that by Protestants, and in any case the Catholic Sunday was relativized by the fact that they had so many other holy days. So far as Protestants were concerned, there was a considerable difference between London and Berlin. The Berlin Sunday was, as a guide of 1905 put it, 'A day of rest, but not of holy rest'.[46] Since the 1840s, Protestant churchmen of many different theological tendencies had been campaigning for a stricter observance of Sunday, including, in particular, restrictions on Sunday work.[47] But their efforts had borne little fruit. Apart from the fact that many people were obliged to work on the Sabbath, Sunday remained throughout the century the great day for outings into the country or to the zoo, for visits to beer gardens or to the theatre. By the early twentieth century, it was also becoming the main day for sporting events.[48]

In London, by contrast, not only were there many more legal restrictions on Sunday activity, Sunday was also recognized as a day apart, requiring distinctive patterns of behaviour, even by many of those who never attended church services. Anyone living above the direst poverty dressed differently on Sundays— and in a society that attached great symbolic meaning to clothes this was in itself important. Sunday was also the great day for family rituals—most notably the Sunday dinner, the best meal of the week, and often the only occasion when all members of the family were together; but also musical evenings, and sometimes visits to relatives. For more religiously minded families, music meant hymn-singing, while other families might prefer music-hall songs—but, either way, music brought together family members who had gone their separate ways all week. So Sunday, apart from being the principal day for religious activities, was also the great family day.[49] For the more religiously minded the two aspects of Sunday merged together; for others, formal religious observances were left to the children, but the rites of family were observed by parents too.

For both kinds of families, there were often strict rules as to what was not permissible on Sunday. A man born in Woolwich in 1899, whose parents, an arsenal labourer and his seamstress wife, were neither of them churchgoers, recalls that Sundays were 'purgatory': the blinds were drawn, and they would go for a walk 'very sedately' or sit in the front room looking at books, 'sort of Pilgrim's Progress and something of that sort'.[50] Many families banned Sunday games, though sometimes they compromised by banning outdoor games or noisy games. A woman brought up in Hackney, where her parents ran a vegetable store, recalls that although her parents were not churchgoers, they would not allow their children to play in the street on Sunday: 'Not Sundays of course. My father wouldn't allow that. Not Sundays. No-one would allow anyone in the street Sundays to play. That was a Sabbath Day, wasn't it?'[51] There were also frequent restrictions on Sunday work. Few went so far as to ban cooking on Sundays; but sewing and knitting were often barred. Stricter families would not read Sunday newspapers.[52] The proper observance of Sunday was thus a subject of considerable confusion, and it is clear that considerations of respectability had as big a role as strictly religious scruples in determining what was permissible. But there were relatively few working-class Londoners around the turn of the century who would have echoed the view stated by a Peckham woman that in her family 'Sunday was just another day of the week'.[53]

For German or English Protestants, there were few holy days of any importance besides the weekly Sabbath. Certainly, Christmas, Easter and Pentecost were the occasions of higher than usual church attendance, as well as being (in the case of Christmas) the occasion of the most important family celebration of the year, and (in the case of Easter) a time for new clothes. Communion at Easter was required of Anglicans; and German Protestants, who generally only took communion once a year, most commonly did so at Easter.[54] Yet there were also some other festivals that had a much smaller part in the church's calendar, but which aroused considerable interest on the part of those on the periphery of the church.[55] There were two different aspects to these temporary booms in churchgoing. On the one hand, there were many people who, in Günther Dehn's terminology, were *kirchenloyal* (loyal to the church), but not *stark kirchlich* (strongly church-minded). The latter group made the church a focal point in their lives; the former group felt that their loyalty to the church required them to turn up on the great festivals, but that to come more frequently might have suggested a degree of fanaticism.[56] On the other hand, there was another group of those who were not particularly loyal to the church, but who had hopes and anxieties and emotions which they could only adequately express or cope with through religious rituals; they had no desire to take part in the regular weekly round of religious worship, but it was very important to them to be able to participate in church services on particular days in the year.

The Capernaum parish in north Berlin recorded attendances at every service, and though the pattern may not be absolutely typical, it gives a clear indication of the way that churchgoing fluctuated during the year.[57] In 1910, for instance, attendance at morning service dipped below 150 on six Sundays in the year, of which two were in January and February, and four in June and July. It seems likely that

the weather, whether exceptionally nasty or exceptionally pleasant, was mainly responsible for these low points. On more average Sundays the attendance rose to
about 200. However, there were eight days or seasons when far more people came.
At the top of the list were Easter, the *Totenfest* (commemoration of the dead) and
the *Busstag* (day of prayer and repentance), all of which attracted congregations of
over 700. Indeed, on Good Friday there were two services attended by over 700
people, and two days later there was another one on Easter Sunday. In the second
group came Christmas when, for three days running, there were congregations of
around 500. Then there were four periods during which, on one or more occasions, there were congregations of over 400: these were Pentecost, New Year's
Eve, and the March and September Confirmations, when large crowds of relatives
would turn up not only for the actual ceremony, but for the formal examination of
the candidates, which would take place on a separate Sunday.[58]

Günther Dehn noted that the only occasions when his church in Moabit was
full were Christmas Eve and New Year's Eve, and he attributed this to the 'senti-
mental character' of these occasions.[59] New Year's Eve attracted large congregations in London too. The themes of reviewing the past and making a new start
evoked a universal response, and Watch Night services mixed solemnity and fes-
tivity in a way that caught the mood of the occasion. One of Charles Booth's team,
who observed the celebrations on New Year's Eve, 1898, in Somers Town, a very
poor district of north London, found that attendance at Watch Night services was
not as universal as he had been led to believe: there was also a more secular
celebration going on at midnight in the market, which consisted of the singing of
'Auld Lang Syne' and 'the clanging of tins and the loud striking of butchers' bar-
rows and boards'. However, he also found a large crowd in the Presbyterian chapel.
Downstairs it was the usual congregation, but in the gallery he found 'the motley
group that the occasion is reputed to attract to the sanctuary'.

> The reporter was next to a muscular, full-blooded ruffian, . . . somewhat in
> liquor, . . . who accompanied the preacher's remarks with a running com-
> mentary of his own, not very complimentary or choice in phrasing. . . . His
> wife was with him and during his little out-breaks was half angry and half
> fearful lest he should be turned out. She was conscious of the occasion, and
> under her bad, scarred face, it was easy to detect the desire for the moment
> to be quiet and subdued.[60]

The other occasion that attracted large numbers of people to London churches
who did not come at other times was the Harvest Festival, which does not seem to
have had any counterpart in Berlin or New York.[61]

A major event in the Berlin religious calendar was the last Sunday in the church
year, known as the *Totenfest* (commemoration of the dead), when special services
were held in church, and the recently bereaved would visit the cemetery where their
loved ones were buried. This commemoration was first introduced in 1816, to re-
member those who had died in the War of Liberation. In the later nineteenth century the churches were full on that day, and huge numbers visited the cemeteries. In

1890, for instance, thirty thousand were counted during the day at the cemetery of one large eastern parish. In 1880 a woman told a city missionary in east Berlin that for her the *Totenfest* was the most important festival in the whole year. She would always begin by going to church in the morning, and she would go without dinner to save money for wreaths to put on her children's graves. In view of the fact that working-class districts of Berlin had infant mortality rates of 25–30 per cent in the later nineteenth century, the number of such grieving mothers was enormous.[62]

Catholics had their own distinctive way of organizing time, and they did so in much greater detail than Protestants.[63] In the first place, rather than the simple dichotomy between Sabbath and workdays, Catholics had a hierarchy of days, with Sunday certainly at the top, but with Friday not too far behind, and Thursday and Saturday also standing out a little. Secondly, while Catholics shared with some other churches the practice of celebrating a variety of festivals and seasons, they were alone in identifying the months with particular saints or devotions. May, the month of Mary, was at the top of the list, but a variety of other months, notably March, June and November, also became identified in the minds of devout Catholics with particular aspects of their faith. Thirdly, the celebration by Catholics of large numbers of saints' days introduced an attractive elective element into this organization of time. The saint's festival, and often the eve of the festival, or even the nine days preceding, became a time of mass celebration for the saint's devotees, who might vary from those who had been or hoped to be healed by the saint, to all those living in a parish named after the saint, to the immigrants originating from a town or nation of which the saint was a patron. New York's annual calendar included numerous celebrations of the latter kind, most notably St Patrick's Day, with its typical mixture of religious rites, public parades, patriotic speeches and eating and drinking. On a more personal note, a New York Italian described her mother's devotion to St Anthony: every day for fifty-four years she went to 'pay her respects' at a church on Bleecker Street on the saint's day, and in her old age, when she lived up in the Bronx, this annual outing was her only one of the year—when she died, her daughter continued to go for her.[64]

In the world of the later nineteenth-century working class, beliefs about good and bad luck played a very important part. One distinctive characteristic of Catholics was the extent to which their ideas about good and bad luck were shaped by their religion. We have seen how Anglicans and German Protestants held 'superstitious' beliefs about baptism; and the same would apply to a number of other rites, for instance churching. But among Catholics this process went much further. The Catholic practice of ranking all aspects of the world on a scale of holiness provided an essential basis for their beliefs about luck. While the secular world was neutral, holy times, places, objects and persons were potent whether for good or for evil, depending on how they were used or on the source of their sanctity. May, as the month of Mary, was of good omen; Friday, as the day on which Jesus was crucified, was of ill omen;[65] whereas Monday had no particular significance either way. The clergy were objects of many such beliefs, though in this case there was no consensus as to the likely effects of contact with them, and different sections of the Catholic population had their own traditions. For instance, it was reported in East Harlem in 1930 that Italian families with members who were sick did not send for a priest, as they believed that to be visited by a priest brought bad luck. This may have been a rationalization of the anti-clericalism that was widespread among the first generation of Italian-Americans; but a Brooklyn Irishman, born in 1922, records that his Mayo-born grandmother held the same belief, tempered in her case by the claim that it also brought misfortune to speak ill of the cloth.[66]

Jews, too, imposed a sharply defined pattern on the week and the year. In the weekly cycle, the Sabbath was separated from workdays as strictly as it was for Protestants—with the difference that Orthodoxy defined the limits of acceptable Sabbath activity even more stringently than the strictest form of Calvinism. During the annual cycle, Jews recognized numerous seasons, requiring special celebrations and observances. Apart from the intensity with which the Sabbath was observed—which had parallels in some branches of Protestantism—there were two distinctive aspects of the Jewish patterning of time. The first was the way in which the annual cycle built up to the climax of the High Holy Days in late September. The nearest Christian parallel, perhaps, would be the role of Easter in Eastern Orthodoxy. In the early twentieth century there were many immigrant Jews in London and New York who had long become accustomed to working on the Sabbath, and who seldom entered a synagogue. But Yom Kippur was different. Even the most religiously indifferent Jew felt the special atmosphere of that day, and only the most determined unbelievers failed to fast. Huge numbers of Jews (especially women) attended public worship for the only time in the year.[67]

The other point that was distinctively Jewish was the role played by food in their celebrations asnd observances. In its division of all foods into clean and unclean, the Jewish religion entered the consciousness of its adherents at the most fundamental possible level. In the East End of London or on the Lower East Side of Manhattan, the Sabbath meal and the kosher kitchen played a crucial role both in binding Jewish families together, and in separating them from the gentiles— and indeed from adherents of rival branches of Judaism. (A major schism in London Judaism occurred in 1893 when the strongly Orthodox *Machzikei HaDath* repudiated the authority of the Chief Rabbi, claiming that he was lax in his interpretation of Jewish law with regard to kosher meat.)[68] But special foods also gave the various times of the week and seasons of the year much of their distinctive character. As synagogue attendance declined, they became even more essential to the defining of these seasons. Thus the Sabbath meant fried fish, Pentecost meant milk, Passover the baking of matzos and so on. Each season had its distinctive flavours and smells, which helped to stamp them on the Jewish consciousness.[69]

III

In London during this period, religion played a part in the upbringing of the overwhelming majority of working-class children. They were compelled to attend day schools in which religious teaching played a part, and few parents took advantage of the conscience clause that allowed them to exempt their children from religious instruction: even those parents who disapproved of religion were usually disinclined to make their children stand out in this way. On Sundays, nearly all working-class parents voluntarily sent their children to a Sunday school or to attend one or more church services.

Jeffrey Cox, pointing to large classes and a lack of discipline in the 'chaotic' Sunday schools, argues that day schools were more effective agencies for imparting religious knowledge, and that as a result of the efforts of the board schools, knowledge of orthodox Christian doctrine may have reached a peak around the end of the nineteenth century.[70] This might be true in a purely intellectual sense. On the other hand, the more relaxed atmosphere of the Sunday schools may have made them more congenial institutions than day schools and ones in which whatever knowledge was acquired had more pleasant associations. As recruiting agencies, the Sunday schools were not quite as ineffective as the churches tended to assume. Oral history evidence suggests that they were popular with most of their customers—mainly because of the treats that they provided, which ranked as major events in the working-class child's calendar.[71] Though the majority dropped out at thirteen, there were also considerable numbers who stayed on, often as a result of personal attachments formed to clergy or teachers.

Girls stayed on more frequently than boys. Some would go to church with a group of their friends. Some would join church clubs for girls, which tended to be better supported than those for boys. Often they would give up regular churchgoing when they began courting, but as mothers they would take the leading part in the religious upbringing of the next generation. The central emphasis of this upbringing was on learning the difference between right and wrong. The strongly ethical character of most people's understanding of religion provided the basis for one of the most popular forms of criticism of the churches—highly 'religious' people were 'no better than anyone else', so that proved that you could be a good Christian without getting involved in the church as a community.[72]

In times of crisis, prayer offered access to supernatural help: above all in times of illness, but also in those of danger, emotional trauma, or financial crisis, large numbers of people turned to God either for strength, or in the hope of a safe escape from whatever was troubling them. Memoirs and oral history give some examples of the situations in which people prayed, though they do not permit us to say how widespread the practice was. One East End memoirist describes her mother (then living in Beckenham) praying for money when her family ran out of food. A Bermondsey memoirist describes a neighbouring woman praying with a sick neighbour. Another Bermondsey woman describes how, when a neighbour died, her mother went to say the Lord's Prayer with the family.[73] She prefaced this account with the phrase 'We weren't religious, but', which tends to occur quite frequently in oral history interviews with working-class people born in Britain around the end of the nineteenth century.[74] By not being religious, she appears to mean that they were not regular churchgoers. While this may have meant that her mother's religion had a somewhat lower priority in her life than it did for many of those who were active in church or chapel, it is clear that like many other non-churchgoing people of her generation, she had a view of the world that was far from secular. She worked all week on her sewing-machine—but never on Sunday: 'And of course at the same time when she was machining she was singing away at the top of her voice. . . . "Tell me the old, old, old story". . . . It was mostly hymns. I think she got it from her own mother. . . . And, oh, another one, oh, the old Easter hymns, you know, those very up and down.' In later life, when the mother was a widow and her children were off her hands, she had more free time and joined a church organization. In this she was typical of quite large numbers of working-class women who had church ties that lay dormant while they had young children, but could be revived when more time was available.[75]

Günther Dehn noted that Protestant Berliners enthusiastically endorsed the biblical maxim that prayer should be a private matter, not something done in public places with the aim of winning a reputation for piety.[76] But it is less clear how far Berliners prayed at all, once they had passed beyond childhood. The subject is better documented in New York. It is clear that for some immigrants, prayer was a vital resource in the face of the loneliness and discouragement that many of them felt. A German Protestant missionary on the Lower East Side described how a Mrs Bahnmiller, when she wanted to 'be alone with God, went up to the roof of her tenement and behind the chimney where only God could see and hear her. There she lifted her eyes and heart up to the sky and it made no difference whether the sky was clouded or covered with bright stars. She felt blessed and newly encouraged when she left the sacred place to take up again the heavy duties of her life.'[77]

Similarly, an Italian immigrant commented that 'You can pray in any place. You can pray in a park, any place. As long as your heart is towards the heaven and you say "God forgive me", if you commit anything bad.' He was typical of Italian males of his generation, in that he was suspicious of the church as an institution, and did not regularly attend services; on the other hand, he was typical of Catholics in that he did like to pray in a church (St Francis's on West 31st Street)—though he preferred to pray alone.[78] In rather similar terms, an elderly Catholic woman of Irish descent recalls: 'I've only been an occasional churchgoer. Only when the load got too heavy to bear did I share it with God.'[79]

Many working-class children during this period were taught to say their prayers each night. We are unusually well informed on this, so far as London is concerned, because of questions asked in the Essex University oral history survey. Out of 45 respondents brought up in working-class families in Greater London, 20 specifically stated that they were taught by their parents or grandparents to say their prayers and 18 said they were not. Clearly the practice was much more widespread than was, for instance, regular churchgoing, but less common than, for instance, the christening of babies or churching of mothers. What it signified is much harder to say. For one woman who was not taught her prayers, and resented the fact, saying prayers together was a moment of peculiar intimacy between mother and child, and its neglect reflected a lack of parental concern: 'My mother had no affection for anybody. No. I brought my children up and taught them to say their prayers. It was something I wanted when I was a child. Love and affection. It's always stuck in your mind, mind you, it leaves a bit of a chip on your shoulder. . . . My mom never kissed us. Never taught us to say a prayer.'[80] A Canning Town man, whose mother, a ship's scrubber, did say a few prayers with him each night, recalls praying fervently on his own account: 'I knelt down by the side of my bed and I prayed. Lots of times. Hoping one day I should be rich enough to send my father to Spain. . . where he could get his health back.'[81]

In Berlin, too, mothers prayed with their children, though one can only surmise from the fragmentary evidence how widespread the practice was. Clergymen were inclined to take a fairly negative view of the religion of their non-churchgoing parishioners. For instance, two pastors interviewed about their memories of the pre-1914 period expressed the view that those who did not go to church seldom read the Bible at home, said grace or taught their children prayers.[82] On the other hand, there is also evidence suggesting that they may have been wrong. For instance, a Berlin teacher recalled that in the 1880s he had taught a class of eighty girls among whom there were a dozen 'young heathen' (those who had never been baptized)—but even they had learnt to say their prayers in the morning and at night. In 1880 a city missionary expressed shock at finding a six-year-old boy who had never learnt a prayer from his mother. And in 1912 the parish helper of the Capernaum Church in Wedding was visiting parishioners who had declared that they intended to resign from the church, and spoke to one woman who stated that although she and her husband were 'enemies of Christian belief', she still prayed with her child every night.[83]

IV

The clergy and other religious professionals also played a role in times of personal crisis: whether as holy men and women, with special access to God, or as people who were bound by the duties of their job to be helpful, they were frequently turned to for support and guidance.

Attitudes to the clergy were often extreme: they might be revered as saints or reviled as hypocrites, but they were not so easily seen with cool objectivity. A clergyman who seems to have fully lived up to popular expectations was Fr St John Groser, the Anglican curate of St Michael's, Bromley, and later Vicar of Christ Church, Watney Street, in Stepney. He was 'really down to earth'. He was different from other East End clergy:

Well, they were alright outside. But when they went inside, they had their wine and a cigar. I'm not so sure. Not like John. He lived like a Labour man—'All I want is two potatoes and a small piece of beef'. He lived a Christian life. He was one of the few who came away from the usual run of vicars, and said we are with the people and should live like the people.[84]

While Groser's radicalism no doubt enhanced his popularity, he was thus admired as much for being a 'real Christian' as for his politics. The qualities emphasized by his admirers are similar to those ascribed to other Anglican clergymen—and, indeed, German Protestant pastors—who are known to have been popular. The most common ground for criticism of the clergymen of these state churches was that they were aloof or patronizing and only mixed readily with the elite. The most popular pastor in east Berlin in the 1920s was said to be Sasse of the Lazarus church, who went on pub-crawls with working-class parishioners, who would address him as 'Du'. Another east Berlin clergyman of the time was said to draw huge numbers to his confirmation classes because of his friendly and humorous manner of conducting these.[85] Friendliness, informality and treating everyone alike seem to have been the salient characteristics of those Anglican clergymen who were most popular. For instance, a Canning Town man, born in 1901, remembers as an outstanding local personality Rev. Varney, who was 'kind', 'gentle' and treated 'everyone on an equal'—he would 'help any waif and stray and all the old children he used to spend his money and give 'em sweets'. Similarly, Fr Bartlett of Poplar 'wasn't stuck up at all'; he was 'for basic Christianity'. [86]

References to admired Roman Catholic priests strike a slightly different note. Here the emphasis was on 'holiness'. A holy priest was not necessarily very gregarious—though he certainly was not aloof or snobbish. He was closer to God than ordinary people were, and this implied a certain degree of set-apartness. Yet at the same time he cared about and understood ordinary people. The principal point of contact was through the confessional, and a holy priest was usually an outstanding confessor—patient, strict where need be, but motivated above all by love for his parishioners and an overriding sense of responsibility for their souls. Such priests served long periods in a single parish, often as assistants, so that a reputation for humility and self-abnegation became a part of the legend that surrounded them.

The Irish-born Fr Murnane was first a curate at Holy Trinity, Dockhead, in south London, and then became pastor in 1896, remaining there for the rest of his life. According to a history of the parish, 'His influence over the people was phenomenal (it is hardly an overstatement to say they "worshipped" him) but was never obtained, as has been known, by bullying.' Appreciative parishioners remembered him as being 'very, very good with the sick', 'with old people extremely good' and 'devoted to the poor'. He 'knew everybody' and was 'always in and out of people's houses', and his reputation for sociability is presumably reflected in the fact that he was said to be keen on smoking, cricket and tea-drinking (though not on alcohol). He was also 'in tremendous demand as a confessor—and at most inconvenient times', and was 'a peacemaker with a wonderful way with him of solving troubles, especially family troubles'. There was a specifically Irish dimension to his persona: he put on 'the brogue when he wanted' and was remembered for having visited the Lord Mayor of Cork, Terence MacSwiney, in Brixton Prison. He was also in touch with the popular Catholicism of Irish London in another way: in 1907 he introduced into his parish the processions through the streets and the blessings of household shrines en route that were a characteristic feature of London Catholicism at that time, and in 1921 he led a pilgrimage to Lourdes. He also introduced a monthly Lourdes service that drew people, including the sick, from many parts of London.[87]

Another such priest was Fr Preis, a Redemptorist serving at the German parish of the Most Holy Redeemer on Manhattan's Lower East Side from 1866 until his death in 1894. In 1885 it was reported that on Wednesday afternoons 'crowds of people came to receive the instructions and blessings of R. P. [Rev. Pater] Preis, to pray and go to confession, and then to bring articles of devotion and to give alms'. It is difficult to get any clear impression of Fr Preis's personality from the cryptic references in the parish chronicles, though it was mentioned that he was 'kind' and did 'most useful work in the confessional'. These were perhaps more than clichés, since his less popular colleague, Fr Saftig, was reported in the chronicles to be 'so strict in the Confessional, so slow at Mass and so solemnly didactic in sermons that some people do not like to be there, and speak about it'.[88] After his death, Preis apparently became the object of a cult. In 1896, the chronicles recorded the contents of a note that the Redemptorists had received:

> Among the many favors obtained through the intercession of good Father Preis, the following is one of the most remarkable: —A child burned both her hands with scalding water, and fearing, from the appearance of the burns, that she would suffer for some time, I immediately had recourse to Fr Preis, saying 'Good Father Preis, you cured so many while on earth, help me now, cure this child within a week and I will say a hundred Rosaries for the Poor Souls.' To our great surprise, the child was able to use one hand that same night, and the other is healing rapidly.[89]

It is clear that by no means all priests inspired this kind of devotion. Indeed, the chronicles give plenty of space to the criticisms and complaints that were frequently the priest's lot. But there is an important distinction between those who made indiscriminate attacks on priests in general, and those who retained an idealized image of 'the good priest', like the 'devout women' at Most Holy Redeemer in 1885 who 'murmured' because 'all the customs of long and holy standing cherished by Rectors Wirth and Anwandt are now done away with' and 'the old fathers are sent off to be followed by inexperienced priests, who are cold to the few that come, and living to themselves never visit the people and (which is worst!) not one is accounted a good preacher'.[90] Thus Catholics, to a greater degree than Protestants, expected specifically priestly qualities of their clergy. Priests who managed to satisfy these expectations were loved, and even revered; those who fell short were subjected to harsh criticism—the more so because of the powers and pretensions of the clergy within the Catholic community. The Protestant clergy were in danger of becoming irrelevant, as much of what they did could in principle be done by a social worker, or a teacher, or a politician or indeed any intelligent and committed Christian layperson. The Catholic clergy were in no danger of being replaced, but there was always the possibility that their people would turn completely against them.

In New York or London in the later nineteenth century, it was potentially helpful to any public cause to have a clergyman among its known supporters—though this support could boomerang if the clergyman did not live up to the qualities popularly demanded of him. The same was true of lay public figures, like, for instance, George Lansbury, known for their strong religious convictions. Reminiscences of Lansbury from elderly residents of his home borough of Poplar are generally highly eulogistic[91]—and most dwell on his personal qualities as much as his political leadership. For instance, Rose notes that he was seen as the embodiment of local ideas of 'neighbourliness' and 'goodness'.[92] On the other hand, the rare critical comments made hostile reference to his religion—but in order to suggest that he was sanctimonious or unreliable.[93] The same kind of ambivalence can be seen in the nineteenth-century British Protestant tradition of mass 'church parades' by such groups as the unemployed, who would march in a body to a local church and demand a sermon on a text of their choice.[94] If the clergyman obliged, they were delighted to feel that they had the moral backing of the church for their cause; if he did not, they could at least enjoy the moral satisfaction of being able to complain about the hypocrisy of the church and its connivance with the powers that be. But in either case, the church was expected to speak up for the oppressed, both in the abstract sense that religion was associated in people's minds with justice and that the Bible was seen as providing added legitimation for the people's cause, and in the more concrete sense that the clergy and religious people generally were seen as having a moral obligation to work actively for justice.[95]

By contrast, when between two and three thousand unemployed Jews from the East End of London marched to the Great Synagogue in 1889, the radical organizers apparently expected to be turned back, and deliberately used the rebuff as a means of discrediting religion in the eyes of the marchers.[96] For many Jewish socialists and anarchists of this period it was axiomatic that 'no step forward, no development can occur for a Jew where the religious fetters are not dismantled or violently hacked away from his hands and feet'.[97] However, there were also more pragmatic Jewish radicals, especially trade union organizers, who were ready to use the Bible and Jewish religious tradition in order to gain the support of their more devout colleagues. No strike speech on the Lower East Side was complete without references to Moses, and recalcitrant employers were inevitably described as 'pharaohs'.[98] In the 1890s a frequent day for the start of strikes in the garment industry was the ninth day of Av, when devout Jews remembered the fall of the Temple. This was partly because the day came in July, at the start of the busy season, and thus at the time when the bargaining position of the tailors was strongest. But there was also another reason why strike calls at that time were particularly likely to meet an enthusiastic response: 'We shed tears on that day, we lament the loss of our independence and glory, we sigh over the fate of the women and children who were outraged and tortured by the brutes of Rome. Well it often happens that while we are at it we also weep over our own misery and utter groans for our own wives and children, who are starved and tyrannized by those brutal bosses of ours.'[99]

The nearest Jewish parallel to the Protestant 'church parade' comes from the New York kosher meat boycott of 1902. The boycott was initiated by a group of housewives on the Lower East Side who were protesting against the high prices charged by kosher butchers. They picketed butchers' shops, and in some cases smashed windows or assaulted women who ignored the boycott. The action spread rapidly to Harlem, Brooklyn and the Bronx, and it ended after three weeks with a substantial drop in prices. On the first Saturday of the boycott, the protesters went from synagogue to synagogue, interrupting services in order to demand support. They justified their action by referring to the tradition whereby the reading of the Torah could be stopped where a matter of justice was at stake. The tactic seems to have worked, as they won the backing of many rabbis, and of the Orthodox *Yiddishes Tageblatt*, as well as the socialist *Forward*.[100]

In Berlin, by contrast, the political use of the Bible had become a conservative monopoly. There were still parts of Protestant Germany, like eastern Westphalia, where trade union organizers went 'Bible in hand', or like the Erzgebirge, where portraits of Luther hung next to those of Bebel on the walls of workers' homes. In Berlin, Social Democratic orators might still distinguish between the Christian church (which was wholly condemned) and the Christian religion (which had at least some good in it),[101] but the party's case was argued in wholly secular terms.

However, periods of national crisis could bring an otherwise submerged religiosity to the surface. One such time was the Franco-Prussian War,[102] and another was the outbreak of the First World War. A memorandum by the Brandenburg Consistory, written in September 1914, noted that the war had 'united all classes and social strata of our people. . . . Even in those circles that were formerly indifferent or hostile to the church, and especially in the working-class world, it has led to a desire for the church, which has found expression in the high attendance at all places of worship in Berlin.'[103] In Wedding a crowd was said to have 'stormed' a church, and demanded a service at a time when none was planned. Crowded services were held in parks, and churches were particularly well attended on New Year's Eve.[104] When statistics of Protestant communicants in Berlin were published, these showed a 32 per cent increase for the year 1914 over the previous year—though there was a drop in 1915, when the figures were only 16 per cent above the pre-war level. The increase seems to have been spread fairly evenly across the city.[105]

The strident patriotism of many Protestant pastors found a much wider acceptance in the early years of the war than in peacetime. The memorandum by the Brandenburg Consistory noted that the war had brought to a halt 'the international, indeed anti-national, current in German Social Democracy'. The predominant tone of Protestant preaching in Berlin throughout the war years was one of enthusiastic support for the German cause, and calls for self-sacrifice. At least in the early years of the war these calls expressed the mood of a large part of the populace. The liberal *Chronik der Christlichen Welt* saw the primary task of the clergy in wartime as being to inspire the people in the way that the liberal hero, Schleiermacher, had done during the War of Liberation: the Berlin church no longer had a Schleiermacher, but instead of the 'soloist' there was now an 'orchestra' of patriotic preachers. The conservative *Kirchliches Jahrbuch* seems to have welcomed the war, seeing it as offering a way out of the religious crisis of the pre-war years: 'Now the people are once more clamouring for the services of the preacher; much distrust has vanished, God be thanked; the church is drawing people in again; bridges have been thrown up between church and people; the point now is to use these bridges. . . . The people *have* been won, God has won them, and is leading them back to the church; may she hold fast to that which God has brought her.'[106] This patriotic religiosity came and went. After the German collapse of 1918, the Berlin church faced a new and even bigger movement of mass resignations; and many of the clergy, their patriotic fervour unabated, turned to the various forms of right-wing nationalism that sought to resurrect the national unity that had briefly flourished in the early days of the war.[107]

In England the statistical pattern was quite different. The first three years of the war brought a continuous, though very gradual, decline in the number of Anglican communicants and Nonconformist church members—the only exception being the Congregationalists, who grew slightly in 1915. Most denominations saw a slight increase in 1918, and a larger upturn in the 1920s.[108] Special services were held in many churches in the period immediately after the outbreak of war; but, according to the *East London Observer*, those in the East End did not attract particularly large congregations.[109] During the first five months of the war, the paper offered no hints that the war might be associated with a church-based religious revival of the kind seen in Berlin, and apparently in France too.[110] Far from claiming that he was witnessing any religious boom, a speaker at the twenty-ninth anniversary of the East End Wesleyan Mission in the autumn of 1914 drew some satisfaction from the fact that 'at the present time of national crisis the church is holding its own'.[111]

This is not to say that the war evoked no religious response in London, but the reaction was rather different from that seen in Berlin. A first major difference was the ambivalence with which an important section of London's religious world faced the war. Berlin's patriotic clergy had their counterpart in the Bishop of London, Arthur Winnington-Ingram, who believed that Britain was fighting 'a holy war'; and the press gave prominent coverage to pro-war sermons, and other declarations of support for the national cause by clergymen.[112] On the other hand, many Nonconformist preachers had been urging British neutrality up to the very last moment; though most were persuaded by the German invasion of Belgium that the Kaiser had got to be stopped, they tended to retain a strong distrust of militarism, and they disapproved of the prevailing hatred of Germany. Even on the Anglican side, there were many clergymen who were felt by superpatriots to be half-hearted in their support for the war.[113] There was also a small, but vocal, element of Christian pacifists.[114] So, in spite of the fact that most London clergy declared their support for the war, London churches were less effective vehicles for the expression of patriotic feeling than their counterparts in Berlin. It may also be that the long years of preaching peace in London churches, and more especially chapels, had left many people with rather mixed feelings about the role of the church in the war. They may themselves have felt that they had a duty to fight; yet at the same time they saw the incongruity in a Christian minister justifying killing. In this feeling that the churches were in a false position may lie one of the causes of the wartime decline in church membership.[115]

However, unease about the public position of the church in wartime, and unwillingness to attend services, did not preclude soldiers and their relatives from expressing religious feelings in other ways. The bishop asked for London churches to be kept open all day for private prayer, and the *East London Observer* reported that parishioners would 'call in at all times, bow down in silent prayer, and then withdraw'.[116] As the casualties mounted, many people sought comfort through spiritualism.[117] And religion also had a role at the front—though in ways that were to quite a large degree independent of churches or clergy. Soldiers were generally said to pray before battle and to thank God afterwards. There was also a great deal of hymn-singing. An army chaplain reported that many men received communion before going into battle: 'In some it means everything we would wish it to mean; in others it is indubitably a superstitious feeling. They believe that having taken Communion they will be safe.' One observer summed up as follows: 'The soldier has got religion. I am not so sure that he has got Christianity.'[118]

Though the religious response to the war of Londoners and of British soldiers differed from that in Germany, there was a fundamental factor at work in both situations. Just as there were certain regularly recurring events such as the birth of a child or the death of a loved one, when most people experienced emotions that were difficult to express without the aid of religious ritual, or when many people turned to God for help, support and comfort, there were less predictable times of individual or collective crisis that could reawaken this normally dormant religiosity. There were many people whose religion played relatively little part in their day-to-day life, but remained an essential part of the resources through which they coped with life as a whole, and a resource that came to the fore at some of life's most important moments.

CONCLUSION

I

BETWEEN THE LATER seventeenth and the late twentieth century, most Western societies have moved from being monolithically Christian (except for the small Jewish minority), to a situation in which a significant proportion of the population professes no religious belief and has little or no connection with any kind of church or synagogue.[1] An essential precondition for this change was the gradual emergence of religious toleration from the later seventeenth century onward. The pioneers were England, the Netherlands and some of the British colonies in North America. But gradually, in the course of the eighteenth century effective toleration spread to most other parts of Western Europe. The crucial significance of this development was that unorthodox religion, or irreligion, or simply religious non-practice, became legally permitted alternatives. It is hardly surprising that at least some people took advantage of these new opportunities. All three forms of religious dissent showed some growth in the eighteenth century. Most notably, deism, and later atheism, began to be popular in some intellectual circles from the later seventeenth century onward, and from that time there was a regular flow of publications questioning various aspects of Christian orthodoxy. As a result, what would previously have been perforce private speculations became generally available to the educated public, at least in those countries that did not have a rigorous censorship. In the eighteenth century religious practice was declining both at the upper and the lower end of the social hierarchy: at the upper end for the intellectual reasons just mentioned, and at the lower end for demographic reasons, notably the growth of poor suburbs with little religious provision in the major towns, and of isolated weaving and mining communities in the countryside. Unreformed established churches were ill-equipped to respond to challenges of the latter kind, and at this stage the state tended to give a low priority to support for religion. Indeed, 'enlightened' monarchs saw the church and popular religiosity as obstacles in the path of their modernizing programmes. On the other hand, the weaknesses of the established churches provided a stimulus, at least in Protestant countries, to evangelistic movements, often led predominantly by laymen, and appealing strongly to craftsmen and small farmers. So the eighteenth century saw important revival movements as well as strong secularizing tendencies.

In the political upheaval that followed the French Revolution of 1789 this tendency toward a polarization between the religious stances of different sections of the population became more marked. Revived religious interest was seen both on the part of the state and of many elite groups, which came to believe that established churches were the only forces strong enough to hold back the tide of revolution. At the same time religious sectarianism held a strong appeal to many middle- and lower-status groups, which were in the process of establishing their own identity and cultural autonomy. However, it was also in this period that the revolutionary government in France conducted the first of the state-directed anti-religious campaigns that have been a major feature of modern European history; in the 1790s political radicals popularized deistic and atheistic ideas, which gained a mass following for the first time; and many people on the political left became strongly anticlerical. The onset of rapid industrialization and urbanization, beginning in Britain, was also two-edged in its religious implications. On the one hand, the massive shifts of population from rural areas to towns and industrial regions presented the churches with major logistical problems which, at least in the short term, most were unable to solve. On the other hand, in Britain and the United States the new industrial communities were often strongholds of Protestant sectarianism. Furthermore, the great mixing of populations from different religious and ethnic backgrounds in many of the new industrial regions often led to a close intertwining of ethnic and religious identity, which enhanced people's religious awareness, and sometimes led to bitter sectarian conflict.

We now reach the period of history covered in the present book. In the second half of the nineteenth century a number of quite separate factors all seemed to be working in the direction of church decline. In the cities and industrial regions intense conflict between the working class on one side and the middle and upper classes on the other made it increasingly difficult for members of different social classes to worship together in the same church. The most frequent result was the alienation from their churches of a large section of the working class, and sometimes the adoption of socialism as a substitute religion. At the same time agnosticism was gaining ground in the middle and upper classes, as a result of new intellectual developments, ranging from Darwinism to biblical criticism, and more generally because of the growing prestige of science and the belief that it had superseded religion. A related development was the progress of agricultural and medical technology, reducing dependence on magic which, especially in rural communities, was sometimes closely bound up with religion. State power was also making rapid strides at this time as a result of increasing resources and improving communications, and the state was tending to take an ever larger role in areas like charity and education previously dominated by the church. Finally, in a less direct and almost imperceptible way, increasing affluence in the industrializing countries was reflected in growing leisure facilities, and a tendency for leisure to become the emotional centre of many people's lives.

At first sight, then, the picture in the later nineteenth century is one of headlong church decline. Yet it appears again that several of the factors making for decline were two-edged in their implications. For instance, the greatest disaster to hit the churches in this period was the massive drop in working-class participation in many areas. On the other hand, fear of the working class and a rediscovery of the social benefits of religion contributed to a 'return to the church' by the bourgeoisie, most notably in France. The growth in state power was even more ambiguous in its religious consequences: at the institutional level the expanding state has been an important source of secularization; but at the popular level resentment of the over-mighty state has provided a major stimulus to religious revival. In the later nineteenth century the best example of this was Bismarck's *Kulturkampf*, designed to cripple the Roman Catholic Church, which had the ultimate effect of strengthening the ties between clergy and people. When the state has turned to direct attacks on religion, the results have generally been counterproductive. Even the rise of leisure may in the short run have done as much to strengthen as to undermine the churches, since religious and political organizations effectively exploited the growing popular obsession with sport and entertainment by forming their own soccer teams and cycling clubs, staging concerts and later building parish cinemas. Meanwhile, the relationship between the decline of religion and the decline of magic has been greatly exaggerated by some historians. In France and Spain in the nineteenth century there were huge differences between the various backward rural regions in the strength of the church, yet magic was at least as strong in the irreligious as in the religious areas. Indeed the more religious areas may have modernized more quickly, as the church often took the lead in setting up credit banks, forming peasant co-operatives and organizing the sale of fertilizers.

In the eighteenth century, church decline was most marked in France; for most of the nineteenth century the front runner was Germany. In the first half of the twentieth century the situation stabilized in France and, to some extent, in Germany. Rapid church decline was now most evident in England and Scandinavia. The crucial group was the middle class and the leitmotif was individual freedom and rejection of the dogmatism and puritanism of nineteenth-century religion and ethics. This phase reached its climax in the 1960s, when the revolt in the name of free personal choice swept across the whole Western world, making its biggest impact in predominantly Catholic countries and communities where changes in the first half of the century had come more slowly. In some West European countries the decline in church attendance and membership, which had been spread over several decades in England and Scandinavia, was compressed into several years. Yet, just as drastic church decline was taking place in many parts of Western Europe, North America and Australasia, religious revival was taking place in the Communist-ruled countries of Eastern Europe.

II

That, in a nutshell, is the story of religious change in the Western world over the last three centuries, of which the phenomena described in this book are a part. In the introduction I summarized some of the major theories in terms of which historians and sociologists have tried to describe and explain these changes. The most widely influential of these theories is that which sees the religious history of the last three centuries in terms of a process of progressive secularization, closely linked with 'modernization'. The most skilful historical exponent of this interpretation is perhaps Alan Gilbert.[2] As critics of the secularization theory have often ruefully admitted, the theory owes much of its popularity to the paucity of clearly articulated alternatives.[3] However, one cogently argued alternative has been advanced by Jeffrey Cox.[4] Cox suggests that the key moment in modern religious history is not the Industrial Revolution or the publication of *The Origin of Species*, but the advent of religious toleration in the later seventeenth and eighteenth centuries. This undermined the artificial religious consensus that had been imposed by the existence of state-supported monopoly churches. It introduced a free market in religion, where state churches were forced to compete against free churches and against secularists. For the first time, religious affiliation became at least partly a matter of personal choice. While accepting that the social and intellectual changes of the modern period have presented the churches with major challenges, Cox rejects the determinism of the secularization thesis. Some religious organizations have responded effectively to the imperatives of the free market, and have prospered accordingly; others have remained stuck in old ways, and have suffered severe decline.

My version of the story is considerably closer to Cox's than to Gilbert's. First, I would stress that there have been many twists and turns in the plot, and I would be much more cautious than Gilbert in assuming that we know how the story will end.[5] It is easy, but probably misleading, to interpret the whole religious history of the last three hundred years in the light of the drastic decline suffered by the churches in the 1960s, and consequently to exaggerate the extent of secularization in the nineteenth century, or even in the first half of the twentieth century.[6] Secondly, I would also stress that the modernizing forces have included some that favoured religious growth, as well as others that fostered secularization, and that the forces making for secularization, rather than forming a coherent 'process', were often unconnected with one another. Finally I would note that the factors that have made for secularization have been very varied, including intellectual, social and especially political factors. Rather than there being some master factor, such as 'modernization' or 'the rise of science', to which all the religious trends in the modern world can be related, the situation has been influenced by the interaction of a complex mix of factors. These have been present in varying proportions in different countries and regions—which is one reason why the religious histories of Western countries have often been so different.

So I would accept a large part of Jeffrey Cox's account of the religious situation in the modern world and his criticisms of the secularization thesis. However, I would argue that his horror of determinism leads him to overstress the specifically English dimensions of the crisis suffered by the English churches in the later nineteenth and early twentieth centuries: he takes insufficient account of the fact that many other Western nations were going through a similar crisis at around the same time.[7] While it is possible that a series of unique local factors explains these various religious crises, this seems unlikely. There is a need therefore to consider both the general factors that have affected nearly all the countries of Europe and North American in some degree, as well as the factors specific to each country.

Among these general factors I would particularly stress three, which had a major effect on the religious situation in most Western countries in the years 1870–1914. First there is the centrality of class conflict in nearly all cities and industrial regions and many rural regions. Periods of most intense class conflict have often been marked by widespread alienation from the established churches, and the growth of sectarianism, secularism, or both.

Second, and related to this, have been the successive movements of emancipation, ranging from the workers' and peasants' movements of the later nineteenth century to the various movements for the emancipation of women, in which oppressed groups have attempted to organize, to build up a sense of common identity and interests and to claim their rights. In view of the important role that established churches have played in legitimating social hierarchies and the close ties that they have often enjoyed with ruling elites, most of these movements had a significant anticlerical dimension—though in some of the movements of workers and peasants the clergy themselves had an important organizing role.

Third, new intellectual developments played a part in making a non-supernatural view of the world more plausible than before and in making traditional Christian and Jewish beliefs less plausible. Most obviously there was the impact of Darwinism. But even more important in Protestant countries was the development of the critical approach to the Bible, which undermined the naive fundamentalism that had been a basic tenet of most of the more democratic Protestant sects. The powerful attraction of this fundamentalism lay in the dual belief that the answers to all of life's problems could be found in the Bible, and that the meaning of the Bible was so transparent that it could be grasped by anyone who was able to read. In the later nineteenth century increasing scientific awareness was making it harder to accept a simple literal understanding of many biblical passages, and liberal Protestantism, with its more scholarly approach to the Bible, made it less accessible to uninitiated readers. Many of the latter were tending either to dismiss the Bible as 'a collection of fairy-tales', or to conclude that the Bible was such a difficult book that there was no chance of them making sense of it.

III

How does the detailed story of working-class religion in great cities in the period around 1900 fit into the picture of long-term change? At first sight the widespread secularism in Berlin and the relatively low levels of involvement in the church by working-class people in both London and Berlin provide excellent examples of the association between modernization and secularization. Closer inspection suggests that the fit between theory and fact is less good. The orthodox theory of secularization suggests that the most 'modern' sections of the population, those most conversant with modern science, technology and business methods, and those enjoying the benefits of an industrial economy are those most likely to reject religion.[8] The evidence for late Victorian London suggests that exactly the reverse was true: the group most involved in organized religion was the upper middle class and the group least involved was the unskilled working class. The evidence from Berlin is more ambiguous. Here again religious involvement was particularly low among the very poor, but was also relatively low in the skilled working class and among business and professional men. In the case of New York the varying levels of 'modernization' in different sections of the population appear to be totally irrelevant, because of the overriding importance of ethnic differences in influencing patterns of religious adherence and practice. In fact the evidence concerning both working-class religion and urban religion more generally in the three cities reveals considerable diversity, so I have sought an explanatory framework that makes sense of these divergences, rather than one which envisages a single dominant pattern.

For long there was a consensus among historians that in most parts of Europe the working class was extensively secularized in the nineteenth century, and controversy focused mainly on the reasons for this secularization; but more recently, many historians, especially in Britain, have challenged this view.[9] My own earlier work showed that oral history evidence suggests higher levels of working-class participation in church and chapel than had previously been recognized, and Callum Brown and Mark Smith have gone considerably further in revising upward the estimated levels of working-class churchgoing and church membership.[10] In particular, many historians have pointed out that church membership was often considerably higher among working-class women than among working men.[11] Meanwhile, Jeff Cox and Sarah Williams have argued that non-churchgoing working-class people were not less religious than middle-class churchgoers, but religious in different ways.[12]

This last point gains strong support from this book, and especially from the material presented in chapter 8. Clearly there were large numbers of working-class people in this period whose connection with any kind of organized religion was fairly tenuous. It has been common to assume that they were 'apathetic' or 'indifferent' in their attitude to religion. Clergymen and other middle-class observers, applying their own very stringent standards of religious observance, frequently made such assumptions at the time. And, for various reasons, most historians have been prepared to take their word for it. On the other hand, there is a good deal of evidence to suggest that the view of the world held by most nineteenth-century working-class people was far from being wholly secular; many of them would have loudly insisted that they were Christians, or Jews, and indeed better Christians or Jews than those who were apparently more pious. I have taken these claims seriously, and have tried to explore some of the different dimensions of this form of religiosity. It seems clear that this group of those who were neither committed church members nor convinced secularists forms both the largest element in the city population of the time, and the section that remains least understood.

As regards working-class churchgoing and church membership, the evidence for Berlin very largely supports the traditional picture. On the other hand, it is clear that in London the level was somewhat higher than has generally been realized—though it was still fairly low—and that in New York the level was considerably higher than in most European cities. As regards gender differences: it should be clear from the evidence presented here that the familiar picture of working-class secularization in the nineteenth century depends too much on evidence about working men, and that far too little consideration has been given to the beliefs and activities of working-class women. Future research will need to explore more fully the relationship between male and female religion—to what extent was female religion accepted or even encouraged by men, and to what extent did it lead to conflict between the sexes? Historians of the twentieth century also need to give more attention to women's religion: it seems likely that the main reason for the accelerated pace of secularization in this century has been that, for the first time, women have been affected as much as men.

Where I would differ from most of the new generation of historians of working-class religion is in laying more stress than they tend to do on class differences and on class antagonisms as a source of tension within the church or chapel, and a source of working-class alienation. My three-stage model, presented in chapter 5, should make it more possible to understand and explain the considerable differences in the extent of this alienation. The first stage was the loosening of ties with the church that was observed in all or nearly all working-class districts of nineteenth-century cities. The second was the marked decline in attendance at regular church services that took place in the majority of such districts. The third was the widespread repudiation even of the Christian rites of passage, which took place in a significant minority of cities.

Even in New York, where working-class religious participation was relatively high, it was lower than that of other classes, and this seems to have been generally the case in this period. Working-class living conditions provide a sufficient explanation for this relative deficiency, but not for the more drastic decline in religious participation seen in many parts of Europe. The second stage, as defined by my model, which is represented by such places as London, saw a major decline in levels of working-class churchgoing and church membership, but in the context of widespread adherence to more informal kinds of religiosity, and without any major growth in militant secularism. A precondition for this second stage was a widespread sense of the separate identity of working-class people, and serious tensions in their relationships with other sections of the population. The third stage, exemplified by Berlin, in which militant secularism was widespread, and a significant minority of working-class people rejected any kind of supernatural religion, was precipitated by political factors. Most of those working-class people who rejected all kinds of religion did so not only for abstract philosophical reasons, but because they were converts to a doctrine of political salvation, and they objected to religion and the churches as obstacles to the achievement of socialism. However, intellectual factors also played a role in this popular irreligion: in Berlin the development of religious scepticism in the educated middle class provided working-class sceptics with much of the basis for their critique of religion, and it is probably true more generally that those cities in which working-class rejection of religion was relatively widespread also contained a large body of middle-class sceptics.

In considering the role of religion in the nineteenth-century city my emphasis has also been on establishing a framework within which the considerable diversity can be explained. Conventional wisdom associates the nineteenth-century city with rapid secularization. But, as I showed in chapter 4, this is in several respects an over-simplification. First, the contrast drawn at the time between 'religious countryside' and 'irreligious city' is misleading. The salient feature of the urban religious life was not secularism but pluralism: certainly, the extremes of collective religious practice were found in rural areas, but equally the extremes of collective non-practice were also found in rural areas; and of course there were many rural areas where the religious situation was more mixed. So the range of different types of religious situation obtaining in the rural regions of any country could be enormous. The degree of variation between the cities of any country was usually much less, but there was generally a great deal of religious diversity within any city. New York, with its enormous variations in the religious patterns obtaining in different ethnic communities, offers a particularly striking example.

Berlin provides a particularly dramatic example of the secularizing trend in nineteenth-century cities. However, the evidence suggests that Berlin was an extreme case. Among the other great cities of the period, Hamburg, Vienna and Paris perhaps came closest to Berlin in such features as the prevalence of giant parishes, the shortage of clergy, the strength of anticlericalism, manifested especially in the press, and the strong anti-religious tendencies in the working-class movement.[13] In the only indicator of secularization that is readily measurable—namely size of parishes and ratios of clergy to people—Berlin clearly outscored its rivals. In the intensity of anticlericalism it probably fell behind such Catholic cities as Paris and Vienna—not to mention Madrid and Barcelona, where there were far more priests around.[14]

But the Berlin model of religious development in the nineteenth-century city is only one among several possibilities. In chapter 4, I suggested five characteristic patterns. The main differences between them were in the political role of the churches, though this in turn was influenced by other factors, such as the extent and significance of ethnic diversity. In comparing the overall religious situation in Berlin and London, I have suggested that the most important factors were the differing religious role of the bourgeois elite in the two cities and the much greater importance of the free churches in London. Differences between the Church of England and the Prussian Evangelical church were also of some significance—for instance, the more decentralized character of the Anglican church and the lesser frequency of state intervention in its affairs made it better able to adapt to local circumstances, notably those of urban working-class parishes. In comparing the Old World cities of Berlin and London with the New World city of New York, differences both in social structure and in the relationship between church and state were relevant. By the later nineteenth century, ties with the state had become a considerable political liability for most of the established churches of Europe; the Liberals and Socialists who, between them, commanded the loyalty of the majority of voters in most European cities, had generally made anticlericalism a standard item in their rhetoric and programmes. The absence of ties between church and state in New York, and indeed the entirely different way in which religion interacted with politics, did not necessarily make the city's churches any more attractive and popular, but it did remove one of the major causes of alienation from organized religion in Europe. Similarly, the less rigid class structure in New York created a situation that was more favourable to the churches. Potentially, the strength of ethnic ties could bring together those from different social backgrounds, and weaken the force of class antagonism which was so potent in Berlin and London—though, as I showed in chapters 3 and 4, the extent to which this actually happened varied considerably. The relatively high levels of upward social mobility in New York and the absence of a hereditary working class had a similar effect.

The much greater strength of Roman Catholicism in New York than in London or Berlin also had an effect on the differing religious situation in the three cities. Where not discredited by political unpopularity, Roman Catholicism was relatively successful, by comparison with Protestantism or Judaism, in resisting the secularizing trend during this period. I have emphasized the popular attractions of Catholicism, and, in particular, the crucial part played by miracles, and the hope for miracles, in the Catholicism of the time. There are certainly many other factors that need to be taken into account. One approach has been indicated by Hugh Jackson in his history of Christianity in Australasia: he has shown that Catholic authoritarianism may have had certain advantages in this period as a means of retaining the loyalty of their people, at a time when Protestant liberalism was making it easier to rebel against orthodox doctrine and morality.[15] It should also be noted that the later nineteenth and early twentieth centuries were a period of political emancipation for the working and lower middle classes, in which large numbers of men and women found a purpose in life and an identity by belonging to great organizations, with popular leaders, heroes and patron saints, shared dogma and ritual, and a passion for marching through the streets with bands playing and flags flying. On the whole, the Catholic Church was far more successful than the Protestants in adopting the contemporary idiom, and Catholicism ranked second only to socialism as a popular political force in Western Europe during this period. It probably is no coincidence that in the later twentieth century both socialism and Catholicism have been vulnerable to the trends toward individualism and privatization, and that the most prosperous branch of Christianity is now evangelical Protestantism.

ABBREVIATIONS

AANY	Archives of the Archdiocese of New York
AKG	Archiv der Kapernaumgemeinde, Berlin
ARBP	Archives of the Redemptorists, Baltimore Province, Shore Road, Brooklyn
BC	Booth Collection (London School of Economics Library)
BSM	*Blätter aus der Stadtmission*
CCNY Interviews	City College of New York, Oral History of the New York Working Class (Tamiment Collection, Bobst Library, New York University)
CMHR	Chronicles of Most Holy Redeemer Catholic parish, New York (Archives of Redemptorists, Baltimore Province)
EOK	Evangelischer Oberkirchenrat
Essex Interviews	Family Life and Work Experience before 1918 (Essex University Oral History Archive)
EZA	Evangelisches Zentralarchiv, Berlin
SJSB	*Statistisches Jahrbuch der Stadt Berlin*

NOTES

Introduction

1. Erhard Lucas, in his well-known comparison between the labour movements in Remscheid and Hamborn, *Zwei Formen von Radikalismus in der deutschen Arbeiterbewegung* (Frankfurt/Main, 1976) somehow avoids any mention of the fact that one city was predominantly Protestant and the other Catholic. Standish Meacham, in his valuable *A Life Apart: The English Working Class 1890–1914* (London, 1977), pp. 15–16, 26, 53, 120, 164–5, 199–200, makes a few references to religion, but only to dismiss the subject as peripheral. Dietrich Mühlberg, ed., *Arbeiterleben um 1900* (Berlin, 1983), p. 126, mentions the importance of the church for many working-class women, but does not develop the point at all.

2. See, for instance, Patrick Joyce, *Work, Society and Politics* (Brighton, 1980); W. Brepohl, *Industrievolk im Wandel von der agraren zur industriellen Daseinsform dargestellt am Ruhrgebiet* (Tübingen, 1957); Klaus Tenfelde, *Sozialgeschichte der Bergarbeiterschaft an der Ruhr im 19. Jahrhundert* (Bonn, 1977); Jürgen Reulecke and Wolfhard Weber, eds., *Fabrik, Familie, Feierabend* (Wuppertal, 1978); S. H. F. Hickey, *Workers in Imperial Germany: The Miners of the Ruhr* (Oxford, 1985); Karl Rohe, *Vom Revier zum Ruhrgebiet* (Essen, 1986).

3. As Gareth Stedman Jones does in his otherwise excellent 'Working-class culture and working-class politics in London, 1870–1900: Notes on the remaking of a working class', *Journal of Social History*, 7 (1974), p. 471.

4. I have summarized the debate in Hugh McLeod, *Religion and Irreligion in Victorian England: How Secular Was the Working Class?* (Bangor, 1993).

5. Some of the exceptions are Wolfgang Köllmann, *Sozialgeschichte der Stadt Barmen im 19. Jahrhundert* (Tübingen, 1960); Vernon L. Lidtke, 'August Bebel and German Social Democracy's relation to the Christian churches', *Journal for the History of Ideas*, 27 (1966), pp. 245–64, and 'Social class and secularization in Imperial Germany: The Working Classes', *Yearbook of the Leo Baeck Institute*, 25 (1980), pp. 21–40; Hugh McLeod, 'Protestantism and the working class in Imperial Germany', *European Studies Review*, 12 (1982), pp. 323–44; Josef Mooser, 'Arbeiter, Bürger und Priester in den konfessionellen Arbeitervereinen im deutschen Kaiserreich, 1880–1914', Jürgen Kocka, ed., *Arbeiter und Bürger im 19. Jahrhundert* (Munich, 1986), pp. 79–105; Richard J. Evans, ed., *Kneipengespräche im Kaiserreich* (Hamburg, 1989), ch. 8; Lucian Hölscher, *Weltgericht oder Revolution* (Stuttgart, 1989).

6. A rare example of a study of working-class religion which is not limited to a specific ethnic group is Bruce C. Nelson, 'Revival and upheaval: Religion, irreligion and Chicago's working class in 1886', *Journal of Social History*, 25 (1991), pp. 233–53.

7. Alan Gilbert, *Religion and Society in Industrial England: Church, Chapel and Social Change, 1740–1914* (London, 1976), and *The Making of Post-Christian Britain* (London, 1980); Robert Currie, Alan Gilbert and Lee Horsley, *Churches and Churchgoers: Pat-*

terns of Church Growth in the British Isles since 1700 (Oxford, 1977); Bryan R. Wilson, *Religion in Secular Society* (London, 1966); Steve Bruce, ed., *Religion and Modernization* (Oxford, 1992).

8. In his lecture on 'Science as a Vocation', as translated in H. H. Gerth and C. Wright Mills, eds., *From Max Weber* (London, 1948), p. 155.

9. See, for instance, some of the comments by historians contributing to Bruce, *Religion and Modernization*, notably Callum Brown.

10. Jeffrey Cox, *English Churches in a Secular Society: Lambeth, 1870–1930* (Oxford, 1982), pp. 3–20, 265–76.

11. Friedrich Engels, *The Condition of the Working Class in England* (1845; repr. Oxford, 1958) p. 141.

12. B. I. Coleman, *The Idea of the City in Nineteenth-Century Britain* (London, 1973), p. 97.

13. Jürgen Boeckh, 'Predigt in Berlin', Kaspar Elm and Hans-Dietrich Loock, eds., *Seelsorge und Diakonie in Berlin* (Berlin, 1990), pp. 317–8.

14. Callum Brown, *The Social History of Religion in Scotland since 1730* (London, 1987), p. 141.

15. Coleman, *Idea of the City*, pp. 87–94.

16. See Gilbert, *Religion and Society*, pp. 110–5, 145–8, 184–7; and the contributions by Steve Bruce and Roy Wallis in Bruce, *Religion and Modernization*.

17. See Callum Brown's contribution to the same volume and his 'Did urbanization secularize Britain?' *Urban History Yearbook* (1988), pp. 1–14.

18. Numerous historians have used the first argument. As one example, see F. Charpin, *Pratique religieuse et formation d'une grande ville: Marseille 1806–1958* (Paris, 1964). The second and third arguments are used by Thomas Nipperdey in 'Religion und Gesellschaft: Deutschland um 1900', *Historische Zeitschrift*, 246 (1988), pp. 591–615. The third of these arguments is developed (though with regard to industrialization generally, rather than specifically to urbanization) in John Bukowczyk, 'The transforming power of the machine: Popular religion, ideology and secularization among Polish immigrant workers in the United States, 1880–1940', *International Labor and Working Class History*, 34 (1988), pp. 22–38. For the second argument, see Gregory Singleton, *Religion in the City of Angels: Los Angeles 1850–1930* (n.p., 1979), pp. 119–46.

19. Roger Finke and Rodney Stark, 'Religious economies and sacred canopies: Religious mobilization in American cities, 1906', *American Sociological Review*, 53 (1988), pp. 41–9.

20. Brown, 'Did urbanization secularize Britain?'

21. Lucian Hölscher, 'Secular culture and religious community in the city: Hannover in the 19th century', *Hispania Sacra*, 42 (1990), p. 407.

22. For a summary of the evidence, see Hugh McLeod, 'The dechristianisation of the working class in Western Europe, c. 1850–1900', *Social Compass*, 27 (1980), pp. 191–214.

23. H. Francis Perry, 'The workingman's alienation from the church', *American Journal of Sociology*, 4 (1898–9), pp. 621–9. See also Nelson, 'Revival and Upheaval'.

24. As quoted by François-André Isambert, *Christianisme et classe ouvrière* (Tournai, 1961), p. 117.

25. Henry J. Browne, *The Catholic Church and the Knights of Labor* (Washington, D.C., 1949), p. xiii.

26. K. S. Inglis, *Churches and the Working Classes in Victorian England* (London, 1963); Herwart Vorländer, *Evangelische Kirche und soziale Frage in der werdenden Industriegrossstadt Elberfeld* (Düsseldorf, 1963).

27. François Houtart, *Les paroisses de Bruxelles, 1803–1951* (Brussels, 1955); William J. Callahan, 'Response to urbanization: Madrid and Barcelona, 1850–1930', *Hispania Sacra*, 42 (1990), pp. 445–51.

28. Allan A. MacLaren, *Religion and Social Class: The Disruption Years in Aberdeen* (London, 1974).

29. Charpin, *Pratique religieuse et formation d'une grande ville*, pp. 56–7, 281–99.

30. Hugh McLeod, *Class and Religion in the Late Victorian City* (London, 1974), ch. 3.

31. Berndt Gustafsson, *Socialdemokratien och kyrkan, 1881–90* (Stockholm, 1953), English summary.

32. See E. J. Hobsbawm, 'Religion and the rise of socialism', *Worlds of Labour* (London, 1984), pp. 33–48.

33. This would apply to some of the major discussions of secularization, such as Owen Chadwick, *The Secularisation of the European Mind* (London, 1975); Thomas Nipperdey, *Deutsche Geschichte* 1800–1866 (Munich, 1983), and *Religion im Umbruch: Deutschland 1870–1914* (Munich, 1988); James Turner, *Without God, Without Creed: The Origins of Unbelief in America* (Baltimore, 1985). Also to the pioneering works on the relationship between the churches and the working class and their approach to the 'social question': Henry F. May, *The Protestant Churches in Industrial America* (New York, 1949); W. O. Shanahan, *German Protestants Face the Social Question: The Conservative Phase, 1815– 1871* (Notre Dame, Ind., 1954); Inglis, *Churches and the Working Classes*; K. E. Pollmann, *Landesherrliches Kirchenregiment und soziale Frage* (Berlin, 1973).

34. Many notable studies of this kind have been published in Britain, e.g. MacLaren, *Religion and Social Class*; Robert Moore, *Pit-men, Politics and Preachers* (London, 1974); Stephen Yeo, *Religion and Voluntary Organisations in Crisis* (London, 1976). An American example is John Bukowczyk, 'Steeples and smokestacks: Class, religion and ideology in the Polish immigrant settlements of Greenpoint and Williamsburg, Brooklyn 1880–1929' (Harvard University Ph.D. thesis, 1980). Less work of this kind has been done in Germany, but see Klaus-Michael Mallmann, '"Aus des Tages Last machen sie ein Kreuz des Herrn . . ."? Bergarbeiter, Religion und sozialer Protest im Saarrevier des 19. Jahrhunderts', Wolfgang Schieder, ed., *Volksreligiosität in der modernen Sozialgeschichte* (Göttingen, 1986), pp. 152–84.

35. Lucian Hölscher, 'Die Religion des Bürgers: Bürgerliche Frömmigkeit und Protestantische Kirche im 19. Jahrhundert', *Historische Zeitschrift*, 256 (1990), pp. 628–9.

36. Hugh McLeod, 'Class, community and region: The religious geography of nine-teenth-century England', Michael Hill, ed., *Sociological Yearbook of Religion in Britain*, 6 (London, 1973), pp. 46–7.

37. For figures, see Kevin J. Christiano, *Religious Diversity and Social Change: American Cities 1890–1906* (Cambridge, 1987), pp. 160–3.

38. So far as Berlin and London are concerned, this theme has been made familiar by such books as Walter Wendland, *Siebenhundert Jahre Kirchengeschichte Berlins* (Berlin, 1930); McLeod, *Class and Religion*; Cox, *English Churches in a Secular Society*. There has been little discussion of this theme by historians of New York. But an article on 'Non-Church Going' in *New York Times*, 21 April 1907, referred to 'a decline in interest in the churches on the part of a vast number of New York's population', and suggested, in particular, that the working class had 'drifted away from the church'.

39. McLeod, *Class and Religion*.

Chapter 1. Berlin

1. Friedrich Sass, *Berlin in seiner neuesten Zeit und Entwicklung, 1846* (Berlin, 1983), p. 93.

2. Wolfgang Ribbe, ed., *Geschichte Berlins*, 2 vols. (Munich, 1987), vol. 2, pp. 759–63; *Berlin und die Berliner: Leute, Dinge, Sitten, Winke* (Karlsruhe, 1905), pp. 293–5.

3. As an example of the conservative tendencies in the latter group, Adolf Stoecker, after failing to win working-class support for his combination of anticapitalism, anti-Semitism and monarchism, turned with much greater success to the lower middle class: Günter Brakelmann, Martin Greschat and Werner Jochmann, *Protestantismus und Politik: Werk und Wirkung Adolf Stoeckers* (Hamburg, 1982), pp. 47–9.

4. *Hohn* and *Spott* featured regularly in accounts of the Berlin character—whether eulogistic, as in *Berliner Typen und Bilder* (Berlin, 1895), pp. 41–3, or more critical, as with Otto von Leixner, *Soziale Briefe aus Berlin* (Berlin, 1891), pp. 3–12.

5. Brakelmann, Greschat and Jochmann, *Protestantismus und Politik*, pp. 90–1, 104.

6. For examples, see *Chronik der Christlichen Welt*, 23 (1913), pp. 165–8; EOK, Acta betreffend die Austrittsbewegung, 1, p. 46, (EZA).

7. K. E. Pollmann, *Landesherrliches Kirchenregiment und soziale Frage* (Berlin, 1973), pp. 19–42.

8. There is a programme for the opening of the church in Chronik der St.-Pauls-Kirche, 2 (Archiv der St.-Pauls-Gemeinde). For a similar example, see Ulrich Mayer, *Die Anfänge der Zionsgemeinde in Berlin* (Bielefeld, 1988), pp. 82–7.

9. Elke Josties and others, *Jetzt geht's rund . . . durch den Wedding* (Berlin, 1984), p. 15. For brief accounts of all the city's Protestant churches, see Gunter Kühne and Elisabeth Stephani, *Evangelische Kirchen in Berlin* (Berlin, 1978); for more detailed accounts of selected churches in the former East Berlin, see Peter Mugay, *Kanzeln, Könige und Kanonen: Evangelische Kirchengemeinden in der Berliner Stadtgeschichte* (Munich, 1991).

10. Karl Kupisch, 'Christlich-kirchliches Leben in den letzten hundert Jahren', Hans Herzfeld, ed., *Berlin und die Provinz Brandenburg im 19. und 20. Jahrhundert* (Berlin, 1968), pp. 481–513; Mayer, Die Anfänge der Zionsgemeinde, pp. 39–43, 81, 127–9; Hans-Dietrich Loock, 'Die evangelische Kirche in Berlin-Brandenburg im 19. Jahrhundert', *Wichmann Jahrbuch*, 30–1 (1990–1), pp. 107–8.

11. Georg von Loebell, *Zur Geschichte der evangelischen Kirchengemeinden Berlins während der Jahre 1875–1908* (Berlin, 1909), p. 11.

12. Lucian Hölscher, *Weltgericht oder Revolution* (Stuttgart, 1989), p. 158.

13. See religious statistics published annually in *SJSB*; von Leixner, *Soziale Briefe aus Berlin*, pp. 367–72.

14. Bernt Satlow, 'Die Revolution von 1848: Die Kirche und die soziale Frage', Günter Wirth, ed., *Beiträge zur Berliner Kirchengeschichte* (Berlin, 1987), pp. 177–83; Ernst Schubert, *Die evangelische Predigt im Revolutionsjahr 1848* (Giessen, 1913).

15. Horst Matzerath, 'Wachstum und Mobilität der Berliner Bevölkerung im 19. und frühen 20. Jahrhundert', Kaspar Elm and Hans-Dietrich Loock, eds., *Seelsorge und Diakonie in Berlin* (Berlin, 1990), pp. 214–5.

16. E. Hirschberg, *Die soziale Lage der arbeitenden Klasse in Berlin* (Berlin, 1897), pp. 18–19; Burkhard Asmuss and Andreas Nachama, 'Zur Geschichte der Juden in Berlin und das Jüdische Gemeindezentrum in Charlottenburg', Wolfgang Ribbe, ed., *Von der Residenz zur City: 275 Jahre Charlottenburg* (Berlin, 1980), pp. 165–228.

17. E. Hülle, *Die kirchlichen Handlungen in der Berliner Gemeinden* (Berlin, 1877), table 1.

18. Walter Wendland, *Siebenhundert Jahre Kirchengeschichte Berlins* (Berlin, 1930),

pp. 285–6, and *Die Entwicklung der christlichen Liebestätigkeit in Gross-Berlin vom Mittelalter bis zur Gegenwart* (Berlin, 1939), pp. 58–9.

19. Wendland, *Kirchengeschichte*, pp. 309–16; Hans Ostwald, *Kultur- und Sittengeschichte Berlins* (Berlin, 1932), p. 224.

20. E. Hülle, *Die kirchliche Statistik von Berlin* (Berlin, 1876), pp. 16, 30–3; Eduard Spranger, *Berliner Geist* (Berlin, 1966), pp. 138-46; Robert Stupperich, 'Berlin als kirchliche Metropole', *Jahrbuch für berlin-brandenburgische Kirchengeschichte*, 50 (1977), p. 35.

21. For the Voigtland, see Johann Geist and Klaus Kurvers, *Das Berliner Mietshaus, 1740–1862* (Munich, 1980); for Luisenstadt, J. Boberg, T. Fichter and E. Gillen, eds., *Exerzierfeld der Moderne: Industriekultur in Berlin im 19. Jahrhundert*, 2 vols. (Munich, 1984), vol. 1, pp. 198–207.

22. See, e.g., Hülle, *Die kirchlichen Handlungen*, p. 42.

23. Wolfgang Ribbe, 'Zur Entwicklung und Funktion der Pfarrgemeinde in der evangelischen Kirche Berlins bis zum Ende der Monarchie', Elm and Loock, *Seelsorge und Diakonie*, p. 252; Hölscher, *Weltgericht*, p. 158; Hülle, *Die kirchliche Statistik*, pp. 29–30.

24. Eugen Baumann, 'Die zunehmende Beweglichkeit der Bevölkerung', p. 14, a lecture delivered 8 May 1885, and contained in Brandenburgisches Konsistorium: Personalia, E. Baumann (EZA); *SJSB*, 27 (1900–2), p. 169; Günther Dehn, *Die alte Zeit, die vorigen Jahre* (Munich, 1962), pp. 166–7; Wolfgang Herzberg, ed., *Ich bin doch Wer: Arbeiter und Arbeiterinnen des VEB Berliner Glühlampenwerk erzählen ihr Leben 1900–1980* (Darmstadt, 1987), pp. 8–15.

25. See biographies in Otto Fischer, *Evangelisches Pfarrerbuch für die Mark Brandenburg seit der Reformation*, 3 vols. (Berlin, 1941).

26. Hsi-Huey Liang, 'The social background of the Berlin working-class movement, 1890–1914' (Yale University Ph.D. thesis, 1959), pp. 195–6.

27. See Martin Greschat, 'Die Berliner Stadtmission', Elm and Loock, *Seelsorge und Diakonie*, pp. 451–74.

28. *BSM*, 1 (1878–9), pp. 139–41.

29. Mayer, *Die Anfänge der Zionsgemeinde*, pp. 153–4.

30. Eugen Baumann, *Der Berliner Volkscharacter in der Seelsorge* (Berlin, 1880), pp. 45–51; Baumann, 'Die zunehmende Beweglichkeit,' p. 19.

31. Hans-Dietrich Loock, 'Bürgerliche Kirche', *Jahrbuch für berlin-brandenburgische Kirchengeschichte*, 49 (1976), p. 49.

32. *BSM*, 2 (1879–80), pp. 180–2; 22 (1900), pp. 209–10.

33. For comments on Zion, see Mayer, *Die Anfänge der Zionsgemeinde*, pp. 44, 93–5; for Nazareth, Hülle, *Die kirchlichen Handlungen*, p. 26, and Loock, 'Bürgerliche Kirche', p. 51.

34. Brandenburgisches Konsistorium: Personalia, Hermann Neubauer (EZA); David Schwartzkopff, *Die Versöhnungskirche in Berlin* (Berlin, 1919); *Kreuz-Zeitung*, 15, 22 October 1894, gave extensive coverage to parish elections, including lists of occupations of those elected.

35. Schwartzkopff, *Versöhnungskirche*, p. 30; *Führer durch das kirchliche Berlin*, 14 (1905–6), pp. 201, 203.

36. *Geschichte der St.-Pauls-Gemeinde zu Berlin N.* (Berlin, 1935), pp. 66–7; David Schwartzkopff, *Der vaterländische Bauverein zu Berlin* (Berlin, 1906), p. 20; Schwartzkopff, *Versöhnungskirche*; Protokollbuch des kirchlich-liberalen Parochialvereins, 21 January 1907, 29 November 1909 (AKG).

37. Hirschberg, *Die soziale Lage*, pp. 22–3; P. Pieper, *Kirchliche Statistik Deutschlands* (Freiburg, 1899), p. 232.

218   *Notes*

38. *BSM*, 2 (1879–80), pp. 180–2.

39. Ibid., 1 (1878–9), pp. 139–41.

40. E.g. a report from Wedding, ibid., 22 (1900), pp. 82–93, contains numerous examples of visits by a missionary to the sick.

41. Herzberg, *Ich bin doch Wer*, pp. 59–98.

42. Günther Dehn, *Proletarische Jugend*, 2nd edn (Berlin, 1930), p. 127; *BSM*, 22 (1900), pp. 179–81, describes a city missionary's conversation on a park bench in the Humboldtshain with an old woman who said that in the village she came from the church had kept the people under.

43. *BSM*, 1 (1878–9), pp. 72–6.

44. See, e.g., W. Ilgenstein, *Die religiöse Gedankenwelt der Sozialdemokratie* (Berlin, 1914).

45. *BSM*, 3 (1880), p. 37.

46. According to Stoecker in a speech reported ibid., 2 (1879–80), pp. 150–1, the Berlin unbeliever referred to the Bible as 'a book of fairy-tales' and to God as 'nothing', but when asked about Jesus, replied that he was 'a good, friendly person, or some kind of socialist'. A similar point was made by a Halle pastor who was the main speaker in a session on 'The religious crisis of the modern working class' at the Evangelical Social Congress in 1904. *Chronik der Christlichen* Welt, 14 (1904), p. 293.

47. Jochen-Christoph Kaiser, 'Sozialdemokratie und "praktische" Religionskritik: Das Beispiel der Kirchenaustrittsbewegung 1878–1914', *Archiv für Sozialgeschichte*, 22 (1982), pp. 268–71.

48. *BSM*, 11 (1889), pp. 26–30.

49. Mayer, *Anfänge der Zionsgemeinde*, p. 66.

50. *BSM*, 1 (1878–9), pp. 72–6, 139–41; 22 (1900), pp. 82–93.

51. Ibid., 3 (1880), pp. 35–8.

52. Eberhard Büchner, *Sekten und Sektierer in Berlin* (Berlin, 1905), pp. 6–9. Annual membership statistics are published in *SJSB*. There is also a useful discussion of the 'sects' in Hölscher, *Weltgericht*, pp. 104–30.

53. Büchner, *Sekten und Sektierer*, pp. 45–9, 63–9.

54. *Die Kirchennot Berlins muss aufhören!*, von einem Hoffnungsvollen (1889), p. 10. There is a copy of this pamphlet in Evangelischer Oberkirchenrat: Generalia, 2, 20, 'Die Korrespondenz über die Hebung der kirchlichen Notständen in Berlin' (EZA). Hölscher, *Weltgericht*, p. 129.

55. Bchner, *Sekten und Sektierer*, pp. 19–20.

56. Ibid., p. 20.

57. Von Loebbel, *Geschichte der evangelischen Kirchengemeinden*, pp. 12–13.

58. There is a summary in Hölscher, *Weltgericht*, pp. 156–60; detailed statistics of communions, baptisms, confirmations, church weddings and funerals with the participation of a clergyman were published annually in *SJSB*. There is impressionistic evidence to suggest that church attendance also rose in the 1880s, but no precise figures: e.g., Hermann Neubauer, *Geschichte der Nazarethgemeinde 1835–1925* (Berlin, 1926), pp. 23–5; *Geschichte der St.-Pauls-Gemeinde*, p. 49.

59. Neubauer, *Nazarethgemeinde*, pp. 23–5.

60. Eugen Baumann, 'Die Unentbehrlichkeit der Stadtmission und ihre sittlich-religiöse Bedeutung für unsere Tage', (1888), pp. 17–19; copy in Brandenburgisches Konsistorium: Personalia, Eugen Baumann (EZA).

61. Von Loebbel, *Geschichte der evangelischen Kirchengemeinden*, pp. 67–8 and passim.

62. *Berlin und die Berliner*, p. 159.

63. Dehn, *Die alte Zeit*, pp. 166–7.

64. Von Loebbel, *Geschichte der evangelischen Kirchengemeinden*, pp. 56–7; Pieper, *Kirchliche Statistik Deutschlands*, pp. 201–4. For illustrations of some of these churches and information on their origins, see Mugay, *Kanzeln, Könige und Kanonen*, pp. 119–22, 131–5.

65. Loock, 'Die evangelische Kirche', p. 112; F. W. Kittlaus, *Das 'Gasthaus zum geduldigen Lamm'* (Berlin, 1988) provides a vivid account of the social work and the *Vereine* associated with Reconciliation parish in Wedding in the 1920s, when the author's father was pastor.

66. Hölscher, *Weltgericht*, pp. 433–5.

67. Helmut Engel, Stefi Jersch-Wenzel and Wilhelm Treue, eds., *Wedding*, Geschichtslandschaft Berlin, 3 (Berlin, 1990), pp. 44–60.

68. Schwartzkopff, *Der vaterländische Bauverein*, p. 3; Engel, Jersch-Wenzel and Treue, *Wedding*, pp. 433–45 (describing the predominantly Social Democratic Friedrich-Ebert-Siedlung in Wedding); one of the East Berliners interviewed by Herzberg (*Ich bin doch Wer*, p. 18) lived in the 1920s and 1930s in a settlement on the eastern edge of Berlin where 'they were all Communist members'. Friedrich Leyden, *Gross-Berlin: Geographie der Weltstadt* (Breslau, 1933), p. 108, noted that the highest proportion of those without religion (*Konfessionslose*) were generally found in the new settlements—most notably, Bohnsdorf on the southeastern edge of the city which had the record figure of 28 per cent.

69. Engel, Jersch-Wenzel and Treue, *Wedding*, pp. 61–78.

70. Neubauer, *Nazarethgemeinde*, pp. 28–33.

71. Wendland, *Die Entwicklung*, p. 22 and passim.

72. Neubauer, *Nazarethgemeinde*, p. 51.

73. Wendland, *Die Entwicklung*, pp. 20–3, 55–6; Wilhelm Witte, *Die Geschichte der Sophienkirche zu Berlin von 1712 bis 1912* (Berlin, 1912), pp. 111–13.

74. Liang, 'The Social Background', pp. 202–5.

75. There is an extensive literature on Stoecker. The study I have found most helpful is Brakelmann, Greschat and Jochmann, *Protestantismus und Politik*.

76. Ibid., pp. 28–9.

77. See Pollmann, *Landesherrliche Kirchenregiment*, pp. 107–23 and passim.

78. *Chronik der Christlichen Welt*, 23 (1913), pp. 165–8, analyzed the voting patterns in the 1912 church elections.

79. Histories of Berlin working-class parishes frequently refer to the influence of Stoecker on the clergy or on parish organizations: Eugen Bethke, *Hundert Jahre St. Elisabeth-Berlin* (Berlin, 1936), p. 57; Witte, *Geschichte der Sophienkirche*, pp. 122–3; Mayer, *Die Anfänge der Zionsgemeinde*, p. 175; Engel, Jersch-Wenzel and Treue, *Wedding*, p. 63.

80. Brakelmann, Greschat and Jochmann, *Protestantismus und Politik*, pp. 68–72.

81. Wilhelm Frank, *Rosen und Dornen in der Berliner Seelsorgsarbeit in zwanzigjähriger Erfahrung* (Breslau, 1909), pp. 10–12.

82. Robert Schlenke, *Die katholische Kirche in Berlin: Ihre Entwicklung in den letzten fünfzehn Jahren* (Berlin, 1904), pp. 24–32.

83. Hugh McLeod, 'Building the "Catholic Ghetto": Catholic organisations 1870–1914', W. J. Sheils, ed., *Voluntary Religion*, Studies in Church History, 23 (Oxford, 1986), pp. 431–4.

84. *SJSB*; Leyden, *Gross-Berlin*, pp. 103–5.

85. Frank, *Rosen und Dornen*, pp. 30–3; Felix Escher, 'Pfarrgemeinden und Gemeindeorganisation der katholischen Kirche in Berlin bis zur Gründung des Bistums Berlin', Elm and Loock, *Seelsorge und Diakonie*, p. 281.

86. Frank, *Rosen und Dornen*, pp. 26–7.

87. Werner Simon, 'Katholische Schulen, Religionsunterricht und Katechese in Berlin im ausgehenden 19. und beginnenden 20. Jahrhundert', Elm and Loock, *Seelsorge und Diakonie*, p. 384; Frank, *Rosen und Dornen*, p. 25; Schlenke, *Die katholische Kirche in Berlin*, p. 30. For discussion of Catholicism in west Germany, see Jonathan Sperber, *Popular Catholicism in Nineteenth-Century Germany* (Princeton, 1984).

88. Frank, *Rosen und Dornen*, pp. 56–9; Escher, 'Pfarrgemeinden und Gemeindeorganisation', pp. 284–6.

89. Schlenke, *Die katholische Kirche in Berlin*, pp. 24–30, describes the early history of St Boniface parish, where the author was pastor. See also Josef Mooser, 'Arbeiter, Bürger und Priester in den konfessionellen Arbeitervereinen im deutschen Kaiserreich, 1880–1914', Jürgen Kocka, ed., *Arbeiter und Bürger im 19. Jahrhundert* (Munich, 1986), pp. 103–4.

90. Konrad Kotterba, *Die evangelisch-katholischen konfessionellen Verhältnisse Berlins* (Berlin, 1906).

91. *SJSB* provided annual statistics of movement between the various religious communities. In this period there were always more Catholics converting to Protestantism than vice versa, and in mixed marriages it was more common for the children to be baptized as Protestants.

92. EOK; Acta betreffend die Austrittsbewegung und die Landeskirchen, 5, report of 6 January 1914 by Brandenburg Consistory (EZA).

93. Gemeinde Helfer Buchholz, Jahresbericht 1913 (AKG).

94. Ibid.; Kirchenaustritte/Übertritte 1908 (AKG).

95. EOK; Acta betreffend die Austrittsbewegung und die Landeskirchen, 4, pp. 146–52 (EZA). See also *Chronik der Christlichen Welt*, 23 (1913), pp. 192–7, for further details.

96. Vernon L. Lidtke, *The Alternative Culture* (New York, 1985). For socialism as 'substitute religion', see Brigitte Emig, *Die Veredelung des Arbeiters* (Frankfurt/Main, 1980), pp. 94–103.

Chapter 2. London

1. According to Shun-Ichi J. Watanabe, 'Metropolitanism as a Way of Life: The Case of Tokyo, 1868–1930', Anthony Sutcliffe, ed., *Metropolis 1890–1940* (London, 1984), p. 406. However, Sutcliffe, in the introduction to the volume (p. 4) suggests that Peking and Canton may have been the leaders.

2. T. H. S. Escott, *Society in London* (London, 1885), pp. 162–3.

3. James Munson, *The Nonconformists* (London, 1991), pp. 101–3; Richard Mudie-Smith, ed., *The Religious Life of London* (London, 1904), p. 291; Sheila Fletcher, *Maude Royden* (Oxford, 1989), pp. 174–5.

4. For which, see Charles Booth, ed., *Life and Labour of the People in London*, 17 vols. (London, 1902–3), 3rd ser., vol. 1, pp. 119–24.

5. B. I. Coleman, 'Church Extension Movement in London, c. 1800–1860' (Cambridge University Ph.D. thesis, 1968), pp. 58–9, 67, 84, 120–1, 182; Alan Bartlett, 'The churches in Bermondsey 1880–1939' (Birmingham University Ph.D. thesis, 1987), pp. 55–8.

6. K. S. Inglis, *Churches and the Working Classes in Victorian England* (London, 1963); D. B. McIlhiney, 'A Gentleman in every slum: Church of England missions in East London 1837–1914' (Princeton University Ph.D. thesis, 1977); Bartlett, 'Churches in Bermondsey', pp. 261–85.

7. Ibid., pp. 119–20; Jeffrey Cox, *English Churches in a Secular Society: Lambeth 1870–1930* (Oxford, 1982), ch. 3, p. 287.

8. Edward Royle, *Radicals, Secularists and Republicans: Popular Freethought in Britain, 1866–1915* (Manchester, 1980), pp. 45–51.

9. Stan Shipley, *Club Life and Socialism in Mid-Victorian London* (Oxford, 1971); Hugh McLeod, *Class and Religion in the Late Victorian City* (London, 1974), pp. 60–2. See also W. H. Reid, *The Rise and Dissolution of the Infidel Societies in This Metropolis* (London, 1800), pp. 12–13, 14, 18–19, 54, 91, which identified Whitechapel, Spitalfields and Hoxton as centres of secularism, of millenarianism and spiritualism, and of numerous forms of Dissent.

10.   Hugh McLeod, 'White-collar values and the role of religion', Geoffrey Crossick, ed., *The Lower Middle Class in Britain 1870–1914* (London, 1977), pp. 61–88.

11.   McLeod, *Class and Religion*, p. 34. The most detailed account of London Catholicism in this period is in Bartlett, 'Churches in Bermondsey', pp. 302–18.

12.   David Feldman, 'Immigrants and workers, Englishmen and Jews: Jewish immigrants to the East End of London 1880–1906' (Cambridge University Ph.D. thesis, 1985), pp. 15–36.

13.   Lloyd Gartner, *The Jewish Immigrant in Britain 1870–1914* (2nd edn, London, 1973), pp. 143–8.

14.   Booth, *Life and Labour*, 3rd ser., vol. 1, p. 213; vol. 3, p. 130.

15.   For comments on the religious censuses and summaries of the results, see McLeod, *Class and Religion*, and Cox, *English Churches*.

16.   McLeod, *Class and Religion*, p. 304.

17.   Ibid., pp. 301–6, 40.

18.   Gartner, *The Jewish Immigrant*, pp. 192–7. *East London Observer*, 3 January 1914, quoted at length from the annual report of the Rector of Whitechapel, who claimed that 'thousands of Jews in the East End are drifting away from the Synagogue and from the restrictions and laws of Judaism'. Many similar comments by Jewish observers in the 1920s are quoted in Elaine R. Smith, 'Jews and politics in the East End of London 1918–39', David Cesarani, ed., *The Making of Modern Anglo-Jewry* (Oxford, 1990), pp. 142–4.

19.   Cox, *English Churches*, pp. 64–6, 294; Bartlett, 'Churches in Bermondsey', pp. 178–9.

20.   Gartner, *The Jewish Immigrant*, pp. 187–214.

21.   David Englander, 'Anglicised but not Anglican: Jews in Victorian Britain', Gerald Parsons, ed., *Religion in Victorian Britain*, 4 vols. (Manchester, 1988), vol. 1, p. 265. For tensions between English-born and immigrant Jews, see also Feldman, *Immigrants and Workers*, pp. 254–8 and passim.

22.   Essex Interviews, no. 417, pp. 23–4; Booth, *Life and Labour*, 3rd ser., vol. 2, p. 34; McLeod, *Class and Religion*, pp. 106–7.

23.   Todd Endelman, 'Communal Solidarity and Family Loyalty among the Jewish Elite of Victorian London', *Victorian Studies*, 28 (1985), pp. 491–526.

24.   Mudie-Smith, *Religious Life of London*, pp. 45–8, 55–7.

25.   George Acorn, *One of the Multitude* (London, 1911), pp. 51, 65, 151, 173–9.

26.   Alexander Paterson, *Across the Bridges* (London, 1911), p. 175.

27.   Essex Interviews, no. 261, pp. 41–2.

28.   Ibid., no. 417, p. 22. See also the discussion of the gap between clergy and people in Colin Marchant, 'Interaction of church and society in an East London borough (West Ham)' (London University Ph.D. thesis, 1979), pp. 262–3.

29.   Bartlett, 'Churches in Bermondsey', pp. 125–9.

30.   McIlhiney, 'A gentleman in every slum', p. 228.

31.   Gillian Rose, 'Locality, politics and culture: Poplar in the 1920s' (London University Ph.D. thesis, 1989), p. 287.

32.   Ibid., p. 288; Bartlett, 'Churches in Bermondsey', pp. 127–8; Raphael Samuel, *East End Underworld: Chapters in the Life of Arthur Harding* (London, 1981), pp. 241–5, 264.

33.   Essex Interviews, no. 113, pp. 23–4.

34.   Ibid., no. 5, p. 27.

35.   Cox, *English Churches*, pp. 167–75.

36.   Alan Bartlett, Interview no. 9 (Tapes and transcripts in his possession).

37.   Inglis, *Churches and the Working Classes*, pp. 79–85.

38.   McLeod, *Class and Religion*, p. 92.

39.   BC, B198, pp. 93–95.

40.   See the coloured maps in the first six volumes of Booth, *Life and Labour,* 3rd series.

41.   See, e.g., Jerry White, *The Worst Street in North London: Campbell Bunk, Islington, Between the Wars* (London, 1986), pp. 78–9. From the 1890s to the 1950s all residents of Campbell Road were stigmatized by outsiders; but the residents themselves were very conscious of the internal division between the bottom end of the street and the more respectable top end.

42.   Essex Interviews, no. 230, p. 38; Raphael Samuel, East London MS: interview with Charles Causon, pp. 22–3.

43.   Janet McCalman, 'Respectability and working-class politics in Late Victorian London', *Historical Studies*, 19 (1980), pp. 108–24.

44.   Essex Interviews, no. 126, p. 32; Hugh McLeod, 'New perspectives on Victorian working-class religion: The oral evidence', *Oral History Journal*, 14 (1986), p. 33.

45.   Raphael Samuel, East London MS: interview with Ethel Vargo, p. 19.

46.   Booth, *Life and Labour*, 3rd ser., vol. 4, p. 145.

47.   Ibid., vol. 3, pp. 142–5.

48.   Raphael Samuel, East London MS: interview with Mrs Stone, p. 32.

49.   In addition to the oral history projects already cited (those organized by Paul Thompson and Thea Vigne at the University of Essex, by Raphael Samuel and by Alan Bartlett), I have also used interviews recorded by Gillian Rose.

50.   Ibid., no. 284, pp. 4, 45, 55.

51.   E.g., ibid., no. 113, p. 17; no. 296, p. 18. See also nos. 5, 71, 205, in all of which the respondent's parents seem to be regarded as a unit.

52.   Ibid., no. 368, p. 26; no. 417, p. 64.

53.   Ibid., no. 368, p. 53.

54.   Ibid., no. 125, p. 17; no. 205, p. 19; no. 417, p. 40.

55.   Ibid., no. 240, p. 17.

56.   Ibid., no. 257, p. 14.

57.   E.g., Essex Interviews, no. 230, p. 30, where the respondent's father lost his job because of his union activities.

58.   Ibid., no. 245, pp. 10, 17, 24, 25, 28.

59.   Ibid., no. 240, p. 25.

60.   Ibid., no. 245, p. 37.

61.   Ibid., no. 70, p. 16; no. 391, p. 45.

62.   Ibid., nos. 76, 333, 407.

63.   Ibid., no. 417, pp. 23–4.

64.   Compare the friendly relations with the local clergy described in Essex Interviews, no. 302 (Canning Town), 368 (Wapping) and 407 (Spitalfields) with the much more distant relationship suggested in no. 53 (where the respondent's family lived in a Paddington mews) and no. 145 (West Norwood). However, since very few of the working-class respondents lived in predominantly middle-class and upper-class areas, it is probably unwise to generalize from these examples.

65.   BC, B196, pp. 19–21.

66.   Essex Interviews, no. 261, p. 28.

67.   Ibid., no. 240, p. 17. For claims from London in the 1890s that working-class Londoners expected church-goers to be teetotallers and questioned their sincerity if they were not, see McLeod, *Class and Religion*, p. 115.

68.   See Edward Royle, *Victorian Infidels* (Manchester, 1974), and *Radicals, Secularists and Republicans*.

69.   Susan Budd, *Varieties of Unbelief* (London, 1977), p. 109.

70.   Royle, *Radicals, Secularists and Republicans*, pp. 333–6.

71.   Shipley, *Club Life and Socialism*, p. 38.

72.   Ibid., pp. 30, 33.

73.   Ibid., pp. 40–1; Paul Thompson, *Socialists, Liberals and Labour: The Struggle for London 1885–1914* (London, 1967), p. 33.

74.   William Rossiter in *Nineteenth Century*, 21 (1887), pp. 262–72, and 22 (1888), pp. 111–26.

75.   Paterson, *Across the Bridges*, p. 218.

76.   Shipley, *Club Life and Socialism*, p. 33.

77.   Ibid., p. 21.

78.   Ibid., pp. 23–4, 40–1; Royle, *Radicals, Secularists and Republicans*, pp. 109–21.

79.   Ibid., pp. 45–51; Royle, *Victorian Infidels*, p. 239; Shipley, *Club Life and Socialism*, pp. 37–8.

80.   McLeod, *Class and Religion*, pp. 35, 40–1.

81.   Ibid., p. 39.

82.   Ibid., p. 309.

83.   Cox, *English Churches*, p. 304.

84.   Bartlett, 'Churches in Bermondsey', pp. 401–3.

85.   Addresses taken from Church Handbooks in BC.

86.   Budd, *Varieties of Unbelief*, pp. 107–8, notes that converts to secularism often came from a strongly Christian background; the biographical appendix in Royle, *Victorian Infidels*, includes several examples of secularists who subsequently reconverted to Christianity.

87.   Royle, *Radicals, Secularists and Republicans*, pp. 130–1.

88.   Bartlett, 'Churches in Bermondsey', pp. 401–3.

89.   McLeod, *Class and Religion*, p. 314. For discussion of the crisis in middle-class religion, see Cox, *English Churches*, and J. N. Morris, 'Religion and urban change in Victorian England: A case study of the borough of Croydon, 1840–1914' (Oxford University D.Phil. thesis, 1985).

90.   Owen Chadwick, *The Victorian Church*, 2 vols. (London, 1966–70), vol. 2, p. 249.

91.   Bartlett, 'Churches in Bermondsey', p. 178.

92.   Cox, *English Churches*, pp. 198-201.

93.   Ibid., pp. 205–7; Bartlett, 'Churches in Bermondsey', pp. 135–44, 153-5; Morris, 'Religion and urban change', pp. 263–84.

94.   Royle, *Radicals, Secularists and Republicans*, pp. 36–43; John Kent, *From Darwin to Blatchford* (London, 1966); Budd, *Varieties of Unbelief*, p. 107.

95.   McLeod, *Class and Religion*, pp. 108–9.

Chapter 3. New York

1.   Diane Ravitch, *The Great School Wars: New York City 1805–1973* (New York, 1974), pp. 70–6.

2.   J. D. McCabe, *New York by Sunlight and Gaslight* (New York, 1882), pp. 622–6.

3.   David C. Hammack, *Power and Society: Greater New York at the Turn of the Century* (New York, 1982), pp. 65–79.

4.   In a sample of 124, 64 stated their religious affiliation. Of these, 28 per cent were Episcopalians, 22 per cent Presbyterians, 13 per cent Methodists, 11 per cent Congregationalists, and 5 per cent Baptists. By contrast, Catholics, Lutherans and Jews totalled 14 per cent. The proportion stating their affiliation varied considerably by profession: lawyers, politicians and editors had a high rate of declared affiliation; writers, artists and educators had a low rate; and businessmen were about average.

5.   J. D. McCabe, *The Secrets of the Great City* (Philadelphia, 1868), pp. 176–9.

6.   Clyde Griffen, 'An urban church in ferment: The Episcopal Church in New York City, 1880–1900' (Columbia University Ph.D. thesis, 1960), pp. 7–10, 38, 220–1.

7.   Hammack, *Power and Society*, pp. 78–9, 101–2; Allen F. Davis, *Spearheads for Reform: The Social Settlements and the Progressive Movement* (New York, 1967), pp. 26–9, 265.

8.   Jay Dolan, *The Immigrant Church: New York's Irish and German Catholics, 1815–1865* (Baltimore, 1975), pp. 129–40; Arthur Goren, *New York Jews and the Quest for Community: The Kehillah Experiment, 1908–1922* (New York, 1970).

9.   Martin Shefter, 'The electoral foundations of the political machine: New York City, 1884–1897', Joel Silbey and Allan G. Bogue, eds., *The History of American Political Behavior* (Princeton, N. J., 1978), pp. 263–98; Steven P. Erie, *Rainbow's End: Irish-Americans and the Dilemmas of Urban Machine Politics, 1840–1985* (Berkeley, Calif., 1988).

10.   Hammack, *Power and Society*, ch. 5.

11.   Daniel Czitrom, 'Underworlds and underdogs: Big Tim Sullivan and Metropolitan Politics in New York, 1889–1913', *Journal of American History*, 78 (1991), pp. 536–58.

12.   J. M. King et al., *The Religious Condition of New York City* (New York, 1889) contains the proceedings of a conference on the evangelization of the city attended by representatives of most of the Protestant denominations. Many speakers implied that the Protestant churches had little hold on the poor (pp. 101, 136, 171, 190–1). However, Griffen, 'An urban church in ferment', p. 34, estimates that about a third of New York City Episcopalians came from lower-income groups in the 1880s and 1890s.

13.   For statistics, see Ira Rosenwaike, *Population History of New York City* (Syracuse, N. Y., 1972). For discussion of the role of ethnicity in New York's history, see Nathan Glazer and Daniel P. Moynihan, *Beyond the Melting-Pot: The Negroes, Puerto Ricans, Jews and Italians of New York City*, 2nd edn (Cambridge, Mass., 1970); Thomas Kessner, *The Golden Door: Italian and Jewish Immigrant Mobility in New York City 1880–1915* (New York, 1977); Melvyn Dubofsky, *When Workers Organize* (Amherst, Mass., 1968), pp. 14–19.

14.   Hammack, *Power and Society*, p. 85.

15.   See Federation of Churches and Christian Workers in New York City, *Sociological Canvass*, 3 vols. (New York, 1897–1901); and the journal *Federation* published from 1901 onwards.

16.   Rosenwaike, *Population History*, pp. 122–3, quotes the contemporary Protestant statistician, Walter Laidlaw, who used the data collected by the Federation of Churches to suggest that the religious composition of Greater New York in 1900 was: Protestant 47 per cent, Catholic 35 per cent, Jewish 17 per cent. While Laidlaw's estimates for some nationalities are fairly close to my own, I believe that he seriously underestimates the proportion of Catholics among immigrants from Germany and Austria-Hungary.

17.   For instance, among those German Protestants declaring a denomination, only 56 per cent of those in the 14th Assembly District of Manhattan, and 53 per cent in the 11th and 13th Districts, were Lutherans.

18.   Oscar Handlin, *The Uprooted*, 2nd edn (Boston, 1973), ch. 5.

19. Timothy Smith, 'Religion and ethnicity in America', *American Historical Review*, 83 (1978), pp. 1155–85, and 'Lay initiative in immigrant religious life', Tamara Hareven, ed., *Anonymous Americans* (Englewood Cliffs, N. J., 1971).

20. For a statement in general terms, see Louis Wirth, 'Urbanism as a way of life', *American Journal of Sociology*, 44 (1938–9), pp. 1–24. For specific examples, see John Bukowczyk, 'The transforming power of the machine: Popular religion, ideology and secularization among Polish immigrant workers in the United States, 1880–1940', *International Labor and Working Class History*, 34 (1988), pp. 22–38; also, most of the literature on the Jews in New York, e.g., Moses Rischin, *The Promised City* (New York, 1962).

21. See Hutchins Hapgood, *The Spirit of the Ghetto* (1902; repr. New York, 1966), pp. 27–47, where Hapgood's strong claims for the influence of the public school are reinforced in Harry Golden's editorial notes. For a study that emphasizes the school's role, but in a much more nuanced fashion, see Deborah Dash Moore, *At Home in America: Second-Generation New York Jews* (New York, 1981), pp. 89–121.

22. Rudolph J. Vecoli, 'Prelates and peasants: Italian immigrants and the Catholic church', *Journal of Social History*, 2 (1969), pp. 217–68; this point is also stressed in the preface to Randall M. Miller and Thomas D. Marzik, eds., *Immigrants and Religion in Urban America* (Philadelphia, 1977).

23. *New York Times*, 24 November 1902.

24. An estimated 15 per cent of heads of household were Jewish.

25. Federation of Churches, *Sociological Canvass*, 3.

26. Hammack, *Power and Society*, p. 83.

27. Dorothy Ross, 'The Irish Catholic immigrant 1880–1900' (Columbia University M.A. thesis, 1959), pp. 1–58.

28. For Manhattan borough a block-by-block ethnic map based on the 1900 census is provided in *First Report of the Tenement House Commission*, 2 vols. (New York, 1903), 2; Edward Ewing Pratt, *Industrial Causes of the Congestion of Population in New York City* (New York, 1911), provides information on the other boroughs drawn from the 1905 state census.

29. This conclusion was reached by comparing the number of church members in each assembly district, published in *Federation*, 2 (1902), with the proportion of Catholics in the population of the district, as reported in the various surveys of religious affiliation published in that journal or in *Sociological Canvass*.

30. J. G. Shea, *The Catholic Churches of New York City* (New York, 1878), pp. 5–6.

31. Jay Dolan, *The American Catholic Experience* (New York, 1985), pp. 302–3; Richard M. Linkh, *American Catholicism and European Immigrants 1900–1924* (New York, 1975), p. 4; Silvano Tomasi, *Piety and Power* (New York, 1975), p. 81.

32. Shea, *Catholic Churches*, states the place of birth of the pastors of all the city's parishes.

33. WPA, 'The Irish in New York', File 9, 'Religion', paper by Harold Wood, pp. 13–14 (New York Municipal Archives).

34. M. A. Gordon, 'Studies in Irish and Irish-American thought and behavior in Gilded Age New York City' (Rochester University Ph.D. thesis, 1977), p. xxxiii, cites a song published in New York in 1882, 'I'm proud I'm an Irishman's son,' which includes bitter references to anti-Irish discrimination.

35. Elsa Herzfeld, *Family Monographs* (New York, 1905), pp. 12–13.

36. Gordon, 'Irish-American thought and behavior', p. 49.

37. Dedicatory sermons at New York churches frequently dwelt on the magnificence of the buildings and the sacrifices required of parishioners during their construction. See

Shea, *Catholic Churches*, pp. 116, 307, 364.

38.   Annual financial reports from parishes, AANY; *Irish World*, 22 January 1887.

39.   H. B. Woolston, *A Study of the Population of Manhattanville* (New York, 1909), pp. 61–2; *Irish World*, 25 June 1887; see also James J. Green, 'American Catholics and the Irish Land League, 1879–82', *Catholic Historical Review*, 35 (1949), p. 39.

40.   WPA, 'The Irish of New York' (Library of Congress, Folk Music Division, Washington, D.C.).

41.   Dick Butler, *Dock Walloper* (New York, 1931), p. 40.

42.   Bourke Cockran took communion every day; 'Mister' Murphy, leader of Tammany Hall from 1902 to 1924, was famous for his refusal to profit from offering protection to brothels or gambling houses. James McGurrin, *Bourke Cockran, A Free Lance in American Politics* (New York, 1948), pp. 305–6; Robert F. Wesser, *A Response to Progressivism: The Democratic Party and New York Politics, 1902–1918* (New York, 1986), p. 23.

43.   Butler, *Dock Walloper*, p. 42.

44.   Ibid., p. 129; Gordon, 'Irish-American thought and behavior', p. 549.

45.   See Henry J. Browne, *One Stop above Hell's Kitchen: Sacred Heart Parish in Clinton* (Hackensack, N. J., 1977), pp. 61–70, for discussion of relations between priests and politicians.

46.   Thomas N. Brown, *Irish-American Nationalism, 1870–1890* (New York, 1966), pp. 34–41.

47.   Robert Emmett Curran, *Michael Augustine Corrigan and the Shaping of Conservative Catholicism in America, 1878–1902* (New York, 1978), pp. 189–93.

48.   Brown, *Irish-American Nationalism*, pp. 34–41, 122; Eric Foner, 'Class, ethnicity and radicalism in the Gilded Age: The Land League and Irish-America', *Marxist Perspectives*, 1 (1978), p. 46; James Paul Rodechko, *Patrick Ford and his Search for America: A Case Study of American Journalism, 1879–1913* (New York, 1976), pp. 166–8.

49.   Foner, 'Class, ethnicity and radicalism', pp. 46–7; Rodechko, *Patrick Ford*, pp. 168–9; Dolan, *American Catholic Experience*, pp. 330–40; Shefter, 'Electoral foundations'.

50.   Parish files: Epiphany (AANY).

51.   John Talbot Smith, *The Catholic Church in the Archdiocese of New York*, 2 vols. (New York, 1905), 2, p. 470.

52.   P. J. Murnion, 'Towards theopolitan ministry: The changing structure of the pastoral ministry, New York, 1920–1970' (Columbia University Ph.D. thesis, 1972), p. 128.

53.   Questionnaire on the history of Sacred Heart parish (Sacred Heart rectory).

54.   Hugh McLeod, 'Building the "Catholic Ghetto": Catholic organisations c. 1870–1914', W. J. Sheils and Diana Wood, eds., *Voluntary Religion*, Studies in Church History, 23 (Oxford, 1986), pp. 411–44.

55.   For general discussion of trends in this period, see Dolan, *American Catholic Experience*, pp. 189, 206.

56.   Butler, *Dock Walloper*, p. 6.

57.   Browne, *One Stop above Hell's Kitchen*, ch. 2.

58.   Ibid., pp. 16–17.

59.   George A. Kelly, *The Story of St Monica's Parish 1879–1954* (New York, 1954), pp. 53–8.

60.   Parish files: Holy Name (AANY).

61.   Murnion, 'Towards theopolitan ministry', p. 129.

62.   *The Year Book and Book of Customs of the Church of Our Lady of Lourdes, Washington Heights, New York* (New York, 1916), p. 83.

63.   Ibid., p. 35.

64.   Richard Burtsell, Diary, 15 February 1887 (AANY).

65. Stanley Nadel, *Little Germany: Ethnicity, Religion and Class in New York City 1845–80* (Urbana, Ill., 1990), pp. 161–2; *New Yorker Staats-Zeitung*, 24 April 1910.

66. See *Federation*, 2 (April 1902), which provided a list of places of worship in each district of New York, with statistics of membership and of the value of their property.

67. Federal Writers' Project, *New York City Guide* (New York, 1939), p. 251.

68. Hammack, *Power and Society*, p. 83.

69. J. S. Billings, *Vital Statistics of New York and Brooklyn* (Washington, 1893), pp. 3, 9, 22, 51.

70. Nadel, *Little Germany*, p. 90.

71. 'The Germans', *Harper's Weekly*, 4 August 1888; at about the same time fairly similar comments were being made by the prominent Lutheran minister Rev. G. U. Wenner, in King et al., *Religious Condition*, pp. 26–32.

72. *Altes und Neues*, May 1902, February 1904, February 1906 (copies at St Luke's Church).

73. *Church of St Joseph in Yorkville, New York City* (New York, 1932).

74. See note 29 for sources and methods used for these calculations.

75. Goren, *New York Jews*, p. 14; Stephen Sharot, *Judaism: A Sociology* (New York, 1976), p. 107.

76. Parish files: Immaculate Conception, Bronx, John Leibfritz to Archbishop Corrigan, 22 July 1892 (AANY).

77. A. B. Faust, *The German Element in the United States*, 2 vols. (New York, 1909), 2, pp. 369–70; Hartmut Keil and Heinz Ickstadt, 'Elemente einer deutschen Arbeiterkultur in Chicago zwischen 1880 und 1890', *Geschichte und Gesellschaft*, 5 (1979), pp. 119–20.

78. Oscar Spengler, *Das deutsche Element von New York* (New York, 1913).

79. H. Kloss, *Um die Einigung des Deutschamerikanertums* (Berlin, 1937), pp. 31–63; Nadel, *Little Germany*, pp. 104–21.

80. Death notices in the *New Yorker Staats-Zeitung* tended to list organizations with which the deceased had been associated and to invite attendance at the funeral by their members.

81. Keil and Ickstadt, 'Elemente einer deutschen Arbeiterkultur', pp. 109–10, 119–20.

82. C. Stürenberg, *Klein-Deutschland* (New York, 1886), pp. 3–11, 62–71, 44–52, 35–43, 53–61, 35–6, 29–33.

83. Lilian Betts, *Leaven in a Great City* (New York, 1902), p. 41; *New Yorker Staats-Zeitung*, 1 January 1886; Billings, *Vital Statistics*, p. 21, showed that in 1889–90 the suicide rate in Brooklyn was about three times higher for those of German stock than those of Irish stock.

84. *Geschichtliche Skizze zum Goldenen Jubiläum der Evangelisch-Lutherischen Immanuelskirche zu Yorkville, New York* (New York, 1913), p. 13; George Haas, *Geschichte der Ev.-Luth. Kirche zu St. Markus* (New York, 1897), pp. 33–9.

85. G. U. Wenner, *The Lutherans of New York* (New York, 1918), pp. 107–9; *Immanuelskirche*, pp. 28–30.

86. Wenner, *Lutherans of New York*, p. 117.

87. Sources and methods used for these estimates as in note 29.

88. Obituaries of leading members of St Luke's Church in *Altes und Neues*; Hermann Hagedorn, *The Hyphenated Family* (New York, 1960), pp. 42–3. For general dicussion of importance of regional differences among German immigrants, see Nadel, *Little Germany*, pp. 13–46.

89. Church records kept at St Luke's Church.

90. *St Luke's Lutheran Church in the City of New York 1850–1940* (New York, 1940);

James Sigurd Lapham, 'The German-Americans of New York City, 1860–1890' (St John's University Ph.D. thesis, 1977), pp. 112–3; Haas, *Ev.-Luth. Kirche zu St. Markus; Immanuelskirche*, pp. 14, 21.

91. Wenner, *Lutherans of New York*, pp. 41–3, 73–8.

92. *Immanuelkirche*, pp. 1–11.

93. *Altes und Neues*, April 1912.

94. Heinrich Paul Suhr, *Hundert Jahre Deutsche Evangelisch-Lutherische St.-Pauls-Kirche in der Stadt New York* (New York, 1940), pp. 114–5; Wenner in King et al., *Religious Condition*, pp. 26–32.

95. Lapham, 'German-Americans', pp. 109–10; *St Luke's Lutheran Church*.

96. Lapham, 'German-Americans', pp. 94–109.

97. *History and Constitution of St Peter's-in-the-Bronx Lutheran* (New York, 1937).

98. Suhr, *Hundert Jahre St.-Pauls-Kirche*, pp. 128–59.

99. Surveys of religious affiliation in *Sociological Canvass and Federation*.

100. Dolan, *Immigrant Church*, pp. 68–98.

101. Parish files: St Anthony of Padua, Bronx, Joseph Moeller to Arcbishop Farley, 29 January and 20 February 1903 (AANY).

102. John K. Sharp, *History of the Diocese of Brooklyn 1853–1953*, 2 vols. (New York, 1954), 2, p. 83, states that only three new German parishes were formed in that diocese after 1890, because the younger generation were getting absorbed into English-language parishes.

103. Dolan, *Immigrant Church*, pp. 94–5.

104. Parish financial reports (AANY).

105. CMHR, 2, p. 1 (ARBP).

106. Ibid., 1, pp. 344, 346.

107. Chronicles of Immaculate Conception Parish, The Bronx, 1, pp. 62–3 (ARBP).

108. Records kept at St Luke's and Immanuel churches.

109. R. E. Helbig, *Auch ein Kirchenbote: Erlebnisse eines Gliedes einer Missourischen Gemeinde, oder Wie man suspendiert wird* (New York, 1911).

110. Rosenwaike, *Population History*, pp. 67, 70, 95.

111. Rischin, *The Promised City*, p. 94. For a good overview of east European Jewish migration and settlement in New York, see Irving Howe, *World of our Fathers* (New York, 1976).

112. Rischin, *Promised City*, pp. 76–8.

113. Ibid., pp. 92–4.

114. Jeffrey Gurock, *When Harlem Was Jewish 1870–1930* (New York, 1979), ch. 2.

115. Howe, *World of our Fathers*, pp. 195–200; Jo Renée Fine and Gerard R. Wolfe, *The Synagogues of New York's Lower East Side* (New York, 1978), p. 31.

116. Gurock, *When Harlem Was Jewish*, p. 23; Jonathan D. Sarna, ed., *People Walk on Their Heads: Moses Weinberger's "Jews and Judaism in New York"* (New York, 1982), pp. 12–14; Alter F. Landesman, *Brownsville* (New York, 1971), p. 76, also notes that American conditions of 'freedom and free enterprise' resulted in sharp competition among ritual slaughterers and circumcisers, sometimes leading to 'unpleasant incidents'.

117. Moses Rischin, ed., *Grandma Never Lived in America: The New Journalism of Abraham Cahan* (Bloomington, Ind., 1985), pp. 79–82, 92–5; Allon Schoener, ed., *Portal to America: The Lower East Side 1870–1925* (New York, 1967), p. 110; Irving Howe and Kenneth Libo, *How We Lived 1880–1930* (New York, 1979), pp. 116–7.

118. Sarna, *People Walk on Their Heads*, passim; Rischin, *Promised City*, pp. 145–8.

119. Ibid., p. 155.

120. *Federation*, 5, no. 4, p. 39; 6, no. 5. Sharot, *Judaism*, p. 106, suggests that in 1915

about a quarter of adult Jewish males in the city were synagogue members.

121. Rischin, *Grandma Never Lived in America*, p. 378.

122. Samuel Chotzinoff, *A Lost Paradise: Early Reminiscences* (New York, 1955), pp. 101–3, 278–9, 290.

123. See his short story *Yekl*, published in 1896, and novel, *The Rise of David Levinsky*, published in 1917.

124. Hamilton Holt, ed., *The Life-Stories of Undistinguished Americans* (New York, 1906), p. 38.

125. Rischin, *Promised City*, ch. 3.

126. Howe, *World of our Fathers*, pp. 287–324; Moore, *At Home in America*, pp. 73–5.

127. Charles Leinenweber, 'The Class and Ethnic Bases of New York City Socialism, 1904–1915', *Labor History*, 22 (1981), p. 39.

128. Leinenweber estimates that 39 per cent of those joining the Socialist Party in Manhattan and the Bronx between 1908 and 1912 were east European Jews, and that 13 per cent were Finns, which was far higher than the proportion of Finns in the population; ibid., p. 43.

129. Rischin, *Promised City*, pp. 90–1, 147; Jenna Weissman Joselit, *Our Gang: Jewish Crime and the New York Jewish Community 1900–1940* (Bloomington, Ind., 1983).

130. Moore, *At Home in America*, pp. 124–9.

131. Jeffrey Gurock, 'The Orthodox Synagogue', Jack Wertheimer, ed., *The American Synagogue, A Sanctuary Transformed* (Cambridge, 1987), pp. 48–9.

132. Rischin, *Promised City*, pp. 146–7.

133. CCNY Interviews, I-49.

134. Hapgood, *Spirit of the Ghetto*, pp. 3–7.

135. Ibid., pp. 53–75; Chotzinoff, *Lost Paradise*, pp. 73–4, describes the struggles of his father, who had made a good living from running a religious school in Russia, but in America faced both poverty and the rebellion against Judaism of two of his children.

136. Jeffrey Gurock, 'Jewish Communal Divisiveness in Response to Christian Influences on the Lower East Side, 1900–1910', Todd M. Endelman, ed., *Jewish Apostasy in the Modern World* (New York, 1987), pp. 255–71.

137. Moore, *At Home in America*, pp. 83–7. Similar points in respect of nonobservant working-class Jews in London are made in Elaine R. Smith, 'Jews and Politics in the East End of London 1918–39', David Cesarani, ed., *The Making of Modern Anglo-Jewry* (Oxford, 1990), p. 144.

138. Jack Wertheimer, 'The Conservative Synagogue', Wertheimer, *American Synagogue*, pp. 112–16.

139. Moore, *At Home in America*, p. 135.

140. Landesman, *Brownsville*, pp. 213–5.

141. For the origins of synagogues established during the period of mass immigration, see many examples in Fine and Wolfe, *Synagogues of Lower East Side*. For instance, out of twenty-one 'small synagogues' discussed, twelve were named after a town in eastern Europe. Moore, *At Home in America*, pp. 129–47, notes the more inclusive character of the Synagogue Center.

142. Ibid., pp. 61–82.

143. Spiritual Reports, Archive of the Diocese of Brooklyn (Brookyn Diocesan Chancery).

144. Ronald H. Bayor, *Neighbors in Conflict: The Irish, Germans, Jews and Italians of New York City, 1929–41* (Baltimore, 1978).

Chapter 4. Religion in the City

1.   For detailed figures, see *Chronik der Christlichen Welt*, 23 (1913), pp. 418–9. For comments, including contemporary criticism of the census, see Joachim Rohde, 'Streiflichter aus der Berliner Kirchengeschichte von 1900 bis 1918', Günter Wirth, ed., *Beiträge zur Berliner Kirchengeschichte* (Berlin, 1987), pp. 219–20. However, the census receives some degree of independent verification from the weekly record of attendance at the Capernaum Church in Kollektenbuch 1907–1913 (AKG): although no record was made on the day of the census, the census figure is very similar to that recorded by the clergy for the Sunday following.

2.   On twenty-five Sundays in the period November 1912–October 1913 when attendance at both services at the Capernaum Church was recorded, there were fifteen cases where the morning congregation was larger, nine where the evening congregation was larger, and one where they were exactly equal.

3.   According to *SJSB*, 32 (1908–11), pp. 869–71, membership of Protestant denominations outside the *Landeskirche* in Berlin in 1910 totalled 23,286, or 1.1 per cent of the population.

4.   In the early twentieth century, the pastor of one Berlin parish gave estimates of mass attendance in his parish that suggested a weekly rate of around 25–30 per cent; another estimated that of those Catholics required to attend mass in his parish, slightly over a quarter did so on any given Sunday. Robert Schlenke, *Die Katholische Kirche in Berlin: Ihre Entwicklung in den letzten fünfzehn Jahren* (Berlin, 1904), p. 30; Wilhelm Frank, *Rosen und Dornen in der Berliner Seelsorgsarbeit in zwanzigjähriger Erfahrung* (Breslau, 1909), p. 25.

5.   By 1913 Protestant church attendance had declined somewhat by comparison with the middle and later nineteenth century. For instance, in the 1850s, a pastor estimated that 4–5 per cent of the members of the *Landeskirche* attended services each week, and in 1869 a census recorded an average attendance of 2 per cent at morning service. F. G. Lisco, *Zur Kirchengeschichte Berlins* (Berlin, 1857), pp. 309–13; Wolfgang Ribbe, 'Zur Entwicklung und Funktion der Pfarrgemeinden in der evangelischen Kirche Berlins bis zum Ende der Monarchie', Kaspar Elm and Hans-Dietrich Loock, eds., *Seelsorge und Diakonie in Berlin* (Berlin, 1990), p. 252.

6.   The New York and London figures are taken from the U.S. census of 1910 and the census of England and Wales in 1911; Berlin figures are taken from *SJSB*, 32 (1908–11), pp. 862–73.

7.   Gérard Cholvy and Yves-Marie Hilaire, *Histoire religieuse de la France contemporaine*, 3 vols (Toulouse, 1985–8), 2, pp. 187, 203.

8.   Hugh McLeod, 'Religion', John Langton and R. J. Morris, eds., *Atlas of Industrializing Britain 1780–1914* (London, 1986), p. 212.

9.   E. Rolffs, *Das kirchliche Leben der evangelischen Kirchen in Niedersachsen* (Tübingen, 1917), pp. 591–2.

10.   Friedrich Sass, *Berlin in seiner neuesten Zeit und Entwicklung, 1846* (Berlin, 1983), pp. 111–2.

11.   Ernst Dronke, *Berlin*, 2 vols (Frankfurt/Main, 1846), 1, pp. 9–10.

12.   Hans Ostwald, *Dunkle Winkeln in Berlin* (Berlin, 1905), introduction.

13.   Julius Bab, *Berliner Boheme* (Berlin, 1905); H. Freimark, *Moderne Geisterbeschwörer und Wahrheitssucher* (Berlin, 1907); Eberhard Büchner, *Sekten und Sektierer in Berlin* (Berlin, 1905).

14.   C. M. Davies, *Orthodox London*, 2 vols (London, 1874–5), *Unorthodox London*, 2 vols (London, 1874–5), *Heterodox London*, 2 vols (London, 1874).

15.   *Berlin und die Berliner: Leute, Dinge, Sitten, Winken* (Karlsruhe, 1905), p. 506.

16.   *Parliamentary Papers* (1852–3), 89, Religious Worship in England and Wales, p. clviii.

17.   Callum Brown, 'Did urbanization secularize Britain?' *Urban History Yearbook* (1988), pp. 1–14; Hugh McLeod, *Religion and the Working Class in Nineteenth-Century Britain* (Basingstoke, 1984), pp. 13–16.

18.   For a guide to some of the literature, see Hugh McLeod, 'Urbanisation and religion in 19th-century Britain', Elm and Loock, *Seelsorge und Diakonie*, pp. 63–80.

19.   Christina Rathgeber, 'The Reception of the Religious Aufklärung in Berlin at the End of the 18th Century' (Cambridge University Ph.D. thesis, 1986), pp. 183–9.

20.   Walter Wendland, *Siebenhundert Jahre Kirchengeschichte Berlins* (Berlin, 1930), p. 334; Rohde, 'Streiflichter', p. 223; tables 4–5.

21.   *Berlin und die Berliner*, pp. 375–6.

22.   Günter Brakelmann, Martin Greschat and Werner Jochmann, *Protestantismus und Politik: Werk und Wirkung Adolf Stoeckers* (Hamburg, 1982), pp. 68–72; Walter Wendland, *Die Entwicklung der christlichen Liebestätigkeit in Gross-Berlin vom Mittelalter bis zur Gegenwart* (Berlin, 1939), pp. 58–9.

23.   David Hempton, 'Competitive Religious Structures in Nineteenth-Century Belfast', *Hispania Sacra*, 42 (1990), pp. 413–22; Frank Neal, *Sectarian Violence: The Liverpool Experience 1819–1914* (Manchester, 1988); Karl Rohe, *Vom Revier zum Ruhrgebiet* (Essen, 1986), pp. 19–29.

24.   Silvano Tomasi, *Piety and Power: The Role of Italian Parishes in the New York Metropolitan Area* (New York, 1975), p. 81.

25.   Adrien Dansette, *Histoire religieuse de la France contemporaine*, 2 vols (Paris, 1948–51), 1, pp. 439–40; Joan Ullman, *The Tragic Week: A Study of Anti-Clericalism in Spain 1875–1912* (Cambridge, Mass., 1968).

26.   For discussion of these changes, see Hans-Dietrich Loock, 'Bürgerliche Kirche', *Jahrbuch für Berlin-Brandenburgische Kirchengeschichte*, 49 (1976), pp. 42–57.

27.   Cf. Lucian Hölscher, 'Die Religion des Bürgers: Bürgerliche Frömmigkeit und Protestantische Kirche im 19. Jahrhundert', *Historische Zeitschrift*, 250 (1990), pp. 607–8; Ralph Gibson, *A Social History of French Catholicism 1789–1914* (London, 1989), pp. 195–9; William J. Callahan, *Church, Politics and Society in Spain, 1750–1874* (Cambridge, Mass., 1984), pp. 131–2.

28.   On the conservative trend in the churches after 1815 see, for instance, ibid., p. 113; Robert M. Bigler, *The Politics of German Protestantism* (Los Angeles, 1972), part 2.

29.   Thomas Nipperdey, *Deutsche Geschichte 1800–1866* (Munich, 1983), pp. 440–51; Wendland, *Kirchengeschichte Berlins*, pp. 287–331.

30.   Thomas Nipperdey, *Religion im Umbruch: Deutschland 1870–1914* (Munich, 1988), p. 141. See also Jim Obelkevich, 'Music and Religion in the Nineteenth Century', Jim Obelkevich, Lyndal Roper and Raphael Samuel, eds., *Disciplines of Faith* (London, 1987), pp. 550–65.

31.   Sylvia Paletschek, *Frauen und Dissens: Frauen im Deutschkatholizismus und in den Freien Gemeinden, 1841–1852* (Göttingen, 1990), p. 34.

32.   Bernt Satlow, 'Die Revolution von 1848: Die Kirche und die soziale Frage', Wirth, ed., *Beiträge zur Berliner Kirchengeschichte*, pp. 185–6.

33.   Liberal anti-Catholicism during this period is well-known. See, e.g., the essay on 'Progress and Piety' in David Blackbourn, *Populists and Patricians* (London, 1987), pp. 143–67. Attitudes to Protestantism were more complex: most Liberals were members of the Protestant church, and for many of them their concepts of 'freedom', 'individual conscience', etc., were closely bound up with their understanding of Protestantism. However, their suspi-

cion of priests, dogma and institutional religion generally strained their relationship with the Protestant as well as the Catholic church. See Dieter Langewiesche, *Liberalismus in Deutschland* (Frankfurt/Main, 1988), pp. 180–7, which stresses the Protestant dimensions of the Liberalism of the 1860s and 1870s, and Brakelmann, et al., *Protestantismus und Politik*, pp. 126–8, which stresses its irreligious dimension.

34. Wolfgang Ribbe, ed., *Geschichte Berlins*, 2 vols (Munich, 1987), 2, pp. 680–3; Ursula Koch, *Berliner Presse und europäisches Geschehen, 1871* (Berlin, 1978); *Berlin und die Berliner*, pp. 204–8, lists Berlin papers in 1905, with information on their circulation, style and politics.

35. *Freisinnige Zeitung*, 29 July 1896.

36. *Berliner Zeitung*, 6 January 1889, as quoted in *BSM*, 11 (1889), pp. 26–30.

37. Karl Erich Pollmann, 'Adolf Stoecker', Gerd Heinrich, ed., *Berlinische Lebensbilder: Theologen* (Berlin, 1990), p. 238; Ludwig Lehmann, *Kirchengeschichte der Mark Brandenburg von 1818 bis 1932* (Berlin, 1936), pp. 136–7; Wendland, *Kirchengeschichte Berlins*, pp. 335–6. As an example of the conservative Protestant critique of Marxist-Jewish-Ultramontane Weimar by a pastor sympathetic to the German Christians: Eugen Bethke, *Hundert Jahre St. Elisabeth-Berlin* (Berlin, 1936), pp. 74–6.

38. Wendland, *Liebestätigkeit*, p. 63; Hsi-Huey Liang, 'The social background of the Berlin working-class movement, 1890–1914' (Yale University Ph.D. thesis, 1959), p. 232.

39. V. L. Lidtke, 'August Bebel and German Social Democracy's Relation to the Christian Churches', *Journal of the History of Ideas*, 27 (1966), p. 249; Alfred Kelly, *The Descent of Darwin: The Popularization of Darwinism in Germany 1860–1914* (Chapel Hill, N. C., 1981), pp. 22–8, 127. See also Karl Birker, *Die deutschen Arbeiterbildungsvereine 1840–1870* (Berlin, 1973).

40. Kelly, *Descent of Darwin*, pp. 123–4, 132, 139–41.

41. Nipperdey, *Deutsche Geschichte*, pp. 449–51; Brigitte Emig, *Die Veredelung des Arbeiters* (Frankfurt/Main, 1980), pp. 184–7.

42. Dietrich Mühlberg, ed., *Arbeiterleben um 1900* (Berlin, 1983), p. 56.

43. *BSM*, 1 (1878–9), pp. 53–9.

44. For the imperial period, there are extensive details in Eduard Bernstein, *Die Geschichte der Berliner Arbeiter-Bewegung*, 3 vols (Berlin, 1907–10).

45. Cf. Gerald Parsons, ed., *Religion in Victorian Britain*, 4 vols (Manchester, 1988), 1, pp. 14–67, and 2, pp. 238–57; Jeffrey Cox, *English Churches in a Secular Society* (Oxford, 1982), pp. 146–9.

46. Hugh McLeod, *Class and Religion in the late Victorian City* (London, 1974), ch. 8.

47. Paul Thompson, *Socialists, Liberals and Labour: The Struggle for London 1885–1914* (London, 1967), pp. 95–6, 168–9.

48. John Davis, 'The Progressive Council, 1889–1907', Andrew Saint, ed., *Politics and the People of London: The London County Council 1889–1965* (London, 1989), pp. 27–48; Cox, *English Churches*, pp. 151–76; Susan Pennybacker, '"The millennium by return of post": Reconsidering London Progressivism 1889–1907', David Feldman and Gareth Stedman Jones, eds., *Metropolis: London* (London, 1989), pp. 129–62.

49. Patrick Joyce, *Work, Society and Politics* (Brighton, 1980), pp. 173–9; Hugh McLeod, 'New perspectives on Victorian working-class religion: The oral evidence', *Oral History*, 14 (1986), pp. 38–9.

50. Essex Interviews, no. 368, p. 28.

51. Alan Bartlett, 'The churches in Bermondsey 1880–1939' (Birmingham University Ph.D. thesis, 1987), pp. 82–3.

52. Cox, *English Churches*, p. 113.

53.   Ibid., pp. 110–9; McLeod, *Class and Religion*, p. 106; David Feldman, 'Immigrants and workers, Englishmen and Jews: Jewish immigrants to the East End of London 1880–1906' (Cambridge University Ph.D. thesis, 1985), pp. 316–7.

54.   Cox, *English Churches*, pp. 136–51.

55.   Ibid., pp. 232–3.

56.   McLeod, *Class and Religion*, p. 66.

57.   Herbert Morrison, *Herbert Morrison* (London, 1960), p. 22.

58.   Cox, *English Churches*, pp. 87–8, 194–7. The best discussion of the role of the churches in adult education is S.J.D. Green, 'Religion and the Rise of the Common Man,' Derek Fraser, ed., *Cities, Class and Communication* (Hemel Hempstead, 1990).

59.   J. F. C. Harrison, *History of the Working Men's College 1854–1954* (London, 1954), pp. 16–57, 143–5; Thomas Kelly, *A History of Adult Education in Great Britain* (Liverpool, 1970), pp. 181–94, 219–32, 240–2, 248–9.

60.   George Lansbury, *My Life* (London, 1928), pp. 37–8; Tom Mann, *Memoirs* (London, 1923), pp. 6–7.

61.   Edward Royle, *Radicals, Secularists and Republicans: Popular Freethought in Britain 1866–1915* (Manchester, 1980), pp. 316–20; Stan Shipley, *Club Life and Socialism in Mid-Victorian London* (Oxford, 1971), pp. 27–8, 41–5; Brian Simon, *Education and the Labour Movement 1870–1920* (London, 1965), pp. 318–44. For Berlin, see Bernstein, *Berliner Arbeiter-Bewegung*, 3, pp. 390–2.

62.   Alexander Paterson, *Across the Bridges* (London, 1911), p. 176.

63.   Carroll Smith Rosenberg, *Religion and the Rise of the American City* (Ithaca, N. Y., 1971), pp. 86–9; Richard Carwardine, 'The Religious Revival of 1857–8 in the United States', Derek Baker, ed., *Religious Motivation: Biographical and Sociological Problems for the Church Historian*, Studies in Church History, 15 (Oxford, 1978), p. 396.

64.   David Hammack, *Power and Society: Greater New York at the Turn of the Century* (New York, 1982), pp. 145–57.

65.   K. A. Scherzer, 'The unbounded community: Neighbourhood life and social structure in New York City 1830–1875' (Harvard University Ph.D. thesis, 1982), p. 416.

66.   Questionnaire on the history of Sacred Heart parish (Sacred Heart rectory).

67.   Interview with Helen Knubel, New York City, 5 September 1978.

68.   Tomasi, *Piety and Power*, pp. 120–6.

69.   John J. Bukowczyk, 'Steeples and smokestacks: Class, religion and ideology in the Polish immigrant settlements of Greenpoint and Williamsburg, Brooklyn, 1880–1929' (Harvard University Ph.D. thesis, 1980), pp. 197–255.

70.   Hammack, *Power and Society*, p. 152.

71.   Oskar Spengler, *Das deutsche Element von New York* (New York, 1913).

72.   Holy Trinity Protestant Episcopal Church, Yorkville: Parish Register 1897–1914; Register of Families 1890–7 (Holy Trinity church office). Cf. Clyde Griffen, 'An urban church in ferment' (Columbia University Ph.D. thesis, 1960); J. P. Peters, *Annals of St Michael's* (New York, 1907), p. 367—at this Upper West Side Episcopalian church in the 1880s, about half those receiving the rites of passage were Germans, and one of the clergy preached in German once a month.

73.   Nathan Glazer and Daniel P. Moynihan, *Beyond the Melting-Pot: The Negroes, Puerto Ricans, Jews, Italians and Irish of New York City*, 2nd edn (Cambridge, Mass., 1970), pp. 201–5, 212–3, 216, discusses the decline of the anticlerical traditions of the New York Italians.

74.   Laurence Glickman, '"The Freeman's best dependence": Henry George, labor and the New York City mayoralty campaign 1886' (Princeton University B.A. thesis, 1985), pp. 6–12, 108–9.

75. Bukowczyk, 'Steeples and smokestacks', pp. 150–63, 173–80.

76. Irving Howe, *World of our Fathers* (New York, 1976), pp. 137–41.

77. Stanley Nadel, *Little Germany: Ethnicity, Religion and Class in New York City, 1845–80* (Urbana, Ill., 1990), pp. 153–4.

78. Feldman, 'Immigrants and workers', pp. 294–8, 316–7, 322.

79. Melvyn Dubofsky, *When Workers Organize* (Amherst, Mass., 1968), pp. 66–72.

80. Clyde Griffen, 'Christian Socialism instructed by Gompers', *Labor History*, 12 (1971), pp. 199–200.

81. For discussion of factors that led to radicalization of clergy, see ibid., pp. 196–7; Klaus Jaehn, *Rauschenbusch: The Formative Years* (Valley Forge, Pa., 1976), pp. 14–20.

82. Stephen Bell, *Rebel, Priest and Prophet: A Biography of Dr. Edward McGlynn* (New York, 1937), pp. 106–7, 163; David Shannon, *The Socialist Party of America* (New York, 1955), pp. 58–61.

83. Henry F. May, *The Protestant Churches and Industrial America* (New York, 1949), pp. 80–7, 175–88.

84. Sarah M. Henry, 'The strikers and their sympathizers: Brooklyn in the trolley strike of 1895', *Labor History*, 32 (1991), pp. 329–53.

85. Sarah Williams, 'Religious belief and popular culture: A study of the South London borough of Southwark, c. 1880–1939' (Oxford University D.Phil. thesis, 1993).

Chapter 5. Religion and the Working Class

1. For a more detailed account of ways in which this came about, see Hugh McLeod, 'The dechristianisation of the working class in Western Europe, c. 1850–1900', *Social Compass*, 27 (1980), pp. 191–214, and 'Protestantism and the working class in Imperial Germany', *European Studies Review*, 12 (1982), pp. 323–45.

2. See Johann Friedrich Geist and Klaus Kurvers, *Das Berliner Mietshaus 1740–1862* (Munich, 1980).

3. Wolfgang Ribbe, 'Zur Entwicklung und Funktion der Pfarrgemeinden in der evangelischen Kirche Berlins', Kaspar Elm and Hans-Dietrich Loock, eds., *Seelsorge und Diakonie in Berlin* (Berlin, 1990), pp. 248–9.

4. Geist and Kurvers, *Berliner Mietshaus*, p. 384; see also pp. 18–19, 314–5.

5. Karin Endert, Manfred Fischer and Rainer Just, *R(T)oter Wedding*, 2 vols (Berlin, 1989), 2, p. 55.

6. Otto von Leixner, *Soziale Briefe aus Berlin* (Berlin, 1891), pp. 348–72.

7. Adolf Levenstein, *Die Arbeiterfrage* (Munich, 1912), pp. 383–403.

8. Erich Schmidt, *Meine Jugend in Gross-Berlin* (Bremen, 1988), pp. 26–7, 39.

9. A fiercely hostile account of Berlin Social Democracy which stresses its irreligion is W. Ilgenstein, *Die religiöse Gedankenwelt der Sozialdemokratie* (Berlin, 1914); Bruno Violet, *Die Kirchenaustrittsbewegung* (Berlin, 1914) is a more balanced account by a Berlin pastor, which reaches similar conclusions.

10. Jochen-Christoph Kaiser, 'Sozialdemokratie und "praktische" Religionskritik: Das Beispiel der Kirchenaustrittsbewegung 1878–1914', *Archiv für Sozialgeschichte*, 22 (1982), pp. 263–98; Alfred Kelly, *The Descent of Darwin: The Popularization of Darwinism in Germany 1860–1914* (Chapel Hill, N. C., 1981), pp. 123–4.

11. Charles Booth, *Life and Labour of the People in London*, 17 vols (London, 1902–3), 3rd ser.

12. Thomas Jesse Jones, *Sociology of a New York City Block* (New York, 1904), p. 95.

13. Hugh McLeod, *Class and Religion in the Late Victorian City* (London, 1974), pp. 55, 71; Ellen Ross, '"Not the sort that would sit on the doorstep": Respectability in pre-

World War I London Neighborhoods', *International Labor and Working Class History*, 27 (1985), pp. 44, 47.

14. McLeod, *Class and Religion*, p. 55.

15. Out of about eighty working-class Londoners born in the later nineteenth or early twentieth centuries who were interviewed by Thompson and Vigne, Raphael Samuel, Alan Bartlett or Gillian Rose, none reported that a parent belonged to the Secularist movement, and only one seems to have had a deliberately secular upbringing. She was one of Gillian Rose's interviewees, who was born in Bow in 1910: her father came back from World War I 'anti-church and anti-war', took her away from Sunday school and sent her to a Socialist Sunday school; a later child was not baptized.

16. Gillian Rose, 'Locality, Politics and Culture: Poplar in the 1920s' (London University Ph.D. thesis, 1989), pp. 209–10; Fenner Brockway, *Bermondsey Story* (London, 1949), pp. 75, 113–4.

17. CMHR, 1, p. 353.

18. E.g., Patrick Quinlan, whose autobiography is included in the WPA collection on New York City Folklore (Library of Congress Folk Music Division, Washington, D.C.)

19. Hugh McLeod, 'Catholicism and the New York Irish, c. 1880–1910', Jim Obelkevich, Lyndal Roper and Raphael Samuel, eds., *Disciplines of Faith* (London, 1987), p. 341; Lawrence J. Taylor, 'Stories of power, powerful stories: The drunken priest in Donegal', Ellen Badone, ed., *Religious Orthodoxy and Popular Faith in European Society* (Princeton, N. J., 1990), pp. 182–3.

20. Robert Orsi, *The Madonna of 115th Street* (New Haven, Conn., 1985), ibid., pp. 163–218, 220, for discussion of attitudes to Mary and the sense of 'being a Catholic' in East Harlem.

21. Ruth True, *The Neglected Girl* (New York, 1914), pp. 12–13; CMHR, 2, pp. 121–4.

22. Columbia Oral History Project: Interview with Joseph Jablonower, pp. 181–9 (Columbia University Library).

23. BSM, 2 (1879–80), pp. 86–90, 150–1.

24. Levenstein, *Arbeiterfrage*, pp. 326–34, 383–403. See also Kelly, *Descent of Darwin*, p. 132.

25. Thomas Jackson, *Solo Trumpet* (London, 1953), pp. 42–9, 59, 92–5.

26. Two contributions to Gerald Parsons, ed., *Religion in Victorian Britain*, 4 vols (Manchester, 1988) provide a useful overview with good bibliographies: James R. Moore, 'Freethought, secularism, agnosticism: The case of Darwin', 1, pp. 274–319; Frank Turner, 'The Victorian conflict between religion and science: A professional dimension', 4, pp. 170–97.

27. BC B196, pp. 43–5.

28. Ibid., pp. 47–9.

29. Robert Moore, *Pit-men, Politics and Preachers* (London, 1974); A. J. Ainsworth, 'Religion in the working-class community and the evolution of socialism in late nineteenth-century Lancashire', *Histoire Sociale*, 10 (1977), pp. 354–80; Hugh McLeod, 'Religion in the British and German labour movements c. 1890–1914: A comparison', *Bulletin of the Society for the Study of Labour History*, 51 (1986), pp. 25–35; W. W. Knox, 'Religion and the Scottish labour movement 1900–1939', *Journal of Contemporary History*, 23 (1988), pp. 609–30.

30. Paul Thompson, *Socialists, Liberals and Labour: The Struggle for London 1885–1914* (London, 1967), pp. 22–38.

31. Stan Shipley, *Club Life and Socialism in Mid-Victorian London* (Oxford, 1971).

32. See, for instance, Alan Bartlett, 'The churches in Bermondsey 1880–1939' (University of Birmingham Ph.D. thesis, 1987), pp. 364–5, which notes the strong Christian Socialist influence on the ILP in Bermondsey.

33.   Herbert Gutman, 'Protestantism and the American labor movement: The Christian spirit in the Gilded Age', *American Historical Review*, 72 (1966), pp. 74–101; Ken Fones-Wolf, 'Religion and trade union politics in the United States 1880–1920', *International Labor and Working Class History*, 34 (1988), pp. 39–55; Clark Halker, 'Jesus was a carpenter: Labor song, poets, labor protest and true religion in Gilded Age America', *Labor History*, 32 (1991), pp. 273–89.

34.   For examples of support by Protestant ministers for strikes by mainly non-Protestant workers, see Melvyn Dubofsky, *When Workers Organize* (Amherst, Mass., 1968), pp. 72–82; John Punnett Peters, *Annals of St Michaels* (New York, 1907), p. 197. Clyde Griffen, 'Christian Socialism instructed by Gompers', *Labor History*, 12 (1971), pp. 195–213, discusses the interest of New York Episcopalian clergy in the Social Gospel; see Paul Minus, *Walter Rauschenbusch* (New York, 1988), for the New York Baptist pastor, and later seminary professor, who was the most famous Social Gospel writer.

35.   For the Irish see Michael Gordon, 'Studies in Irish and Irish-American thought and behavior in Gilded Age New York City' (Rochester University Ph.D. thesis, 1977); for the Jews, Moses Rischin, *The Promised City* (New York, 1962); for the Germans, Stanley Nadel, *Little Germany: Ethnicity, Religion and Class in New York City 1845–1880* (Urbana, Ill., 1990), pp. 104–54.

36.   See the discussion in Fones-Wolf, 'Religion and trade union politics', on differences between Protestant and Catholic attitudes to trade unions.

37.   Rischin, *Promised City*, ch. 3.

38.   CCNY Interviews, I–9.

39.   Max Ravage, as quoted in Irving Howe and Kenneth Libo, *How We Lived 1880–1939* (New York, 1979), p. 163.

40.   Karl Vorländer, 'Sozialdemokratische Pfarrer', *Archiv für Sozialwissenschaft und Sozialpolitik*, 30 (1910), pp. 455–513.

41.   K. E. Pollmann, *Landesherrliches Kirchenregiment und soziale Frage* (Berlin, 1973), pp. 75–84, 170–2, 232–51.

42.   A useful discussion of the relationship between Social Democracy and the churches, with the emphasis on Berlin, is Kaiser, 'Sozialdemokratie und "praktische" Religionskritik'.

43.   Günter Brakelmann, *Kirche, soziale Frage und Sozialismus* (Gütersloh, 1977); Pollmann, *Landesherrliches Kirchenregiment*.

44.   Ibid., pp. 232–51. There is a detailed account of disciplinary procedures in the Hanover church in E. Rolffs, *Das kirchliche Leben der evangelischen Kirchen in Niedersachsen* (Tübingen, 1917), pp. 95–8; disciplinary action peaked in the period 1893–8, when forty-five pastors were proceeded against, including twelve for political reasons.

45.   Günther Dehn, *Proletarische Jugend* (Berlin, 1930), p. 28; see also Manfred Gailus, *Kirchengemeinden im Nationalsozialismus* (Berlin, 1990), pp. 112–3.

46.   This is a recurrent theme in Günter Wirth, ed., *Beiträge zur Berliner Kirchengeschichte* (Berlin, 1987): see especially Hans-Jürgen Gabriel, 'Im Namen des Evangeliums gegen den Fortschritt: Zur Rolle der "Evangelischen Kirchenzeitung" unter E. W. Hengstenberg von 1830 bis 1849', pp. 154–76. See also Walter Wendland, *Siebenhundert Jahre Kirchengeschichte Berlins* (Berlin, 1930), pp. 338–9; Robert M. Bigler, *The Politics of Prussian Protestantism* (Los Angeles, 1972).

47.   Ibid.; Sylvia Paletschek, *Frauen und Dissens: Frauen im Deutschkatholizismus und in den freien Gemeinden 1841–1852* (Göttingen, 1990), pp. 62–6.

48.   Lucian Hölscher, *Weltgericht oder Revolution* (Stuttgart, 1989), pp. 105, 127–8.

49.   Dudley Bahlman, 'The Queen, Mr Gladstone and church patronage', *Victorian Studies*, 3 (1960), pp. 349–80.

50. Dudley Bahlman, 'Politics and church patronage in the Victorian age', ibid., 22 (1979), pp. 253–96.

51. See G. I. T. Machin, *Politics and the Churches in Great Britain 1869–1921* (Oxford, 1987) for detailed analysis of the role of religious issues in parliamentary politics.

52. Peter d'A. Jones, *The Christian Socialist Revival 1877–1914* (Princeton, N.J., 1968), p. 246; Hugh McLeod, *Class and Religion in the Late Victorian City* (London, 1974), pp. 118–20, 176; Alan Bartlett, 'Churches in Bermondsey', pp. 362, 365.

53. Thompson, *Socialists, Liberals and Labour*, pp. 22–5.

54. Jones, *Christian Socialist Revival*, p. 24.

55. Ronald Ross, *Beleaguered Tower* (Notre Dame, Ind., 1976); Michael Schneider, *Die Christlichen Gewerkschaften* 1894–1933 (Bonn, 1982); E. D. Brose, *Christian Labor and the Politics of Frustration in Imperial Germany* (Washington, D.C., 1985).

56. Thompson, *Socialists, Liberals and Labour*, pp. 180, 313; Bartlett, 'Churches in Bermondsey', pp. 363–4.

57. M. McDermott, 'Irish Catholics and the British Labour movement: A study with particular reference to London' (Kent University M.A. thesis, 1979), pp. 21–37.

58. Ibid., pp. 93–130, 169–71; Marchant, 'Interaction of church and society in an East London borough (West Ham)' (University of London Ph.D. thesis, 1979), pp. 181, 193; McLeod, *Class and Religion*, p. 76.

59. Levenstein, *Arbeiterfrage*, p. 339.

60. Hugh McLeod, 'Building the "Catholic Ghetto": Catholic Organisations 1870–1914', W. J. Sheils and Diana Wood, eds., *Voluntary Religion*, Studies in Church History, 23 (Oxford, 1986), pp. 431–40. See also the chapters by William Callahan on Spain and Carl Strikwerda on Belgium in Hugh McLeod, ed., *European Religion in the Age of Great Cities, 1830–1930* (London, 1995).

61. McLeod, '"Catholic Ghetto"', pp. 417–23.

62. Josef Mooser, 'Arbeiter, Bürger und Priester in den konfessionellen Arbeitervereinen im deutschen Kaiserreich, 1880–1914', Jürgen Kocka, ed., *Arbeiter und Bürger im 19. Jahrhundert* (Munich, 1986), pp. 103–4.

63. As a local example, a Berlin Catholic priest complained of the excessive number of workers on his parish council—not a problem that would have worried any of his Protestant colleagues: William Frank, *Rosen und Dornen in der Berliner Seelsorgsarbeit in zwanzigjähriger Erfahrung* (Breslau, 1909), pp. 56–9. For a more general discussion of Catholic economic and educational disadvantage in Germany c. 1900, see Thomas Nipperdey, *Religion im Umbruch: Deutschland 1870–1918* (Munich, 1988), pp. 38–42.

64. Richard O'Connor, *Hell's Kitchen* (Philadelphia, 1958), pp. 194–5; P. J. Dooley, *Fifty Years in Yorkville* (New York, 1917), pp. 103–5; True, *Neglected Girl*, p. 91; McLeod, *Class and Religion*, p. 74.

65. See Ann Taves, 'Relocating the sacred: Roman Catholic devotions in midnineteenth-century America', (Chicago University Ph.D. thesis, 1983), pp. 132–3, 148–60.

66. Orsi, *Madonna of 115th Street*, p. 87. For similar comments, see Hamilton Holt, ed., *The Life Stories of Undistinguished Americans* (New York, 1906), p. 50; G. Longo, *Spoiled Priest: The Autobiography of an Ex-Priest* (New York, 1966), p. 6.

67. CMHR, 2, p. 26.

68. Henry J. Browne, *St. Ann's, New York City* (New York, 1952), pp. 41–9; Taves, 'Relocating the sacred', p. 164; Ralph L. and Henry F. Woods, *Pilgrim Places in North America: A Guide to Catholic Shrines* (New York, 1939), pp. 108–9.

69. Taves, 'Relocating the sacred', pp. 148–160; Orsi, *Madonna of 115th Street*, pp. 174–6.

70.   Elsa Herzfeld, *Family Monographs* (New York, 1905), pp. 44–6.

71.   Orsi, *Madonna of 115th Street*, p. 86.

72.   The standard hagiography is Stephen Bell, *Rebel, Priest and Prophet: A Biography of Dr. Edward McGlynn* (New York, 1937). Sylvester Malone, *Dr. Edward McGlynn* (New York, 1918) is a useful compilation of reminiscences and excerpts from speeches. The best account of the 'McGlynn affair' is in Robert Emmett Curran, *Michael Augustine Corrigan and the Shaping of Conservative Catholicism in America* (New York, 1978). See also Hugh McLeod, 'Edward McGlynn', Stuart Mews, ed., *Modern Religious Rebels* (London, 1933), which does not add to Curran's narrative, but offers some new points of interpretation.

73.   Martin Shefter, 'The electoral foundations of the political machine: New York City 1884–97', Joel H. Silbey and Allan G. Bogue, eds., *The History of American Electoral Behavior* (Princeton, N. J., 1978), pp. 289–91; Laurence Glickman, '"The freeman's best dependence": Henry George, labor and the New York City mayoralty campaign, 1886,' (Princeton University B.A. thesis, 1985), p. 97.

74.   Charles Leinenweber, 'The class and ethnic bases of New York City socialism 1904–15', *Labor History*, 22 (1981), pp. 29–56; Ronald Bayor, *Neighbors in Conflict: The Irish, Germans, Jews and Italians of New York City, 1929–41* (Baltimore, 1978), pp. 92–3.

75.   *New York Herald*, 22 April 1887.

76.   *New York Times*, 31 December 1894.

77.   Diary of Rev. Richard Burtsell, 5 August 1888; parish files: Immaculate Conception, Bronx, Rev. John Leibfritz to Archbishop Corrigan, 22 July 1892 (AANY).

78.   *New York Times*, 12 December 1886.

79.   Shefter, 'Electoral foundations', p. 287.

80.   Names of McGlynn's leading supporters are listed in Bell, *Rebel, Priest and Prophet*. I have identified many of them in city directories. They come from a wide range of occupations from labourer to physician, but with a concentration in the lower middle class.

81.   Cf. *Irish World*, 13 November and 11 December 1886.

82.   Ibid., 29 October 1887.

83.   McLeod, 'Catholic Ghetto', pp. 411–44.

84.   Eric Foner, 'Class, ethnicity and radicalism in the Gilded Age: The Land League and Irish America', *Marxist Perspectives*, 1 (1978), pp. 22–8, 43–4.

85.   Thomas N. Brown, *Irish-American Nationalism, 1870–1890* (Philadelphia, 1966), pp. 34–8; for discussion of attitudes of Catholic clergy to trade unions, see Fones-Wolf, 'Religion and trade union politics', pp. 39–42.

86.   J. P. Rodechko, *Patrick Ford and His Search for America* (New York, 1976), pp. 168–9.

87.   Shefter, 'Electoral foundations', pp. 265–6.

88.   Leinenweber, 'New York City socialism', pp. 47–9.

89.   Steven P. Erie, *Rainbow's End: Irish-Americans and the Dilemmas of Urban Machine Politics 1840–1985* (Berkeley, 1988); Daniel Czitrom, 'Underworlds and underdogs: Big Tim Sullivan and metropolitan politics in New York, 1889–1913', *Journal of American History*, 78 (1991), pp. 536–58, analyzes the political style and policies of a prominent Tammany politician.

90.   Melvyn Dubofsky, 'Organised labor and the immigrant in New York City, 1900–1918', *Labor History*, 2 (1961), pp. 182–201.

91.   Robert F. Wesser, *A Response to Progressivism: The Democratic Party and New York Politics, 1902–1918* (New York, 1986), p. 112.

92.   Bell, *Rebel, Priest and Prophet*, pp. 125–84; Elizabeth Gurley Flynn, *The Rebel Girl* (New York, 1973), pp. 42–3; Thomas Sugrue, *A Catholic Speaks his Mind on America's*

Religious Conflict (New York, 1952), p. 44.

93.   Curran, *Corrigan*, p. 310.

94.   John Talbot Smith, *History of the Catholic Church in the Archdiocese of New York*, 2 vols (New York, 1905), 2, pp. 542–54; Curran, *Corrigan*, p. 514.

95.   Leinenweber, 'New York City socialism', pp. 51–6.

Chapter 6. Heart of a Heartless World?

1.   Michael Gold, *Jews Without Money* (1930; repr. New York, 1965) pp. 6–7, 47–8, 88–99, 160–1, 179–82, 201–5.

2.   Charles Booth, ed., *Life and Labour of the People in London*, 17 vols. (London, 1902–3), 1st series, 2, Appendix, table 2; Mrs Pember Reeves, *Round About a Pound a Week* (1913; repr. London, 1979).

3.   Robert C. Chapin, *The Standard of Living among Workingmen's Families in New York City* (New York, 1909), p. 245; *Report of the Immigration Commission*, 41 vols. (Washington, D.C., 1911), 26, p. 226.

4.   Figures for London were published in *Annual Report of the Registrar-General* and for Berlin in *Statistisches Jahrbuch der Stadt Berlin*. For discussion, see Ellen Ross, 'Labour and Love: Rediscovering London's Working-Class Mothers, 1870–1918', Jane Lewis, ed., *Labour and Love: Women's Experience of Home and Family 1850–1940* (Oxford, 1986), p. 81; Sigrid Stöckel, 'Säuglingssterblichkeit in Berlin von 1870 bis zum Vorabend des Ersten Weltkriegs—Eine Kurve mit hohem Maximum und starkem Gefälle', *Berliner Forschungen*, 1 (1986), pp. 222, 224.

5.   *Statistisches Jahrbuch der Stadt Berlin*, 27 (1900–2), plan 1; *Census of England and Wales (1901): County of London, Area, Houses and Population*, p. 58.

6.   The quotation comes from the introduction to Marx's *Contribution to the Critique of Hegel's Philosophy of Law*, Karl Marx and Friedrich Engels, *Collected Works*, 32 vols. so far published (London, 1975–), 3, p. 175.

7.   Stephen Yeo, *Religion and Voluntary Organisations in Crisis* (London, 1976), pp. 118–25.

8.   *Parliamentary Papers* (1852–3), 89, p. clviii.

9.   *BSM*, 3 (1880), pp. 134–5.

10.   George Acorn, *One of the Multitude* (London, 1911), p. 51.

11.   Charles Stelzle, *Christianity's Storm Center* (New York, 1907), pp. 21–3.

12.   Mission Chronicles, 9–23 December 1894, 30 November–18 December 1879 (Archives of the Paulist Fathers, St Paul's rectory).

13.   Elsa Herzfeld, *Family Monographs* (New York, 1905), p. 23.

14.   Ibid.; Henry J. Browne, *One Stop above Hell's Kitchen: Sacred Heart Parish in Clinton* (Hackensack, N. J., 1977), p. 10; Federation of Churches and Christian Workers in New York City, *Sociological Canvass*, 3 vols. (New York, 1897–1901), 1, p. 44.

15.   Herzfeld, *Family Monographs*, p. 23.

16.   Case files of the New York Charity Organisation Society, R–133; R–138; R–136, 8 February 1901; R–127 (Archives of the Community Service Society, New York City).

17.   The diary is kept at St Giles-in-the-Fields church, London. For fuller discussion of the diary and information about Oppenheimer, see Donald M. Lewis, *Lighten Their Darkness: The Evangelical Mission to Working-Class London 1828–1860* (Westport, Conn., 1986), ch. 6.

18.   *BSM*, 22 (1900), pp. 82–93.

19.   H. H. Gerth and C. Wright Mills, *From Max Weber: Essays in Sociology* (London, 1948), pp. 275–6; Günther Dehn, *Proletarische Jugend* (Berlin, 1930), pp. 140–5.

20. *BSM*, 1 (1878–9), pp. 72–6.

21. Essex Interviews, no. 296, p. 54.

22. BC, B197, pp. 3–11. See also Hugh McLeod, *Class and Religion in the Late Victorian City* (London, 1974), pp. 128–9; Alan Bartlett, 'The churches in Bermondsey 1880–1939' (Birmingham University Ph.D. thesis, 1987), p. 284.

23. Raphael Samuel, East London MS: Interview with Mr Causon, pp. 22–4.

24. Eugen Baumann, *Der Berliner Volkscharacter in der Seelsorge* (Berlin, 1880), pp. 75–7.

25. Otto von Leixner, *Soziale Briefe aus Berlin* (Berlin, 1891), p. 195; BSM, 8 (1886), p. 102.

26. J. M. King and others, *The Religious Condition of New York City* (New York, 1889), pp. 136, 190–1.

27. Questionnaire on the history of Sacred Heart parish (Sacred Heart rectory).

28. Herzfeld, *Family Monographs*, pp. 33–4.

29. Raphael Samuel, East London MS: Interview with Mrs Stone, p. 35.

30. Essex Interviews, no. 126, pp. 27, 32, 38, 56.

31. My emphasis. Ibid., no. 235, p. 66.

32. *Calendar* of St Paul's parish, January 1908, October 1907, October 1910, March 1898 (copies in Archives of the Paulist Fathers).

33. Alter Landesman, *Brownsville* (New York, 1971), pp. 69, 208; Irving Howe, *World of our Fathers* (New York, 1976), pp 183–90; Samuel Chotzinoff, *A Lost Paradise* (New York, 1955), pp. 34–5. A more satirical view of the subject is provided by Gold, *Jews Without Money*, pp. 148–52.

34. Dietrich Mühlberg, ed., *Arbeiterleben um 1900* (Berlin, 1983), p. 126; Hsi-Huey Liang, 'The social background of the Berlin working-class movement, 1890–1914' (Yale University Ph.D. thesis, 1959), pp. 60–1.

35. Mühlberg, *Arbeiterleben*, pp. 74–6.

36. Ibid., pp. 155–9; Eberhard Büchner, *Variété und Tingel-Tangel in Berlin* (Berlin, 1905), pp. 5–22; Tobias Bohm and Udo Gosswald, *Anfänge der Arbeiterfreizeit* (Berlin, n.d.), pp. 103–4, 124–9, 149–52.

37. Johann Friedrich Geist and Klaus Kurvers, *Das Berliner Mietshaus 1740–1862* (Munich, 1980), p. 323; Rosmarie Beier, 'Leben in der Mietskaserne: Zum Alltag Berliner Unterschichtsfamilien in den Jahren 1900 bis 1920', Gesine Asmus, ed., *Hinterhof, Keller und Mansarde: Einblicke in Berliner Wohnungselend 1901–20* (Hamburg, 1982), pp. 267–8.

38. Von Leixner, *Soziale Briefe*, p. 87.

39. *Chronik der Christlichen Welt*, 25 (1915), pp. 161–6.

40. Browne, *One Stop above Hell's Kitchen*, pp. 61–4; W. L. Riordon, *Plunkitt of Tammany Hall* (New York, 1905).

41. Mary Simkhovitch, *The City Worker's World in America* (New York, 1917), p. 182.

42. There are no systematic discussions of this topic with regard to New York. For another northeastern city, see James O'Toole, 'Prelates and politicos: Catholics and politics in Massachussets, 1900–1970', Robert E. Sullivan and James M. O'Toole, eds., *Catholic Boston: Studies in Religion and Community, 1870–1900* (Boston, 1985), pp. 15–65; for a more general discussion, see D. N. Doyle, 'Catholicism, politics and Irish America since 1890: Some critical considerations', *Irish Studies*, 4 (1985), pp. 192–230, which highlights tensions in the relationship between clergy and politicians.

43. *Calendar* of St Paul's parish, November 1888. For Archbishop Corrigan's sensitivity to claims that he was too close to Tammany Hall, see Browne, *One Stop above Hell's Kitchen*, p. 65; Robert Emmett Curran, *Michael Augustine Corrigan and the Shaping of*

Conservative Catholicism in America (New York, 1976), pp. 197–8.

44. Ibid., pp. 60, 314, 403, 478; Browne, *One Stop above Hell's Kitchen*, pp. 61–70; *New York Times*, 5 November 1894.

45. Hugh McLeod, 'Catholicism and the New York Irish, c. 1880–1910', Jim Obelkevich, Lyndal Roper and Raphael Samuel, eds., *Disciplines of Faith* (London, 1987), pp. 346–7.

46. *New York Times*, 5–6 November 1894.

47. Gillian Rose, 'Locality, politics and culture: Poplar in the 1920s' (London University Ph.D. thesis, 1989), pp. 319–26.

48. Franz Linden, *Sozialismus und Religion* (Leipzig, 1932), pp. 113, 123–5.

49. H. J. Hammerton, *This Turbulent Priest* (London, 1952); Alison Ravetz, *Model Estate* (London, 1974).

50. Raphael Samuel, East London MS: Interview with Bill Brinson; Geoff Richman, *Fly a Flag for Poplar* (London, 1976), pp. 87–90.

51. Alan Bartlett, interview no. 9 (tape and transcript in his possession).

52. BC B221, interview with Rev A. E. Dalton, vicar of St Dunstan's, Stepney; ibid., B287, p. 109. For the association in Britain as a whole between working-class Anglicanism and voting Conservative, see Hugh McLeod, 'New perspectives on Victorian working-class religion: The oral evidence', *Oral History*, 14 (1986), p. 36.

53. *Chronik der Christlichen Welt*, 19 (1909), p. 291.

54. Liang, 'Berlin working-class movement', p. 181; W. Ilgenstein, *Die religiöse Gedankenwelt der Sozialdemokratie* (Berlin, 1914), p. 73.

55. *Führer durch das kirchliche Berlin*, 14 (1905–6), pp. 200–4; *Jahresbericht des Verbandes Evangelischer Arbeiter* (1906), p. 59. For an overview of the Protestant and Catholic workers' organizations, see Josef Mooser, 'Arbeiter, Bürger und Priester in den konfessionellen Arbeitervereinen im deutschen Kaiserreich, 1880–1914', Jürgen Kocka, ed., *Arbeiter und Bürger im 19. Jahrhundert* (Munich, 1986), pp. 79–105.

56. Liang, 'Berlin working-class movement', p. 181.

57. Ingrid Kraus, 'The Berlin Catholic Church 1871–1910: Its social and political endeavors' (Nebraska University Ph.D. thesis, 1981), pp. 66–79.

58. Ibid., pp. 100–51.

59. Johannes Schauff, *Das Wahlverhalten der deutschen Katholiken im Kaiserreich und in der Weimarer Republik* (Mainz, 1975), pp. 174–5, 198–200, showed that the proportion of Catholics voting for the Centre Party in Berlin was among the lowest of any German city. He estimated that the proportion peaked at 39 per cent in 1874 and again in 1924, but that it was below 20 per cent for most of the intervening period.

60. According to a police report, 11.7 per cent of those leaving the church in four Berlin districts in 1912 had been Roman Catholics, which was exactly the same as the proportion of Catholics in the general population. EOK: Acta betreffend die Austrittsbewegung und die Landeskirchen, 4, pp. 181–2 (EZA).

61. Schauff, *Wahlverhalten der deutschen Katholiken*, pp. 64–8.

Chapter 7. Male and Female

1. Rosmarie Beier, 'Leben in der Mietskaserne: Zum Alltag Berliner Unterschichtsfamilien in den Jahren 1900 bis 1920', Gesine Asmus, ed., *Hinterhof, Keller und Mansarde* (Hamburg, 1982), p. 251. For further discussion of the role of pubs in the life of working-class men of this period, see Dieter Mühlberg, ed., *Arbeiterleben um 1900* (Berlin, 1983), pp. 127–41; Kathy Peiss, *Cheap Amusements: Working Women and Leisure in Turn-of-the-Century New York* (Philadelphia, 1986), pp. 17–21; Brian Harrison, 'Pubs',

H. J. Dyos and M. Wolff, eds., *The Victorian City*, 2 vols. (London, 1973), 1, pp. 161–90.

2.   Mrs Pember Reeves, *Round about a Pound a Week* (London, 1979), pp. 154–8; Beier, 'Leben in der Mietskaserne', pp. 250–3; Elsa Herzfeld, *Family Monographs* (New York, 1905), pp. 51–2.

3.   Ellen Ross, 'Survival Networks', *History Workshop* 15 (1983), pp. 4–27; '"Not the sort that would sit on the doorstep": Respectability in pre-World War I London neighbourhoods', *International Labor and Working Class History*, 27 (1985), pp. 39–59; 'Labour and love: Rediscovering London's working-class mothers, 1870–1918', Jane Lewis, ed., *Labour and Love: Women's Experience of Home and Family 1850–1940* (Oxford, 1986), pp. 72–96; '"Fierce questions and taunts": Married life in working-class London, 1870–1914', Gareth Stedman Jones and David Feldman, eds., *Metropolis: London* (London, 1989), pp. 219–44; 'Hungry children: Housewives and London charity', Peter Mandler, ed., *The Uses of Charity: The Poor on Relief in the Nineteenth-Century Metropolis* (Philadelphia, 1990), pp. 161–96.

4.   Otto von Leixner, *Soziale Briefe aus Berlin* (Berlin, 1891), p. 98.

5.   Charles Booth, ed., *Life and Labour of the People in London*, 17 vols. (London, 1902-3), 3rd ser. 1, pp. 89–90, 27–8.

6.   Gillian Rose, 'Locality, politics and culture: Poplar in the 1920s' (London University Ph.D. thesis, 1989), pp. 266–9.

7.   The material on Lancashire in the Essex University archive can be compared with the interviews conducted by Elizabeth Roberts, tapes and transcripts of which are kept at the Centre for North-West Regional Studies, Lancaster University. So far as churchgoing is concerned, the Essex University and Lancaster University interviews show very similar patterns, though levels of churchgoing may have been slightly higher in the north Lancashire towns covered by Roberts than in the south Lancashire areas covered by Thompson and Vigne. See also Hugh McLeod, 'New perspectives on Victorian working-class religion: The oral evidence', *Oral History*, 14 (1986), pp. 31–49.

8.   Elizabeth Roberts, *A Woman's Place* (Oxford, 1984), pp. 118–9.

9.   Standish Meacham, *A Life Apart* (London, 1977), p. 95, notes wide variations in the proportions of married women reporting an occupation in the 1911 census. Among those towns and counties he cites, Blackburn had the highest figure (44 per cent) and Co. Durham the lowest (3 per cent). For discussion of distinctive culture patterns in the north-east, see D. J. Rowe, 'The North-East', F. M. L. Thompson, ed., *The Cambridge Social History of Britain*, 3 vols. (Cambridge, 1990), 1, pp. 443, 467–9.

10.   Gareth Stedman Jones, *Outcast London* (Oxford, 1971), pp. 84–7, 125; Ross, 'Fierce Questions', p. 220.

11.   Booth, *Life and Labour*, 3rd ser., 1, pp. 87–8.

12.   W. H. Reid, *The Rise and Dissolution of the Infidel Societies in this Metropolis* (London, 1800), pp. 18–19, 21.

13.   See the description of a summer Sunday in 1900 on Peckham Rye in Booth, *Life and Labour*, 3rd ser., 6, pp. 185–95.

14.   John Kent, *From Darwin to Blatchford* (London, 1966), pp. 17–20.

15.   D. B. McIlhiney, 'A gentleman in every slum: Church of England missions in the East End of London 1837–1914' (Princeton University Ph.D. thesis, 1977), p. 306.

16.   Henrietta Barnett, *Canon Barnett*, 2 vols. (London, 1918), 2, p. 10.

17.   See Edward Royle, *Radicals, Secularists and Republicans: Popular Freethought in Britain, 1866–1915* (Manchester, 1980), pp. 154–5, for the parallels with modern soccer matches—which even include some associated vandalism.

18.   BC, B206, p. 68.

19.   Richard Mudie-Smith, ed., *The Religious Life of London* (London, 1904), p. 322.

20.   Hugh McLeod, *Class and Religion in the Late Victorian City* (London, 1974), p. 66.

21.   Mudie-Smith, *Religious Life of London*, p. 176; for discussion of Watts-Ditchfield, vicar of St James the Less, see McIlhiney, 'A gentleman in every slum', ch. 5.

22.   McLeod, 'The oral evidence', p. 43.

23.   McLeod, *Class and Religion*, p. 73.

24.   BC, B280, p. 7.

25.   For the earlier period, see Norman Vance, *Sinews of the Spirit* (Cambridge, 1985); for the period around 1900, see John Springhall, 'Building character in the British boy: the attempt to extend Christian manlinesss to working-class adolescents, 1880–1914', J. A. Mangan and James Walvin, eds., *Manliness and Morality: Middle-Class Masculinity in Britain and America 1800–1940* (Manchester, 1987), pp. 52–74.

26.   For the high popularity of amateur boxing in working-class areas of London from the 1880s onwards, and for the important role of church-based clubs among the places for boxing, see Stanley Albert Shipley, 'The boxer as hero: A study of social class, community and the professionalisation of the sport in London, 1890–1905' (London University Ph.D. thesis, 1986), pp. 251–3, 290–300, 334–56.

27.   BC, B228, p. 37.

28.   *East London Observer*, 13 August 1892, reported a fight between two gangs in Bethnal Green in which one of 'Father Jay's Boys' was killed.

29.   BC, B228, p. 47.

30.   *East London Observer*, 1 August 1896, 7 November 1896, 21 August 1897.

31.   Rose, 'Locality, politics and culture', pp. 268–9. Alan Bartlett, however, comments (in a letter to me, dated 20 August 1992) that his work on Bermondsey suggests that the political orientation of the clergy was a less important factor in their relationship with working men than the degree to which they were regarded as easygoing and approachable. A similar point, with regard to east Berlin in the 1920s, is made in Jörg Kniffka, *Das kirchliche Leben in Berlin-Ost in der Mitte der zwanziger Jahre* (Münster, 1971), pp. 164–5.

32.   Rose, 'Locality, politics and culture'.

33.   Essex Interviews, no. 302, pp. 67–78, 108–9; no. 417, pp. 28, 65.

34.   Ibid. For households where father said grace, see no. 71, pp. 18–19; no. 302, p. 68. But no. 298, pp. 20–1 reports it being said by mother, and no. 333, p. 21, and no. 145, p. 55 report it being said by the children. For father reading the Bible to the family, see no. 5, p. 6; no. 284, p. 25. But no. 71, pp. 18–19, and no. 368, p. 26 report it being read by mother.

35.   Ibid., no. 113, p. 15; no. 302, p. 69.

36.   This subject will be discussed more fully in chapter 8.

37.   Alan Bartlett, 'The churches in Bermondsey, 1880–1939' (Birmingham University Ph.D. thesis, 1987), p. 185.

38.   See ibid., for a brief discussion, noting both the frequency of churching and the sparsity of evidence about it. According to two Bethnal Green clergymen, interviewed in the 1890s, churchings in their parishes were at least as numerous as baptisms: see BC, B182, p. 171, B228, p. 131.

39.   Ross, 'Hungry children', pp. 170–1.

40.   F. K. Prochaska, 'Body and soul: Bible nurses and the poor in Victorian London', *Historical Research*, 60 (1987), pp. 336–48.

41.   Ross, 'Hungry children', p. 169.

42.   Jerry White, *The Worst Street in North London: Campbell Bunk, Islington, Between the Wars* (London, 1986), pp. 130–2.

43. Essex Interviews, no. 261, pp. 5, 30.

44. McLeod, *Class and Religion*, p. 113.

45. Essex Interviews, no. 298, pp. 22–3.

46. F. K. Prochaska, 'A mother's country: Mothers' meetings and family welfare in Britain, 1850–1950', *History*, 74 (1989), pp. 379–99.

47. Ibid., p. 388.

48. BC, B198, pp. 96–8.

49. Bartlett, 'Churches in Bermondsey', pp. 166–7; Prochaska, 'Mother's Country', pp. 384–5.

50. Ibid., pp. 383–8; Bartlett, 'Churches in Bermondsey', pp. 165–8.

51. Essex Interviews, no. 261, pp. 66, 80–1. See also no. 105: this respondent was herself a churchgoer, and continued to be so, but when she answered an advertisement for a 'Christian' servant, her Methodist employers treated her badly, and did not give her the opportunity to go to church; on the other hand, she got on much better with a nonreligious couple, whose main interest was in golf and tennis.

52. For detailed figures, see Mudie-Smith, *Religious Life of London*. For discussion, see McLeod, *Class and Religion* and Jeffrey Cox, *English Churches in a Secular Society* (Oxford, 1982). The census-takers defined anyone aged fifteen and over as an adult.

53. Rosemary Chadwick, 'Church and people in Bradford and district 1880–1914' (Oxford University Ph.D. thesis, 1986), p. 145.

54. Ibid., p. 163.

55. This is discussed more fully in Hugh McLeod, 'Weibliche Frömmigkeit— männlicher Unglaube? Religion und Kirchen im bürgerlichen 19. Jahrhundert', Ute Frevert, ed., *Bürgerinnen und Bürger* (Göttingen, 1988), pp. 134–56.

56. Elizabeth Isichei, *Victorian Quakers* (Oxford, 1970), pp. 86–7, 107–9; Ann R. Higginbotham, 'Respectable sinners: Salvation Army rescue work with unmarried mothers, 1884–1914', Gail Malmgreen, ed., *Religion in the Lives of Englishwomen, 1760–1930* (Beckenham, 1986), p. 217; Clive D. Field, 'Methodism in Metropolitan London c. 1850–1920' (Oxford University Ph.D. thesis, 1974), p. 63. See also the wide-ranging collection of papers in W. J. Sheils and Diana Wood, eds., *Women in the Church*, Studies in Church History, 27 (Oxford, 1990).

57. Glenn Horridge, 'The Salvation Army in England 1865–1900' (London University Ph.D. thesis, 1989) has analyzed the religious backgrounds of early Salvation Army officers: whereas converts from Methodism were predominantly male, two-thirds of converts from Anglicanism were female.

58. For information on the social characteristics of London denominations, see McLeod, *Class and Religion*; Cox, *English Churches*; Field, 'Methodism in Metropolitan London'.

59. Rickie Burman, '"She looketh well to the ways of her household": The changing role of Jewish women in religious life, c. 1880–1930', in Malmgreen, *Religion in the Lives of English Women*, pp. 234–57.

60. Burman's model is explicitly endorsed in Sydney Stahl Weinberg, *The World of our Mothers: The Lives of Jewish Immigrant Women* (New York, 1988), p. 140.

61. Ibid., pp. 105–48.

62. Marion Kaplan, 'Priestess and Hausfrau: Women and tradition in the German-Jewish family', Steven M. Cohen and Paula E. Hyman, eds., *The Jewish Family: Myths and Reality* (New York, 1986), pp. 62–81.

63. For comments on London Jewish geography, see Lloyd P. Gartner, *The Jewish Immigrant in England, 1870–1914*, 2nd edn (London, 1973), pp. 142–5; Booth, *Life and Labour*, 3rd ser., 1, pp. 152, 213; 3, p. 130.

64. Cf. Gartner, *The Jewish Immigrant*, p. 198.

65. P. Pieper, *Kirchliche Statistik Deutschlands* (Freiburg, 1899), p. 233.

66. See figures published in *Chronik der Christlichen Welt*, 23 (1913), pp. 418–20.

67. Josef Mooser, 'Arbeiter, Bürger und Priester in den konfessionellen Arbeitervereinen im deutschen Kaiserreich, 1880–1914', Jürgen Kocka, ed., *Arbeiter und Bürger im 19. Jahrhundert* (Munich, 1986), p. 85; *Führer durch das kirchliche Berlin*, 14 (1905–6), p. 201.

68. Ibid., pp. 40–102 provides a comprehensive list of Berlin parish organizations. Gerlinde Böpple, *Kapernaum: eine evangelische Kirchengemeinde "auf dem Wedding"* (Berlin, 1992), pp. 27–31 provides a detailed discussion of the women's organizations and their role in parish life.

69. Protokollbuch des Frauenhilfs-Vereins, (AKG); *BSM*, 22 (1900), pp. 82–93.

70. Ursula Baumann, 'Protestantismus und moderne Gesellschaft: "Frauenfrage" und Frauenbewegung in der evangelischen Kirche des Deutschen Kaiserreiches (1870–1918)' (Berlin Technical University Ph.D. thesis, 1991), pp. 79, 318 and passim.

71. For a liberal view see *Chronik der Christlichen Welt*, 23 (1913), pp. 165–8; for a conservative view, see reports of election meetings in *Kreuz-Zeitung*, 28 August, 7 September and 20 September 1894. See also Ulrich Mayer, *Die Anfänge der Zionsgemeinde in Berlin* (Bielefeld, 1988), pp. 93–6 and passim.

72. Joachim Rohde, 'Streiflichter aus der Berliner Kirchengeschichte von 1900 bis 1918', Günter Wirth, ed., *Beiträge zur Berliner Kirchengeschichte* (Berlin, 1987), pp. 222–6.

73. Protokollbuch des kirchlich-liberalen Parochialvereins (AKG).

74. Protokollbuch des ev. Männer- und Jünglingsvereins; Gemeinde-Helfer Buchholz, Jahresbericht 1911 (AKG). Günther Dehn also regarded his work with the young men's group as the highlight of his pastorate in Moabit: see his *Die alte Zeit: Die vorigen Jahre* (Munich, 1962), pp. 185–9.

75. Eugen Baumann, *Der Berliner Volkscharacter in der Seelsorge* (Berlin, 1880), p. 87.

76. Günther Dehn, *Proletarische Jugend* (Berlin, 1930), pp. 110–16, 136.

77. Alexander Paterson, *Across the Bridges* (London, 1911), pp. 174–82.

78. Federation of Churches and Christian Workers in New York City, *Sociological Canvass*, 3 vols. (New York, 1897–1901), 3.

79. Raphael Samuel, East London MS: Interview with Mrs Howard.

80. Orsi, *The Madonna of 115th Street* (New Haven, Conn., 1985), p. 205.

81. Section on parish organizations in *The Year Book and Book of Customs of the Church of Our Lady of Lourdes, Washington Heights, New York* (New York, 1916); interview with Miss Caroline Kolb, New York City, 21 November and 5 December 1983.

82. *BSM*, 2 (1879–80), pp. 86–90.

83. Baumann, *Berliner Volkscharacter*, p. 104.

84. *BSM*, 22 (1900), pp. 82–93; 8 (1886), p. 133.

85. Gemeinde-Helfer Buchholz, Jahresbericht, 1913 (AKG); for a similar story in Hamburg, see Richard J. Evans, ed., *Kneipengespräche im Kaiserreich* (Hamburg, 1989), pp. 171–2.

86. Ralph Gibson, *A Social History of French Catholicism 1789–1914* (London, 1989), pp. 187–8.

87. *New York Times*, 24 November 1902. For France, see Gibson, *Social History of French Catholicism*, p. 181.

88. The major studies of New York Italian Catholicism are Silvano Tomasi, *Piety and Power* (New York, 1975); Orsi, *The Madonna of 115th Street*; and Mary Elizabeth Brown, 'Italian immigrants and the Catholic Church in the Archdiocese of New York, 1880–1950' (Columbia University Ph.D. thesis, 1987).

89.   Henry J. Browne, 'The "Italian Problem" in the Catholic Church of the United States 1880–1900,' *Historical Studies and Records of the Catholic Historical Society*, 35 (1946), pp. 46–72.

90.   Brown, 'Italian immigrants', p. 122.

91.   Orsi, *The Madonna of 115th Street*, pp. 84–5.

92.   CCNY Interviews, II–7.

93.   Ibid., II–20.

94.   Ibid., II–9.

95.   For a detailed account, see Orsi, *The Madonna of 115th Street*, pp. 6–11.

96.   Daniel Czitrom, 'Underworlds and underdogs: Big Tim Sullivan and metropolitan politics in New York, 1889–1913', *Journal of American History*, 78 (1991), pp. 537–40; Willie Sutton, *Where the Money Was* (New York, 1976), p. 14.

97.   As in Hutchins Hapgood, ed., *The Autobiography of a Thief* (New York, 1903), where the author follows the example of his uncle, rather than his parents, or William Callahan, *Man's Grim Justice* (New York, 1928), where the Boston-born author follows the example of his criminal father, rather than his pious mother.

98.   For the emphasis on sport in New York Catholic parishes in the period around World War I, see George A. Kelly, *The Story of St Monica's Parish, New York City 1879–1954* (New York, 1954), pp. 53–8, 66–7, 74; Henry J. Browne, *One Stop above Hell's Kitchen: Sacred Heart Parish in Clinton* (Hackensack, N. J., 1977); St Paul's *Calendar*, February 1911 (copy in the Archive of the Paulist Fathers, at St Paul's rectory). For the Holy Name Societies as a distinctive aspect of American Catholic culture, see Jay Dolan, *The American Catholic Experience* (New York, 1985), p. 257.

99.   In the 1930s, Michael Quill, the radical Transport Workers Union leader, said: 'Our going to church did no harm either. Many a fellow who thought me a dangerous agitator found me more to his taste after meeting me at the Paulist Fathers.' Joshua B. Freeman, 'Catholics, Communists, and Republicans: Irish workers and the organization of the Transport Workers Union', Michael H. Frisch and Daniel J. Walkowitz, eds., *Working-Class America* (Urbana, Ill., 1983), p. 271.

100.   Hasia Diner, *Erin's Daughters in America* (Baltimore, 1983), p. 67, notes the frequency with which Catholic writers praised Irish-American mothers, while being much more critical of their husbands.

101.   Most of the evidence on this is by hostile witnesses, such as those cited in Peiss, *Cheap Amusements*, pp. 20–1; but see also Hapgood, *Autobiography of a Thief*, pp. 26–8.

102.   Mission Chronicles, 6–20 January 1889 (Archives of the Paulist Fathers, St Paul's rectory).

103.   Augustine Fitzgibbon Folder, WPA Collection on New York City Folklore (Library of Congress Folk Music Division, Washington, D.C.).

104.   Colleen McDannell, '"True men as we need them": Catholicism and the Irish-American male', *American Studies*, 27 (1986), pp. 23, 28.

105.   St Ignatius Church Bulletin, May 1905 (St Ignatius parish library, New York).

106.   See J. W. James, ed., *Women in American Religion* (Philadelphia, 1980).

Chapter 8. Religion in a Half-Secular Society

1.   Elke Josties et al., *Jetzt geht's rund . . . durch den Wedding* (Berlin, 1984), pp. 46–57.

2.   Manfred Gailus, ed., *Kirchengemeinden im Nationalsozialismus* (Berlin, 1990), pp. 14–15, analyzes the polarization in Berlin between supporters of the German Christians and of the Confessing Church: in a sample of eighty pastors working in Berlin parishes in the period 1933–6, thirty-four belonged to the former and thirty-two to the latter.

3. Paul Piechowski, *Proletarischer Glaube* (Berlin, 1927). See also Günther Dehn, *Proletarische Jugend* (Berlin, 1930).

4. Jörg Kniffka, *Das kirchliche Leben in Berlin-Ost in der Mitte der zwanziger Jahre* (Münster, 1971), pp. 96–112, 132–4, 149–53, 158–66.

5. Dehn, *Proletarische Jugend*, pp. 23–4.

6. Eugen Baumann, *Der Berliner Volkscharacter in der Seelsorge* (Berlin, 1880), pp. 44–51.

7. Elsa Herzfeld, *Family Monographs* (New York, 1905), pp. 15–28, 118, 120, 139. Herzfeld stresses (p. 23) that many of the families studied did not attend church, and that a major reason for this was poverty—but she does not say what proportion of the families were churchgoing.

8. Wolfgang Herzberg, ed., *Ich bin doch Wer: Arbeiter und Arbeiterinnen des VEB Berliner Glühlampenwerk erzählen ihr Leben 1900–1980* (Darmstadt, 1987), p. 10; Dehn, *Proletarische Jugend*, pp. 120–2.

9. Alter Landesman, *Brownsville* (New York, 1971), p. 78; Jonathan Sarna, ed., *People Walk on Their Heads: Moses Weinberger's 'Jews and Judaism in New York'* (New York, 1980), pp. 14–15, 76–7.

10. Wilhelm Frank, *Rosen und Dornen in der Berliner Seelsorgsarbeit in zwanzigjähriger Erfahrung* (Breslau, 1909), pp. 26–7.

11. *BSM*, 2 (1879–80), pp. 86–90.

12. See annual statistics in *SJSB*.

13. Herzfeld, *Family Monographs*, p. 20.

14. For analysis of these differences, see Gerald Parsons, ed., *Religion in Victorian Britain*, 4 vols. (Manchester, 1988), 1, pp. 14–67; Thomas Nipperdey, *Deutsche Geschichte 1800–1866: Bürgerwelt und starker Staat* (Munich, 1983), pp. 423–32 (where he suggests that the division between liberals and *Positiven* was so deep that German Protestantism had effectively split into two new confessions), and *Religion im Umbruch: Deutschland 1870–1918* (Munich, 1987), pp. 67–76.

15. Essex Interviews, no. 5, p. 15.

16. *Jahresbericht der St.-Sophiengemeinde* (1905), p. 4.

17. Baumann, *Berliner Volkscharacter*, p. 61. For similar coments from the 1880s, see *Geschichte der St.-Pauls-Gemeinde zu Berlin N.* (Berlin, 1935), p. 50.

18. *BSM*, 3 (1880), pp. 134–5.

19. Karl Julius Müller, *Aberglaube und Occultismus in Berlin und der Provinz Brandenburg* (Berlin, 1899), p. 13; F. G. Lisco, *Zur Kirchengeschichte Berlins* (Berlin, 1857), p. 327.

20. Karl Grünberg, *Episoden: Sechs Jahrzehnten Kampf um den Sozialismus* (Berlin, 1969), pp. 30–1; Ulrich Mayer, *Die Anfänge der Zionsgemeinde* (Bielefeld, 1988), pp. 199–201.

21. Erich Schmidt, *Meine Jugend in Gross-Berlin* (Bremen, 1988), p. 39.

22. Alan Bartlett, 'The churches in Bermondsey 1880–1939' (Birmingham University Ph.D. thesis, 1987), pp. 182–8; Select Committee of the House of Lords appointed to inquire into the Deficiency of means of spiritual instruction and places of Divine Worship in the Metropolis and other populous places, *Parliamentary Papers* (1857–8) 9, QQ. 547, 1070; Gillian Rose, 'Imagining Poplar in the 1920s: Contested concepts of community', *Journal of Historical Geography*, 16 (1990), p. 429.

23. Federation of Churches and Christian Workers in New York City, *Sociological Canvass*, 3 vols. (New York, 1897–1901), 3; Herzfeld, *Family Monographs*, pp. 20–1.

24. For an example of a Jewish atheist who insisted on her son being circumcised, see Irving Howe and Kenneth Libo, eds., *How We Lived Then: A Documentary History of*

Immigrant Jews in America 1880–1930 (New York, 1979), pp. 89–90.

25. Todd M. Endelman, 'The social and political context of conversion in Germany and England, 1870–1914', Todd M. Endelman, ed., *Jewish Apostasy in the Modern World* (New York, 1987), pp. 83–107. Peter Hönigmann, *Die Austritte aus der Jüdischen Gemeinde Berlin 1873–1941* (Frankfurt/Main, 1988), p. 109, cites a study of patterns of promotion in German universities in 1909–10, which placed faculty in three categories, which were (in order of the likelihood of their achieving the rank of professor): 'Christians', 'baptized Jews' and 'Jews'.

26. Helmut Engel, Stefi Jersch-Wenzel and Wilhelm Treue, eds., *Charlottenburg*, Teil 2, *Der Neue Westen* (Berlin, 1985), p. 184.

27. Lucian Hölscher, *Weltgericht oder Revolution* (Stuttgart, 1989), p. 157.

28. Kniffka, *Das kirchliche Leben in Berlin-Ost*, pp. 124–6.

29. Dehn, *Proletarische Jugend*, p. 23.

30. Hsi-Huey Liang, 'The social background of the Berlin working-class movement, 1890–1914' (Yale University Ph.D. thesis, 1959), p. 206.

31. Olive Anderson, 'The incidence of civil marriage in England and Wales', *Past & Present*, no. 69 (1975), p. 55.

32. *Annual Report of the Registrar-General* (1883). See also Jeffrey Cox, *English Churches in a Secular Society: Lambeth 1870–1930* (Oxford, 1982), p. 304; Hugh McLeod, *Class and Religion in the Late Victorian City* (London, 1974), p. 309–11; Gareth Stedman Jones, *Outcast London* (Oxford, 1971), pp. 132–4.

33. Alexander Paterson, *Across the Bridges* (London, 1911), pp. 199–200.

34. C. Stürenberg, *Klein-Deutschland* (New York, 1886), pp. 14–23. Ellen Badone, ed., *Religious Orthodoxy and Popular Faith in European Society* (Princeton, N. J., 1990) provides a valuable discussion of Roman Catholic and Orthodox popular religion in various parts of rural Europe, much of which is relevant to the themes discussed in this chapter. Caroline Brettell's paper on 'The Priest and His People: The Contractual Basis for Religious Practice in Rural Portugal' (pp. 54–85) analyzes saint's-day celebrations in a way that is in some respects similar to Stürenberg's account of the wedding celebration. 'Sacred' elements (processions and church services) and 'secular' elements (eating, drinking and dancing) were both integral parts of the festival: some anti-clericals organized a purely secular carnival, but most people felt that something essential was missing; some priests kept up a running battle against the 'sensual and pagan' aspects of the celebrations, but with equally little effect. In Stürenberg's story, the pastor accepts his allotted role, so conflict is avoided.

35. Christel Lane, *Christian Religion in the Soviet Union* (London, 1978), pp. 60–1.

36. Standish Meacham, *A Life Apart: The English Working Class 1890–1914* (London 1977), pp 62–3; John R. Gillis, *For Better, For Worse: British Marriages, 1600 to the Present* (New York, 1985), pp. 240, 256–8.

37. Herzfeld, *Family Monographs*, pp. 23, 26–7; Robert A. Orsi, *The Madonna of 115th Street* (New Haven, Conn., 1985), p. 101.

38. See annual figures in *SJSB*.

39. Georg von Loebell, *Zur Geschichte der evangelischen Kirchengemeinden Berlins während der Jahre 1875–1908* (Berlin, 1909), pp. 12–13.

40. Kniffka, *Das kirchliche Leben in Berlin-Ost*, p. 129.

41. Eduard Bernstein, *Die Geschichte der Berliner Arbeiter-Bewegung*, 3 vols. (Berlin, 1907–10), 1, p. 353.

42. Kirchenaustritte/Übertritte, 1908 (AKG).

43. *BSM*, 11 (1889), pp. 163–8. *Jahresbericht der St.- Sophiengemeinde* (1905), pp. 6–7, stressed that the clergy would always conduct a funeral if available, would not charge a

fee, and would travel to the cemetery by streetcar if there were no vehicles, but that it was essential to book a clergyman in advance, especially if the funeral was to be on a Sunday. See Baumann, *Berliner Volkscharacter*, p. 57, for description of a mass baptism.

44. Lisco, *Zur Kirchengeschichte Berlins*, pp. 327–8.

45. *BSM*, 11 (1889), pp. 163–8.

46. *Berlin und die Berliner: Leute, Dinge, Sitten, Winke* (Karlsruhe, 1905), pp. 374–5.

47. Lisco, *Zur Kirchengeschichte Berlins*, pp. 286–7.

48. *Berlin und die Berliner*, pp. 387–8.

49. Essex Interviews, no. 284, p. 56; no. 391, pp. 8, 44.

50. Ibid., no. 236, pp. 15–16.

51. Raphael Samuel, East End MS: Interview with Gladys Bradford.

52. Essex Interviews, no. 296, p. 18.

53. Ibid., no. 230, pp. 27–8.

54. Kollektenbuch 1907–1913 (AKG) lists the numbers of the congregation, the numbers taking Communion, and the money collected at each service (though there are some gaps). The most thorough analysis of communicant statistics in this period is Lucian Hölscher and Ursula Männich-Polenz, 'Die Sozialstruktur der Kirchengemeinden Hannovers im 19. Jahrhundert. Eine statistische Analyse', *Jahrbuch der Gesellschaft für niedersächsische Kirchengeschichte*, 88 (1990), pp. 159–211. In the years 1876–8 only 2 per cent of communicants in the parishes studied took communion more than once a year.

55. See Cox, *English Churches in a Secular Society*, pp. 102–4, for discussion of this phenomenon.

56. Günther Dehn, *Die alte Zeit, Die vorigen Jahre* (Munich, 1962), pp. 174–5.

57. See note 54.

58. Baumann, *Berliner Volkscharacter*, pp. 79–97.

59. Dehn, *Die alte Zeit*, pp. 174–5. Dehn also stated that his father, as a state official, believed that the principal religious festival of the year was the Kaiser's birthday, and made his only appearance in church on that day. However, the day does not seem to have attracted large congregations in Capernaum parish.

60. BC, B386, pp. 85–95.

61. Cox, *English Churches in a Secular Society*, pp. 103–4; Richard Mudie-Smith, *The Religious Life of London* (London, 1904), pp. 29–30, 207; a Bethnal Green vicar reported in the later 1890s that his church was crammed for the only time in the year at Harvest Festival—though he said that he regarded this festival as 'superstition': BC, B182, pp. 79–87.

62. *BSM*, 3 (1880), p. 58; 12 (1890), pp. 163–7.

63. A valuable discussion of this theme is Ann Taves, 'Relocating the sacred: Roman Catholic devotions in mid-nineteenth-century America' (Chicago University Ph.D. thesis, 1983), pp. 44–9, 72–5. A useful primary source is *The Year Book and Book of Customs of the Church of Our Lady of Lourdes, Washington Heights, New York* (New York, 1916), which lists the many devotions practised in the parish and the seasons with which they were associated.

64. CCNY Interviews, II–10; for St Patrick's Day parades, see Colleen McDannell, '"True men as we need them": Catholicism and the Irish-American male', *American Studies*, 27 (1986), pp. 25–7; the best account of the role of the saints in New York Catholic life is Orsi, *Madonna of 115th Street*.

65. This belief was sufficiently widespread to be among those singled out for condemnation in an article on superstition in the *Calendar* of St Paul's parish, New York, August 1898 (copies at St Paul's rectory).

66. M. C. Marsh, 'The life and work of the Church in an interstitial area' (New York

University Ph.D. thesis, 1932), p. 338; T. C. Wheeler, ed., *The Immigrant Experience* (New York, 1971), p. 21.

67. Moses Rischin, ed., *Grandma Never Lived in America: The New Journalism of Abraham Cahan* (Bloomington, Ind., 1985), pp. 97–8; Deborah Dash Moore, *At Home in America: Second Generation New York Jews* (New York, 1981), pp. 61–2, 127, 140–1; Lloyd Gartner, *The Jewish Immigrant in Britain 1870–1914*, 2nd edn (London, 1973), pp. 192–7.

68. Ibid., pp. 209–14.

69. Rischin, *Grandma Never Lived in America*, pp. 82–9, 100–2; Sydney Stahl Weinberg, *The World of our Mothers* (New York, 1990), p. 140. There is a vivid evocation of Passover in Howe and Libo, *How We Lived Then*, pp. 120–1. See also the discussion of 'Jewish domestic culture' and 'Kitchen Judaism' in Susan L. Braunstein and Jenna Weissman Joselit, eds., *Getting Comfortable in New York: The New York Jewish Home, 1880–1950* (New York, 1990).

70. Cox, *English Churches*, pp. 95–7.

71. Raphael Samuel, ed., *East End Underworld: Chapters in the Life of Arthur Harding* (London, 1981), pp. 26–7; Bartlett, 'Churches in Bermondsey', p. 196.

72. Essex Interviews, no. 145, p. 59; Mudie-Smith, *Religious Life of London*, p. 39.

73. Dolly Scannell, *Mother Knew Best* (London, 1975), p. 16; Kathleen Woodward, *Jipping Street* (London, 1928), p. 131; Essex Interviews, no. 235, pp. 12, 47.

74. Hugh McLeod, 'New perspectives on Victorian working-class religion: The oral evidence', *Oral History*, 14 (1986), p. 32.

75. Essex Interviews, no. 236, p. 12, 47; no. 298, pp. 29–30.

76. Dehn, *Proletarische Jugend*, pp. 128–9.

77. Ella Beyer, *Valiant is her Name* (n.p., n.d.), p. 28.

78. CCNY Interviews, II–20.

79. Questionnaire on the history of Sacred Heart parish (Sacred Heart rectory).

80. Raphael Samuel, East London MS: Interview with Mrs Prentice, p. 36.

81. Essex Interviews, no. 302, p. 37.

82. Liang, 'The social background of the Berlin working-class movement', p. 188.

83. Johannes Tews, *Berliner Lehrer* (Berlin, 1907), pp. 26–7; *BSM*, 3 (1880), p. 59; Gemeindehelfer Buchholz, Jahresbericht, 1912 (AKG).

84. Interview by Gillian Rose; Geoff Richman, *Fly a Flag for Poplar* (London, 1976), p. 44.

85. Kniffka, *Das kirchliche Leben in Berlin-Ost*, pp. 103–12, 164–5.

86. Essex Interviews, no. 334, p. 77; Richman, *Fly a Flag for Poplar*, p. 44.

87. L. E. Whatmore, *The Story of Dockhead Parish* (n.p., 1960), pp. 72–9.

88. CMHR, 1, pp. 311–3, 321, 351.

89. Ibid., 2, pp. 68–9.

90. Ibid., 1, p. 314.

91. Richman, *Fly a Flag for Poplar*, pp. 30, 36, 40, 92–3.

92. Gillian Rose, 'Locality, politics and culture: Poplar in the 1920s' (London University Ph.D. thesis, 1989), pp. 209–10.

93. Richman, *Fly a Flag for Poplar*, pp. 54, 89.

94. See McLeod, *Class and Religion*, pp. 179, 181, for examples from London in 1887 and 1908; for discussion of an earlier period, see Eileen Yeo, 'Christianity and Chartist struggle 1838–42', *Past & Present*, no. 91 (1981), pp. 109–39.

95. See, e.g., the sermon by Tom Mann, the secretary of the Independent Labour Party, in a Hackney chapel, cited in McLeod, *Class and Religion*, p. 63.

96. David Feldman, 'Immigrants and workers, Englishmen and Jews: Jewish immigrants in the East End of London 1880–1906' (Cambridge University Ph.D. thesis, 1985), pp. 322–3.

97. Ibid., pp. 321–2.

98. Rischin, *Grandma Never Lived in America*, pp. 321–2.

99. Ibid., p. 380.

100. Paula Hyman, 'Immigrant women and consumer protest: The New York kosher meat boycott of 1902', Jonathan Sarna, ed., *The American Jewish Experience* (New York, 1986), pp. 135–46.

101. Karl Ditt, *Industrialisierung, Arbeiterschaft und Arbeiterbewegung in Bielefeld 1890–1914* (Dortmund, 1982), p. 239; Hugh McLeod, 'Protestantism and the working class in Imperial Germany', *European Studies Review*, 12 (1982), p. 331; Bruno Violet, *Die Kirchenaustrittsbewegung* (Berlin, 1914), pp. 7–8.

102. C. F. Bellermann, *Die St. Pauls–Gemeinde in Berlin (1848–85)* (Berlin, 1885), pp. 5–10.

103. EOK: Acta betreffend die kirchlichen Notstände in Berlin, 6, memo dated 21 September 1914 (EZA).

104. *Chronik der Christlichen Welt*, 25 (1915), pp. 161–6.

105. EOK: Acta betreffend die kirchlichen Notstände, 6, Statistische Übersicht über die kirchlichen Verhältnisse der Evangelischen in Berlin (EZA).

106. Joachim Rohde, 'Streiflichter aus der Berliner Kirchengeschichte von 1900–1918', Günter Wirth, ed., *Beiträge zur Berliner Kirchengeschichte* (Berlin, 1987), p. 229.

107. Ibid., pp. 236–7.

108. Robert Currie, Alan Gilbert and Lee Horsley, *Churches and Church–Goers: Patterns of Church Growth in the British Isles since 1700* (Oxford, 1977), pp. 128, 143, 150.

109. *East London Observer*, 29 August 1914. However, the paper noted larger congregations in other parts of London; and later in the war there were claims that the early days of the war had indeed seen exceptionally large congregations—though these had long since dwindled. See Stuart Paul Mews, 'Religion and English society in the First World War' (Cambridge University Ph.D. thesis, 1973), pp. 50–1.

110. Ibid., pp. 51–3.

111. *East London Observer*, 31 October 1914.

112. Ibid., 14 November 1914. For discussion of Winnington–Ingram's role, see also Alan Wilkinson, *The Church of England and the First World War* (London, 1978), pp. 180–2.

113. Alan Wilkinson, *Dissent or Conform? War, Peace and the English Churches 1900–1945* (London, 1986), p. 30; Mews, 'Religion and English Society', pp. 59–63.

114. Wilkinson, *Dissent or Conform?*, pp. 48–53, and *First World War*, pp. 46–56.

115. See, for instance, ibid., pp. 114–8.

116. *East London Observer*, 29 August 1914.

117. Geoffrey K. Nelson, *Spiritualism and Society* (London, 1969), pp. 155–7; J. M. Winter, 'Spiritualism and the First World War', R. W. Davis and R. J. Helmstadter, eds., *Religion and Irreligion in Victorian Society* (London, 1992), pp. 185–200.

118. David S. Cairns, ed., *The Army and Religion* (London, 1919), pp. 9, 172; Wilkinson, *First World War*, pp. 156–8.

Conclusion

1. This section draws on material from Hugh McLeod, *Religion and the People of Western Europe 1789–1970* (Oxford, 1981).

2. Alan D. Gilbert, *Religion and Society in Industrial England 1740–1914* (London, 1976), and *The Making of Post-Christian Britain* (London, 1980).

3. Jeffrey Cox, *The English Churches in a Secular Society: Lambeth 1870–1930* (Oxford, 1982), p. 266.

4.   Ibid., pp. 266–68. Similar arguments are used in Hugh McLeod, *Class and Religion in the Late Victorian City* (London, 1974), pp. 214–18, and Callum Brown, 'A revisionist approach to religious change', Steve Bruce, ed., *Religion and Modernization: Sociologists and Historians Debate the Secularization Thesis* (Oxford, 1992), pp. 31–58.

5.   In his contribution to S. Gilley and W.J. Sheils, eds., *A History of Religion in Britain* (Oxford, 1994), Gilbert offers confident predictions about the nature of our religious future.

6.   Some recent attempts to re-evaluate in a more positive light the religious history of the period 1900–1960, or parts of that period, include: N.-J. Chaline, *Les catholiques normands sous la Troisième République* (Roanne, 1985); Callum G. Brown, 'Religion and secularisation', Tony Dickson and James H. Treble, eds., *People and Society in Scotland, 1914–1990* (Edinburgh, 1992), pp. 48–79; Adrian Hastings, *A History of English Christianity 1920–1985* (London, 1986) (emphasizing revival in the 1930s and 1940s); David Hilliard, 'The religious culture of Australian cities in the 1950s', *Hispania Sacra*, 42 (1990), pp. 469–81.

7.   Some of the parallels are noted in McLeod, *Class and Religion*, pp. 284–5.

8.   Gilbert, *Religion and Society*, pp. 147, 186.

9.   See Hugh McLeod, ed., *European Religion in the Age of Great Cities, 1830–1930* (London, 1995), especially the chapters by Carl Strikwerda, Sarah Williams and Callum Brown.

10.   Hugh McLeod, 'New perspectives on Victorian working-class religion: The oral evidence', *Oral History Journal*, 14 (1986), pp. 31–49; Mark Smith, 'Religion in industrial society: Oldham and Saddleworth 1780–1865', (University of Oxford D.Phil. thesis, 1987); Callum Brown, *The Social History of Religion in Scotland since 1730* (London, 1987), pp. 154–67; Callum G. Brown and Jayne D. Stephenson, '"Sprouting wings?" Women and religion in Scotland 1890–1950', Esther Breitenbach and Eleanor Gordon, eds., *Out of Bounds: Women in Scottish Society 1800–1945* (Edinburgh, 1992), p. 101.

11.   Cox, *English Churches*, pp. 34–5; Rosemary Chadwick, 'Church and people in Bradford and district 1880–1914' (University of Oxford D.Phil. thesis, 1986).

12.   Cox, *English Churches*, p. 92; Sarah C. Williams, 'Religious belief and popular culture: A study of the South London borough of Southwark c. 1880–1939' (University of Oxford D.Phil. thesis, 1993), p. 295.

13.   For statistics see P. Pieper, *Kirchliche Statistik Deutschlands* (Freiburg, 1899), pp. 150–61; J. Weissensteiner, 'Wien', Erwin Gatz, ed., *Pfarr- und Gemeindeorganisation: Studien zu ihrer Entwicklung in Deutschland, Österreich und der Schweiz seit dem Ende des 18. Jahrhunderts* (Paderborn, 1987), pp. 27–44; Y. Daniel, *L'équipement paroissial d'un diocèse urbain* (Paris, 1957). For more general comments on the religious character of these cities, see, for instance, Richard J. Evans, *Death in Hamburg* (Harmondsworth, 1990), pp. 100–103, 356–63; John W. Boyer, *Political Radicalism in Late Imperial Vienna* (Chicago, 1981); Gerard Jacquemet, 'Déchristianisation, structures familiales et anticléricalisme: Belleville au XIXe siècle', *Archives des Sciences sociales des Religions*, 57 (1984), pp. 69–82.

14.   See William Callahan's contribution on Madrid, Barcelona and Valencia to Hugh McLeod, ed., *European Religion in the Age of Great Cities, 1830–1930*, pp. 43–60.

15.   H. R. Jackson, *Churches and People in Australia and New Zealand 1860–1930* (Wellington, 1987).

BIBLIOGRAPHICAL NOTE

Since London was considerably bigger than New York and Berlin during this period, it is hardly surprising that more sources are available on London than on the other two cities. But London also has the edge in terms of quality. In particular, there are the incomparable riches of Charles Booth's *Life and Labour of the People in London*, 17 vols. (London, 1902–3), and of the Booth Collection at the London School of Economics, which contains the notebooks on which the work was based. Other outstanding sources for London include Richard Mudie-Smith, ed., *The Religious Life of London* (London, 1904), with its comprehensive data on church and synagogue attendance; the collections of visitation returns for the London, and for the Rochester and Southwark dioceses, which are respectively at Lambeth Palace Library and at the Greater London Record Office; and the tapes and transcripts of interviews conducted by various oral historians. These latter have been my most important London source. In particular, Paul Thompson and Thea Vigne's project on Family and Work Experience before 1918, tapes and transcripts from which which are held at the Department of Sociology, Essex University, are of immense value to anyone researching the social history of Britain in the early twentieth century. Though religion was not one of the principal themes of the project, information was systematically collected on such subjects as churchgoing and Sunday schools, and much information about religion and irreligion emerges incidentally. I have discussed this material and some of the problems in its interpretation in Hugh McLeod, 'New perspectives on Victorian working-class religion: The oral evidence', *Oral History*, 14 (1986), pp. 31–49.

There are three areas in which Berlin has the advantage over the other two cities so far as sources for a study of this kind are concerned. First, it has in the Evangelisches Zentralarchiv an outstanding church archive, with material compiled by the Prussian church authorities on many aspects of church life. Second, the fact that the state took a closer interest in the religion of its citizens in Prussia than in England or the United States meant that a wider range of statistical information about religious affiliation and practice is available for Berlin, and that some types of records exist that have no parallel in the other cities. The *Statistisches Jahrbuch der Stadt Berlin*, published annually, included an extensive section on religion, so that long runs of statistics are available for Berlin when often only more fragmentary data are available for London or New York. Information is also available about those changing denomination, or leaving the church altogether, as they were required to complete forms, some of which have been retained in parish archives. And third, numerous histories of Berlin parishes are available, and they tend to be of higher quality than their counterparts in London and New York. Two other kinds of source, which are also available for London and New York, but seem to me to be of exceptional quality in Berlin, are city mission journals (I found *Blätter aus der Stadtmission* invaluable), and writings by clergymen, describing their work or commenting on aspects of religion in the city—here I found books by two pastors of north Berlin parishes, the conservative Eugen Baumann and the radical Günther Dehn, very helpful.

In New York I was able to find much more evidence than in the other cities on the social composition of religious denominations and of specific congregations. There were two reasons for this: first, the invaluable surveys conducted in the years around 1900 by the Federation of Churches and Christian Workers in New York City published in *Socio-*

logical Canvass, 3 vols. (New York: 1897–1901) and the journal *Federation*; and second, the availability of considerable numbers of lists of members of churches or contributors to their funds. In particular, Catholic parishes used lists of contributors as a way of encouraging more people to pay up; but many churches, especially Lutheran ones, also have unpublished lists of members or communicants. In several cases it has been possible to identify those listed in these church sources in the manuscript schedules of the federal or state censuses. Zion Lutheran Church, which has good records generally, has a list of communicants at Easter 1910 which fell very close to the time of the federal census of that year. It has been possible to identify about 70 per cent of those listed. Unfortunately, it seems that a certain proportion of those listed will always elude identification in the census, not only because of removals and deaths, but also because of the omission of some households or buildings by the census-takers, and also because some households were included, but recorded separately from the rest of the street to which they belonged. It is also possible to use city directories to obtain occupations of church members, etc., as many historians have done. These have the great advantage of appearing annually, but they provide far less information than the census. They also need to be used with considerable care, since there is reason to think that those identified in this way will include a disproportionate number of the church's wealthier members. To illustrate this point: the German Catholic parish of the Assumption on Manhattan's West Side published a list of contributors to their jubilee collection (see *Zur Erinnerung an die Feier des Goldenen Jubiläum der Mariae-Himmelfahrt-Kirche* [New York, 1908]); 73 per cent of those giving more than fifty dollars could be identified in the city directory, but only 49 per cent out of a sample of those giving smaller sums. City directories are still a useful source if due account is taken of this social bias, and possibly of ethnic bias as well.

Three other kinds of source proved very useful in my work on New York: the records kept by two religious orders active in the city, the Paulists and the Redemptorists—in particular, the latter order, who were responsible for the running of several German Catholic parishes, kept highly detailed parish chronicles, now preserved in their archives in Brooklyn; the files on city parishes in the Archives of the Archdiocese of New York at St Joseph's seminary in Yonkers; and the various pioneering social surveys published in this period, most notably Elsa Herzfeld's invaluable *Family Monographs* (New York, 1905).

The secondary literature available to the student of London's religious history is far larger than that which exists for the other two cities: there are many specialized studies of London religion; and works on other aspects of London history are more likely to include useful material on religion. In the former category, the two works on which I have depended most heavily have been Jeffrey Cox, *English Churches in a Secular Society: Lambeth 1870–1930* (Oxford, 1982), and Alan Bartlett, 'The churches in Bermondsey 1880-1939' (Birmingham University Ph.D. thesis, 1987). In the latter category, those that have influenced me most have included Ellen Ross's work on working-class women: see now *Love and Toil: Motherhood in Outcast London, 1870–1918* (Oxford, 1993); Paul Thompson, *Socialists, Liberals, and Labour: The Struggle for London 1885–1914* (London, 1967); David Feldman, 'Immigrants and workers, Englishmen and Jews: Jewish immigrants to the East End of London, 1880–1906' (Cambridge University Ph.D. thesis, 1986); and Gillian Rose, 'Locality, politics and culture: Poplar in the 1920s' (London University Ph.D. thesis, 1989). Among the many other works on London religion in this period are Hugh McLeod, *Class and Religion in the Late Victorian City* (London, 1974); Clive Field, 'Methodism in Metropolitan London, 1850–1920' (Oxford University Ph.D. thesis, 1974); D. B. McIlhiney, 'A gentleman in every slum: Church of England missions in the East End of London 1837–1914' (Princeton University Ph.D. thesis, 1977); C. Marchant, 'Interaction of church and society in an East London borough (West Ham)' (London University Ph.D. thesis, 1979); Edward Royle, *Radicals, Secularists and Republicans: Popular Freethought in Britain 1866–1915* (Manchester, 1980); Roger Swift and Sheridan Gilley, eds., *The Irish in the Victorian City* (London, 1985) (which includes three excellent chapters on Catholicism); and J. N. Morris, *Religion and Urban Change: Croydon, 1840–1914* (Woodbridge, 1992). An important study which appeared too late for me to use is Sarah Williams, 'Religious belief and popular culture: A study of the South London borough of Southwark c. 1880–1939' (Oxford University D.Phil. thesis, 1993).

In the history of religion, as in other branches of history, Berlin has attracted far more general surveys than the other two cities. Among the general histories of the city, the only one with a good section on religion in this period is Hans Herzfeld, ed., *Berlin und die Provinz Brandenburg im 19. Jahrhundert* (Berlin, 1968). Two studies that I found helpful for their discussion of the everyday life of the city's working class were Hsi-Huey Liang, 'The social background of the Berlin working-class movement, 1890–1914' (Yale University Ph.D. thesis, 1959) (one of the few such studies to include discussion of religion), and Dietrich Mühlberg, ed., *Arbeiterleben um 1900* (Berlin, 1983). Two books by Walter Wendland are still useful: *Siebenhundert Jahre Kirchengeschichte Berlins* (Berlin, 1930); and *Die Entwicklung der christlichen Liebestätigkeit in Gross-Berlin vom Mittelalter bis zur Gegenwart* (Berlin, 1939). Among the many historical volumes inspired by the city's 750th anniversary in 1987 were two collections of papers on church history, one from East Berlin and the other from the West. The former volume, Günter Wirth, ed., *Beiträge zur Berliner Kirchengeschichte* (Berlin, 1987) adopted a more conventional narrative approach; the latter, Kaspar Elm and Hans-Dietrich Loock, eds., *Seelsorge und Diakonie in Berlin* (Berlin, 1990) was more experimental—it covered both Catholics and Protestants, and ventured further into the field of social history. For the Catholics, see also Ingrid Kraus, 'The Berlin Catholic church 1871–1910: Its social and political endeavors' (University of Nebraska Ph.D. thesis, 1981); and for the Jews, Burkhard Asmuss and Andreas Nachama, 'Zur Geschichte der Juden in Berlin und das Jüdische Gemeindezentrum in Charlottenburg', Wolfgang Ribbe, ed., *Von der Residenz zur City: 275 Jahre Charlottenburg* (Berlin, 1980), pp. 165–228. See also the superbly illustrated *Wegweiser durch das jüdische Berlin* (Berlin, 1987). A valuable interpretative essay is Hans-Dietrich Loock, 'Die evangelische Kirche in Berlin-Brandenburg im 19. Jahrhundert', *Wichmann Jahrbuch*, 30–1 (1990–1), pp. 101–16. Local studies of Berlin religious life during this period are sadly rare. A pioneering venture is Ulrich Mayer, *Die Anfänge der Zionsgemeinde* (Bielefeld, 1988); two very useful local studies of the inter-war period are Jörg Kniffka, *Das kirchliche Leben in Berlin-Ost in der Mitte der zwanziger Jahre* (Münster, 1971) and Manfred Gailus, ed., *Kirchengemeinden im Nationalsozialismus: Sieben Beispiele aus Berlin* (Berlin, 1990). Other studies relating partly to Berlin that I found particularly valuable were Horst Ermel, *Die Kirchenaustrittsbewegung im deutschen Reich 1906-14* (Cologne, 1971); Klaus Erich Pollmann, *Landesherrliches Kirchenregiment und soziale Frage* (Berlin, 1973); Günter Brakelmann, Martin Greschat and Werner Jochmann, *Protestantismus und Politik: Werk und Wirkung Adolf Stoeckers* (Hamburg, 1982); Lucian Hölscher, *Weltgericht oder Revolution: Protestantische und sozialistische Zukunftsvorstellungen im deutschen Kaiserreich* (Stuttgart, 1989).

Among those more general studies of New York history that I found most useful were Nathan Glazer and Daniel P. Moynihan, *Beyond the Melting-Pot: The Negroes, Puerto Ricans, Jews, Italians, and Irish of New York City*, 2nd edn (Cambridge, Mass., 1970); David C. Hammack, *Power and Society: Greater New York at the Turn of the Century* (New York, 1982); Melvyn Dubofsky, *When Workers Organize* (Amherst, Mass., 1968).

Ira Rosenwaike, *Population History of New York City* (Syracuse, N. Y., 1972) is an invaluable work of reference.

Studies of New York religion tend to focus on specific ethnic groups or denominations. Of the former, the Italians have been best served, and among the latter, the Roman Catholics. Jay Dolan pioneered the social history of New York Catholicism with *The Immigrant Parish: New York's Irish and German Catholics 1815–65* (Baltimore, 1975), and he subsequently drew partly on New York material in *Catholic Revivalism: The American Experience 1830–1900* (Notre Dame, Ind., 1978). Two of the best studies of New York Catholicism in this period, the former a view from the top down, and the latter from the bottom up, are Robert Emmett Curran, *Michael Augustine Corrigan and the Shaping of Conservative Catholicism in America* (New York, 1978) and Robert Orsi, *The Madonna of 115th Street* (New Haven, Conn., 1985). At an even more local level, the series of Catholic parish histories written by Henry J. Browne are excellent value, the best of all being *One Stop above Hell's Kitchen: Sacred Heart Parish in Clinton* (Hackensack, N. J., 1977). Other useful studies that focus on specific ethnic groups include W. Welty, 'Black shepherds, A study of leading Negro clergymen in New York City, 1900–40' (New York University Ph.D. thesis, 1969); Silvano M. Tomasi, *Piety and Power: The Role of the Italian American Parishes in the New York Metropolitan Area, 1880–1930* (New York, 1975); J. S. Lapham, 'The Germans of New York City 1860–1890' (St John's University Ph.D. thesis, 1977); John J. Bukowczyk, 'Steeples and smokestacks: Class, religion, and ideology in the Polish immigrant settlements of Greenpoint and Williamsburg, Brooklyn, 1880–1929' (Harvard University Ph.D. thesis, 1980); Mary Elizabeth Brown, 'Italian immigrants and the Catholic church in the Archdiocese of New York, 1880–1950' (Columbia University Ph.D. thesis, 1987). A useful denominational study is Clyde Griffen, 'An urban church in ferment: The Episcopal church in New York City, 1880–1900' (Columbia University Ph.D. thesis, 1960).

In most respects the literature on the history of the Jews in New York is far superior to that on any other ethnic or religious group. However, their religious history remains relatively neglected. For instance it is only a minor theme in Irving Howe, *World of our Fathers* (New York, 1976). The three studies that I found most useful for their discussion of New York Jewish religion in this period were Jeffrey Gurock, *When Harlem was Jewish 1870-1930* (New York, 1979), Deborah Dash Moore, *At Home in America: Second Generation New York Jews* (New York, 1981), and Jonathan Sarna, ed., *People Walk on their Heads: Moses Weinberger's 'Jews and Judaism in New York'* (New York, 1982). Three more general works on American religion that I found particularly helpful were Ann Taves, 'Relocating the sacred: Roman Catholic devotions in mid-nineteenth-century America' (Chicago University Ph.D. thesis, 1983); Jay Dolan, *The American Catholic Experience* (New York, 1985); Jack Wertheimer, ed., *The American Synagogue, A Sanctuary Transformed* (Cambridge, 1987).

INDEX

Maida Vale, 32; Mile End, 39, 140; Paddington, 163; Peckham, 46; Poplar, 30, 35–8, 42, 115, 142–3, 145, 151, 156, 195; Queens Park, 39; St Giles, 134–5; St Johns Wood, 32; Somers Town, 189; Southwark, 92, 130; Southwark Park, 39; Spitalfields, 31, 38–9; Stepney, 35, 130; Strand, 130; Tottenham, 29, 37, 144; Walworth, 37; Wapping, 40, 42, 156; West Ham, 29, 115; Westminster, 29–30; Willesden, 29; Wood Green, 32; Woolwich, 29, 115, 183, 188
London places of worship and Secular halls: All Hallows, Poplar, 145, 167; Bermondsey Central Hall, 154; Bow Wesleyan Mission, 156; Brixton Independent, 93; Chapel Royal, 30; Christ Church, Stepney, 194; Christ Church, Westminster Bridge Road, 93; City Temple, 30; East End Wesleyan Mission, 199; Great Synagogue, 163, 197; Hall of Science, 31, 44; Holy Trinity, Dockhead, 195; Holy Trinity, Shoreditch, 155; New Court Congregational, 153; St Dunstan, Stepney, 42, 182; St Gabriel, Canning Town, 156; St James the Less, Bethnal Green, 144, 154, 167; St John, Wapping, 42; St Margaret, Westminster, 30; St Matthew, Bethnal Green, 37; St Michael, Poplar, 156, 194; St Paul, Bethnal Green, 37; St Paul's Cathedral, 30; St Peter, Vauxhall, 115; St Philip, Stepney, 152; St Stephen, Poplar, 144; Trinity, Congregational, Poplar, 156; Westminster Abbey, 30
Lösche, A. and S., 21
Lourdes, 195
lower middle class, 5, 31, 86
luck, 178, 181–2, 190–1
Luther, M., 68, 74, 198
Lutherans (U.S.A.), 50, 63–73, 77, 96, 112, 179

McCabe, J., 50
McCloskey, Cardinal, 58, 121, 143
McGlynn, Fr E., 58, 112, 120–4, 143
McIlhiney, D. B., 36
MacSwiney, T., 195
Magnes, Rabbi, 99
Maguire, J., 122
Manchester, 162

Mann, H., 85–6, 130
Mann, T., 94
Manning, Cardinal, 122
Mansbridge, A., 94
Marseilles, xxvi
Marx, K., 110–11, 130
Massachusetts, 49
Maurice, F. D., 94
Mecklenburg, 15
Messer, F., 144–5
Methodists, 31–2, 50, 95, 100, 111, 159–62
middle class, xxx, 5, 8–10, 12, 21, 35, 51, 72–4; *see also* lower middle class, urban elites
Moleschott, J., 90
Mooney, Mgr J., 61
mobility: social, 62, 74, 117, 123–4, 138, 178; spatial, xxviii, 10–12, 15–16, 47; and religion, 54–6, 70–4, 76–80, 96, 107–8, 119–20
Morgan, Rev. G. C., 153
Morgan, J. P., 51
Morris, Rev. W. A., 115
Morrison, A., 155
Morrison, H., 93
Most, J., 17, 107
mothers' meetings, 158–9
Mühlberg, D., 141
Murnane, Fr, 195

nationalism and religion, 58–60, 64, 116, 122–3, 198–200
Netherlands, 117, 201
New Jersey, 133
Newark, N.J., 99
New York, xxix–xxxi, 25, 29, 49–80, 83, 88, 91, 95–101, 107–10, 136, 149, 176, 185–6, 207; elites, 50–2; immigration, 49, 52–3, 79–80, 95–8, 119; politics, 52, 95, 97–9, 120–5, 142–3
New York city districts: Blackwell's Island, 167; Borough Park, 79; Bronx, 49, 69, 74, 78, 133, 190, 198; Brooklyn, 49, 50, 57, 63, 74–5, 77, 79, 95–6, 98–100, 142, 166, 198; Brooklyn Heights, 50, 68; Brownsville, 74, 78, 141, 178; Clinton Hill, 50; East Harlem, 118–19, 167, 169–71, 190–1; Fifth Avenue, 50; Flatbush, 78; Greenpoint, 96–7, 100; Greenwich Vil-